Ancient Israel's Faith and History

Ancient Israel's Faith and History
An Introduction to the Bible in Context

George E. Mendenhall

Edited by Gary A. Herion

Westminster John Knox Press
LOUISVILLE
LONDON • LEIDEN

Book design by Savitski Design
Composition by Bookcomp, Inc.
Cover design by Mark Abrams

On the cover: *Diana of the Ephesians* (Greek, Artemis), the chief goddess of the eastern Mediterranean world in the first century (Acts 19:28). She represented prosperity, fertility, and productivity—values worshiped then, during the late Bronze Age, and now.

First edition

Published by Westminster John Knox Press
Louisville, Kentucky

This book is printed on acid-free paper that meets the American National Standards Institute Z39.48 standard.♾

PRINTED IN THE UNITED STATES OF AMERICA

01 02 03 04 05 06 07 08 09 10 — 10 9 8 7 6 5 4 3 2 1

Library of Congress Cataloging-in-Publication Data is on file at the Library of Congress, Washington, D.C.

ISBN 0-664-22313-3

Dedicated to the villagers (*'am ha'arets*) of Palestine, Jordan, Syria, and Lebanon, from whom I have learned so much.

Contents

Illustrations

Abbreviations

AEL	M. Lichtheim, *Ancient Egyptian Literature*. 3 vols. Berkeley, Calif.: University of California Press, 1973.
AL	W. L. Moran, *The Amarna Letters*. Baltimore: Johns Hopkins University Press, 1992.
ANET[3]	J. B. Pritchard, ed., *Ancient Near Eastern Texts Relating to the Old Testament*. 3d ed. Princeton, N. J.: Princeton University Press, 1969.
ANEP	J. B. Pritchard, ed., *Ancient Near East in Pictures Relating to the Old Testament*. Princeton, N. J.: Princeton University Press, 1954.
ARM	Archives royales de Mari
BA	*Biblical Archaeologist*
BAR	*The Biblical Archaeologist Reader*. 3 vols. Garden City, N.Y.: Doubleday, 1961–70.
BASOR	*Bulletin of the American Schools of Oriental Research*
CBQ	*Catholic Biblical Quarterly*
DocStGos	D. R. Cartledge and D. L. Dungan, eds., *Documents for the Study of the Gospels*. Rev. and enl. ed. Minneapolis: Fortress Press, 1994.
DOTT	D. W. Thomas, ed., *Documents from Old Testament Times*. New York: Harper & Brothers, 1958.
EA	El Amarna letter
EB	Early Bronze Age
JBL	*Journal of Biblical Literature*
JSOT	*Journal for the Study of the Old Testament*
KJV	King James Version

LB	Late Bronze Age
MB	Middle Bronze Age
Mélanges Dussaud	G. Dossin, *Mélanges syriens offerts à Monsieur René Dussaud*. 2 vols. Paris: P. Guethner, 1939.
NRSV	New Revised Standard Version
NT	New Testament
OT	Old Testament ·
OTP	J. Charlesworth, ed., *The Old Testament Pseudepigrapha*. 2 vols. New York: Doubleday, 1983.
OTPar	V. Matthews and D. Benjamin, *Old Testament Parallels*. 2d ed. New York: Paulist Press, 1992.
RDSS	L. Schiffman, *Reclaiming the Dead Sea Scrolls*. Philadelphia: Jewish Publication Society, 1994.
RSV	Revised Standard Version
SAC	M. D. Coogan, ed., *Stories from Ancient Canaan*. Philadelphia: Westminster Press, 1978.
SEM	E. Chiera, *Sumerian Epics and Myths*. Chicago: University of Chicago Press, 1934.
TEV	Today's English Version
v(v).	verse(s)
WD	Hesiod, *Works and Days*. Trans. D. Wender. Harmondsworth, Middlesex: Penguin Books, 1973.

Foreword

In the pages that follow, one of the most creative minds of twentieth-century biblical scholarship offers general readers the fruits of sixty years of groundbreaking research into the history, language, and religious thought of the Bible.

In 1986, George Mendenhall retired after thirty-four years as professor of Near Eastern Languages and Literature at the University of Michigan. His scholarly articles and books—often published in specialized journals read by a handful of scholars—have had revolutionary impact on the way historians approach the Bible. One American colleague observed that few others have so successfully changed the perspective from which scholars view ancient Israel's faith and history, while a German scholar called him one of the two most influential American Old Testament scholars of the twentieth century. At last, popular audiences can read and evaluate for themselves the basic features of his pioneering approach to the Bible.

Of course, George Mendenhall has been controversial, as anyone will see who engages the "Suggestions for Further Reading" at the end of each chapter. But Mendenhall's youth in small-town Nebraska, coupled with years spent among village populations in the Near East, have given him an ethnographer's sensitivity to social and cultural dynamics in the past—and in the Bible—that many others miss. Along the way he mastered a dozen languages, developing a keen awareness of the suppleness of language: whether it be modern Japanese, ancient Akkadian, or biblical Hebrew, he has understood that words have meanings not just in dictionaries but in concrete historical and social contexts. His rigorously historical approach to the Bible, combining archaeology, social science insights, and historical linguistics, has challenged many conventional views, and not a few scholars attempting to refute one of his claims have ended up conceding that "Mendenhall was probably right."

He has also challenged many religious approaches to the Bible. His fresh perspective not only means that there are new things to be learned; it also means that there are old things that must be *unlearned*. This may prove unsettling to some readers who are relatively content with established religious views and interpretations. Indeed, for several hundred years here in the West both the church and the synagogue have nurtured traditional ways of thinking about every element in this book's title: ancient Israel, faith, history, the Bible, and most important, the proper context within which all these things should be approached. One need only glance at Mendenhall's discussion of "Ten Commandments or Ten Commitments?" (in chapter 2) to see what a fresh perspective can do— and why some people with established ways of thinking may find this sort of approach unsettling.

Mendenhall's study has been energized by his belief that the religious ethic of ancient Israel urgently commends itself to thinking people today. But his is not the voice of a preacher or theologian. In fact, he has repeatedly voiced frustration with theologians—conservative, liberal, or in-between—who demonstrate less interest in understanding the Bible in its own context than in straining to make it either support traditional doctrines or speak "relevantly" to modern times and issues. Even for Christians and Jews, he argues, the context for understanding the Bible today is still the world of the biblical writers themselves.

These chapters began as informal lectures delivered to various church groups and other popular (nonreligious) audiences across southeast Michigan beginning in the mid-1980s. That Mendenhall consistently received enthusiastic responses indicates that the ordinary layperson— accompanied by a seasoned guide with a fresh perspective—can indeed follow a meaningful trail through archaeological ruins, clay tablets, and papyrus scrolls. It also indicates that average laypeople and students, with no background whatsoever, are capable of understanding the Bible generally in its ancient historical and cultural context. And because the problems confronting people in ancient times—especially problems relating to personal integrity and the use of power—were not all that different from those confronting us in modern times, the average thinking person is also capable of finding meaningful connections to the contemporary world. Some even acquire a deepened connection to their own religious heritage.

Mendenhall's lectures were frequently tape-recorded, and beginning in the early 1990s they were transcribed electronically. A sabbatical from Hartwick College, coupled with an appointment as visiting scholar at

Princeton Theological Seminary, provided me the time and resources this past year to edit those transcripts, organizing the lectures for the printed page and preparing the various boxes, maps, tables, appendixes, list of suggested readings, and bibliographies. Along the way, both of us received valuable assistance from two wonderful editors, Jeff Mortimer and Leslie Barkley. Mendenhall then read everything, deleting, adding, and transposing material to create the finished text, beginning with his preface.

In most other respects, this book is the result of the love and dedication of the Mendenhall family: son Stephen transcribed the initial lectures, daughter-in-law Robin provided the illustrations, wife Eathel supplied not only constant encouragement but also original artwork, and son David gave early feedback on our preliminary efforts. A special word of thanks goes to another son, Stan, who was in most respects the managing editor, facilitating the correspondences and the work flow, consulting with the publisher, and providing helpful feedback and guidance every step of the way. Together, he and I identified a pool of readers on whom we could "test" the manuscript, including Dan Capper, Karen Cass, Jane Cook, David MacGregor, Maria Megnin, Jonathan Shah, James F. Smith, Tiernan Sykes, David Weed, and Burton Wolfe. The candid reactions and suggestions we received from all these people have helped ensure that the final text does what the original lectures intended: provide a popular audience with a coherent introduction to ancient Israel's faith and history. Carey C. Newman, our editor at Westminster John Knox, has been a constant and much-appreciated source of help and enthusiasm for bringing George Mendenhall's work to a wider, popular audience. Daniel Braden has done a marvelous job overseeing this book's production.

Unless indicated otherwise, all Bible quotations come from the New Revised Standard Version, following its chapter and verse designations. However, we have departed from traditional translations in one significant respect: whenever ancient Hebrew manuscripts mention the name of the Israelite god, we have chosen to render the ancient name itself—Yahweh—rather than follow the later Judeo-Christian tradition of substituting "the LORD." We feel this is essential to setting biblical religion in its proper historical and cultural context. Desiring not to sidetrack into technical minutiae, we have avoided exact transliterations of foreign words that might otherwise intimidate general readers. Also, we have decided against including any footnotes citing scholarly publications. For those who wish to continue their studies, each chapter concludes with a related list of readable and generally accessible works by other scholars; bibliographies in those works will guide students who wish to dive deeper still. For those who wish to integrate their study with readings from the Bible itself, we have begun each chapter with a recommendation of some relevant passages.

It has been a privilege this year to immerse myself fully in a role I have enjoyed playing for the past twenty-five years—a George Mendenhall student. His sharp mind, his depth and breadth of learning, his sensitivity to issues of power and ethic, and his own personal integrity and concern for human beings over human systems have been a constant source of inspiration for me.

Gary A. Herion
Oneonta, New York
November 24, 2000

Preface

The present work is an attempt to condense and incorporate sixty years of study into a clear and comprehensible overview of the biblical tradition, particularly as it pertains to ancient Israel's faith and history. Born in the ruins of the Late Bronze Age, the biblical tradition provides a critical perspective on the value systems of that doomed age, especially its deification of political power and wealth. In many respects, the values that led to the collapse of that civilization are not much different from those held and celebrated by many people today. And if the biblical tradition, which arose as an alternative framework of values, could speak meaningfully to people then, perhaps it can do the same for us now.

But there are significant challenges to understanding the Bible, especially in its own context. Through the ages, whether through ignorance or malice, the Bible has frequently been misinterpreted, misunderstood, and misused. And because the Bible has frequently been used to justify much mischief (and worse), there has been an understandable intellectual backlash against it. Modern biblical scholars—who should be in the best position to help our understanding—are themselves frequently hamstrung by the enormously broad range of requisite knowledge (including ancient history and languages) and by the inability or unwillingness to separate their scholarship from the presumptions and orthodoxies of their peer groups.

When it comes to biblical history, scholarship today extends along a spectrum that ranges between two religiously motivated extremes. On one extreme are those who insist that the Bible is absolutely true in every respect: if scripture says the sun and moon stood still, then they will insist that this actually happened, even if it requires a reorganization of the solar system. On the other extreme are those who dismiss the entire Bible as fairy tales and fictions, assuming it addresses readers merely on the aesthetic plane, if at all, and not on an intellectual or moral plane: "Do you *like* what the Bible says?" rather than "Does the Bible engage us to re-examine our world and ourselves?"

Both these extremes reflect an antipathy to real history that seems pervasive in the modern West, where many people would probably agree with Henry Ford: "History is bunk." In my own undergraduate days, I would have agreed, too. For years I have felt that responsible historical work in biblical studies is similar to my experiences in New Guinea during World War II. Stationed at a camp on the shore of Lake Sentani, my unit (which comprised Brits, Australians, and Americans) was responsible for translating, analyzing, and evaluating captured Japanese documents for useful tactical or strategic information. Every few weeks a courier would arrive bringing yet another gunnysack filled with scraps of paper recovered from the battlefield.

The Old Testament (or Hebrew Bible) in particular—especially the traditions contained in its so-called historical books—is the gunnysack of documents retrieved from the battlefield of ancient times, but with one important contrast: the soldiers on the front lines in New Guinea were instructed to send us every piece of raw data on which there was writing, while the Old Testament documents come to us preselected and preinterpreted by ancient Israelite scribes interested in showcasing the traditions and having the documents understood in a certain way. Many decades of study have convinced me that those ancient scribes themselves often had a poor and incomplete understanding of the ancient traditions they were preserving. Under those circumstances, they could not avoid being "creative" (as modern scholars correctly observe) in the attempt to make those ancient traditions meaningful and relevant to their own time. These scribes were less interested in understanding their own history than they were in exploiting it.

This is what accounts for the plethora of misunderstandings, discrepancies, and absurdities sometimes encountered in the Bible. To cite one brief example: these scribes did not understand the archaic Hebrew word *'elef,* used to designate a military unit of six-to-twenty men. Assuming it to represent the common numeral "thousand," the result was the historically absurd picture (in Exod. 12:37) of Moses rescuing several million Israelites in a column that would extend from Cairo to Canaan.

Similarly, a more significant misinterpretation concerns the so-called Ten Commandments (or Decalogue), which most people automatically regard as divine imperatives (God says, "Thou shalt not do X, Y, and Z"). Not only has this obscured their original nature and purpose, but it has also justified countless attempts to use the Bible coercively to legislate morality, usually doing more harm than good. In fact, the Decalogue simply describes patterns of ethical behavior that freely flow out of a relationship with God ("Because you have entered this sacred covenant, you will not do X, Y, and Z"). They are actually ten basic commitments voluntarily undertaken by individuals rather than imposed by force. An underlying theme of the Bible—from Genesis through Revelation—is that true faith does not result from the use of force. The biblical tradition arose and grew around an awareness that religion and politics are best thought of as reciprocals. In other words, voluntary religious controls of behavior and compulsory legal ones are reciprocal—the less we have of the one, the more critically civilization depends on the other.

On the other hand, the Old Testament tradition is rife with examples of what happens when people choose not to undertake the ethic described in the Decalogue (see, for example, Judges 19–20). The "wrath of God" described in the Hebrew Bible is simply a description of the real historical processes that result.

This, of course, runs contrary to the popular notion—shared by the Bible's friends and foes alike—that the biblical tradition, by nature, is tyrannical, an age-old instrument of social control. After all, both Judaism and Christianity have used it as such for centuries. But there is now sufficient evidence from antiquity to cast a radically different light on the Bible and its traditions. I will present here as much of that evidence as can realistically be provided, given the limitations of time and space. Although the Bible is often quoted as the main source in the following chapters, this is only because it remains our only written source attesting to the critical early centuries of the biblical faith and community (approximately 1200–850 B.C.). Both arose simultaneously after an almost total collapse of civilization, a "dark age" when illiteracy was the norm across the Near Eastern and Mediterranean worlds, and when the usual institutions producing writing lay in ruins.

There has also emerged over the past fifty years an academic enterprise known as religious studies. It involves a cluster of disciplines whose various methods are employed to increase our analytical understanding of so-called "religious" phenomena. Simply stated, it differs from more "theological" approaches to religion that tend to arise less from a desire to *understand* a religious system than to *obtain a certain commitment* to it. In short, the academic study of religion does not shield faith from disturbing and disquieting questions. Just as a responsible study of ancient Israel's faith and history must "make sense" with respect to the growing body of evidence from antiquity, so it must also "make sense" with respect to our growing awareness of what religion, generally and academically speaking, is and does.

I have tried to introduce readers to some of the insights resulting from the past century of research into ancient Israel. Throughout this book, whole scholarly monographs, technical papers, and even decades of debate are sometimes condensed to a sentence or two. This is certainly not meant to disparage this important work but merely to assist the general reader who may have little if any knowledge about ancient Near Eastern languages, literature, archaeology, and history. I have tried to emphasize what is important in understanding the Bible and to separate that from scholarly discourse that most readers would find overly technical. A bibliography listing some general and accessible works has been provided for those readers interested in advancing to the next level of study.

In treating the social and religious history of ancient Israel, I have been privileged to work alongside scholars in many university departments, including my own academic home in the Department of Near Eastern Studies at the University of Michigan. I have also benefited enormously from years of personal experience living and traveling in the cities, villages, and hinterlands of the Near East, when they were still relatively unspoiled by Western culture. This experience has helped open my eyes to many aspects of the Bible and biblical history that I would never have appreciated had my studies remained locked in books and guided by the intellectual fads and fashions of the Western academy.

Finally, I wish to express my deepest gratitude and appreciation for the initiative, intelligence, effort, and persistence that Dr. Gary Herion has dedicated to this work, which otherwise would certainly have never seen the light of day.

George E. Mendenhall
Ann Arbor, Michigan
November 24, 2000

Introduction

Religious systems are perhaps the most widespread and universally attested human phenomena, and also perhaps the oldest and most complex. So, how does one begin to understand religion from a "religious studies" perspective?

It might be helpful to begin with the observation that religion is an aspect of culture, which in turn is a meaningful arrangement of technology (the means by which people provide for material needs), society (people's relationships), and ideology (people's ways of thinking, including religion). These three are so interconnected that a change in one will induce corresponding changes in one or both of the other two. This truism was humorously depicted in the South African film *The Gods Must Be Crazy:* When a glass bottle casually tossed from a low-flying airplane lands in a local village, it is immediately welcomed as a heaven-sent gift, a tool with a variety of constructive uses (technology). But disputes over the bottle soon violently disrupt the normally peaceful village (society), leading the elders to conclude that the gods who gave them the bottle must be crazy (ideology).

Five Questions about Religion

Before examining the Bible, ancient Israel, and early Judaism and Christianity, it may be helpful to look at religion more generally by considering five basic questions that could be directed toward any religious system, whether "Western," "Eastern, "primitive," or "modern." (The discerning reader will note that much of what is said here about religion applies equally to other cultural phenomena, including government bureaucracies, business corporations, university systems, organized athletics, and even street gangs.)

1. *What is one's "religion"?* Religion may be defined as the combination of an individual's values, experience, and actions, meaningfully brought together and focused upon something considered sacred or holy. For fundamentalists, scripture (or a particular way of viewing scripture) may be holy. For others, the holy may be a sacred place (such as Jerusalem's Wailing Wall) or a sacred time of year (Easter, Passover, Ramadan). In the business world, corporate profits might be sacred; in politics, it might be the national self-interest. Regardless, values seem to lie close to the core of religion—not only the values to which people give verbal assent in formal worship settings, but also the (unspoken) priorities that shape their daily choices and actions. People's values are related to their "gods," who are frequently regarded as the source of (and the authority behind) their values. As Martin Luther once observed, a "god" is simply whatever one is most afraid of losing. Its degree of holiness may be indicated by the degree of resistance one encounters when questioning or challenging it.

2. *What are religious communities?* If people were never drawn together by their shared values, it is doubtful that religious systems would ever arise. At best, each individual would possess his or her own personal spirituality. Initially, the basic criterion for fellowship is whether one identifies his or her own values with those of others. In time, however, as the group grows and comprises people with different values, other criteria may arise for identifying who belongs and who does not (for example, who worships in a particular building on a particular day of the week).

3. *What does religion actually do?* Religion's functions range from the therapeutic (effecting physical as well as emotional or spiritual healing) to the social (creating community, dividing it, or giving people a sense of belonging). Because values determine how resources are allocated, religion also has an economic function. Thus, religious factors ultimately underlie the construction of not only the ancient pyramids and medieval cathedrals but also modern sports complexes. Religion almost always functions to provide legitimacy to the norms and principles to which the faithful must adhere. Thus, the architectural maxim "Form follows function" has a religious antecedent: "Function follows value." Values and priorities determine functions (i.e., what people do), and functions give rise to specific forms. For example, if on the one hand the care of widows and orphans is a religious value, then functions will naturally follow as people enact those values and actually begin providing support to these people. Forms will follow from this, whether it be the development of charitable institutions or of religious liturgies invoking God's compassion for the poor. Everything works to affirm the value. On the other hand, if

social control and group distinctiveness become "sacred" values, such things as political power and ethnic solidarity can become "religious," and formal structures will arise to promote those values.

4. *How are religious values transmitted?* Religious systems foster identity by communicating their views and values in different ways, including narratives (myths, legends, and sacred histories); rituals and enactments (such as dance and song); the arts; and formal doctrines and creeds. Religious systems always intend to communicate explicit "truths" (such as "There is no god but Allah, and Muhammad is his prophet"). But often, in the way members of the community are either praised or ostracized, other subtler messages are communicated about the sanctity of the group and the value of complying with its norms. Participation (or nonparticipation) in public ritual can be especially effective in communicating one's affection for (or disaffection from) the group. Given this, it is not surprising that institutions of social control not only latch onto religion but manipulate sacred (or "patriotic") images to legitimize themselves.

5. *How does a religious system change over time?* Contrary to pious claims that they are timelessly unchanged and supernaturally revealed or "lowered from heaven," religions and religious systems actually have complex human histories, and they respond to all sorts of historical forces that bear upon them. We will say more about this historical factor in a moment.

Five Observations about Religion	Even the casual observer often notices certain features about religion that seem to occur frequently. In fact, they occur with such predictability in religious systems that they justify our labeling them "laws." By no means does this mean that anyone mandates these; rather, they seem to occur naturally and are largely unpreventable.

1. *The Law of Transference.* Religious language is metaphorical, not literal. It uses images transferred from daily human experience. For example, all statements about the divine—whether conventional Judeo-Christian ones about God ("the Lord who rules") or pop-cultural *Star Wars* ones about the Force ("an energy field that surrounds us and penetrates us")—are actually analogies transferred from the realm of normal human experience, whether the ancient world of feudal lords and masters or the modern world of science and technology. Similarly, "covenant"—the principal symbol describing the Israelite attachment to its religious ethic—was transferred from the world of international politics, where it designated a loyal subject's attachment to (or treaty with) his overlord (see chapter 2).

2. *The Law of Functional Shift.* Religious rituals and symbols acquire new meaning and significance over time; and their forms endure, in part, because their meaning has evolved to address changing circumstances. In short, their functions have shifted. The Christian Eucharist is a good example: Prior to the time of Constantine (early 300s A.D.), participants in this rite risked their lives and livelihoods because the rite functioned to signal allegiance to something other than the political order. But a thousand years later people risked their lives and livelihoods if they did *not* participate (as the Spanish Inquisition dramatically proved), because the rite now functioned to signal allegiance to the power structure. Another example is Sabbath observance, whose original purpose was to provide rest for farm animals and laborers. Subsequent Jewish and Christian officials elevated this commandment to proscribe all work, using it socially to measure people's piety and obedience. Very often the original meaning or significance of religious rituals and symbols is completely lost even to the practitioners of the faith.

3. *The Law of Elaboration.* Given sufficient time and resources, religious specialists will engage in endless elaboration on their specialty, regardless of its (ir)relevance. For example, in times of prosperity ancient Egyptian priests specialized in mummifying cats. In New Testament times Jewish scribes debated the circumstances by which a ceremonially "clean" jar became "unclean." And one need only compare the Gospel of Mark's brief sixteen chapters with the thousands of books on systematic theology written in the twentieth century alone to see the Law of Elaboration at work within the Christian household of faith.

4. *The Law of Contrast.* In time, religious communities will develop certain traits that serve no real purpose other than to distinguish them from "outsiders." The most common trait is ritual itself, where and how people choose to gather for worship. But under certain circumstances, the contrasts can become exaggerated to the point of becoming stereotypical—such as the dress of the Hasidic Jew or of the Amish farmer. In other words, these markers of the group are signs of piety and loyalty to the community. When the community itself becomes a central value— regardless of whether it is a religious sect, a street gang, a sports team, or a fraternal organization—the symbols emblematic of the group are treated as if they were sacred, and they are sacred because they belong to "us" and not to "them."

5. *The Law of Finality.* Certain concepts or rituals, even peripheral ones, come to enjoy a "holiness" that is considered "final" and therefore no longer subject to debate or change. However, because people often lose sight of what is properly sacred or confuse it with something that seems important at the moment, certain things that were once incidental or relatively peripheral become sacred, "once and for all." An extreme

example of this is the hurt feelings that often surface when an old liturgy or hymnal is replaced by a new one: for some, the "old way" had become the only, truly sacred way. Likewise, the Jewish prohibition of intermarriage, which was not a concern in early biblical times, later became an ultimate and unchallengeable tenet; even though a majority of Jews today actually practice intermarriage, there are still many traditionalists who passionately consider intermarriage the single greatest threat to Judaism. But the classic example of this is perhaps the Bible itself. The faithful devotees of Yahweh in ancient Israel had no Hebrew scripture to guide their faith, nor did the early Christians have a New Testament; yet today the words of scripture have become the indispensable core of many people's religious life, something that dare not be questioned. And to the extent that they fear most to lose it, it has become, in effect, their "god."

| How Religions Develop | Religious systems are not timeless or eternally fixed; like living organisms, they change and adapt as they encounter new situations. And those changes, while rarely correlating with precise moments in time or dates on a calendar, broadly but typically follow a regular pattern. There are five stages of development associated with the birth, growth, and sometimes death of a religious system. |

1. *Prologue to the Religion.* The history of culture and society in the days prior to the appearance of a new religion is crucial background providing a key to understanding which of its elements the new religion retained (and why) and which ones it rejected (and why). The choices people made with respect to their cultural antecedents help reveal what they valued—in other words, what *constituted* their religion. In fact, this may give us a more accurate picture of their faith than historical (or even scriptural) accounts written centuries later by descendants who had little appreciation of the actual context within which the religion emerged. The collapse of civilization at the end of the Bronze Age helps us understand the rise of the Old Testament tradition, just as the dysfunctional religious systems at the time of Jesus help explain the rise of the New.

2. *The Formative Period.* The formative period is the time when significant numbers of people consciously reject the old religious systems and embrace a new vision of religious community, usually articulated by an inspired individual (Moses, Muhammad, the Buddha, Zarathustra). Initially, the new religious community may be comparatively small but acutely aware of the gap between its values and those of others. Two social processes appear to be at work as religious communities are forming: *fission* and *fusion*. The formation of a new religious fellowship inevitably

entails the weakening, if not severing (or fissioning), of old attachments to those who do not share the same values. Many "prophets" in different cultural, historical, and religious contexts have correctly predicted that religious commitments can even drive wedges between the faithful and their beloved family members (see Matt. 10:34–37). At the same time, processes of fusion exist, because in its early stages many religions are quite ecumenical (that is, open to new members).

3. *The Adaptive Period.* To grow and endure, a religious value system must adapt to linguistic, geographical, and cultural settings different from that of its original adherents. For example, Buddhism enjoyed limited success in its homeland India, but it flourished in China, Tibet, and Southeast Asia, where it was adapted to the cultures, societies, and histories there. Likewise, immediately after its formation Christianity was adapted to the broad range of Mediterranean cultures, to the point that the language of the first Christians, Aramaic, was largely neglected. A religious system that does not so adapt, for whatever reason, will eventually die.

4. *The Traditional Period.* This is a comparatively uncreative period in a religious system, although it may be the most long-lasting. Here, the religious system has evolved to the point that institutions now exist with a hierarchy of officials responsible for receiving, preserving, and transmitting without change the sacred tradition. Religious unity and fellowship are largely organizational, superficial, and formal at this stage, expressed mainly in ceremonial gatherings for ritual purposes. *The tradition itself* may become sacred—in other words, something people are most afraid to lose. The Laws of Elaboration, Contrast, and Finality (see above) are most likely to come into play during this period.

5. *The Reform Period.* Some people, frustrated with the perceived meaninglessness of traditional religious forms, become reinvigorated by connecting with the functions and values of the religion's formative or adaptive periods. For example, in the sixteenth century Martin Luther appealed to first-century scriptures and to Saint Augustine (fourth century) as his guidelines for religious renewal, bypassing the thirteenth-century scholastic theology of Thomas Aquinas and the church traditions of his own day. Reform movements seem to fall into one of two classes. *Imitative* reforms attempt to shore up the tradition by reviving certain conventional forms—but not the values—of earlier days. This sort of nostalgia for the past is actually quite common: there is nothing quite so conventional as a restored convention. *Creative* reforms actually manage to recover the complex of values and meanings from the earlier periods, without much concern for retaining traditional forms.

The subtitles of the eight chapters to follow deliberately invoke the five stages just described, to help readers better understand the biblical tradition as it unfolded historically. This tradition is preserved in what Judaism has called Tenakh (the Law, Prophets, and Writings) and what Christianity has called the Old Testament, supplemented by the New. Drawing on the best available evidence and sensitive to the aspects of religion briefly sketched above, the following chapters will explore the numerous factors that, over time, resulted in the production of these scriptures.

One

The World from Abraham to Moses: Prologue to the Emergence of the Biblical Tradition

Suggested Reading

Creation Story: Genesis 1–4
Flood Story and Tower of Babel: Genesis 6–9; 11:1–9
Abraham: Genesis 12:1–9; 13:1–12; 15:1–6; 17:1–8
Joseph: Genesis 37:1–36; 39:1–41:45

Introduction

It is a curious fact that Exodus is not the first book of the Bible. Biblical scholars today acknowledge that Hebrew religion—the worship of the god Yahweh—appeared relatively late in the history of the ancient Near East. Numerous hymns, prayers, and prophetic oracles throughout the Bible poetically describe how a group of Hebrews, led by Moses, escaped slavery in Egypt and shortly thereafter became constituted at Mount Sinai as the people of Yahweh. The prose narrative account of these formative events is found in the book of Exodus.[1]

Yet the Bible begins not with Exodus but with the book of Genesis, which tells of persons and events *prior to* the formation of this religious community. Its first eleven chapters contain incredible stories about the creation of the universe, a garden paradise called Eden, a race of semidivine giants, a cataclysmic flood at the time of Noah, and a man-made tower at Babel so high that it threatened to interfere with God's heavenly abode. A more credible scale prevails through the remainder of Genesis, beginning with a man named Abraham who emigrated from southern Mesopotamia (Ur of the Chaldees) to northern Syria (Haran) and then to Palestine with his wife Sarah and his flocks and herds. Stories of their descendants follow, and the book ends with them finding their way into Egypt, thus setting the stage for their enslavement there and for the events described in Exodus.

The placement of Genesis at the beginning of the biblical canon seems paradoxical, until we view it as testimony to the Hebrews' own

1. The Exodus-Sinai traditions will be covered in the next chapter. The name "Yahweh" was apparently unattested prior to the time of Moses (Exod. 6:3). During the millennium after Moses, however, all sorts of traditions associated with this god Yahweh and the people Israel would be compiled and written down, many finding their way into the Hebrew Bible, or Old Testament. The form "Jehovah" is a recent corruption of this ancient name.

2. The stories in Genesis contain numerous inconsistencies, repetitions, and even contradictions. This has led the scholarly mainstream to conclude that it is actually a pastiche of different documents or sources that have been woven together to form a unified story. Because these different documents were first written down perhaps a thousand years or more after the time of Abraham, scholars today disagree sharply over the extent to which they preserve accurate historical memories.

recognition that their cultural roots were older than their religion. Consequently, our study of the religion of ancient Israel must begin by examining this larger Near Eastern cultural background. This background serves as prologue to the emergence of the biblical tradition. Fortunately, we have abundant textual and artifactual evidence from the Near East prior to 1200 B.C. (the approximate date of Moses and the exodus) and need not rely solely on the traditions of Genesis for that background.[2] Although abundant, this ancient evidence is also incomplete, limited by the accidents of historical discovery and by the momentary interests that prompted ancient people in the first place to record things in writing, always reflecting their own limited perspectives, biases, and conventions. The challenge is to piece these data together in such a way as to catch a glimpse into this ever-elusive past.

Specifically, we hope to clarify five ancient phenomena that are crucial to a well-balanced understanding of the Bible's background:

1. *Amorite Culture.* Most people have never heard of the Amorites, although many scholars have written a great deal about them and the connections between their culture and the Bible. By the time biblical Israel emerged, archaic elements of Amorite culture were spread across the Near East, leaving their mark (in varying degrees) on almost every culture in the lands of the Bible, including that of the Israelites.

2. *Pagan Religion and Social Control.* While ancient governments, kings, bureaucrats, armies, judges, and courtrooms are intelligible to most of us, their integration of religion and politics seems strange, at least to those of us raised on the separation of church and state. By the time ancient people began to develop writing, the religion attested in these texts had apparently lost whatever autonomy it may have once enjoyed and had become essentially an arm of political control. Some gods symbolized the state or empire, while others symbolized the various social, political, and economic interests of different segments and subcultures of society. Like many people today, many ancient Near Easterners seem to have had a difficult time conceiving of religion apart from some social enforcement system. We label as "paganism" this tendency to assume not only that the chief concern of deity is to compel obedience but also that the chief instruments for this are the powerful institutions of control in society. In other words, the social application of coercive force was considered to be the typical concerns of the gods.

3. *Social Disintegration and Collapse.* There has been a prevailing tendency among scholars to explain the destruction of major social organizations (e.g., states and empires) in terms of *external forces*, such as invading armies. Social organizations also became vulnerable to collapse and

destruction from *internal processes,* such as the disintegration of loyalties into competing factions within the organization. When this occurred, there is evidence of immigrants and refugees fleeing from economically unstable and increasingly violent trouble spots. Although often downplayed or ignored by most biblical scholars, this phenomenon contributed to the historical processes out of which Israelite community and religion emerged.

4. *Village Life.* Historians understandably focus on the affairs of the major urban centers of political and economic power, and the elites there who produced written records. Unfortunately, the agricultural village has been largely ignored and sometimes even disparaged by historians, even though this is where—year-in and year-out—the economic staples of *everyone's* existence (food and clothing/textiles) were produced. This is also where 80 percent of the people were born, raised families, struggled with daily hardships, paid taxes, tried to enjoy the simple pleasures of life, and died. Not only in the ancient Near East but almost everywhere, the village was also the locus of cultural continuity, in which one could find vestiges of older ways of life, including simpler technologies, more archaic social patterns, and older ways of thought (see Figs. 3.3, 8.2, and 8.4).

5. *Ethnic Diversity.* A century ago, Western scholars interpreted most biblical references to Edomites, Assyrians, Hebrews, and so forth as references to discrete *ethnic groups,* an interpretation reinforced by then-current beliefs that each was originally a distinctive tribe or group of desert nomads. This was also reinforced by numerous biblical passages depicting each group as having a single, literal, biological ancestor (e.g., Esau is presented as the father of all Edomites in Gen. 36:1, 43). It is widely conceded today that references to common ancestors were almost always fictive and symbolic, not literal or biological. It now seems preferable to view these biblical references instead as the names of *political regimes* and *social organizations* whose members could, in fact, be quite diverse ethnically. Rather than an amalgam of discrete ethnic groups, each associated with a distinct geographical center or homeland, the Near East was an ethnic melting pot in the centuries prior to Moses. Even the word "Hebrew" did not originally designate an ethnic group, and the evidence is sufficiently strong today to suggest that the Jewish concern for ethnicity appeared only a few centuries before the time of Christ. Perhaps most radical of all is evidence (discussed in chapters 2 and 3) suggesting that the Israelites themselves originally comprised a mix of people from different ethnic backgrounds. If true, the conventional picture of Yahwism as the religion peculiar to a distinctive ethnic group will have to be radically revised.

The Early Bronze Age

Historians refer to the pre-Israelite era as the Bronze Age. The recurring and massive disruptions of civilization in the Near East during that time are used to subdivide it into Early, Middle, and Late periods, each of which can be further subdivided into discrete phases. Inspired largely by nineteenth-century romantic writings about Arab bedouin, most historians throughout the twentieth century believed that these major cultural disruptions were the work of outside forces, specifically masses of land-hungry, Semitic-speaking nomads sweeping out of the Arabian desert and overwhelming these civilizations. According to this theory, the Israelites were one such group, invading Palestine around 1200 B.C. and overrunning Canaanite civilization. Although it has been largely dismissed by most scholars, this theory still manages to capture the imagination of popular audiences and some scholars (see Box 1.1).

The characteristic features of both Egyptian and Mesopotamian civilizations arose during the Early Bronze Age (3400–2000 B.C.), the time of the great pyramids of Egypt and the powerful Sumerian city-states of southern Mesopotamia. We know comparatively little about

Table 1.1 Chronology of the Ancient Near East (Early Bronze Age)

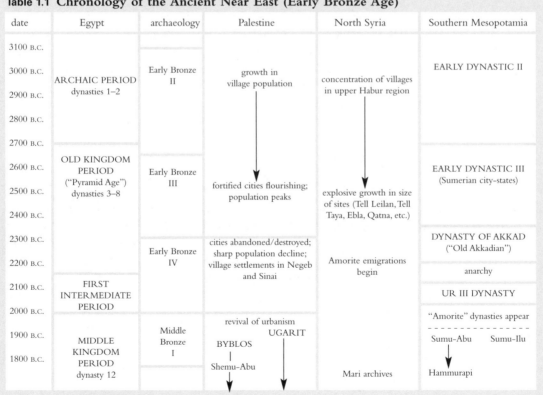

date	Egypt	archaeology	Palestine	North Syria	Southern Mesopotamia
3100 B.C.					
3000 B.C.	ARCHAIC PERIOD dynasties 1–2	Early Bronze II	growth in village population	concentration of villages in upper Habur region	EARLY DYNASTIC II
2900 B.C.					
2800 B.C.					
2700 B.C.					
2600 B.C.	OLD KINGDOM PERIOD ("Pyramid Age") dynasties 3–8	Early Bronze III	fortified cities flourishing; population peaks	explosive growth in size of sites (Tell Leilan, Tell Taya, Ebla, Qatna, etc.)	EARLY DYNASTIC III (Sumerian city-states)
2500 B.C.					
2400 B.C.					
2300 B.C.		Early Bronze IV	cities abandoned/destroyed; sharp population decline; village settlements in Negeb and Sinai	Amorite emigrations begin	DYNASTY OF AKKAD ("Old Akkadian")
2200 B.C.					anarchy
2100 B.C.	FIRST INTERMEDIATE PERIOD				UR III DYNASTY
2000 B.C.			revival of urbanism UGARIT		"Amorite" dynasties appear
1900 B.C.	MIDDLE KINGDOM PERIOD dynasty 12	Middle Bronze I	BYBLOS | Shemu-Abu	Mari archives	Sumu-Abu Sumu-Ilu Hammurapi
1800 B.C.					

Box 1.1—Nomadism as a Scholarly "Invention"

To explain cultural change in the ancient Near East, nineteenth-century scholars developed the notion of invading waves of Semitic-speaking desert nomads. The following excerpt preserves the flavor of this image, in which most population groups were assumed to be ethnically homogeneous, and in which the most fertile part of the "fertile crescent" seems to have been the heart of the sandy desert!

> The heart of the Arabian peninsula and of the Syrian desert north of it was inhabited from time immemorial by bedouins who eked out a near-starvation existence roaming with their herds of sheep and goats over the vast expanses of sand in search of better pastures. Under the pressure of hunger or the lust of adventure bedouin groups would raid from time to time adjacent areas of the "sown." . . . It is possible to follow . . . the arrival of wave after wave of nomads from the desert. . . . The first Semites to abandon nomadism seem to have been the Akkadians. . . . Next came the *Amurru* (Biblical Amorites). . . . Late in the second millennium the Arameans begin to give up their nomadic habits, and by and by occupy the territory around Damascus in Syria.
> — S. Schwantes, *The Ancient Near East* (1965), 11–12

Today, modified versions of this discredited view substitute the nondescript word "seminomad" and tone down the warlike image of these allegedly distinct ethnic groups:

> A bewildering role [*sic*] call of ethnic groups and social groups has passed before us. In Mesopotamia there does seem to be a trend for seminomadic groups to come from the west down the Euphrates and to establish themselves first on the fringes of the cultivated areas and then to penetrate, usually peacefully, into the settled land. The Guti, the Amorites, the Kassites, and the Arameans probably all conformed to that pattern.
> — D. Snell, *Life in the Ancient Near East* (1997), 121

This outdated model for explaining cultural change has inspired the romantic subtitle of Thomas Cahill's popular book, *The Gifts of the Jews: How a Tribe of Desert Nomads Changed the Way Everyone Thinks and Feels*. It periodically surfaces in archaeological literature, such as the 1994 collection of essays entitled *From Nomadism to Monarchy: Archaeological and Historical Aspects of Early Israel*. Many years ago my colleague, Professor William Schorger, an anthropologist specializing in the Near East, observed that many people in the Near East and modern scholars considered their cultures to have originated with the bedouin, who were believed to have preserved archaic traits that the other cultures had given up.

Palestine at this time, however, because we have unearthed no texts there dating from this period. But the archaeological study of the Early Bronze (EB) Age has shed some important light. For example, we now know that the population density in Palestine in the EB Age was higher than at any other period in its history until the Byzantine Empire (fourth–seventh centuries A.D.). The first two phases of the EB Age in Palestine were characterized by a growing number of small agricultural villages based almost entirely on the combination of agriculture and herding (sheep and goats), a combination going as far back as 8000 B.C. Whether in Italy or Palestine—or Nebraska a century ago—people would farm the land that could be cultivated, with the rest being used for grazing domestic animals. It was not until the third phase of the EB Age (2650–2300 B.C.) that large fortified cities first began to be built in Palestine, many covering areas 25–50 acres in size with defensive walls 25–30 feet thick. But all these large cities, like the cities and empires elsewhere in the ancient Near East, depended on the economic productivity of small agricultural villages for such basics as food and clothing. The economic vitality of small agricultural villages is one of the keys to understanding the history and culture of the ancient Near East.

Between 2300 and 2100 B.C., these large fortified cities of Palestine fell into ruin for reasons that remain a mystery. One after another was destroyed or simply abandoned. It is estimated that during this period the population of Palestine dropped 65 to 85 percent. By 2000 B.C., settlement had reverted to small unwalled villages, including new settlements farther south in the wildernesses of the Negeb and Sinai. Thus, the population levels in EB Age Palestine start low, rise, reach a climax, and then decline sharply after 2300 B.C. Such fluctuations in population are also attested in Syria at this time.

So-called Nomads

The region around the Euphrates River is a desert fringe area. While it does not receive enough annual rainfall to support dry farming (i.e., cultivation without irrigation), it *does* receive enough (at least four inches per year) to support wild grasses on which animals can graze. The northernmost arch of the critical ten-inch annual rainfall line (the minimum for dry farming) lies some miles south of the modern Syria-Turkey border (see Map 1.1); north of it, the number of mounds of ruins is astonishing, virtually all yielding EB Age pottery fragments. The shape of these mounds is characteristic of unwalled villages, not fortified cities, so it seems that the dense settlement here in the region of the upper Habur River consisted largely of agricultural villages, not political power centers. There was also a series of cities along the river valleys of eastern

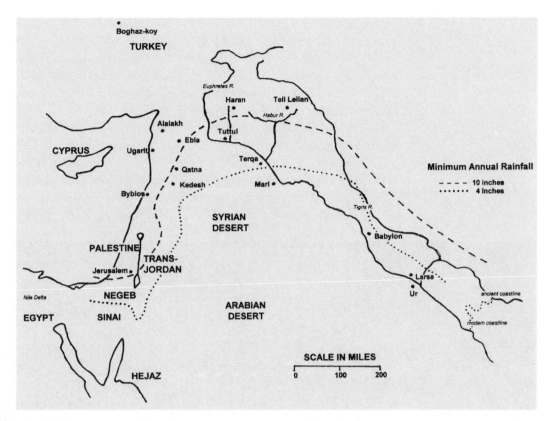

Map 1.1
The Ancient Near East in the Bronze Age. Rain is sufficient above the 10-inch rainfall line to support agriculture. Hundreds of unexcavated village mounds—many dating to the EB Age—can be seen north of this line between the Tigris and Euphrates rivers. Below the 4-inch line (the Syrian and Arabian deserts) rainfall will support occasional pastoralism. Residents there rely on complex irrigation systems. Between the two rainfall lines is the steppeland, where enough rain falls to support pastoralism.

Syria, which seem to have functioned as trading sites and also as centers for manufacturing textiles. About 25 percent of the Ebla texts, which date from about 2300 B.C., deal with the production and sale of textiles, as do a great many of the texts from Mari five hundred years later. The major textile commodity then was wool, the production of which required vast flocks of sheep and goats.

For many scholars, the mere presence of such flocks was enough to prove that these people were landless nomads. However, it actually constitutes evidence of exactly the reverse situation: highly productive, large-scale sheepherding. The fringe area between the 10-inch and 4-inch rainfall lines is much like western Kansas and eastern Colorado in North America: it is prime territory for large-scale sheepherding. Documents from the Middle Bronze Age site of Mari (ca. 1800–1760 B.C.) indicate that its king alone owned 20,000–30,000 sheep, all entrusted to the care of professional shepherds, who would be away from home, out in the steppes, for weeks at a time. But the point is that they *had* a home: they were not wandering nomads (see Box 1.4).

This sort of village-based pastoralism, often called "transhumance," has been confused with bedouin "nomadism" ever since the nineteenth century, a confusion perpetuated by the continued use of the meaning-less word "seminomad." Careful historical and anthropological study of bedouin nomadism indicates that the bedouin cultures of the diverse Arabian peninsula probably did not exist much before the eighth century B.C.; therefore, bedouin nomadism is essentially irrelevant to the origins of the Israelites four or five centuries earlier.

The archaeological record also refutes the nomadic-invasion theory: there is simply no evidence of anyone living in the areas where all these nomadic invasions were supposedly originating. Furthermore, linguistic evidence from the MB Age site of Byblos (in modern-day Lebanon) reveals an extremely archaic Semitic language there that can be tentatively characterized as a common ancestor of both Arabic and

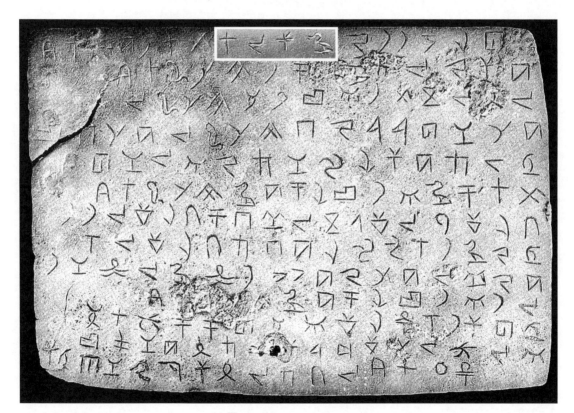

Figure 1.1

Syllabic Text from Bronze Age Byblos. It took the author over forty years to decipher a half-dozen texts such as this copper tablet from Byblos, dating to around 1800 B.C. These signs correspond to spoken syllables, and some were later used in the development of the alphabet. A concordance of recurring sign-combinations helps establish words whose roots can be compared with those in other Semitic languages. The language of the Byblos texts is an archaic forerunner of both Hebrew and Arabic. (Adapted from *ANEP*, Fig. 287, p. 89.)

Hebrew. Thus, the forerunner of the language of the desert Arabs was not some remote dialect of the northwest Arabian peninsula but actually the language of the highly urbanized Bronze Age civilization along the Mediterranean coast. This suggests a population movement from the settled areas *out to* the desert, not vice versa.

The Importance of Linguistic History

Between the language of the Byblos texts and the fact that these "staging" areas were unoccupied at the time, it is clear that neither the periodic disruptions of Bronze Age (and later) cultures nor the differences in the various Semitic languages can be adequately explained by the theory of successive waves of land-hungry nomads emerging from the desert, settling down, and becoming "civilized." For example, the Sumerian language of the Early Dynastic texts was replaced by the Old Akkadian language around 2300 B.C., and that language gave way, after the disruptions at the end of the EB Age, to Old Babylonian in the south and Old Assyrian in the north. Even in Egypt the Old Egyptian language of the EB Age was replaced after the First Intermediate Period by Middle (or Classical) Egyptian. What accounts for the significant linguistic changes that usually accompanied such major cultural transformations? If one population group was not invading and supplanting another one, how do we explain this change in language?

In the first place, the only reason we know anything at all about these ancient languages is because the urban political regimes of Mesopotamia

---

Box 1.2—The Writings of Scribal Bureaucrats

Grassroots contempt for the writings of the bureaucratic elite is illustrated in this second-millennium-B.C. text. Historians disagree on whether its description of social chaos preserves actual memories of Egypt's First Intermediate period.

> Lo, offices are opened,
> Their records stolen,
> . . . .
> Lo, [scribes] are slain,
> Their writings stolen,
> Woe is me for the grief of this time!
> Lo, the scribes of the land-register,
> Their books are destroyed,
> . . . .
> Lo, the laws of the chambers are thrown out,
> Men walk on them in the streets,
> Beggars tear them up in the alleys. (*AEL*, 1:155)

Figure 1.2
Ancient Scribes. A professional corps of writers, such as these depicted on a wall carving from EB Age Giza (in Egypt), existed in royal courts and temples across the Near East, including Jerusalem in biblical times. In addition to routine record-keeping duties, government officials such as these also created and preserved all sorts of literature (such as in the Old Testament) on behalf of their royal patrons.

and Egypt relied heavily on written records. A class of highly trained scribes developed specialized systems of writing—hieroglyphics in Egypt and cuneiform in Mesopotamia—that endured for several centuries with little change. The same was true of the languages expressed by this writing. In contrast, the language of the common folk was constantly evolving as it always does in every language, so that over time the gulf widened considerably between the official language of the written documents and the vernacular of the common folk (including perhaps the vernacular of the scribes themselves). Some evidence indicates that at times of social collapse grassroots populations expressed great contempt for professional scribes and their official documents (see Box 1.2).

The biblical story of the Tower of Babel (Genesis 11) may express a popular awareness of this gap between the official language of the power structure and the common dialects of the regions that fall under its control—and under its language. It recognizes the connection between sociopolitical collapse and linguistic diversity, although it interprets the latter to be the cause of collapse rather than a concurrent phenomenon.

The destruction or collapse of a civilization is often followed by several centuries when there is almost no writing at all because everyone is struggling daily simply to secure the basic necessities of life. This is what historians call a "dark age." When a bureaucracy reemerges and official writing resumes, the new class of professional scribes bases its writing system not on the outdated (and perhaps even unintelligible) language of centuries past, but on the common vernacular spoken *at the time*. The person unaware of historical linguistics might mistakenly attribute changes of this magnitude to some new foreign group invading, destroying, and replacing the old native one. The new regime inevitably became as conservative linguistically as its predecessor, so that once again, over time, the gap would widen between the official language of the elite and the grass-roots dialect of the common folk. Because local factors can explain such linguistic change, there is no need *necessarily* to attribute it to foreign invaders, much less marauding nomads. Consequently, biblical scholars no longer have a solid basis for depicting the early Israelites as such nomads (or seminomads).

The End of the Early Bronze Age

However, we do have evidence of two notable population movements around the end of the Early Bronze Age (labeled "EB IV"), neither of which are instances of nomadism. The first involves Palestine proper. We noted previously that, although the collapse of the large EB III settlements decimated the population, there was apparently a population *increase* between 2300 and 2100 B.C. farther south, in the more arid Negeb and Sinai wilderness regions. It seems reasonable to conclude that these people relocated here because this was one of the few places of refuge from the violence and chaos associated with the collapse of urban, political civilization. The archaeological record shows miserable stone huts, grinding stones (suggesting some limited agriculture), and the remains of animal bones and pens, confirming that sheep/goat husbandry was the mainstay of their economic livelihood. Anthropologists have noted that the goat is an extremely efficient "factory" for converting inedible cellulose (such as wilderness stubble) into human food (milk, yogurt, cheese, and meat).

Scholars have theorized that the collapse of EB III Palestine was precipitated by external forces such as invasion, plague, climatic catastrophe, or the withdrawal of Egyptian control. But we should not be too quick to dismiss *internal* social causes, which have often been overlooked by scholars. There is evidence elsewhere that the breakdown of familial and personal relationships almost always accompanies the destruction of political organizations and the consequent radical drop in population. An ancient text lamenting the destruction of Ur around 2000 B.C. describes in rather stark terms the concurrent collapse of family relationships.

Social processes of fissioning (or disintegration) often follow sharp increases in population density (such as occurred in EB III Palestine), as competition for resources intensifies. The challenges of social control become acute. In the absence of internalized ethical restraints, the political structure increasingly relies on force (military, police, courts) to regulate a growing and increasingly complex society. An ever larger proportion of its total productivity is directed toward its institutions and structures of control, especially the military, straining the whole economic system further. If its use of coercive force (law and order) is successful in achieving short-term political interests, then people with such interests increasingly begin to value their own exercise of power, further accelerating social disintegration. Consequently, society begins to break down into smaller and smaller units, each of which conceives of itself as a power base eager to acquire control or influence over the political institutions and structures that govern its affairs. It then matters little whether the final destruction eventually comes from within or without, because such fissioning itself is already the first and perhaps most incorrigible stage in the destruction of the social unity.

Meanwhile, the productive segment of society—the submerged 80 percent of the population who are village agriculturalists and pastoralists—is increasingly subjected to the ruinous confiscation of its produce. The *expenses* of a small farmer in the Euphrates River valley during the Old Babylonian period—including taxes, rent for the land, water rights, and sharecropping arrangements (50 percent of his produce could go to the landowners)—theoretically amounted to 110 percent of his *income*. It is no wonder that a system like this breaks down in violence, or that farmers start investing more heavily in transportable livestock and emigrate to more remote areas, out of the reach of the increasingly dysfunctional urban power centers.

The Amorites

The second notable population movement involved north Syria. Earlier we noted the large number of EB Age village ruins north of the 10-inch rainfall line, and the large tracts of grazing land in the steppes south of it. This area, called "Amurru" (or "The West") by the Mesopotamians, could sustain a relatively dense population, and indeed, there is evidence of increasing population density in the region between 2500 and 2300 B.C. (see Table 1.1). For example, the site of Tell Leilan grew from 37 acres to 247 acres, suggesting a population increase from 4,000 to 25,000. We may infer that, in time, social fissioning followed such an increase in population density, creating tensions among the people of Amurru. The Bible calls these people "Amorites."

The population growth in this region stimulated Amorite migrations to the southeast, which the Mesopotamians did not welcome. One of the kings of Ur even built a wall to check the flow of these newcomers. But the Amorites had a transforming impact on Mesopotamian culture: by 1900–1800 B.C., virtually every major Mesopotamian city-state had a king with an Amorite name. The founder of the Old Babylonian dynasty—Hammurapi's great-great grandfather—was Sumu-Abu, an Amorite name. His contemporary, the king of Larsa, was Sumu-Ilu, another Amorite name identical to that of the great Israelite prophet Samuel (*shemu-'el*).

3. When this kingdom was destroyed around 1200 B.C. and some of its rogue soldiers set up petty regimes in Palestine and Transjordan, the name Amurru once again migrated farther south. Since this coincided with the appearance of biblical Israel in the same region (see chapter 3), early biblical traditions sometimes refer to portions of Palestine and Transjordan as the land of the Amorites (Num. 21:31; Judg. 11:21; also Josh. 10:6).

The fact that such names also surface among the biblical Israelites strongly suggests that Amorites not only migrated east. Apparently, those Amorites unwilling to abandon life on the steppes for the congestion of the Mesopotamian cities would have found plenty of hospitable territory and fertile farmland to the south and west, in southern Syria and Palestine. Although direct evidence for such migrations is lacking, there are all sorts of indirect clues. For example, by about 1800 B.C. the city-states of Byblos and Ugarit on the Mediterranean coast had kings with Amorite names. Indeed, the name of the first known Amorite king at Byblos was Shemu-Abu, a dialect variant of the same name held by the founder of the Old Babylonian dynasty (Sumu-Abu). The southwesterly migration of some Amorite groups is also suggested by the southwesterly migration of the geographical name "Amurru." In the EB Age, it originally designated northeast Syria (i.e., the area around the Habur River). Several centuries later, the Mari letters refer to the area south of Qatna as the "land of Amurru," consisting of several small kingdoms. Later still, tablets excavated at Alalakh refer to a kingdom named "Amurru" that flourished in the Late Bronze Age around Kadesh (see Map 1.1).[3]

Box 1.3 — A Sumerian View of the Amorites

One Sumerian satire describes Amorites (represented by the logogram MAR.TU) as uncivilized barbarians:

> The MAR.TU who know no grain . . . who know no house nor town. . . . The MAR.TU who digs up truffles . . . who does not bend his knees (to cultivate the land), who eats raw meat, who has no house during his lifetime, who is not buried after his death. (*SEM*, nos. 58 and 112)

Some have erroneously assumed that this text provides an ethnographically sober description of the Amorites as nomads.

The Amorites must have been extremely good at agriculture and at developing sheep-herding technology to exploit the desert fringe. As competition for grazing land increased, those Amorites disinterested in the city life of Mesopotamia had to relocate their sheep to the vast steppelands farther south. The abandonment of the EB III urban centers of Palestine around 2300 B.C. would have opened up vast tracts of unregulated steppeland where, for the next several centuries, Amorite shepherds could thrive by greatly expanding their production of sheep. Many biblical scholars today correlate the stories of Abraham's migrations (Gen. 12:1–9) with just such a southwesterly emigration of Amorites.

The Middle Bronze Age

By 1800 B.C., many Amorite families had accommodated themselves to urban culture, amassed wealth and influence, and become power brokers in the politics of the Near East. One noteworthy Amorite kingdom of the Middle Bronze (MB) Age was Mari, located on the Euphrates River near the modern border of Syria and Iraq. Archaeologists have unearthed archives there containing more than twenty-five thousand tablets, including many

Figure 1.3

Pastoralism. A phenomenon in the Near East unchanged since antiquity is the grazing of sheep in uncultivated steppeland. This is not nomadism, though the shepherd may be away from his village weeks at a time. In the 1970s, a teenage boy of the village of Hadidi could earn one Syrian pound (= 25 cents) per sheep per month. If he tended one hundred sheep, he could earn about $300 per year, the average annual income at that time. By the early 1990s, one ewe alone generated about $100 per year in income from the lambs, wool, and milk. The livestock of biblical characters such as Abraham and Jacob constituted real wealth in a society requiring no cash expenses at all. (Painting by Eathel Mendenhall)

letters revealing features of Amorite culture and society that may have been carried southwest by immigrants whose descendants centuries later constituted a major component of Israelite society. Their "Amorite legacy" is still evident in vast portions of the Old Testament.

Most scholars believe that some Canaanite myths and epics recounted in the Late Bronze (LB) Age texts from Ugarit actually originated several centuries earlier in the MB Age, when they circulated orally. (See Box 1.6 for an excerpt of the Canaanite myth of Baal.) If so, then the MB Age appears to have been a sort of Canaanite "Heroic Age," the term applied by the great Sumerologist S. N. Kramer to periods in a society's history when royal courts would host a variety of festivities for visiting ambassadors, trade delegations, and other dignitaries, at which professional singers would recite epic tales about ancient heroes and royal ancestors[4] (see Fig. 1.4).

Among the MB Age ballads recited at the royal festivities of Ugarit were those recounting the exploits of epic characters such as Keret and Dan'il, both of whom were royal figures imperiled by lack of an heir. In this respect, they resemble the biblical Abraham, a man likewise childless but destined to sire a royal dynasty (Gen. 15:1–6; 17:1–8). The original form of his name, Abram, is clearly Amorite, leading many scholars to speculate that, along with his kinsmen and livestock, he may have been an actual historical person who joined the southwesterly migration toward the land of Canaan. If he became a locally renowned figure, he, too, may have become the subject of some MB Age oral ballad centuries before Israelite scribes transformed it into the stories now found in the book of Genesis.

4. The so-called Age of Homer in Greece would be another example of this. Some scholars believe that Bronze Age merchants from Mycenae may have regularly heard such performances at the royal court of Ugarit and carried this tradition back to their Greek homeland.

Box 1.4—Mari and the Bible

Some of the Mari letters, written by provincial officials to the king, describe prophets resembling some of those of ancient Israel (see Box 5.3). Others reveal tensions between the government and villagers who often identified themselves tribally. One such tribe was the Hanaeans. Another, the Benjaminites (*banu-yamina*), had the exact same name as a later Israelite tribal group (*ben-yamin* in Hebrew). (The following are translations of texts published in *Mélanges Dussaud* II, 988; ARM 3:38; and ARM 2:48.)

To: Zimri-Lim
From: Yassi-Dagan
   Ever since I acquired the steppelands of the Euphrates, Benjaminites have been continuously conducting raids. On one occasion, they stole many sheep. I sent armed soldiers after them and they killed them, so that no one got away and all the stolen sheep were recovered.

To: Zimri-Lim
From: Kibri-Dagan
   I notified the people of Terqa and they assembled labor crews. I also wrote to the Benjaminite villages, and the tribal representative of Dumteti replied: "Let the enemy come and drag us away from our villages!" This was his response. Consequently, no one from the Benjaminite villages helped me with the harvest.

To: Zimri-Lim
From: Bahdi-Lim
   The Hanaeans arrived from the steppes and are dwelling in their villages. Twice I sent notice to their villages summoning them, but they did not assemble. Now, if it please my lord, let someone execute one of the criminals in prison, cut off his head, and parade it through their villages. Their contingents will be intimidated by this and will quickly assemble.

The first letter may allude to lingering disputes over whether the royal flocks legitimately belonged to the king. The other two letters suggest that villagers had their own important chores to do, especially at harvesttime when shepherd youths had returned from the winter pastures. The royal work projects were a low priority, and being conscripted for them apparently caused deep resentment.

The Amorite Legacy in the Bible

At the dawn of the twentieth century, a number of scholars claimed that anything of importance in the Bible had been copied or derived from southern Mesopotamia, since civilization there was obviously superior. *Materially* speaking, of course, it was: Palestine has always been a relatively poor provincial backwater. But the fact remains that the Bible—the product of this impoverished backwater—is the only important aspect of *any* of these ancient civilizations that survives to the present day. Everything else died and was largely forgotten until the archaeologist's spade dug it up.

Figure 1.4

Female Singers. Women were almost always present at royal festivities. The pharaohs often demanded singing girls and beautiful women from Palestine, and several dozen singing girls served at the Mari palace. This fifteenth-century tomb painting from Thebes shows women serving as entertainers and "hostesses." Daily administrative texts from Mari reveal the physical toll these festivities could exact on the "weaving women," who also served as hostesses: the day after one party, five pints of perfumed oil were distributed to "the weaving women who are sick."

5. The Babylonian version (translated in *ANET*³, 93–95 ["*Tablet XI*"], *DOTT,* 17–24, and *OTPar,* 25–28) cited Mount Nisir in eastern Mesopotamia as the place where the ark landed. When the Hurrians took over this Amorite flood story, they had the ark land in the mountains of Ararat, their ancestral homeland in northeast Turkey. When some Hurrians later governed Jerusalem during the LB Age, their version of the flood story became established there. Centuries later, Israelite scribes in Jerusalem periodically revised it to address Israelite religious concerns, adding references to their God Yahweh, to "clean" and "unclean" animals, and to the so-called "covenant" with Noah. This Israelite updating of the Hurrian version of an Amorite flood story eventually found permanent expression in Genesis 6–9. See note 10 below.

Nevertheless, the parallels between the Bible and the civilization of southern Mesopotamia are significant. Already a century ago, two were perceived to be most striking:

First, there are similarities, sometimes verbatim, between the famous law code of the Babylonian king Hammurapi and the laws recorded in the so-called Covenant Code of Exodus 21–23. Both include such phrases as "an eye for an eye and a tooth for a tooth" (the *lex talionis*). (For an explanation of the *lex talionis*, see chapter 3, note 14.)

Second, the parallels between the biblical story of Noah's ark (Genesis 6–9) and the story of the legendary Mesopotamian king Gilgamesh are remarkable. Gilgamesh's quest for eternal life brought him to a remote corner of the world, where he met Utnapishtim. Utnapishtim had been granted immortality by the gods because, when a flood had threatened to engulf the world, he had built an ark and brought aboard a pair of each animal. This story predates the Bible by more than a thousand years but is similar in numerous details, including the releasing of birds to see if the flood waters had subsided.⁵

Such parallels can no longer be explained as ancient Israelite borrowing from a superior Babylonian civilization in southern Mesopotamia because there was hardly any contact between these two areas until after

Box 1.5—Biblical and Ancient Near Eastern Law

There are many parallels between the law code of Hammurapi's Amorite dynasty of Babylon and biblical laws in Exodus, Leviticus, and Deuteronomy. Both probably reflect ancient Amorite legal traditions. Some of the parallels are noteworthy (excerpted from *OTPar*, 101–109).

Code of Hammurapi	Biblical Law
No. 14—If a citizen kidnaps and sells a member of another citizen's household into slavery, then the sentence is death	Whoever kidnaps a person, whether that person has been sold or is still held in possession, shall be put to death. (Exod. 21:16)
No. 57—If a herder does not have a covenant with the owner of a field to graze his sheep on it, but has grazed his sheep on the field without the consent of the owner, when the owner of the field harvests it, then the fine is one hundred forty bushels of grain for every sixteen acres of land.	When someone causes a field or vineyard to be grazed over, or lets livestock loose to graze in someone else's field, restitution shall be made from the best in the owner's field or vineyard. (Exod. 22:5)
No. 209—If one citizen beats the daughter of another and causes her to miscarry, then the fine is six ounces of silver.	When people who are fighting injure a pregnant woman so that there is a miscarriage, and yet no further harm follows, the one responsible shall be fined what the woman's husband demands, paying as much as the judges determine. (Exod. 21:22)
No. 196—If a citizen blinds an eye of an official, then his eye is to be blinded. No. 197—If one citizen breaks a bone of another, then his own bone is to be broken.	If any harm follows, then you shall give life for life, eye for eye, tooth for tooth, hand for hand, foot for foot, burn for burn, wound for wound, stripe for stripe. (Exod. 21:23–25)

586 B.C., when the biblical traditions were already well established. Rather than accepting the so-called pan-Babylonianism of a century ago (i.e., the claim that Israelite traditions were directly dependent on Babylonian ones), we can now see that *both* cultures—the Babylonian and the Israelite—independently inherited and preserved many elements of the more-archaic Amorite culture.

These and other originally Amorite cultural elements (such as the myth of cosmic combat) were already deeply embedded in the culture of

Box 1.6—The Myth of Cosmic Combat

The Mesopotamian form of the Amorite myth of cosmic combat is reflected in the Babylonian creation epic *Enuma elish*, which describes the hero-god Marduk's battle against the serpentine Tiamat, who represents chaos:

> They strove in single combat, locked in battle.
> ....
> With his unsparing mace he [Marduk] crushed her [Tiamat's] skull.
> ....
> He split her like a shellfish into two parts:
> half of her he set up and ceiled it as sky,
> ....
> He determined the year by designating the zones:
> He set up three constellations for each of the twelve months.
> ....
> The Moon he caused to shine, the night (to him) entrusting. (*ANET* [3], 67–68)

In the Canaanite form of this myth, chaos is represented by Yam (or "Prince Sea"), who is vanquished by the hero-god Baal.

> And the club danced in Baal's hands,
>   like a vulture from his fingers.
> It struck Prince Sea on the skull,
> ....
> Sea stumbled;
>   he fell to the ground;
> ....
> Baal captured and drank Sea;
>   he finished off Judge River. (*SAC*, 89)

Note how the Israelites modified this myth (still retaining references to Yam, "Sea") to extol the power and glory of Yahweh:

> O Yahweh, God of hosts,
>   who is as mighty as you, O Yahweh?
> ....
> You rule the raging of the sea [Hebrew *yam*];
>   when its waves rise, you still them.
> You crushed Rahab like a carcass. (Ps. 89:8–10)
>
> You divided the sea [*yam*] by your might,
>   you broke the heads of the dragons in the waters.
> You crushed the heads of Leviathan;
> ....
> Yours is the day, yours also the night;
>   you established the luminaries and the sun. (Ps. 74:13–14, 16)

many of the people who later embraced the worship of the Hebrew god, Yahweh. These people were free to retain or modify any of their traditions, so long as they were not incompatible with Yahwism. Consequently, it is not surprising that many of these traditions surface in the Old Testament.

Egypt and the Hyksos	The MB revival of Canaan coincides with the reunification of Egypt during the so-called Middle Kingdom period. The pharaohs of the Twelfth Dynasty restored trade relations with the coastal cities of Canaan, which had been interrupted during the First Intermediate period. Commercial and cultural exchanges between Egypt and Palestine date back to the EB I period, leading some archaeologists to speculate that an Egyptian military colony existed in southern Palestine long before the Pyramid Age. Moreover, hundreds of Semitic words entered the Egyptian vocabulary, and many Canaanite gods were "Egyptianized" and worshiped along the Nile.

Increasing numbers of Semites from Canaan immigrated into the eastern Nile Delta in the nineteenth century B.C. In time, some of them gained significant political and economic influence. The demise of the Twelfth Dynasty shortly after 1800 B.C. marks the beginning of the Second Intermediate period, during which political instability and decentralization returned to Egypt, and a line of Asian immigrants established themselves as a dynasty of pharaohs, extending their rule across the Nile Delta. The Egyptians contemptuously referred to these Asiatics as *heqaw khasut* (or *Hyksos,* in Greek), "rulers from foreign lands." Some scholars believe that the Joseph story in Genesis 37–50 preserves traditions from this period, when northern Egypt was essentially an extension of Canaan itself and when Semites from Canaan—such as Joseph and Jacob—could enjoy favorable treatment and even career advancement in the courts of the Hyksos pharaohs.

The Empires of the Late Bronze Age	Personal names in fourteenth-century-B.C. documents reveal that there was tremendous ethnic diversity in many parts of Syria-Palestine, with roughly 40 percent being Semitic, 35 percent Hurrian, and 20 percent Indo-European. The situation then was probably not much different from reading the names listed in the telephone directory of a typical American city today. In other words, Syria-Palestine was a cultural melting pot, the new home of many populations displaced during this period by the

6. Some frequently over-
looked biblical passages
suggest that early Israel
likewise comprised a pot-
pourri of different peoples
(see chapters 2 and 3),
which is exactly what one
would expect in Palestine
at this time. Indeed, the
notion of an ethnically
distinct Israelite (or
"Jew") arose more than
seven hundred years
later, under radically different historical circum-
stances (see chapter 7).

expansion and collision of the large empires of the day.[6] Three of those empires were particularly important:

1. *Egyptian.* By 1550 B.C., the native Egyptians had reunited and driven the Hyksos from power. Especially significant were the punitive military campaigns that the Eighteenth Dynasty pharaohs conducted across Canaan (see Box 2.1). Egypt was beginning to emerge as a major imperial power, its military expansion driven, in part, by a desire to ensure that Asiatics would never again wield power over Egypt. This period, roughly 1550–1200 B.C., is called the "New Kingdom" or "Empire" period in Egypt, and the LB Age in Canaan. The areas of Lebanon and Damascus marked the northernmost extension of uncontested Egyptian control.

2. *Mitanni.* Farther north, Egypt's main rival was initially the Mitanni. This north Syrian empire was ruled by Hurrians whose society was dominated by the *maryannu*, a military aristocracy providing much of the muscle for Mitanni military expansion. Treaties with Egypt shortly after 1400 B.C. established a boundary between the two empires. But the Mitanni Empire, squeezed between two expansionist rivals, the Assyrians and the Hittites, had collapsed by 1350 B.C., and the surviving *maryannu* were enlisted in the service of other empires.

3. *Hittite.* Until recently, the Hittites were little more than names in the Bible, but we can now reconstruct a fairly detailed history of their civilization. The Hittite capital at Boghaz-koy in central Anatolia has been excavated, and important Hittite archives have been uncovered, containing several dozen treaties that will be discussed in the next chapter. Around 1350 B.C., the Hittite king Shuppiluliumash I conquered the Mitanni capital and annexed their territory. The Hittites also gained control of some smaller kingdoms that had previously been under Egyptian control, including Ugarit and Amurru, setting the stage for a clash of the Egyptian and Hittite superpowers.

Power Politics and "Hebrews" in the Amarna Age

A cache of 380 tablets discovered in the archives at Tell el-Amarna in Egypt, where the heretic king Amenophis IV, or Akhenaten, established his capital, illuminates the situation of some of the smaller states caught up in this clash of superpowers. Most were letters written by various kings to Akhenaten and his predecessor, Amenophis III, informing them of urgent matters affecting their respective kingdoms (see Box 1.8). One such kingdom was that of Amurru, located around Kadesh. As its name suggests, the ruling regime there traced its ancestry to the Amorites of north Syria, even though by this time its population was as ethnically diverse as the rest of the region.

Table 1.2 Chronology of the Ancient Near East (Late Bronze Age)

date	Egyptians	Hittites	Syria-Palestine	Ugarit	Amurru
1400 B.C.	Thutmose IV	Ammishtamru Shuppiluliumash I			Abdu-Ashirta
1380	Amenophis III		Rib-Addi of Byblos		
1360	"AMARNA AGE"			Niqmaddu II	Aziru
1340	Akhenaten	*defeat of Mitanni*	Abdu-Hepa of Jerusalem	*Ugaritic myths & epics written down*	
	Ay	Mursilis II			DU-Teshub
1320	Tutankhamun Haremhab			Niqmepa	Duppi-Teshub
1300 B.C.	Seti I	Muwatallis			
					Bente-shina I
1280	Ramesses II		*Battle of Kadesh*		Shapilish
1260		Hattusilis III	*Egyptian-Hittite Treaty*	Ammishtamru	Bente-shina II
1240		Tudhaliyash IV			Shaushga-muwash
1220		Arnuwandas		Niqmaddu III	
	Merneptah		*Hazor and Gezer destroyed?*	Ammurapi	
1200 B.C.	*(chaos)*	Shuppiluliumash II *Hattusas destroyed*	*Ashdod, Bethel, Tell Beit-Mirsim destroyed?*	*Ugarit destroyed*	
		(depopulated)			
1180	Ramesses III		*Philistine settlement*		*(depopulated)*

migrations from north Syria (with arrow spanning Syria-Palestine column from 1280 to 1220)

7. Akhenaten is often erroneously portrayed as the world's first monotheist who paved the way for Moses and Yahwism. Akhenaten was not a monotheist but actually worshiped three gods: (1) the sun-disk, Aten, which was most important, (2) a deified abstraction of *Ma'at* (often translated "Truth" or "Order"), and (3) himself. This pantheon was radically different from anything associated with Moses and Yahwism.

The political turmoil evidenced in these letters was triggered by Egypt's increasing inability to maintain control over the international political scene during the half century when Amenophis III and Akhenaten reigned (1390–1336 B.C.), due, in part, to Akhenaten's religious idiosyncrasies. Preoccupied with the worship of the sun-disk Aten, he rejected the ancient gods of Egypt and moved the capital south to el-Amarna.[7] In the political vacuum that resulted, various kings in Syria and Palestine scrambled to extend their own political power bases as far as possible, even to the point of trying to unify the diverse population by covenant. It was a time of shifting loyalties, palace intrigues, political assassinations, and internecine fighting, with each king blaming the others for provoking the instability.

As Syria-Palestine disintegrated into chaos, each local king wrote to Egypt to solicit Pharaoh's aid. Each presented himself as Pharaoh's loyal vassal, whose highest priority was protecting Egyptian interests. Each also accused other local kings of anti-Egyptian hostility, and each knew that his rivals were writing similar letters complaining about him. Pharaoh

Box 1.7—Political Attempts to Unify Syria-Palestine by Covenant

Covenants are alliances solemnly sealed by sworn oaths. In EA 74, Rib-Addi, king of Gubla (Byblos), describes how a rival king, Abdu-Ashirta (or 'Abdi-Aširta) of Amurru, has attempted to unify disaffected segments of society ('Apiru) by means of covenant.

> All my villages that are in the mountains or along the sea have been joined to the 'Apiru. . . . 'Abdi-Aširta said to the men of Ammiya, "Kill your leader, then you will be like us and at peace." They were won over, following his message, and they are like 'Apiru. So now 'Abdi-Aširta has written to the troops: "Assemble in the temple of NINURTA, and then let us fall upon Gubla. . . . Then let us drive out the mayors from the country that the entire country be joined to the 'Apiru. . . . Then will (our) sons and daughters be at peace forever." . . . Accordingly, they have made an alliance among themselves and, accordingly, I am very, very afraid, since [in] fact there is no one who will save me from them. (*AL*, 143)

A couple of generations later, Pharaoh Seti I described how one of his foes was similarly attempting to unify various peoples of Palestine against Egyptian interests:

> On this day one came to speak to his majesty [i.e., to Seti I], as follows; "The wretched foe who is in the town of Hamath is gathering to himself many people, while he is seizing the town of Beth-shean. Then there will be an alliance with them of Pahel." (*ANET* [3], 253)

Such politically motivated covenants were apparently short-lived. In the hill country of Palestine a century after Seti I, a more lasting unification of people under covenant was accomplished by Yahwism, creating the community known as Israel (see chapter 3, especially Box 3.4). Unlike the earlier attempts, the Yahwist covenant was not an instrument wielded by ambitious politicians bent on expanding their domains.

and his bureaucrats, understandably, would have had trouble determining who was loyal and who was not, but as long as tribute continued to flow, the Egyptians seem to have paid little attention to these Canaanite power struggles.

The letters of a dozen of these kings, written in cuneiform, mention hostile forces called *habiru*. Throughout the first half of the twentieth century, historians mistakenly imagined these Habiru to be nomadic invaders. Some even went so far as to equate their activities with the (supposedly nomadic) Israelites' invasion of Canaan. But cuneiform texts all across the Near East refer to Habiru as early as the MB Age, making it unlikely that this is the name of a single, distinct ethnic group. Egyptian texts call them '*apiru,* representing the actual Semitic consonants of the word more accurately than the cuneiform rendering. There is little doubt that the root of this word is identical to Hebrew '*br,* "to cross over," especially to pass beyond some sort of established boundary. The word would therefore mean something like "transgressor." In the ancient Near East, the word "Habiru/Apiru" was apparently a label disparaging anyone who, for whatever reason, no longer identified with or belonged to any of the established, politically defined social organizations. Such a person *became* Apiru, that is, a transgressor or "outlaw" who was no longer considered part of the established social and political order.

Such detachment seems to be a constant in human history, an inevitable consequence of large-scale social organizations (such as state governments) whose activities and policies always seem irrational or tyrannical to at least some of their own members. For example, as early as the Code of Hammurapi, the Babylonians had to deal with such

Box 1.8—Amarna Letters

Rib-Addi frequently complained to Pharaoh about Abdu-Ashirta, whom he villified as an "Apiru dog." Abdu-Ashirta, on the other hand, accused people like Rib-Addi of slandering him. Each wrote to Pharaoh concerning Abdu-Ashirta's military intervention in the city of Sumur. The conflicting information undoubtedly made it difficult for Pharaoh to determine which of the two was the more trustworthy vassal.

EA 91 *(letter of Rib-Addi to Pharaoh)*
Why have you sat idly by and done nothing, so that the 'Apiru dog takes your cities? When he took Sumur, I wrote you, "Why do you do nothing?" Then Bit-arqa was taken. When he saw that there was no one that said anything to him about Sumur, his intentions were reinforced, so that he strives to take Gubla. . . . I go on writing like this for archers and an auxiliary force, but my words go unheeded. (*AL,* 165)

EA 62 *(letter of Abdu-Ashirta to Pharaoh)*
What do your words . . . mean . . . [when you say to me], "You are an enemy of Egypt and you committed a crime against Egyptians." May my lord listen. There were no men in Sumur to guard it as he had ordered. . . . So I myself hastened to the rescue from Irqat. . . . There were only 4 men that had stayed on in the palace, and they said to me, "Save us from the hand of the troops of Šehlal." . . . the mayors lie to you [about me], and you keep on listening to them? (*AL,* 133–134)

persons who said, "I hate my king and my city," in effect renouncing their citizenship.[8] Across the ancient Near East, such persons could earn a livelihood by working regular jobs or as day laborers, by participating in some black market economy, or by enlisting as mercenaries. Also, they could band together and stockpile weapons for self-protection, since they did not rely on society to protect them and, in fact, probably expected armed confrontation with it. Sometimes—but not always—their social and political detachment was accompanied by a physical relocation to some hinterland where they could eke out a living away from the despised political authorities.

Like many other ancient Near Eastern documents, the Amarna letters allude to such Apiru groups. Obviously they further frustrated the already beleaguered kings of Canaan, and Apiru ranks may have swollen as the Canaanite power struggles, which many common folk probably wanted no part of, raged on.

9. The Bible preserves an archaic poem roughly contemporaneous with the emergence of Yahwism at the end of the LB Age. It says of the Yahweh worshipers: "Here is a people living alone, and not reckoning itself among the nations [Hebrew *goyim*]!" (Num. 23:9).

Although many scholars dispute this, there are sound linguistic and historical reasons for finding in the word "Apiru" (*'apiru*) the origin and equivalent of the term "Hebrew" (*'ibri*). Initially, the word "Apiru/ Hebrew" was applied by their enemies to the early Israelites, who likewise did not identify with or belong to any established, politically defined social system.[9] In the eyes of others, the early Yahweh worshipers were Apiru/Hebrews in the old and familiar sense of the word: they were alienated persons who refused to extend their loyalties to any of the existing political regimes (or "nations") of the time. Centuries later, when these Yahweh worshipers established their own political state, the archaic word "Apiru/Hebrew" would be forced to take on a new meaning, no longer a disparaging social label (roughly equivalent to "outlaw") but eventually a respectable ethnic label virtually synonymous with "Jew" (as in Phil. 3:5).

Abdu-Hepa and the Kashites

10. The Hurrian impact on Palestinian politics became so noticeable that the Egyptians sometimes referred to Palestine as "Hurri-land" or "Hurru." The Bible refers to these people as "Horites."

The king of Jerusalem during the Amarna Age was Abdu-Hepa, whose name indicates his Hurrian ancestry (Hepa was a Hurrian goddess). From his Amarna letters we learn that he was not originally a politician but a soldier owing his royal position to Pharaoh's benevolence. The language of his letters indicates that Abdu-Hepa's scribe had come from either north Syria or southern Turkey. If this scribe had come to Jerusalem as part of Abdu-Hepa's entourage, it would reinforce the conclusion that Abdu-Hepa was a former Mitanni *maryannu* now established as some sort of king or governor protecting Egyptian interests in and around Jerusalem.[10]

There is also evidence of at least one other group of northern transplants in the Jerusalem area. In his letters, Abdu-Hepa refers to Kashites (*Kashiya*) who had previously attempted to assassinate him in Jerusalem. The

Box 1.9—"Hebrews" in Early Israel

Some biblical passages describing events in eleventh-century-B.C. Palestine use the word *'ibri,* "Hebrews," exactly as the word *'apiru* was used there three centuries earlier:

> Then Saul and all the people who were with him rallied and went into the battle; and every sword was against the other, so that there was very great confusion. Now the *'ibri* who previously had been with the Philistines and had gone up with them into the camp turned and joined the Israelites who were with Saul and Jonathan. (1 Sam. 14:20–21)

The *'ibri* here were people who identified themselves with neither Israelite nor Philistine society, and consequently had no formal place within either. The term (usually translated "Hebrews") refers to their *social and political status* as outsiders, not to their *ethnicity* as Israelites.

> As . . . David and his men were passing on in the rear [of the military column] with Achish, the commanders of the Philistines said, "What are these *'ibri* doing here?" Achish said to the commanders of the Philistines, "Is this not David, the servant of King Saul of Israel, who has been with me now for days and years? Since he deserted to me I have found no fault in him to this day." (1 Sam. 29:2–3)

It is noteworthy that the Philistines, in essence, label David and his followers as Apiru, not Israelites. The biblical tradition here recalls that the Philistine commanders were acutely aware of David's ambiguous social status: he was not a full-fledged member of Philistine society, yet he had "deserted" Israelite society and was now an outlaw being hunted down by the Israelite king Saul.

Kashites were unknown until Hittite sources were discovered, revealing that Kashites originally inhabited the territory between the Hittite and Hurrian (Mitanni) Empires, probably along the Euphrates River in what is now south-central Turkey. During the New Kingdom period, the Egyptians apparently defeated and captured Hurrian and Kashite military units (one led by Abdu-Hepa?), resettling elements of both groups in the environs of Jerusalem, where old animosities resurfaced in political violence.

These references to the *Kashiya* may also help clarify a much-discussed biblical passage pertaining to Moses' wife: "And Miriam and Aaron spake against Moses because of the Ethiopian [Hebrew *kšy*] woman whom he had married: for he had married an Ethiopian [*kšy*] woman" (Num. 12:1, KJV). In other passages, Moses' wife, Zipporah, is said to have been a Midianite (Exod. 2:15–21), and there is archaeological and linguistic evidence that, like Abdu-Hepa, some Midianites originated in the area of north Syria/south-central Turkey. But what do we make of the word *kšy?* Given what we now know, it seems that Zipporah must have been a Kashite whose ancestors had emigrated from south-central Turkey along with others who subsequently formed the Midianite confederation of tribes. Traditionally, however, *kšy* has been interpreted as "Cushite," the Egyptian name for the Nubians of Ethiopia. This inspired a much later tradition that Moses had married a Black woman. But the evidence now clearly indicates that Moses' wife was *not* Ethiopian.

Religious Values in the Late Bronze Age

11. A more contemporary functional equivalent might be the upraised, clinched fist that adorned the banners, bumper stickers, and letterheads of various political movements of the 1960s and 1970s. In America in the 1980s and 1990s, a popular buzzword was "empowerment." In some segments of American culture today, power is esteemed as the necessary prerequisite for all other social virtues, including love, justice, and civility. Value is placed on the political will and ability to *compel* people to behave consistent with desired norms.

12. This insight characterized the prophetic tradition of Israel, from Isaiah's observation (29:13) that people honor Yahweh with their lips even though their religious values demonstrably lie elsewhere, to Jesus' claim that one can discern a person's true religious character by observing his or her "fruit" (Matt. 7:15–20; also Matt. 6:1–18 and 25:31–46). See also chapter 2, note 9.

Because religion and politics were so closely intertwined in the LB Age, the Apiru rejection of a politically defined social organization likely entailed the rejection of the religious systems and values that undergirded it, and vice versa. The LB Age witnessed an increasing concentration of wealth and power, ironically at the expense of the village population who produced the goods and services necessary for any political organization in the first place. The acquisition of wealth and power seems, in fact, to have been the dominant value in this period, religiously personified and deified in such gods as Baal and Asherah. Statues of Baal were everywhere, and they apparently served as deified symbols of power.[11]

Understanding ancient religion becomes much easier once we realize that deities such as this—and their symbols and rituals—were merely state-sanctioned expressions of entrenched social values. In other words, a social value does not initially receive its impetus or derive its legitimacy because religion espouses it; from the outset its legitimacy is unquestioned, and the fact that it is considered legitimate and authoritative induces people to represent it symbolically in religious forms and terms, even to the point of personifying it as a god. For example, Asherah was one of three Canaanite goddesses usually referred to as fertility goddesses, but to call them that misses the point. They personified *productivity*, not fertility. To worship Asherah was to celebrate wealth and prosperity. At the same time, indulging in a luxurious lifestyle was just as much "worship" as offering prayers and sacrifices at one of her shrines. Thus, the worship of Asherah, in a sense, remains alive and well even in contemporary America—advertising encourages it all the time. The driving religious ideology of people is often manifested more clearly and candidly in their characteristic behavior and choices than in their formal rituals, doctrines, and myths.[12]

Baal personified power, overwhelming any enemy who threatened the status quo. To worship him was to celebrate power (which was highly valued in the LB Age) and to extol the role that coercive force plays in human affairs. To describe Baal worship as the veneration of power is to recognize it as a universal phenomenon that can neither be localized in one part of the world, nor limited to one particular historical era, nor characteristic of one particular culture. Likewise, its presence need

Figure 1.5
Baal and Asherah. Carved and molten images of deities such as Baal and Asherah were extremely common in antiquity. Baal's characteristic pose became a virtual icon for political force. At the left is a MB limestone relief of Baal discovered at Ugarit, in the middle is a LB Age gold-covered bronze statuette of Baal discovered at nearby Minet el-Beida, and at the right is a cast, made from a MB Age stone mold, of a "fertility goddess," probably Asherah.

not be restricted to formal liturgies invoking the name Baal. The Canaanite theology of Baal frankly conceded that power is worshiped under many names; and that even though Baal inevitably dies, in time he springs back to life again. That is the nature of power and of systems devoted to it. When some Israelites later came to value their own social exercise of political power, they began to regard their god, Yahweh, as if he were Baal.

For modern Western audiences, this theology of power is probably articulated more intelligibly and succinctly in the fifth-century-B.C. reply of the Athenians to the Melos delegation than in the fourteenth-century-B.C. Ugaritic myth of Baal. The Athenians had forcibly seized the small island of Melos, whose delegates pleaded that it was wrong of Athens to dominate them this way. The historian Thucydides contrasted the dignity of the Melians with the rapacity of the Athenians, who addressed the Melians as follows:

> "Of the gods we believe, and of human beings we know, that there is a natural imperative for them to extend their rule wherever they can. We are not the first people to invent this principle, nor are we the first ever to act upon it. It existed long before us, and it will exist long after we are gone. We are merely acting upon this imperative, knowing that you and everyone else would do exactly what we are doing, if you had the same measure of power as we." (*The Peloponnesian Wars* V.105)

The Athenians were not interested in "right" or "wrong"; for them, morality was secondary to the interests of power:

> "Everyone knows that justice is relevant only among those who are equal in power, while the strong take whatever they can, and the weak concede whatever they must." (V.89)

For the Athenians, this was a "natural imperative"; the Canaanites called it the "worship of Baal." Nowadays, among other things, we call it "national self-interest."

Almost all ancient literary and artistic sources clearly and consistently illustrate this deification of power. Although power was recognized in and identified with many forms (e.g., the storm, the hunt, the battle), the clearest and most common form in which it was extolled was always kingship (i.e., the exercise of political authority). It should come as no surprise that, from Greece to India, the most common theme of ancient myth has characteristically involved the conflict between competing power systems.

Martin Luther once observed that your "god" is that which you most fear to lose. More recently, Paul Tillich defined a "god" as an "Ultimate Concern."[13] For the influential citizens and decision makers of the LB Age, the "Ultimate Concerns" they most feared losing were power and prosperity, and the political apparatus that was believed to guarantee both. For the elite, these concerns took precedence over almost every other consideration. Like many modern folk, they found it impossible to conceive of the reality of the divine apart from some social system of coercion and force. To worship Baal and Asherah was to affirm the supreme value that power and wealth played in making all human life and experience meaningful.[14]

13. People in a pluralistic society obviously have diverse concerns (which must be prioritized) and therefore diverse gods (which must be ranked). For example, the tenants of the Bolan apartment house in ancient Rome set aside a room for the cult of their apartment-house god, which represented their shared interests. Part of the role of the ancient state was to maintain the pantheon, the regular ranking of the gods. The chief gods were, of course, the ones who symbolized the state itself and its political interests.

14. As we shall see in subsequent chapters, the biblical tradition originated both in the Hebrew belief that worship of these things was dangerously wrong and in the claim that human life and experience can be made more meaningful by something else.

The End of the Late Bronze Age

15. Jesus summarized this succinctly when he said, "All who take the sword will perish by the sword" (Matt. 26:52). Paul echoed this thought: "If, however, you bite and devour one another, take care that you are not consumed by one another" (Gal. 5:15).

This sort of pagan religious ideology almost inevitably sows the seeds of its own demise. Where power and wealth are the predominant concerns and sacred ends, society dissolves into a self-destructive struggle to obtain them. And the more widely held such a religious ideology, the more widespread the violence will likely be, destroying especially those who most faithfully embrace it.[15]

Fighting between the Hittite and Egyptian superpowers intensified by the thirteenth century B.C. Political stability returned to Egypt soon after the death of Akhenaten, as did the Egyptian resolve to recapture its imperial holdings. Egyptian and Hittite armies clashed in a major battle outside Kadesh in 1274 B.C., and the exhausted Egyptians and Hittites ratified a peace treaty about fifteen years later. But a century of warfare had impoverished much of the population, while the movement of armies across devastated regions spread epidemic disease. Whole communities were uprooted as people fled the approaching violence and plague. The deployment of Egyptian forces against the Hittites to the north exposed Egypt's western flank to destabilizing pressures from the Libyans. In the Aegean, trade was disrupted and ships became weapons for warrior gangs similar to those romantically depicted in Homeric epic. Troy was destroyed, and the once-great Mycenaean civilization of Greece fell into a three-hundred-year-long dark age. Roaming freebooters preyed on defenseless populations.

Box 1.10—The Collapse of Civilization

Some scholars believe the Greek poetry of Hesiod (ca. 700 B.C.) preserves vivid memories of the social disintegration and moral collapse that attended the end of the LB Age:

> Father will have no common bond with son,
> Neither will guest with host, nor friend with friend.
> The brother-love of past days will be gone
> . . . .
> Men will destroy the towns of other men.
> The just, the good, the man who keeps his word
> Will be despised, but men will praise the bad
> And insolent. Might will be right and shame
> Will cease to be. Men will do injury
> To better men by speaking crooked words
> And adding lying oathes, and everywhere
> Harsh-voiced and sullen-faced and loving harm,
> Envy will walk along with wretched men. (*WD,* 182–195)

The heartland of the Hittite Empire was so completely depopulated by the end of the thirteenth century B.C. that only in the last several years has evidence emerged of a few survivors dwelling among the ruins of its capital. Much of central Syria, as well as the Euphrates and Orontes River valleys, became virtually uninhabited. At Ugarit, clay tablets were discovered still in palace kilns (where they were being baked for transport), offering grim testimony to the city's dramatic fall. In one, the Hittite king requests a ship to transport urgently needed grain for areas ravaged by famine. In another, the king of Cyprus requests the same. In a third, the king of Ugarit writes that his soldiers are all deployed farther north, and that he has no ships to spare because enemies are even now attacking his coast. Apparently these enemies suddenly reached and plundered the palace before these tablets could be removed from their kilns.

Not everyone believed these LB political organizations and their gods were worth living or dying for. Population actually increased in three areas where newly arrived refugee immigrants began building new lives and communities:

1. *Arabian Hejaz.* In the thirteenth century B.C., Syrian populations were already emigrating to the remote area between the Jordanian border and Mecca. This historical record reveals that they brought with them such cultural traits as Mycenaean pottery traditions and names with Hurrian, Luwian (southern Anatolian), and Amorite etymologies. A tribal confederation known as "Midian" soon arose among these newcomers.

2. *South-Central Turkey.* Recent archaeological surveys reveal that, as LB civilization collapsed, this area just north of the Syrian border witnessed an influx of population. These newcomers seem to have been refugees from the Hittite heartland, since the political regimes that arose here three hundred years later were called "Hatti" by the Assyrians. Indeed, these Iron Age kingdoms preserved enough LB Age Hittite cultural traits for modern scholars to label them "Neo-Hittite states."

3. *Hill-Country Palestine and Transjordan.* New villages proliferated here beginning around 1200 B.C. In the past, it was fashionable to attribute these new settlements to waves of desert nomads becoming sedentary, but it is now clear that the material culture of these villages retained north Syrian and indigenous Canaanite elements. They, too, for the most part appear to have been refugees. A federation of a dozen or so tribes soon arose among the diverse people who settled here, people who named their larger social unit "Israel."

The origins of the unprecedented religion that came to be associated with Israel—the so-called formative period of the biblical tradition—will be the subject of the next chapter.

A Research Plan for Further Study

Dictionaries and Commentaries

Most Bible dictionaries have articles on the peoples, places, individuals, topics, and biblical books mentioned in this book. The following are good places to start for getting an overview of the topic:

Harper's Bible Dictionary (1985)
Anchor Bible Dictionary (1992; 6 vols.)
Interpreter's Dictionary of the Bible (1962; 4 vols. with Supplement)

Bible commentaries provide discussion of biblical passages and books:

Harper's Bible Commentary (1988)
New Jerome Bible Commentary (1990)
The Anchor Bible (multivolume)
The New Interpreter's Bible (1994; multivolume)

Overviews of the Bible

Students desiring to develop a more complete reading list should consult the annotated bibliographies provided in the following texts:

B. Anderson, *Understanding the Old Testament*. Abr. 4th ed. Upper Saddle River, N.J.: Prentice-Hall, 1998.

R. Friedman, *Who Wrote the Bible?* New York: Harper & Row, 1987.

S. Harris, *Understanding the Bible*. 5th ed. Mountain View, Calif.: Mayfield, 2000.

J. Sheler, *Is the Bible True?* San Francisco: HarperSanFrancisco/Zondervan, 1999.

Overviews of Israelite History and Religion

Students desiring to obtain more complete discussions of specific periods or issues in Israelite history should consult the relevant chapters in the following books:

J. Bright, *A History of Israel*. 4th ed. Louisville, Ky.: Westminster John Knox Press, 2000.

R. De Vaux, *Ancient Israel: Its Life and Institutions*. New York: McGraw-Hill, 1961.

J. Hayes and M. Miller, eds., *Israelite and Judean History*. Philadelphia: Westminster Press, 1977.

G. W. Ramsey, *The Quest for the Historical Israel*. Atlanta: John Knox Press, 1981.

H. Shanks, ed., *Ancient Israel: From Abraham to the Roman Destruction of the Temple*. Rev. and exp. ed. Washington, D.C., and Upper Saddle River, N.J.: Biblical Archaeology Society and Prentice-Hall, 1999.

Atlases

The following contain helpful maps and geographical discussions related to the ancient Near Eastern world of the Bible.

Y. Aharoni and M. Avi-Yonah, *The Macmillan Bible Atlas*. 3d ed. New York: Macmillan, 1993.

J. Baines and J. Malek, *Atlas of Ancient Egypt*. New York: Facts on File, 1980.

M. Roaf, *Cultural Atlas of Mesopotamia*. New York: Facts on File, 1990.

J. Rogerson, *Atlas of the Bible*. Oxford: Phaidon, 1989.

The Ancient Near East

These resources contain more focused presentations about subjects related to the peoples and cultures of antiquity.

M. Coogan, ed., *The Oxford History of the Biblical World*. New York: Oxford University Press, 1998.

O. R. Gurney, *The Hittites*. Harmondsworth, Middlesex: Penguin Books, 1962.

S. N. Kramer, *The Sumerians*. Chicago: University of Chicago Press, 1963.

A. Kurht, *The Ancient Near East, c. 3000–330 B.C.* New York: Routledge & Kegan Paul, 1996.

G. Roux, *Ancient Iraq*. 2d ed. Harmondsworth, Middlesex: Penguin Books, 1980.

N. Sandars, *The Sea Peoples: Warriors of the Ancient Mediterranean*. Rev. ed. London: Thames & Hudson, 1987.

J. Sasson, ed. *Civilizations of the Ancient Near East*. 4 vols. New York: Simon & Schuster/Macmillan, 1995.

J. Wilson, *The Culture of Ancient Egypt*. Chicago: University of Chicago Press, 1963.

Suggestions for Further Reading

The following are suggested readings for further study of the topics covered in chapter 1.

Dictionary/Encyclopedia Entries

Anchor Bible Dictionary: Agriculture; Akhenaten; Amarna Letters; Amorites; Asherah; Baal; Byblos Syllabic; Canaan, Religion of; Education; Egypt, History of; Egyptian Relations with Canaan; Hittite History; Hittite Religion; Hyksos; Hurrians; Literacy; Mari Texts; Mesopotamia, History of; Military Organization in Mesopotamia; Mitanni; Negeb; Sheep; South Arabia, Religions of; Ugarit; Writing and Writing Material

Two

Moses and the Exodus: The Formative Period of the Biblical Tradition

Suggested Reading

Moses: Exodus 1:1–3:15; 5; 11
Flight from Egypt: Exodus 12:29–38; 14:5–15:21
The Sinai Covenant: Exodus 19:1–20:17; 24:3–8

Early Biblical Traditions: Fact or Fiction?

Although Genesis is the first book of the Bible, it is Exodus that describes the actual origins of the Hebrew religion. Historians disagree on the time and circumstances in which this religion originated. The majority, in one way or another, agrees that it originated at the time of Moses and the exodus, usually dated to the end of the LB Age (about 1200 B.C.). Others insist that it actually originated later, whether at the time of David and Solomon (tenth century B.C.), or with the Hebrew prophets (eighth century B.C.), or around the reign of King Josiah (seventh century B.C.). Some even date its origins as late as the Persian period (fifth century B.C.), viewing the religion as an instrument consolidating Judaean ethnicity.

The scholars who insist on these later dates claim that the traditions associating the origins of this religion with Moses and the exodus are more or less fictional. Some feel that the legendary and supernatural character of some of the story's elements "proves" the fictional character of these traditions. They argue that one cannot glean historical information from a narrative that never intended to report it in the first place. This argument has some popular appeal, perhaps because it constitutes such a direct attack on disagreeable fundamentalist views of the Bible and religion.

However, this argument also has some notable weaknesses. Because the Israelites used history-writing conventions different from ours does not mean that they were unable or unwilling to preserve traditions about historical people and events. At the same time, it is understandable that many modern Western readers find it impossible to believe a story that reports a flaming bush that never actually burns (Exod. 3:2), a miraculous series of plagues (Exodus 7–12), and a large body of water being split apart (Exod. 14:21–22). Of course, we are not constrained to interpret such reports literally. But other ancient peoples also used similar mythic language and imagery to celebrate otherwise real (and momentous) historical events. Therefore, the incorporation of supernatural imagery was not just a convention of ancient *fiction* writing, but also one of ancient *history* writing.

Furthermore, too many problems (and too few solutions) are created by the assumption that these biblical traditions are complete fictions. The Exodus narrative simply diverges too much from too many of the well-known conventions of ancient fiction writing. In other words, no one has yet explained why Israelite fiction writers would create a narrative about Israel's origins in this particularly unusual way, inventing a character named Moses and fabricating a plotline such as the exodus. The simplest explanation—and currently the best—is that these Israelite writers *were constrained to tell the story this way*. The most obvious constraint would have been a well-known body of tradition about past people, places, and events in which all these "cluttering" details were not trivial. Their story had to acknowledge and incorporate (some of) those older traditions. This is not to say that every element in that tradition is historically accurate. As we shall see in subsequent chapters, later Israelite scribes often felt inspired to revise and embellish the tradition with fictional, mythic elements, crafting a narrative structure to make the tradition more "relevant" to their readers.

We have no extrabiblical evidence corroborating the specific details of the exodus story. Nevertheless, disciplined historical speculation about people and events mentioned in the exodus tradition—speculation guided by an understanding of ancient Near Eastern culture and history—seems preferable to the outright dismissal of this tradition as mere fiction. This equally applies to other biblical traditions about Israel's past. Therefore, in the following pages we provide a theoretical reconstruction of the origins and history of Israel's religion, believing that beneath the story's use of legendary motifs, miracle, and mythic language and imagery, there was indeed a bona fide attempt by Israelite scribes to preserve traditions rooted in history, many of which they clearly did not understand.

| Population Changes in the Near East | Archaeological evidence confirms that at the end of the LB Age the population of hill-country Palestine and Transjordan skyrocketed. Already before 1200 B.C., large numbers of immigrants and refugees were streaming southward from Anatolia and north Syria into Egyptian-controlled territory, some by oxcart with families, others—professional military units comprising skilled warriors—by boat. Some, *along with the existing population,* established a series of fortified cities in the Arabian |

Figure 2.1
Immigrants from the North. Some Egyptian reliefs depict boatloads of
Mediterranean warriors (called "Sea Peoples") entering Egyptian-held territories.
Others (like this from Medinet Habu) show families arriving in ox-drawn carts. As
political order began collapsing at the end of the Bronze Age, the Egyptians considered all immigrants a threat. The artist here, portraying the chaos of the times,
has depicted civilian refugees alongside Mediterranean warriors (in plumed head-
dresses), as Egyptian soldiers (with spears) try to drive them all off.

Hejaz, engaging in large-scale agriculture and metallurgy. Their pottery
imitated Mycenaean wares, suggesting that these particular people—
whom the Bible calls "Midianites"—had cultural roots in the more cosmopolitan north.

This period was characterized both by the destruction of civilization and by the populating of areas that had previously been sparsely
settled, if at all. Some sociologists would associate such demographic
changes with a "frontier" mentality, in which people are receptive to new
value systems and new patterns of social organization different from those
of the societies they have abandoned. There is little doubt that the
destruction of those LB Age social and political organizations—and the
religious ideologies that legitimized them—was almost complete. As we
seek to understand the sudden appearance of the Israelite religious community, we should not underestimate the world-shattering impact this
civilization-wide collapse had on those who survived it.

The early Iron Age pottery of hill-country Palestine and
Transjordan is revealing. It is crudely made—thick, coarse, poorly fired,
and cheaply manufactured. But ceramicists agree that LB Age forms and
shapes persist in these pieces. This suggests that although the people who
settled there eked out a simple living, they were also familiar with some
features of "Canaanite" culture, including not only its pottery traditions but presumably also its religion, art, and international politics.
Undoubtedly, these settlers came to this frontier hoping for a new and
better life. Because this settlement occurred prior to and independent of
Moses and the exodus, it was part of the prologue to the formation of
Israelite religion.

Table 2.1 Chronology of Egypt at the End of the Bronze Age

date	Egypt	Other Events	Archaeology of Palestine
1300 B.C.			
	SETI I (1295–1279)		
1290			
1280	RAMESSES II (1279–1213)		
	Egyptians vs. Hittites at Kadesh (1274)	earliest (Midianite) settlements in Arabian Hejaz	
1270			LATE
1260	Egyptian–Hittite Treaty (1259)		BRONZE
1250 B.C.			AGE
1240			
1230			
1220		depopulation of central Turkey and northern Syria settlements in hill-country Palestine begin to appear	
	MERNEPTAH (1213–1203)		
1210	Libyan–Sea Peoples attack (1208)	"Israel is laid waste; his seed is not."	
1200 B.C.	(chaos) *Moses and the exodus?*		
1190			EARLY
	RAMESSES III (1184–1153)		
1180			IRON
	Sea Peoples attack (1176)	Philistines occupy coastal Palestine	
1170		*"Israel" as Yahwist federation of tribes emerges?*	AGE

The Decline of the Egyptian Empire

1. It has become conventional to regard Ramesses II as the pharaoh of the exodus, a view popularized by the 1956 epic film *The Ten Commandments*. A successful escape by several hundred slaves would have been less likely during Ramesses's long and stable reign than during the reign of weaker successors such as Merneptah or Ramesses III.

Throughout Egypt's Eighteenth and Nineteenth Dynasties (around 1550–1200 B.C.) a large, ethnically diverse population from Syria-Palestine resided in Egypt, particularly in the Nile Delta. Some arrived peacefully, voluntarily, and temporarily: reports regularly filed by ancient Egyptian border guards noted the seasonal passage of shepherds and flocks from the Sinai and Palestinian hinterlands to the lush grasslands of the Delta. Various inscriptions show that others, such as prisoners of war, were brought to Egypt as slaves. They tell of agricultural workers from Palestine toiling in Egyptian vineyards, and Apiru/Hebrews laying bricks for Pharaoh's building projects. The group of slaves who followed Moses out of Egypt came from this ethnically diverse reservoir of Syro-Palestinian peoples.

One of the best-known pharaohs of the New Kingdom period was Ramesses II (1279-1213 B.C.).[1] His son and successor, Merneptah, ruled for about a decade (1213–1203 B.C.), after which there seems to have been a twenty-year period of chaos. During the fifth year of Merneptah's reign, and again during the eighth year of Ramesses III (reigned 1184–1153 B.C.), Egyptian-controlled areas were invaded. The Egyptians

Box 2.1—Asiatics in Egypt

During the LB Age, various pharaohs of the Eighteenth Dynasty conducted military campaigns into Syria-Palestine (or "Retenu"). This first text describes one way that Asiatics could be brought into Egypt by conquering Egyptian kings such as Thutmose III:

> List of the tribute brought to the glory of his majesty by the princes of Retenu in this year. Now the children of the princes and their brothers were brought to be hostages in Egypt. Now, whoever of these princes died, his majesty was accustomed to make his son go to stand in his place. List of the children of princes carried off this year: 36 men; 181 male and female slaves; 188 horses; and 40 chariots. . . . (*ANET*[3], 239)

The following text celebrates Amenophis II's victorious return to Egypt. It mentions Apiru and also Shasu (shepherds):

> His majesty reached the town of Memphis, his heart appeased over all countries, with all lands beneath his soles. List of the plunder which his majesty carried off: princes of Retenu: 127; brothers of princes: 179; Apiru: 3,600; living Shasu: 15,200; Kharu: 36,300; living Neges: 15,070; the adherents thereof: 30,652. . . . (*ANET*[3], 247)

During the chaotic times around 1200 B.C., the borders of Egypt were being closely patrolled. Border guards filed regular reports about Asiatic people voluntarily entering Egypt:

> [We] have finished letting the Shasu-tribes of Edom pass the Fortress . . . (in) Tjeku, to the pools of Per-Atum . . . which are in Tjeku, to keep them alive and to keep their cattle alive. (*ANET*[3], 259)

referred to these invaders as "Sea Peoples" and "northerners from all lands," listing five or six different groups who formed alliances hoping to gain control of Egyptian holdings. One such group was the "Philistines" mentioned frequently in the Old Testament:

> The foreign countries made a conspiracy in their islands. All at once the lands were removed and scattered in the fray. No land could stand before their arms. . . . They were coming forward toward Egypt. . . . Their confederation was the Philistines, Tjeker, Shekelesh, Denye(n), and Weshesh, lands united. They laid their hands upon the lands as far as the circuit of the earth, their hearts confident and trusting: "Our plans will succeed!" (*ANET*[3], 262)

Both Merneptah and Ramesses III succeeded in keeping the invaders out of Egypt proper, but a greatly weakened Ramesses III conceded territory in Palestine to some of these groups. For example, the Tjeker acquired territory around Byblos, while the Philistines settled in the southern coastal plain of Palestine. Many of these groups had apparently originated in the area around the Aegean Sea and were seafarers at the time their homelands fell into ruin.

Whether they arrived by sea or by land, these and other bands of professional soldiers took control over local village populations wherever they moved in. Cut off from their native Aegean homelands, they were no longer accountable to anyone but themselves. These gangs roamed the eastern Mediterranean world, searching for political vacuums they might fill, establishing themselves at various locales as a military elite. Typically, their leader (or warlord) would proclaim himself "king," or some such equivalent, and would deploy his squads throughout the surrounding villages to "pacify" the land and collect taxes to support himself and his soldiers. They would take local women as wives and, within two generations, very little would remain of them but their ancestral name, preserved as the name of the political regime they had bequeathed to their sons.

This is precisely what the Philistines were. Assyrian texts often give *Canaanite* names to later Philistine kings, which is not surprising since these kings would have been raised by Canaanite mothers and would have adopted their mothers' language, customs, and worldview. Within a couple of generations, little, if anything, remained of the distinctively Aegean elements of Philistine culture. Even their characteristic pottery, some of which was probably used as part of their native rituals, had ceased being produced. They had been thoroughly assimilated into the Canaanite population.

Pharaoh Merneptah and "Israel"

The Victory Stela of Merneptah, discovered more than a century ago at Thebes, celebrates Merneptah's defeat of the Libyan-Sea Peoples coalition during his fifth year (1208 B.C.). It concludes by praising him for keeping the Egyptian Empire intact. This text is also called the "Israel Stela" because of these concluding lines:

> Israel is laid waste, his seed is not;
>   Hurru is become a widow for Egypt! (*ANET*[3], 378)

The Egyptian hieroglyphs here suggest that this "Israel" was not the name of a politically organized or geographically centralized group of people but of a looser social network (such as a tribe or a coalition) comprising

Figure 2.2
Merneptah Stela. The reference to "Israel" is highlighted on the next-to-bottom line of the stela. Left of the name is a "determinative sign" showing a man and woman crouched above three short slash marks. Since the Egyptians used other determinative signs to indicate politically organized or geographically localized groups, this text here identifies "Israel" as a different type of social organization.

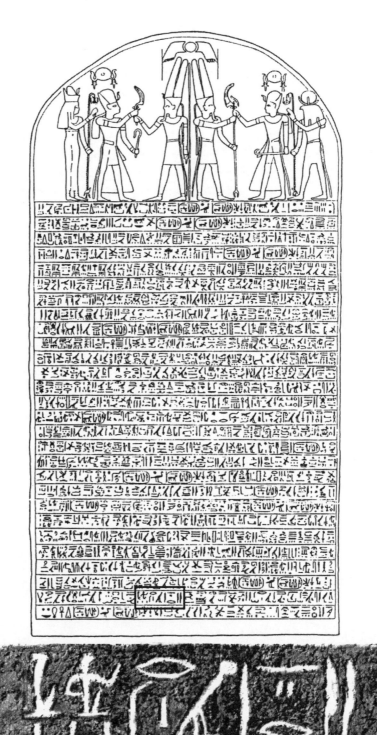

people scattered in different villages and areas of Palestine. It was apparently not the name of any group (free or slaves) within Egypt proper, and there is no indication that this social group yet had a particular religious character. It was only *after* the time of Moses—when many members of this social network joined others in forming a federation of Yahweh-worshiping tribes—that the name "Israel" became associated with the biblical religious community (see chapter 3). It was not unusual for a prominent social group or tribe to transfer its name to a larger federation of which it had just become a member. Merneptah's "Israel," therefore, likely had nothing to do with the worship of the biblical god Yahweh; it was merely part of the prologue to the biblical tradition.

Moses and the Exodus	There is evidence outside the Bible that the Egyptians used Syro-Palestinian slaves to work on state-sponsored building projects. By 1200 B.C., large concentrations of such slaves could be found in the Nile Delta. We also know that the Egyptians at this time had not forgotten how the bitterly hated Asiatics (Hyksos) had exploited Egyptian weakness several centuries earlier and gained control of portions of the Nile Delta. It is likely that they did not want to see that disaster repeated. Consequently, Egyptian control over these slaves in the Nile Delta undoubtedly grew increasingly severe as Egyptian political control once again began to unravel.

The evidence also shows that groups of runaway slaves would periodically flee east into the Sinai wilderness to escape their increasingly harsh treatment. For example, around 1200 B.C. an Egyptian military commander wrote to other officers concerning the pursuit of a couple of runaway slaves:

> I was sent forth . . . following after these two slaves. . . . When my letter reaches you, write to me about all that has happened to [them]. Who found their tracks? Which watch found their tracks? What people are after them? Write to me about all that has happened to them and how many people you send out after them. (*ANET*[3], 259)

Thus, the biblical tradition concerning the oppression of Apiru/Hebrew slaves in Egypt at this time (Exod. 1:8–14) seems plausibly rooted in this historical context. The story of Moses as an infant being floated down the Nile and adopted by Pharaoh's daughter (Exod. 2:1–10) is demonstrably the stuff of legend, for which there are clear ancient parallels. However, this legend and Moses' Egyptian name encourage us to locate the histor-

Figure 2.3
Egyptian Slaves
Making Bricks. This
scene appears on a
fifteenth-century-B.C.
Egyptian tomb painting
from Thebes.

ical man socially among the oppressors and not the oppressed. However, he subsequently came to identify himself sympathetically with the slaves.

The series of events leading up to the formation of the biblical community and its religion apparently began unexpectedly. Moses killed an Egyptian overseer who was beating one of the slaves. It is difficult to imagine this being a fictional invention, especially since the biblical writers never chose to comment on this noteworthy aspect of the protagonist's dark past. When Moses later tried to intervene between two quarreling slaves, one of them responded, "Who made you a ruler and a judge over us? Do you mean to kill me as you killed the Egyptian?" (Exod. 2:11–15). In other words, who authorized Moses to exercise coercive control over others?[2] Is the monopoly of force—*the ability to coerce other human beings*—truly the ultimate basis of social authority? If it seems undesirable to ground social authority on something that essentially boils down to the superior ability to commit murder, then what is the alternative?

Realizing that this murder was common knowledge, Moses fled into the Sinai desert where he subsequently joined a Midianite sheepherding family, whose patriarch is given various different names throughout the Bible—Jethro, Hobab, or Reuel. Midianite society comprised a complex federation of urban and tribal groups who had withdrawn into the desert fringe area, probably to escape from the violence accompanying the end of the LB Age. Their culture apparently encouraged hospitality and a willingness to accept new members. The tradition that Moses married a Midianite woman (Exod. 2:21) can hardly have been a later fiction, particularly since the Israelites later had developed extremely negative stereotypes of the Midianites—especially of Midianite women (as in Numbers 22–25; Numbers 31; and Judges 6–8).

Moses subsequently returned to Egypt to rescue whom he could from among the Apiru/Hebrew slaves. Numbers 11:4 notes that Moses brought with him out of Egypt *'asaf-suf,* a pejorative label meaning "mixed rabble." Similarly, Exodus 12:38 mentions the *'ereb-rab,* or "mixed

2. It is no accident that Jesus dealt with the same question. Two brothers quarreling over their father's estate asked Jesus to determine how they should fairly divide it. Jesus replied, "Who made me a judge or divider over you? Take heed, and beware of all covetousness" (Luke 12:13–15, RSV). As we will see, the notion that religion and politics are reciprocals is the core of the biblical tradition: if political rule (by legal force) is to be renounced, this renunciation must be preceded by a value system that successfully nurtures human integrity—Thou shalt not covet. Paul called such a value system the "still more excellent way" of love (1 Cor. 12:31). See note 14.

crowd" of people, who left Egypt with Moses. This strikes many scholars as an authentic historical tradition, particularly since the later Israelite scribes preparing the final version of these traditions (now enshrined in scripture) apparently went to great lengths to emphasize exactly the opposite, namely, the *ethnic homogeneity* of Israel's enslaved ancestors. These scribes were apparently successful, because most Bible readers today gloss over these references to the diverse ethnic backgrounds of the Apiru/Hebrew slaves and assume that Moses led an already-established, homogeneous "nation" out of Egypt. Given what we know about the Syro-Palestinian melting pot at this time, this popular assumption is completely untenable.

What also seems wrong is the conventional interpretation of the biblical statement that "six hundred thousand [Hebrew *'elef*] men on foot" left Egypt with Moses (Exod. 12:37), where *'elef* is believed to mean "thousand." This statement was apparently based on census data preserved in Numbers 1 and 26, data apparently collected a century or so after the exodus when the Israelites in Palestine had to muster young men ("men on foot") to defend against invaders. In Numbers 1 and 26, the word *'elef* actually means "military unit." In other words, a century after Moses the Israelite federation of tribes was capable of mustering about six hundred fighting units (of six-to-twenty soldiers each), totaling five thousand men on foot. The usual tendency to translate *'elef* as "thousand" reinforces the common but erroneous assumption that Yahweh delivered a large number of people—an entire nation—from slavery in Egypt.[3] Other biblical passages may hint that the escaping slaves comprised closer to seventy families—perhaps several hundred people (Exod. 1:5).

Even the narrative portrait of Moses as their dynamic "leader" is likely overblown: these slaves would have probably regarded him more as an opportunity to be exploited than a leader to be followed. In fact, the biblical traditions describe organizational chaos among the slaves, as well as their periodic insistence that no one should have to defer to Moses on anything (see Exod. 16:2; 17:2–3; Num. 12:1–2; etc.). What seems more likely from a historical standpoint is that Moses, assisted by a fortunate turn of events, was able to help several hundred Apiru slaves of diverse ethnic backgrounds escape and elude the soldiers dispatched to retrieve them.

3. If the exodus group comprised 600,000 young men, then the whole group (including women, children, and older men) would have totaled two or three million people. This is implausibly high. Marched twenty-five abreast, this many people would form a column almost two hundred miles long, meaning that the front of the line would have reached Mount Sinai before the back of the line had left Egypt.

"Acts of God"

The exodus from Egypt took place under circumstances that are often labeled "acts of God." This phrase survives today in the language of lawyers and insurance companies, for whom an act of God is an event that no one could have caused or prevented. When such an act of God occurs, nobody can take credit for it if the outcome is desirable, and nobody can be blamed if it isn't. Loosely speaking, "God" made it happen, even though supernatural forces need not be involved.

Actually, this is not much different from the biblical understanding. In the case of the exodus, the act of God was the fortunate turn of events enabling some Apiru slaves to escape. This is celebrated in Exodus 15:1–18 in a poem describing the escape from Egypt. Its language is clearly more archaic than that of the surrounding narrative, suggesting that the poem might even be dated to the time of the exodus itself. If so, its author may have experienced firsthand the act of God enabling the slaves to escape from the Egyptian troops across a body of water, probably during a storm. On the basis of Exodus 15:21, some scholars suggest that this poem was actually composed by Moses' sister, Miriam. The poem includes no mention, much less celebration, of Moses: because "God" made it happen, the focus is exclusively on deity. Consequently, the use of figurative language, mythic motifs, and symbolic imagery was entirely appropriate. Whether reporting history or creating fiction, this was simply the way ancient scribes expressed their belief that deity was participating in human events.

We have already seen that the Israelites inherited such mythic language and imagery from their pre-Yahwist, pagan past (see Box 1.6). Similar continuity of language and imagery is apparent in the biblical account of the slaves' arrival at Mount Sinai soon after their escape from Egypt. There, Yahweh is said to have appeared, accompanied by thunder and lightning, blazing smoke and fire rising into the sky, the blast of a trumpet, and people cowering in fear (Exod. 19:16–19).[4] Yahweh's appearance is also associated with the 'anan, an archaic word that later biblical writers misunderstood as a reference to a natural phenomenon, a "thick cloud." Actually, this word—attested from Bronze Age Ugaritic to modern Arabic—referred to a supernatural phenomenon, the means through which a deity's power, authority, word, and glory are revealed to humans. The 'anan is roughly equivalent to what the ancient Greeks called the aegis of a god and what later generations of Israelites would call an "angel." Like halos in later European art, the 'anan simultaneously signaled the presence of the deity while keeping the deity masked from mortal eyes.

This is all the archaic and metaphorical language of the religious imagination. But that does not mean that the story it recounts is entirely the product of someone's imagination, especially since other ancient Near Eastern peoples frequently wove such imagery into their narration of historical events. If that is the case here, it would seem that Exodus 19 preserves an archaic tradition, replete with mythic imagery, perhaps of a powerful thunderstorm generally coinciding with the slaves' arrival at the foot of the mountain. Such storms can be extremely dramatic and

4. This mountain is usually identified with Jebel Musa in the southern Sinai peninsula, even though this site lacks water. Some have argued that the mountain should be identified with a volcano in the Arabian Hejaz, assuming that the reference to "smoke and fire" is not a mythological motif but a literal description of an active volcano. The location of Mount Sinai remains unknown.

Box 2.2—Ancient Theophanies

The Sinai theophany (Exod. 19:9–19) resembles those described in Homeric legend. Yahweh's 'anan, like the aegis of a Greek god, was not a mere "cloud"; like halos in medieval paintings, they signal to human senses the presence of the deity itself. In the Iliad, different aegises appear, each attesting to the presence of different gods competing to determine the outcome of the battle of Troy. For example, on hearing that his Trojan countrymen have failed to capture the corpse of their enemy Patroclus,

> [a] dark cloud of grief fell upon Hector . . . , and he made his way to the front clad in full armour. Thereupon the son of [the god] Saturn seized his bright tasseled aegis, and veiled Ida in cloud; he sent forth his lightnings and his thunders, and as he shook his aegis he gave victory to the Trojans and routed the Achaeans. (Iliad 17.591–595)

In other words, accompanied by a divine theophany, Hector captured the corpse of Patroclus. Meanwhile, on the other side, Achilles resolved to help the Achaeans steal back the captured corpse from Hector:

> [The goddess] Minerva flung her tasseled aegis round [Achilles'] strong shoulders; she crowned his head with a halo of golden cloud from which she kindled a glow of gleaming fire. As the smoke that goes up into heaven from some city that is being beleaguered . . . even so did the light flare from the head of Achilles. . . . Ringing as the note of a trumpet that sounds alarm when the foe is at the gates of the city, even so brazen was the voice of the son of Aeachus, and when the Trojans heard its clarion tones, they were dismayed: . . . awe-struck by the steady flame which the grey-eyed goddess had kindled above [Achilles'] head. . . . Thrice did Achilles raise his loud cry as he stood by the trench, and thrice were the Trojans and their brave allies thrown into confusion. . . . The Achaeans to their great joy then drew Patroclus out of reach of the weapons and laid him on a litter. (Iliad 18.196–236)

Surrounded in the divine glory of Minerva, Achilles routed the Trojans. The Sinai theophany uses similar archaic imagery, including a description of fire and smoke ascending into the sky and (an otherwise awkward reference to) trumpets blaring.

5. The word "numinous" refers to the feelings of fear, awe, and fascination people experience in the overwhelming presence of the powerful yet mysterious supernatural "Other," ranging from beatific rapture to paralyzing terror. The ability of Near Eastern people to see deity revealed in the thunderstorm is illustrated by this personal anecdote: In 1973, we were in rural Yemen, which was suffering severe drought. One day, storm clouds moved in and a few insignificant drops of rain fell. When a strange fringe of light appeared behind the clouds, a village boy pointed to it and said, "Allah." He was exhibiting an extremely ancient pattern of thought preserved in remote Yemen, where even benign storm clouds can represent a theophany in a drought-stricken land.

frightening in the wilderness regions of the Near East. If so, for the escaped slaves trying to weather it out, this one particular storm had a numinous quality.[5] For them, it was a theophany, and subsequent descriptions of it required the use of mythic imagery.

Figure 2.4
Sinai Wilderness. (Painting by Eathel Mendenhall)

The Sinai Covenant

A numinous experience lacking further significance quickly degenerates into mere superstition, easily rationalized or forgotten over time. What prevented this particular experience from such a fate was its connection with something of urgent significance to this diverse group of escaped slaves: a covenant. The covenant revealed at Mount Sinai directly addressed their wilderness predicament by proposing a framework on which this heterogeneous collection of individuals could see beyond their differences and together build a future, no longer as a "mixed rabble" but as "one people." The thunderstorm at the mountain powerfully reinforced the sacred quality and value of the covenant delivered there by Moses, and the value of this covenant, in turn, powerfully reinforced the escaped slaves' belief that, in this particular thunderstorm, they had indeed witnessed the presence and voice of a god.

In antiquity, the revelation of a new religious insight or system was not described in terms of human inspiration or innovation but rather as a divine revelation associated with a theophany. The theophany was the typical motif used to explain the origin of something new and meaningful. But something new can only become meaningful if it is also expressed and described in terms and analogies that are already well-known to everyone concerned. Despite its religious novelty, the Sinai covenant Moses delivered was readily intelligible to these ex-slaves because it employed well-known concepts and images, in this case concepts and images drawn from the familiar world of LB Age international politics. Naturally, they were adapted so that they now served *religious* as opposed to *political* ends, providing a basis for a community whose cohesion did not require any political enforcement mechanism or monopoly of force.

This revelation of covenant as the basis for community was also timely since virtually all social and political organizations were in shambles. Many people lacked faith in their ability to serve as desirable bases for community. At the same time, this new god, Yahweh, could not serve as the usual authority symbol or divine patron for some such organization simply because there was no organization here at the mountain with which he could be identified. And Moses himself, "credentialed" or otherwise, was remembered as being characteristically "meek" (Num. 12:3, RSV), in other words, personally and temperamentally unwilling to wield power or exercise controlling influence over this group.[6]

6. Later biblical writers recast the meek Moses into a more dynamic and commanding authority. He was eventually regarded as an "unusual kind of prophet" (Deut. 34:10–12), an intermediary through whom divine leadership was exercised.

A passage in the book of Isaiah illustrates how covenant-related ideas in the Bible often employed and adapted images similar to those attested in the LB Age world of international politics. When castigating the Israelites for abandoning God, Isaiah observed that even dumb animals are loyal to their masters:

> The ox knows its owner,
>   and the donkey its master's crib. (1:3)

The same "barnyard" imagery appears in Hittite political correspondence with regard to a border group that had been switching loyalties between the Hittites and the Mitanni. After defeating the Mitanni, the Hittite king boasted that the border group had now "chosen his stable" (i.e., recognized him as master, or lord). This shows that religious ideas in the Bible are the product of neither specialized theological reflection nor a distinct ethnic group's particular customs and peculiar worldview; rather, most of the Bible's basic religious ideas originated as simple adaptations of familiar concepts widely known across the Near East.

The Treaty Structure

The Sinai covenant, identified in Exodus 20 and Deuteronomy 5 with the so-called Ten Commandments, had almost exactly the same structure as LB international treaties, which were probably widely known throughout the eastern Mediterranean world. Although the treaty structure is best known from the Hittite archives, it clearly did not originate with the Hittites. A copper plate excavated at Byblos and perhaps dating to the end of the EB Age was inscribed with the text of a treaty made by Huruba'ilu, king of Byblos, containing almost all the features of the later Hittite treaties. This treaty structure was likely a thousand years old by the time of Moses and was part of the common knowledge of people throughout the region. Because such treaties were required to be read publicly across the realm, sometimes several times a year, their basic structure was probably well known, not only to Moses but to Syro-Palestinian peoples everywhere. The structure of these treaties had six sections, each of which has a clear parallel in biblical traditions describing the Sinai covenant: a preamble, a historical foundation, a list of stipulations, a list of witnesses, a list of curses and blessings, and (implicitly) a concluding oath activating the treaty.

1. *Preamble*. International treaties before the time of Moses were highly formalized, usually beginning with a preamble identifying the overlord with all his elaborate titles. The purpose of this opening line was to identify the supreme authority with whom the relationship was about to be established. Depending on the treaty, this could be any authority figure, whether King Huru-ba'ilu of Byblos, the Hittite emperor Mursilis, or even the god Yahweh. The preamble of the Sinai covenant is simple: "I am Yahweh your God" (Exod. 20:2).

The covenant then proceeds to shift the basis of the relationship away from coercive force and on to mutual interests, hoping to unite the concerns and commitments of the vassal with those of the overlord. Simply put, a covenant brings about a merger. Such written treaties were probably based on earlier oral marriage contracts. The Bible often portrays the covenant relationship between Yahweh and Israel as if it were a marriage (see Hosea 1–3). Sometime in the EB Age, or perhaps earlier, the concept of a binding of shared commitments was transferred from the *private* realm of marriage (husband and wife) to the *political* realm of international treaties (lord and subject). At Mount Sinai, it was transferred from that to the *spiritual* realm of religious relationship (God and his people).

The norm in the ancient Near East was to depict the relationship between deity and common folk as involving a whole set of intermediaries. But here the Hebrew god is shown establishing a relationship directly with each person, by addressing each individual personally: "Thou shalt not. . . . " There is no charge here given to any king or social authority. The biblical faith begins with this historically unprecedented charter of autonomous and free individuals—unprecedented because such individualism elsewhere or at a later time would surely concern and offend the governing authorities.

2. *Historical Foundation*. The next words in the Sinai covenant are "who brought you out of the land of Egypt." Imagine the situation of this heterogeneous collection of individuals now stuck in the howling desert, their future uncertain. Can they even survive in this unfamiliar environment? Should they perhaps now go their separate ways, each family trying to make it on its own? Some might want to return to Egypt. Or should they remain together and, if so, what basis of unity can transcend their differences? What do they really have in common? Who should have authority in this new community, and how should it be exercised?

Only the recent past—a miraculous deliverance from slavery—was positive, but the past can be used in all sorts of ways for all sorts of purposes. In the treaty tradition, the past was consistently used to emphasize the benefits that an overlord has already conferred on a vassal. The phrase "[who brought you] out of the house of bondage" (Exod. 20:2, RSV) referred to such a benefit. Objectively speaking, this was one tangible thing the ex-slaves undoubtedly held in common. The foundation of the *future*, however, is the gratitude for such benefits (or blessings) received. This gratitude at least ought to shape one's outlook or perspective on life, which in turn might inspire one's future choices and commitments. Gratitude was thus something else they all held in common.

This use of the past to stimulate a sense of gratitude is evident in the LB Age international treaties, such as the covenant between the Hittite king Mursilis and Duppi-Teshub, king of Amurru (see Box 2.3). There are about thirty of these Hittite treaties, in which past history is cited to anchor the vassal's future loyalty more firmly in his gratitude for benefits received. Someone reading selected passages in these treaties and substituting "God" for the name of the Hittite king would think they were reading excerpts from the Bible. And that is precisely the point: for the Hebrews, God *was* a king—they were his vassals, and he was their *lord*.

3. *Obligations or Stipulations*. Loyal gratitude is reflected in the vassal's desire to embrace the principles and values of the overlord who has shown such favor. The Hittite treaties sometimes translate these principles and values into a long list of obligations a grateful vassal should embrace. Many concern the extradition of refugees, attesting to the political volatility, widespread social dislocations, and mass movements of people toward the end of the LB Age. In the Sinai covenant, the list of stipulations contained ten items called the "Decalogue" or, more popularly, the "Ten Commandments." Before examining the final three sections of the treaty structure, we should examine the Decalogue in more detail.

Box 2.3—The Hittite Emperor's Treaty with the King of Amurru

[*Preamble*]
"These are the words of the Sun Mursilis, the great king, the king of the Hatti land, the valiant, the favorite of the storm-god. . . .

[*Historical Foundation*]
"Aziras was the grandfather of you, Duppi-Teshub. Aziras remained loyal to my father [as his overlord]. . . . My father was loyal toward Aziras and his country. . . . When my father became a god and I seated myself on the throne of my father, Aziras behaved toward me just as he had behaved toward my father. . . . Aziras, your grandfather, and DU-Teshub, your father, . . . they remained loyal to me as their lord. . . . When your father died, in accordance with your father's word I did not drop you. . . . I sought after you. To be sure, you were sick and ailing, but although you were ailing, I, the Sun, put you in the place of your father. . . .

[*Obligations*]
"But you, Duppi-Teshub, remain loyal toward the king of the Hatti land. . . . The tribute which was imposed upon your grandfather and your father . . . you shall present them likewise. . . . Do not turn your eyes to anyone else! . . . If anyone utters words unfriendly toward the king or the Hatti land before you, Duppi-Teshub, you shall not withhold his name from the king. . . . [All sorts of military clauses, etc., follow.]

[*Witnesses*]
[Over seven dozen gods are listed, including the gods of the Apiru.] ". . . all the olden gods, . . . the mountains, the rivers, the springs, the great Sea, heaven and earth, the winds (and) the clouds—let these be witnesses to this treaty and to the oath.

[*Curses and Blessings*]
". . . should Duppi-Teshub not honor the words of the treaty and the oath, may these gods of the oath destroy Duppi-Teshub together with his person, his wife, his son, his grandson, his house, his land and together with everything that he owns. But if Duppi-Teshub honors these words of the treaty and the oath that are inscribed on this tablet, may these gods of the oath protect him together with his person, his wife, his son, his grandson, his house (and) his country." (*ANET*[3], 203–205)

Ten Commandments or Ten Commitments?

There is nothing particularly profound or original about the actual content of the Decalogue, and some of its "commandments" strike many people today as somewhat petty or irrelevant. Some of the commandments simply reiterate rather basic social obligations already acknowledged worldwide. For example, people who have never heard of the Bible nevertheless condemn killing, the dishonoring of parents, adultery, theft, bearing false witness, and coveting. They apparently did not need Yahweh to reveal this to them. Other commandments seem to establish doctrines and practices peculiar to Judaism (e.g., monotheism, anti-idolatry, respect for the divine name, and Sabbath observance). It would seem that if God were going to bequeath ten statements to the human race, he might do better than this.

But it would be a mistake to look for the profundity of the Decalogue in its *content*. If it is profound, it must be so with respect to its *context and application*. The embracing of these so-called "commandments" by a heterogeneous mix of people suggests that—in addition to a shared sense of gratitude for past good fortune—these were the only commitments they held in common, or felt they needed to hold in common. Political authorities, most of whom were now extremely weakened if not dead, would certainly have given subjects a longer and more explicit list of do's and don'ts. Voluntary compliance with the basic statements of the Decalogue may well have been regarded as an alternative to—or even a safeguard against—other more coercive forms of social or political control.

It is therefore ironic that Jews and Christians have often used the Decalogue—and the God who published it—coercively as such an instrument of social control, warning people to be good or else face dire consequences. This misuse of the Decalogue has been facilitated by the mistaken view that its statements are indeed "commandments" uttered by a demanding deity—a view that has unfortunately become deeply embedded in the consciousness of both Jews and Christians, and consequently of much of the world. In Deuteronomy, this text is referred to as the "ten words" (Hebrew *'asar debarim;* Greek *deka logoi*), understood generally as "statements," not specifically as "commands." This is reinforced by the fact that, grammatically speaking, the verbs used in the Decalogue are not commands (imperatives or prohibitives). Instead, they are simple future tense verbs or infinitive forms. No one is *commanding* anyone here in the Decalogue.[7] The Decalogue simply lists the basic principles that a lord—in this case, Yahweh—offers for the vassal's endorsement. In other words, a person who values and embraces these is poised to enter a covenant relationship with the one who proclaims them, namely Yahweh.

The Decalogue thus provides not a *proscription* against bad conduct but a *description* of a religious value system, in this case, the ethical obliga-

7. Some people who already feel a covenant bond with the biblical God may "hear" these ten statements as universal commands, even though they are not commands at all. Such a person might more correctly choose to "hear" them posed as personal questions: "Will you reject other gods, honor your father and mother, not commit adultery, etc.?" Within Judaism there is a tradition of viewing these statements in such a way, as if they were marriage vows between God and his people.

tions and personal commitments that provide the foundation of any and all human communities. These obligations are stated, not demanded. As in any covenant, the commitments must be voluntarily embraced and undertaken freely and gladly in grateful response for benefits and blessings already received. Technically speaking, at this point in the covenant-making process no relationship yet exists from which an overlord can boldly issue *commands*; here, in the stipulations, the overlord can only state the *principles* of central concern for the potential vassal to consider. Vassals must embrace the stipulations for their intrinsic merit alone, not because they are afraid of what will happen to them if they do not. In other words, people must see for themselves that these principles are compelling and good.

These are therefore not Ten *Commandments*. It would be much more accurate, and perhaps much better, to think of them as Ten *Commitments*, since Yahweh's rule becomes an effective and tangible reality only when human beings freely embrace them also *as their own personal commitments*. In other words, when people act on these *commitments*—all of which restrict self-interest—the rule of God becomes a tangible reality, establishing a religious basis (i.e., faith) on which human differences can be transcended and community achieved.

At the same time, these ten statements are flexible enough to accommodate wide-ranging cultural differences, not only in what they do say but also in what they leave unaddressed. For example, the Decalogue insists that the honoring of parents is a universal and unquestioned value, but it says nothing about how this should concretely manifest itself. Putting one's parents in a nursing home may be the honorable thing to do in one set of circumstances but not in another. "Adultery" is an unquestioned wrong always and everywhere, but legitimate marriage practices are never defined in the Bible: polygamy is not here outlawed, nor is Western-style monogamy mandated. The Decalogue says nothing about whether teenagers can drink alcohol, permitting coreligionists in, say, France, the United States, and Saudi Arabia to frame and decide the issue as seems appropriate to their different cultures. There is nothing here about how women should dress (veiled from head-to-toe as in traditional Yemeni society, or bare-breasted as in the Maldives), again permitting coreligionists to defer to prevailing cultural norms.

Of course, the Hebrew slaves could not have foreseen such a myriad of possible scenarios. Accepting this covenant simply meant that none of them were required to surrender his or her cultural heritage or distinctiveness, so long as it did not clash with these Yahwist principles. The "glue" that bound their community was not a common culture, ethnicity, or governing political structure, but a religious commitment to these obligations. While the biblical tradition will be quick to criticize any Yahwist with a halfhearted commitment to these obligations, it also originally allowed

8. Centuries later, parochializing forces in Israel would append to the Decalogue all sorts of law codes mandating specific cultural norms, creating the impression that Yahweh was over-weening in his demands, as concerned with what Israelites ate and how they dressed as with whether or not they told → the truth, stole, cheated, or harmed others. To salvage an emphasis on the latter (ethical matters), the early Jewish Christians felt compelled to jettison all emphasis on the former (ethnic matters). See chapters 7 and 8.

tremendous latitude for cultural differences, historical contexts, and personal autonomy in areas unrelated to these ten covenant principles. Most people inclined to view Yahweh as a dictator fail to appreciate this. The goal was not to issue commands restricting, regulating, and standardizing behavior per se, but to enumerate those basic but universal *commitments* (or ethical obligations) that were both fundamental to human integrity in *everyone's* culture and essential to human community *everywhere*.[8]

These statements do not serve the ends of social control as such commandments would in almost all other societies. Instead, these ten commitments cross-culturally define human integrity, making possible a community based on that integrity. Such religious teachings (e.g., "God says not to steal") usually seem unnecessary or, at best, supplemental in a society whose cohesion is actually based on something other than integrity, such as nationalism, blood kinship, ethnic homogeneity, solidarity of interests, or simply externally imposed force (i.e., law and order). But the Decalogue insists that these (religiously grounded) commitments are always the *primary and essential* control mechanisms making any community possible. Unless people possess integrity in these fundamental aspects of life, no community can long endure, regardless of how strong its nationalism, ethnicity, tribal bonds, or social institutions may be. In other words, the Decalogue describes Yahweh's will simply as those ten basic commitments necessary to maintain human community with a minimum of conflict and coercion.

What made these obligations profound—and *religious* as opposed to merely *social*—is that at Sinai they stood not as supplemental commandments *alongside* other mechanisms of social control but rather *in place of* such mechanisms altogether. The existence of community is staked precariously on nothing more than people's commitment to these obligations and to the faith that inspires that commitment. There is no other fail-safe mechanism that can salvage community if that faith and commitment should wane (a sociologically sobering insight). That is what made the Sinai community religiously based, as opposed to culturally or politically based. The only homogeneity that existed among these people was their shared commitment to a very fundamental definition of human integrity and religious obligation—in other words, their basic value system.

The Decalogue thus constituted a religious *value system* that was genuinely "transcendent" in the sense that it actually *rose above* or *superseded* existing social and cultural differences. People with a frontier mentality might eagerly embrace something akin to this as a desirable basis for building a new community and future on the ruins of the discredited past.

In discussing "value systems," it is important to remember that a "value" is not simply an agreeable idea but something that actually determines one's commitments, choices, and activities. The Latin word for this was *valuta*, which corresponds to Anglo-Saxon *worth-ship*, the antecedent of our word "worship." In this sense, any time a person acts either on the basis of a commitment or to uphold a value, *by definition* that person is engaging in "worship." As we saw with Baal and Asherah (chapter 1), so it was with Yahweh: embracing a value system and worshiping are essentially one and the same thing—the "god" being worshiped, of course, varies, depending on what is specifically being valued.[9]

What Are the Yahwist Religious Commitments?

9. People are therefore always "worshiping," whether they realize it or not. The important question is, What are the specific core values that inform and characterize one's pattern of living—in other words, What is one's god? Paul understood this when he wrote that "in fact there are many gods" (1 Cor. 8:5) and that the god worshiped by those who live as enemies of the cross (i.e., those incapable of self-sacrificial love) is "the belly," that is, their own self-centered desires and appetites (Phil. 3:19). Unfortunately, this *dynamic* sense of worship usually succumbs to a more *formal* sense (worship as stylized ritual behavior performed in sacred places on certain cultic occasions), making worship seem more "special." Formal worship becomes a means for monitoring one's own piety, as well as that of others, transforming religion into just another instrument of social control.

When viewed in the light of what we know about ancient patterns of thought, the connotations and significance of each covenant stipulation, when correctly translated, become dramatically different from the usual popular interpretations:

"You will have no other gods before me." In his treaty with Duppi-Teshub, Mursilis says, "Do not turn your eyes to any one else." Jesus echoes this in the NT: "No one can serve two masters" (Matt. 6:24). To reject Yahweh is to enter into a conflicting covenant with someone or something else, to reject all Yahwist commitments and obligations altogether. "Turning to other gods" means embracing alternative values and commitments, thus threatening the community by rejecting the ethical bond that holds it together. To place other gods ahead of Yahweh is to legitimize value systems rivaling that of the Decalogue, substituting another value system that may, for example, be less tolerant of cultural differences or encourage one group's domination of another. It has nothing to do with participating in the rituals of the wrong denomination. Most reasonable people today are far more concerned about their neighbors' operating value systems than about which rituals they practice or where they practice them. The coreligionist across the street who neglects or mistreats his or her children is a far more serious *spiritual* matter than the agnostic next door who has always been a good parent and reliable neighbor.

"You will not make for yourself an idol . . . you will not bow down to them or serve them." This stipulation makes perfect sense when viewed in the context of the end of the LB Age, when all political power structures were discredited and in ruins. Monumental art and statuary typically had been commissioned to cast an aura of sacredness around official political organizations and to thereby sanctify particular socioeconomic agendas. "Graven images" of gods were symbols of power structures and interest groups. To "bow down" to them would be to ascribe value ("worship") to that which they represent—the old ways of political domination and social control by coercion.

At the same time, it was forbidden to make an image of Yahweh that, given the context, surely meant transforming Yahweh into just

10. Having rejected artistic abstractions, the Israelites apparently believed that only human characters can serve as proper images of God. This is reflected, first, in every biblical passage that "imagines" God through heightened anthropomorphism, and second, in the claim that human beings were created "in the *image* of God" (Gen. 1:27). The Hebrew word for "image," *tselem*, is often synonymous with "idol." This notion probably underlies the later Christian claim that Jesus "is the image of the invisible God, the firstborn of all creation" in whom "all the fullness of God was pleased to dwell" (Col. 1:15, 19).

11. In time, the Sabbath would lose its *cross-cultural* significance and become something more *parochial*, a holy day whose "proper" rituals marked membership in one particular culture (Judaism). See chapter 7. It became so important that the later author of the Genesis creation story depicted everything being created in six days so that God, too, could properly observe the Sabbath. Ironically, Sabbath observance became a bitterly divisive issue within Judaism and later Christianity, as different sects bickered over who observed it most properly. Viewed as a command, this stipulation expects (if not demands) that people adjust their lives around

another "divine patron" symbolizing and promoting a particular social group or political agenda.[10] The Sinai covenant forbids imagining—or "imaging"—Yahweh in such sociopolitical terms. Political authority and coercion, in some contexts, may be legitimate, but they can never be "sacred" (i.e., viewed as the supreme arbiter of good and evil), a point that both Jewish and Christian martyrs have given their lives to affirm.

"You will not make wrongful use of the name of Yahweh your God." In its ancient setting, this had nothing to do with foul language or obscene words, but with legal acts and what it meant to swear an oath either to the truth of a statement (when rendering testimony in a dispute) or to the reliability of a promise (when drafting a contract with someone). Among the diverse mix of people at Sinai, it was essential to know that someone's sworn word was his or her bond. It was an extremely serious matter formally and deliberately to invoke the name "Yahweh." You shall not swear an oath by Yahweh to something if you are insincere or know it to be false. Any invocation of the name "Yahweh" to advance or promote something incompatible with Yahwism is a serious breach of covenant faith. It is taking that name "in vain" (i.e., wrongly).

"To remember the Sabbath and to keep it holy." Of all the covenant stipulations, this one initially seems to lack much moral profundity or cross-cultural value. But the Sabbath (Hebrew *shabbat*) has a long and complex history. Ancient Mesopotamian texts refer to the fifteenth day of the month as *shapattum*, which one text identifies as "a day of resting of the heart." In farm villages, a day of rest for farmers and animals is widely recognized and highly advisable to prevent injury to overworked draft animals, especially during the plowing season. Originally, the Sabbath (*shabbat, shapattum*) was a humanitarian institution for the well-being of laborers and working animals, and as such would have been especially meaningful to a group of people only recently escaped from servitude. Understood in this context, its cross-cultural application is obvious.[11]

"To honor your father and mother." It is curious that this command is presented as an interest of Yahweh, especially since such adages are commonly used everywhere socially to control children. At the same time, like all the other obligations, this is addressed not to youngsters but to adults, presumably with elderly parents. We know far too little about family relationships in the LB Age to know whether this command sought to rectify disturbing patterns of parental neglect that accompanied social disintegration. The family has been the primary economic unit throughout history, and because its survival is based as much on economic interests as personal attachments, the elderly are sometimes vulnerable to neglect.

But here, parent-child relationships are given an expressly *religious* foundation. In other words, the family is said to serve purposes that tran-

the observance of ritual ceremonies, a notion Jesus criticized (see Mark 2:27). The history of Sabbath observance is a classic example of the Law of Functional Shift (p. 4), where a religious form is preserved long after its original function has been lost and replaced by another.

12. Abraham Heschel once pointed out that this covenant stipulation also speaks to parents. If parents lack integrity, how can their children obtain and value it? If parents conduct themselves in dishonorable ways, then how can their children be expected to honor them?

13. Since the Decalogue is addressed to individuals ("you" singular) and not to corporate bodies (such as governments), it would be improper to use this passage to prohibit the government from exercising its legitimate functions of waging war and punishing criminals.

scend the economic and emotional needs of its members, meaning that one must care for one's aged parents even after they have lost their economic usefulness and value. Family solidarities are thus made subordinate to covenant solidarity with Yahweh, and are therefore not ends unto themselves. Consequently, one cannot let familial bonds—no matter how precious—supersede one's covenant obligations to God. This is the key to understanding some of Jesus' disturbing sayings about family (see Matt. 10:37; Luke 9:59–62; 14:26). As an interest of Yahweh, the solidarity of the family must in some way also serve to nurture personal character and moral integrity among the next generation.[12]

"You will not kill. You will not commit adultery. You will not steal. You will not bear false witness against your neighbor." Murder, adultery, theft, and lying about another person whose well-being is at stake were prohibited in all ancient law. But this is not law, because these rather terse stipulations, despite their straightforward language, lack the precision and specificity required of legal injunctions. Consequently, they are inadequate as bases of externally enforced social control because they do not address (much less "command" or "prohibit") specific acts. The key Hebrew terms for these four prohibitions—*ratsah, na'af, ganab,* and *'anah 'ed shaqer*—are, in many respects, more general and elastic than would seem from our various English translations. For example, the Hebrew *ratsah* does not refer to the legal concept of "murder" (despite the misleading NRSV translation). Any time a human life is taken through the agency of a private individual—regardless of whether the law would classify it as murder, manslaughter, depraved indifference to human life, or even accidental homicide—the religious obligation to Yahweh has been violated. This means that whenever a human life is taken by another human being, the religious community must insist that religion not be used to sanction, excuse, or gloss over the death. Regardless of the extent of the *legal* guilt or innocence of the killer, *religious* guilt existed in all cases except those where a person's accidental death was regarded as an "act of God."[13]

In the Sermon on the Mount, Jesus recognized that such elastic terms have broad implications (Matt. 5:21–37). Criticizing those who sought to reduce them to precise legal definitions—creating convenient loopholes along the way—Jesus said that whoever harbors ill will toward his brother is as guilty under God of destroying human life as someone who bludgeons another person to death, and that whoever relates to a woman in any way on the basis of improper lust is as guilty under God of sexual impropriety as the man who actually has illicit sexual intercourse with her. Such elastic terms as *ratsah* and *na'af* provide no useful basis for socially enforced sanctions because the prohibited actions are not clearly specified. Consequently, persons with integrity are committed to avoiding *all* these things, and therefore are under obligation not even to start down a path leading in these directions. If they do, they are accountable to God. It would seem from this that Jesus was not innovatively "reframing" Old Testament law but simply recognizing (in an insightful way) the built-in flexibility of the covenant commitments.

Like the Sermon on the Mount, these statements are part of a *personal* ethic, whose enforcement has not been delegated publicly or socially to any human judges or juries. Because these obligations were intended to define the core of human integrity, deviation from them was a private matter of conscience between God and the individual. Putting human life in jeopardy, sexual impropriety, taking things that do not belong to you, and distorting the truth are always wrong, regardless of whether the culprit is hauled into a court of law to answer to the community. Individuals who stand in covenant with Yahweh are constantly responsible, much more so than if their actions were merely accountable to the law. This insight alone accounts for the overwhelmingly moralistic tone of the Bible.

Of course, no human community can long endure the behavior of rogue individuals who bludgeon others to death or jeopardize the family—and therefore society—with inappropriate sexual conduct. These concerns eventually migrate from the realm of the private (i.e., the individual's conscience) to the public (community-enforced legal sanctions). The Bible contains numerous such legal codes in Exodus, Leviticus, and Deuteronomy—all from later times—in which social sanctions were extrapolated from the religious ethic expressed in the Decalogue. When the personal and voluntary commitments of private individuals to the religious ethic fail to inspire a minimum level of tolerable behavior, society becomes increasingly tempted to establish a legal monopoly of force (or human government, with legislators and judges). By this, they hope to establish and enforce laws regulating behavior, thereby helping guarantee public order through fear of tangible penalties.[14]

"You will not covet your neighbor's house." The final proof that the Decalogue was not intended as the basis of community-enforced law or commandment is the commitment not to covet (*hamad*)—in other words, not to want something belonging to someone else. Clearly, obligations to Yahweh encompass not only objective behaviors that human witnesses can observe and testify to but also inner attitudes. No law court could possibly enforce this stipulation, because no witness can credibly testify that another person is "desiring" something.

The "something" specified here is the neighbor's "house" (Hebrew *bayit*), which is not simply a domicile but an estate, anything and everything that belongs to another family. The principle here is that socioeconomic ("profit") motives cannot be a legitimate basis for Yahwist behavior, especially when such behavior jeopardizes community rela-

14. If a value system nurturing human integrity and rejecting self-centeredness loses its popular appeal, then it must be succeeded either by the political exercise of legal force or by the violence of anarchy. This also seems to be the point of Jesus' remark that biblical laws—usually attributed to God—were actually written to accommodate human "hard-heartedness" (= lack of covenant integrity; Matt. 19:7–8). At best, they are divine concessions made because people who are no longer willing to do what is right out of a sense of ethical obligation will do so out of fear of *social* sanctions.

15. Prestige based on socioeconomic status would likely have been considered legitimate in the worship of Asherah. Because this classless society results either from people's internal commitments not to covet or from historical catastrophes reducing everyone to a subsistence level, it is unrelated to those socialist visions of a classless society created by the government's exercise of legal force.

tionships by introducing rivalry and jealousy. Also, personal relationships within the covenant community must transcend socioeconomic differences, which was probably not a problem for the former slaves in the Sinai wilderness or for the Israelite villagers in Palestine a generation later, who all lived at approximately the same subsistence level. The principle here is that prestige based on socioeconomic status must not be allowed to stratify society, and when it eventually did in Israel centuries later, Yahwist prophets condemned it.[15] The covenant stipulations therefore conclude with the statement that a person ruled by Yahweh will have an integrity that precludes grasping ambitions.

Like the other nine commitments, this is an obligation to Yahweh, not to the society per se. Its intent was not to control human behavior through socially enforced rules but to define personal character and integrity.

Concluding the Covenant

The final three sections of ancient treaties underscore the solemnity of the new merger and the sacred character of the vassal's obligations. Each is also found in the biblical covenant tradition:

4. *List of Witnesses.* Even though overlords were militarily much stronger than their vassals, the treaty itself would never be so crass as to suggest that their relationship was actually established upon intimidation and threats of military reprisal. Because the treaty, as a covenant, was an oath (see no. 6 below), it was the *gods* who were expected to punish any violation. The Hittite treaties invoked by name every imaginable god, the overlord's as well as the vassal's, to underwrite the treaty. In other words, all religions were called on to uphold the sanctity of the promise the vassal was about to make. The sanctity of a promise is nothing less than the sanctity of human integrity, and any religion promoting that was acceptable to the Hittite state. Various natural phenomena were also invoked: mountains, rivers, streams, the great sea, heaven and earth, the winds, and the clouds. "Let these be witnesses to this treaty and this oath."

The Hebrews, of course, could not imagine other (discredited) gods witnessing their covenant with Yahweh. But later prophetic tradition poetically expresses the curious notion that nature, as an agent of God, was a witness to the covenant who could be summoned to indict Israel for breach of covenant. The biblical idea that creation itself has a stake in human integrity apparently also goes back to these ancient treaties.

In the biblical account of the later covenant ceremony at Shechem, Joshua tells the Israelites, "You are witnesses against yourselves that you have chosen Yahweh, to serve him." The Israelites reply, "We are witnesses" (Josh. 24:22). Instead of nature or some supernatural power enforcing

Box 2.4—Nature as "Witness" to Israel's Covenant Loyalty

Give ear, O heavens, and I will speak;
    let the earth hear the words of my mouth.
. . . .
Do you thus repay Yahweh,
    O foolish and senseless people?
Is not he your father, who created you,
    who made you and established you? (Deut. 32:1, 6)

Hear, O heavens, and listen, O earth;
    for Yahweh has spoken:
I reared children and brought them up,
    but they have rebelled against me. (Isa. 1:2)

Hear what Yahweh says:
Rise, plead your case before the mountains,
    and let the hills hear your voice.
Hear, you mountains, the controversy of Yahweh,
    and you enduring foundations of the earth;
for Yahweh has a controversy with his people. (Mic. 6:1–2)

compliance, the community itself has become the witness. Adherence to the covenant is to be self-policing.

5. *Curses and Blessings.* The treaties conclude with a list of the benefits and punishments that the gods will bestow or inflict on the vassal, depending on his compliance with the stipulations. Failing to fulfill one's commitments to one's overlord had dire consequences. Death, disease, crop failure, and defeat in war were prominently listed among the curses, the ultimate curse being the complete destruction and scattering of the body politic. The blessings of the gods included long life, peace, and prosperity. Lists of curses and blessings were appended to several later legal texts in the Bible, reminding the Israelites of the solemn nature of their obligation to Yahweh (see Leviticus 26 and Deuteronomy 28). The biblical tradition also recalls that ceremonial renewals of Yahweh's covenant with Israel included a recitation of curses and blessings (see Deut. 27:11–26; Josh. 8:30–35, especially v. 34).

The authors of the Former Prophets (see Appendix A), writing about six hundred years after the time of Moses, used these blessings and curses as the basis for interpreting Israel's history: whenever tradition recalled a plague or military defeat befalling Israel, these writers explained it as the consequence of some prior covenant violation. But the *original* purpose of covenant blessings and curses was not to rationalize historical events in this way or to promote a rigid historical determinism. Rather, they provided an incentive for the individual actively to embrace the commitments, since neglecting them would have serious consequences for future generations, who would have to grow up in a community where people are untrustworthy, self-seeking, uncommitted to fundamental ethical principles, and graspingly ambitious. This is presented as an empirically demonstrable aspect of the historical processes of social decay:

> "I, Yahweh your God, am a jealous God, punishing children for the iniquity of parents, to the third and fourth generation of those who reject me, but showing steadfast love to the thousandth generation of those who love me and keep my covenant stipulations." (Exod. 20:5–6)

6. *Oath of Compliance.* A treaty is a text, but an oath is the actual mechanism whereby the text is ratified and brought to life, no longer just words in a document but a functioning reality in the lives of actual people. We have ample evidence of treaties concluding with rituals of compliance—usually spoken oaths but sometimes physical gestures. In much the same way, treaties today are ratified by signatures and handshakes activating the new relationship and its terms. It should not be surprising that the biblical story of the covenant at Mount Sinai reaches its climax with the escaped slaves pledging to abide by the covenant obligations, thereby defining and activating themselves as the people of Yahweh (see Exod. 24:3–8).

A New Vision, a New Religion

With this ceremony, the covenant took effect. A treaty form that, in centuries past, had been the basis for relationships between political states and other social groups now became the basis for a religious community born in the wilderness of Sinai. For those assembled there, an image or metaphor that originally functioned in the context of political governance came to function in the context of religious accountability. They, too, now had an overlord—a king—whose "government" bound them together.

For these first devotees of Yahweh, religion supported the unprecedented claim that human community is actually not dependent ultimately on *commandments* or any other organization of coercive social force (or inducements of social prestige) but on people's *commitments* to integrity and personal character. From this, it follows that no religion claiming Moses and the exodus as part of its heritage can be used to sanction social control interests; such interests must stand—or fall—on their own. Instead, in this its formative period, the role of Yahwism was to promote the fundamental values that cultivate—across cultures—the sort of personal character and integrity desired by Yahweh, because *that* is ultimately the true and only foundation of human community.

The Sinai covenant provided a basis for community to reemerge from the ash heaps of civilization-wide destruction. The centuries that followed brought rapid and exceedingly far-reaching changes to this particular community now regarding itself as the people of Yahweh. In fact, the attempt to preserve the values and commitments of its formative period in changing historical and social contexts eventually resulted in the production of all sorts of Israelite religious literature, some of which was later collected for inclusion in that body of sacred scripture today called the Bible (see Appendix A).

About half of that later literature is history writing. The need to present the faith to later generations and to new circumstances induced many ancient scribes to revise the picture of Israel's formative period—for example, fictitiously depicting Yahweh leading an entire nation of ethnically homogeneous people out of Egypt. This is why critical readers of the Bible cannot and should not take its historical reporting at face value. But the image of Moses going up Mount Sinai to receive the Decalogue—the centerpiece of Yahwist faith—remained a powerful image for later Israelite storytellers. And when some of them would later be tempted to add something new to the centerpiece of that faith, they could revise the Sinai story, portraying Moses taking yet another trip up the mountain to receive some authoritative new directive making the faith more "relevant." This helps explain the curious fact that, in the Bible, Moses makes repeated trips up Mount Sinai.

The following chapters focus on the subsequent history of this Yahwist tradition during biblical times, examining both the impact this faith had on later generations of Israelites, and the impact these later Israelites had on the structure of this faith.

Box 2.5—Moses the Mountain Climber

Between Exodus 19:3 and 34:29, Moses makes perhaps eight or nine trips up Mount Sinai to meet Yahweh. But the story is so garbled that it is impossible to say how many times he went up, or even why. Some verses describing Moses' ascent do not seem to have a corresponding reference to his descent, and sometimes an account of an ascent may simply elaborate on a previous one, creating the impression he went up twice when he only went up once.

ascent	descent	accompanied by	what Moses received from Yahweh
1. Exodus 19:3	Exodus 19:14	no one	the Decalogue (Exod. 20:1–17)
2. Exodus 19:20	Exodus 19:25	no one	the command to bring Aaron up with him the next time
3. Exodus 24:9	Exodus 32:15?	Aaron, Aaron's two sons, seventy elders	specifications for building the ark of the covenant and the tabernacle, and for observing the Sabbath?
4. Exodus 24:13	unclear	Joshua?	unclear? two tablets?
5. Exodus 34:4	Exodus 34:29	no one	Ritual Decalogue (Exod. 34:10–28)

If nothing else, this confusion discounts the theory that all this is the simple work of creative writers inventing a coherent story. It seems better to assume that the tradition of Moses ascending Mount Sinai was constantly being modified by later scribes trying to piggyback onto it something they considered important. The confusion results from attempts to preserve in the book of Exodus *all* these traditions—the original one about the Decalogue (no. 1) and all the later revisions.

In almost all cases, we cannot determine when and why the later traditions arose. For example, the tradition of Aaron (the prototypical Yahwist priest) accompanying Moses up Sinai (no. 2) might have arisen among later Israelites who wanted to confer legitimacy on the priestly family administering the Yahwist shrine at Shiloh. The tradition of Moses (joined by Aaron, Aaron's sons, and the seventy elders) receiving specifications for the ark of the covenant (no. 3) may have arisen at the time of David to sanctify the ark that David brought into Jerusalem (2 Samuel 6). Perhaps the clearest revision is the giving of the so-called Ritual Decalogue (no. 5): the tradition that ritual commandments were given at Sinai to supersede the ethical ones likely arose during the reign of Solomon, when the old covenant and its tribal federation had been superseded by the Davidic covenant and the Solomonic kingdom (see 1 Kings 4:7–19). By piggybacking this onto the Sinai tradition, Yahweh is shown giving divine approval to the reduction of religion to mere ritual, which is in fact what happened during Solomon's reign.

Even though some degree of literary license was permitted, it is worth noting that no scribe felt comfortable depicting Moses making a trip up the mountain with a representative of the tribe of Benjamin (Saul's tribe) or Judah (David's tribe) to receive anything like a divine charter authorizing some human king to be named in the future. The tradition was simply too insistent that Saul had been installed at the behest of Samuel (1 Samuel 9–10), and that David had received his divine right to rule from Nathan, who may have been the court prophet from the Jebusite regime in Jerusalem that preceded David. Apparently Israelite culture had some constraints preventing Israelite kingship from being linked to Moses.

Suggestions for Further Reading

Additional information on the topics discussed in this chapter can be found in the following sources.

Dictionary/Encyclopedia Entries

Anchor Bible Dictionary: Adultery; Blessings and Curses; Covenant; Exodus, The; Idol; Image of God; Merneptah; Midian; Mosaic Covenant; Moses; Philistines; Ramesses; Theophany in the OT; Treaties in the ANE; Wanting and Desiring

Interpreter's Dictionary of the Bible: Covenant; Election

Encyclopedia Britannica (14th rev. ed., 1964): Decalogue

The Exodus

E. Campbell, "Moses and the Foundations of Israel." *Interpretation* 29 (1975): 141–154.

E. Frerichs and Leonard Lesko, eds., *Exodus: The Egyptian Evidence.* Winona Lake, Ind.: Eisenbrauns, 1997.

J. Hoffmeier, *Israel in Egypt: The Evidence for the Authenticity of the Exodus Tradition.* New York: Oxford University Press, 1996.

The *'Anan* of Yahweh

G. Mendenhall, *The Tenth Generation.* Baltimore: Johns Hopkins University Press, 1973. Chapter 2: "The Mask of Yahweh."

Covenant

D. Hillers, *Covenant: The History of a Biblical Idea.* Baltimore: Johns Hopkins University Press, 1969.

D. McCarthy, *Old Testament Covenant: A Survey of Current Opinions.* Richmond: John Knox Press, 1972.

G. Mendenhall, "Covenant Forms in Israelite Tradition." *BAR* 3: 25–53.

Three

The Twelve-Tribe Federation: The Adaptive Period (I)—Yahweh Becomes "King" of Israel

Suggested Reading

Sojourn in the Wilderness: Numbers 10:29–36; 14; 21
"Conquest" of Canaan: Joshua 6–7; 9–10; 24
The Non-Israelite Regimes: Judges 1–2; 4–8

Obstacles to Understanding Early Israel

There is little agreement among biblical scholars about the nature of Israelite society from the time it is first mentioned in the Merneptah Stela (ca. 1208 B.C.) to the time of kings David and Solomon two hundred years later. Even the Israelite scribes six hundred years later who wrote about it had difficulty comprehending its original social character. For example, the author of the book of Joshua envisioned it less as a religious community and more along the lines of a political state or "nation," whose leader Joshua is depicted as (but never actually labeled) a king. Most historians agree that the author of Joshua, writing centures later and trying to make the tradition more "relevant" to his contemporaries, anachronistically projected a later monarchist perspective onto this early period. They further agree that we must pay more careful attention to other biblical traditions portraying early Israel as a more or less loose confederation of approximately twelve different tribes, clans, and other smaller social groups. However, these same scholars sharply disagree about most of the specifics concerning this federation.

This twelve-tribe federation existed during a "dark age" that archaeologists label the Iron Age IA–B period, roughly 1200–1000 B.C. If it arose simultaneous to the Philistine confederation along the coast, and if it began to collapse after the Israelite defeat at the battle of Ebenezer (see chapter 4), then we might date the federation more precisely to 1175–1025 B.C. After this, it was transformed into a political state (or "nation") ruled by a king.

Box 3.1—Joshua as Israel's Surrogate "King"

The author of the book of Joshua, writing after four hundred years of Israelite kingship, anachronistically imagined Joshua as a sort of warrior-king and Israel as the loyal subjects who can be put to death if they do not obey him. Like a king, Joshua symbolically represents the entire Israelite community:

> After the death of Moses the servant of Yahweh, Yahweh spoke to Joshua son of Nun, Moses' assistant, saying, "My servant Moses is dead. Now proceed to cross the Jordan, you and all this people, into the land that I am giving to them, to the Israelites. Every place that the sole of your foot will tread upon I have given to you, as I promised to Moses. . . ."
>
> Then Joshua commanded the officers of the people, "Pass through the camp, and command the people: 'Prepare your provisions; for in three days you are to cross over the Jordan, to go in to take possession of the land that Yahweh your God gives you to possess.'" . . .
>
> They answered Joshua: "All that you have commanded us we will do, and wherever you send us we will go. Just as we obeyed Moses in all things, so we will obey you. Only may Yahweh your God be with you, as he was with Moses! Whoever rebels against your orders and disobeys your words, whatever you command, shall be put to death. Only be strong and courageous." (Josh. 1:1–3, 10–11, 16–18)

During this period authority within this federation resided ultimately in the religious tradition of Sinai, so much so that the Israelites themselves regarded Yahweh, the god of Sinai, as their functional equivalent to a king. Consequently, in many important respects early Israel was the domain of Yahweh, or "kingdom of God." In other words, this federation appears to have been a community whose morale and cohesion—to the extent such existed—was provided solely by a religious ethic regarded as the "royal policy" of Yahweh.

Thus, this chapter shifts attention away from the structure and substance of the Sinai covenant's new way of thinking about God (chapter 2) to the impact this had, not on the several hundred ex-slaves in the Sinai wilderness, but on the members of the federation of Israel who, a generation later, appeared in the land of Palestine as "the people of Yahweh."

There are two obstacles to this understanding of early Israel. The first is the lack of sources outside the Bible that can provide a check against these biblical stories. All this is, after all, set in a historical dark age, when written sources were virtually nonexistent. From this, some scholars infer that the stories about this early federation are sheer fiction. However, as with the exodus story, these stories contain names and details that seem to serve no literary or theological purpose, reinforcing the likelihood that they preserve archaic traditions about real people and events.

The second obstacle is our own modern vantage point, which bombards us with all sorts of potentially misleading stereotypes. For example, many modern folk instinctively equate religion with superstition, and tribes with primitive exclusivism.[1] Consequently, this chapter's claim that an ancient tribal federation was based on religion can be misinterpreted as a claim that, among the Israelites, narrow group loyalty was reinforced by ignorance and primitive superstition, which was clearly *not* the case. Also, many modern Western folk have a difficult time either conceiving of gods apart from some social enforcement system or imagining that people can actually achieve a civic unity without the political monopoly of force we call government. Consequently, this chapter's claim that a god "ruled" in early Israel can be misinterpreted: it neither assumes that a supernatural being was interrupting naturally occurring, human, historical processes in early Israel nor implies that someone somewhere in this confederation was politically exploiting religion. Only by moving beyond such modern and Western biases is it possible to appreciate the impressive synthesis of religion and culture achieved within this confederation of Israelite tribes.

1. Anthropologists correctly understand that "tribes" are fragile social bodies (compared to states) composed of economically self-sufficient residential units. They are usually geographically based networks of villages providing effective economic and military counterweights to the demands of urban power centers. Their fragile unity is often bolstered symbolically by the claim that everyone in the tribe descends from a common ancestor. In fact, actual blood kinship hardly ever exists.

The Diversity of the Twelve Tribes

Archaeological excavations in the hill country of Palestine and Transjordan, where the federation of tribes was strongest, reveal a standard of living greatly reduced from the LB Age. As pointed out in the previous two chapters, the number of villages here increased rapidly beginning around 1200 B.C., suggesting a sudden influx of refugee immigrants as Bronze Age civilization was collapsing. By the eleventh century B.C. the population had risen to about a quarter of a million, covering territory roughly half the size of Vermont. Most of the villages were unfortified, and there is little evidence of weaponry, suggesting that some sort of regional social polity was operating to ensure some measure of order within this densely concentrated population. Curiously, there is no archaeological evidence of any such polity. What was it, then, that made it possible for these different hill-country tribes, clans, and other subgroups to coexist with some degree of peace and security during this period?

It is much easier to say what it was *not*. First, it could not have been *blood kinship*. The so-called "shibboleth" incident in Judges 12 describes how the Transjordanian Yahwists demanded the Palestinian Yahwists to pronounce the password "shibboleth," knowing that it contained a type

Map 3.1

The Israelite Tribes.
By and large, villagers of hill-country Palestine and Transjordan embraced Yahwism, while those controlled by regimes in the lowlands did not. In addition to Philistine-controlled areas on the southern coastal plain, other towns (listed in Judges 1) resisted the new faith, such as those in the fertile valley that arched south and east from Aphek to Megiddo and Beth-shean. Because early Israel's fundamental concern was the religious ethic controlling personal conduct (and not political or military power to control territory), it would be as inappropriate to draw boundary lines on this map as it would be to draw "Christian" boundary lines on Map 8.1. There may have been Yahweh worshipers in non-Israelite towns, just as there were non-Yahwists in otherwise Israelite villages.

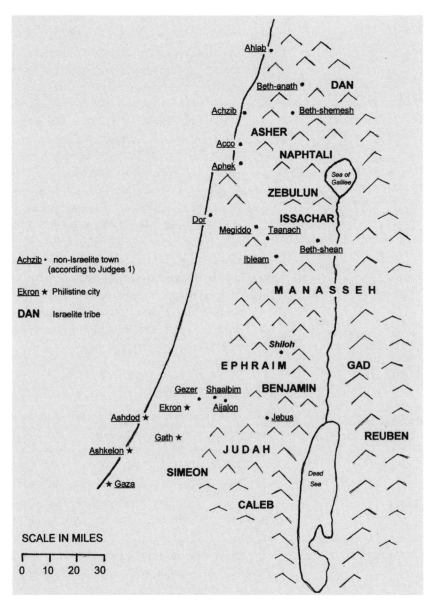

of "sh" sound they could not pronounce. This provides graphic evidence that even though they all spoke the same West Semitic language as non-Israelites, they did not all speak the same dialect. This would be unlikely if they were biologically related to one another.

Nor could their confederation have been based on a *common ethnic heritage*. Proper names suggest that the Israelite forebears came from diverse ethnic backgrounds, just as one would expect given the ethnic melting pot that existed at the time and place. Consequently, the basis of

Israelite unity could not have been *common cultural practices*. For example, the tradition about the Zelophehad clans (Num. 27:1–11), where a daughter could inherit property in the absence of sons, is radically different from the custom of levirate marriage preferred by some other Israelites, under which, if a deceased man left no sons, his brother would sire sons on his behalf so that property would *not* be inherited by daughters (Deut. 25:5–10). Here was a significant difference in customs among Israelites involving an issue basic to the solidarity of the family.

Finally, Israelite unity could not have been based on *shared economic interests.* Palestine and Transjordan contain numerous different regions and microenvironments, each sustaining different economic modes of life. For example, the chief economic activity in the arid regions of southern Judah was animal husbandry (sheepherding), whereas the grainfields in northern Transjordan can be very much like Kansas in a good year, ripe for farming.[2] Different still are the valleys in the northern hill country of Palestine, which support the cultivation of grapes, olives, and vegetables. The only economic interest shared across regions was the desire of villagers to keep as much of these scarce resources as possible out of the hands of political bureaucrats, who produced essentially nothing valuable in return.

Pottery forms from the time also suggest regional differences between north and south. This is confirmed by biblical traditions that recount the periodic flare-up of regional rivalries and antagonisms (but only later, after the bonds of the federation had already begun to loosen).

2. There could be significant tensions between these two different economic modes. The natural antagonism between farmers and shepherds in the ancient Near East was well known and may provide a background motif in the biblical story of Cain and Abel (Genesis 4).

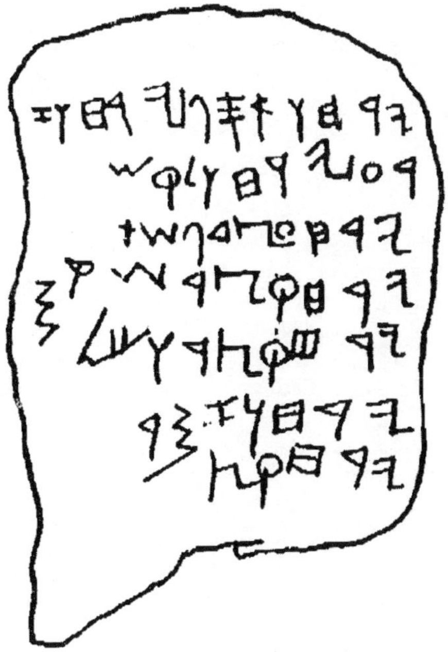

Figure 3.1
Gezer Calendar. The earliest example of Hebrew writing is attested in this "calendar" discovered at Gezer, about twenty miles from Jerusalem. Dating to the tenth or eleventh century B.C., it simply lists in order the seasonal agricultural cycle of activity (sowing, harvesting, pruning, etc.).

Despite all this, throughout most of the early Iron Age this assemblage of different peoples and tribes did not devolve into the chaos and anarchy that routinely result when governmental control disintegrates. Unlike the warlords who rushed to fill the ensuing power vacuum, this federation of tribes not only shunned imperial expansion but also lacked even the basic political apparatus to govern its own internal affairs. As far as we can tell, this federation seems to have been the largest, most widespread, diverse population group in ancient history that was *not* held together by

3. We are, of course, interested here only in this *early* period of Israel. Before long, the Israelites would establish a political state and begin pursuing imperialistic goals (see chapters 4, 5, and 6). Writing within that later context, the author of Joshua 1–11 anachronistically portrayed the Israelites behaving exactly like typical imperialists, storming into other people's lands, taking control of their resources, and slaughtering everyone around. See note 13.

some sort of power structure. As Egyptian influence waned after 1200 B.C., why didn't early Israel respond like most of the non-Israelites—the Jebusites, Amorites, and Philistines?[3] The answer: the very fact of being "Israelite" at this early time precluded such behavior because early Israel (not unlike the early Christian community) was "self-selected," that is, composed of people who did not value power politics. A frontier mentality may help account for such an orientation, but the point is that these hill-country villagers had little use for political power structures, great contempt for the value systems that necessitated them, and deep dissatisfaction with the old Bronze Age religious cults that legitimized them. Traces of their antipathy are laced throughout the biblical texts written by their descendants.

Box 3.2—The Parable of Jotham

The early Israelite antipathy toward political power and the sort of people willing (if not eager) to wield it found picturesque expression in Jotham's Parable of the Trees. Noteworthy is the movement from the productive and valuable trees to the worthless one:

> "The trees once went out
>   to anoint a king over themselves.
> So they said to the olive tree,
>   'Reign over us.'
> The olive tree answered them,
>   'Shall I stop producing my rich oil
>   by which gods and mortals are honored,
>   and go to sway over the trees?'
> Then the trees said to the fig tree,
>   'You come and reign over us.'
> But the fig tree answered them,
>   'Shall I stop producing my sweetness
>   and my delicious fruit,
>   and go to sway over the trees?'
> . . . .
> So all the trees said to the bramble,
>   'You come and reign over us.'
> And the bramble said to the trees,
>   'If in good faith you are anointing me king over you,
>   then come and take refuge in my shade;
>   but if not, let fire come out of the bramble
>   and devour the cedars of Lebanon.'" (Judg. 9:8–11, 14–15)

The bramble is small, dried up scrub, good for nothing but kindling. If ignited, it has the potential to destroy even the most valuable and magnificent of all trees.

The Unifying Factor—Yahweh

We must take seriously the possibility that the so-called twelve tribes of Israel were held together only by *ideology*, that is, a shared but fragile vision or hope. In the absence of other factors, this may well have been the intangible "polity" conferring predictability to the corporate affairs of these diverse people. Being intangible, it has left virtually no trace in the archaeological record. The later author of the book of Judges, in his own characteristic way, agreed that the health and viability of the early federation had indeed been linked to its members' commitment to this intangible religious factor. When different values became paramount (in other words, people began worshiping other gods), social fissioning resulted and the community became vulnerable to exploitation:

> Then the Israelites did what was evil in the sight of Yahweh and worshiped the Baals; and they abandoned Yahweh, the God of their ancestors, who had brought them out of the land of Egypt; they followed other gods, from among the gods of the peoples who were all around them, and they bowed down to them; and they provoked Yahweh to anger. They abandoned Yahweh, and worshiped Baal and the Astartes. So the anger of Yahweh was kindled against Israel, and he gave them over to plunderers who plundered them, and he sold them into the power of their enemies all around, so that they could no longer withstand their enemies. (Judg. 2:11–14)

What these twelve tribes shared was their voluntary acceptance of a covenant of obedience to a divine king, namely Yahweh. In the absence of *political* mechanisms of social control, they embraced a *religious* mechanism. They considered the Yahwist ethic expressed in the commitments of the Sinai covenant to be paramount. While the imprecision of these ethical principles rendered them useless as legal statutes, they nevertheless defined principles of personal integrity enabling people of different tribal and ethnic backgrounds to consider as "brothers" anyone who likewise shared a commitment to the paramount nature of those principles. At the same time, this also enabled members of the different tribes, clans, and subgroups to interact with one another while retaining those aspects of their respective cultures (such as inheritance practices) that did not conflict with or supersede their shared Yahwist commitments. This was not unlike what happened in early Christianity as well, which cut across the tremendous cultural diversity of the first-century Mediterranean world and permitted Christians to retain any aspect of their indigenous cultures that did not clash with Christian faith and life.

These ethical commitments were made compelling not by *social* forces but by a spiritual one that the Bible calls the "fear of Yahweh" (Hebrew *yir'at YHWH*), what we call "conscience." This "spiritual force" was linked with historical processes: it was not a matter of people's "souls" being supernaturally cleansed of all self-interest (not even the Bible makes that claim). Rather, the *historical context* made the embrace of this new religious structure an extremely attractive—and therefore a somewhat reasonable and "natural"—choice to make.[4] At the opportune moment, community was in fact attained across the hill country of Palestine and Transjordan when enough people became committed to this ethic, trusting each other to act conscientiously in the fundamental areas of life associated with the obligations of the Sinai covenant. Sworn to by the individual and integrated into the fabric of social life, this religious ethic made it possible for the Israelite federation of tribes to exist for almost two centuries without resort to or reliance on any organized monopoly of coercive force.

A covenant is a binding promise, *voluntarily* made. The Yahwist covenant was not a mere social contract, in which people made promises to one another, thereby essentially helping guarantee each other's legitimate interests. Instead, each person was bound individually to *Yahweh*—in other words, to something intangible, to a value system that transcends material self-interest. Thus it was that a community was created. The vital question then becomes, *How much* do these Israelites "fear Yahweh"? If the religious commitment to this ethic wanes, relationships deteriorate and community begins to disintegrate, eventually resulting in tension, conflict, anarchy, and chaos.[5] In biblical terms, future generations would suffer as a result of improper choices made in the present (Exod. 20:5). This is also the key to the later Israelite fascination with history: they saw clear cause-and-effect links between their religious ethic and the normal processes of continuity and change that human beings experience.

4. By associating a divine being (Yahweh) with the historical process itself (see Appendix B), the Israelites (in their own ancient Near Eastern way) were insisting that historical contexts are essential to understanding expressions of religious faith. As we shall see, when the historical context of later generations changed, so did their respect for the values and choices of their ancestors.

5. As voluntarily embraced religious controls over behavior wane, it becomes increasingly necessary to impose more coercive political and legal controls.

How the Twelve Tribes Were Formed

6. The Egyptians would never have tolerated such a system among the Apiru slaves. Indeed, the Israelite king Solomon two hundred

The twelve-tribe system was an aspect of frontier village life in Palestine and Transjordan. It is extremely unlikely that it existed among the escaped slaves of the Sinai peninsula.[6] Indeed, the biblical traditions themselves vaguely hint at a difference between the Hebrew slaves of Egypt and Sinai on the one hand and the Israelite villagers of the Promised Land on the other. They report that of all the slaves who came out of Egypt with Moses, only Joshua and Caleb ever actually entered Palestine. All the rest, Moses included, lived out their lives either in the Sinai wilderness or in the steppe of Transjordan. With a two-step literary maneuver later biblical authors removed the distinction between these two groups: first, they

years later apparently did not tolerate it either and proceeded to dismantle the tribal system (1 Kings 4:7–19). The typical imperial policy is to prohibit such organization from the outset. For example, Pliny the Younger, governor of Asia Minor, wrote to the Roman emperor Trajan in A.D. 110, asking whether the people of a certain town might form a volunteer fire brigade. Trajan wrote back refusing permission, saying that, once organized, the members of the fire brigade would start talking politics, and all sorts of trouble would follow.

7. We can actually trace the history of the kingdom of Amurru through the eight successive kings who ruled there prior to its destruction (see Table 1.2). We do not know whether Sihon was of the royal house or simply a ranking military officer with no more superiors to report to. Their Amurru (Amorite) homeland in ruins, he and his troops found the newly established villages of Transjordan to be easy prey. Sihon established himself there as legitimate successor, adopting the title "king of the Amorites." Numbers 21:27–30 preserves a very archaic poem recalling Sihon's earlier victory over a rival (Moabite) warlord, giving Sihon uncontested control of the region.

portrayed these escaped slaves as "destined" for the land of Canaan (i.e., Palestine); and second, they portrayed the Israelite villagers of Palestine literally as the "children" of those slaves forty years later. Biblical scholars have questioned the historical accuracy of both these elements of the biblical story.

The establishment of the twelve-tribe federation in Canaan is usually equated with the so-called Hebrew conquest of Palestine recounted in the much later stories of Joshua 1–11. An overwhelming number of biblical scholars today agree that those bloody stories are historically inaccurate (see notes 3 and 13). The linguistic and archaeological evidence, combined with a reexamination of the biblical traditions themselves, today support an alternative historical reconstruction. Briefly (and therefore simplistically) stated, it is possible to reconstruct the processes and sequence whereby a community of Yahweh worshipers appeared in Palestine as a two-stage development.

Stage One: Sinai to Transjordan. After departing Mount Sinai, life in the Sinai desert could not have been easy for the several hundred ex-slaves and their meager livestock. They managed to eke out their livelihood in the wilderness, partly through "miracles" (finding water at the right moment, not to mention "manna" and quails) and partly through a symbiotic relationship with the Midianite clan of Moses' father-in-law, a group apparently well adapted to wilderness living (see Num. 10:31). While they may not have felt themselves "destined" for any Promised Land, the Bible does not really depict them as homeless wanderers—their "home" for much of that time was the well-watered site of Kadesh-barnea. In fact, a close reading of the wilderness narratives shows that the escaped slaves spent virtually all their wilderness years there. From Kadesh-barnea they could take their flocks out into the steppes for seasonal grazing.

The biblical tradition suggests that these pastoralists periodically attempted to negotiate grazing rights with various local political regimes that were patrolling portions of the steppe. At some point, some of these Yahwists brought their flocks and herds to the pastures of eastern Transjordan, where they were confronted by Sihon, a petty warlord operating out of Heshbon (Num. 21:21–32). Sihon and his gang of soldiers had probably recently migrated from the LB Age kingdom of Amurru, which had collapsed along with everything else around 1200 B.C.[7] Sihon dispatched perhaps half a dozen of his professional warriors to attack and despoil these Yahwist shepherds. We often fail to appreciate what a small number of professionally armed soldiers were required to establish dominion over vast territories of defenseless villagers. Sihon's troops

Map 3.2
**The Wilderness
Wanderings.** The Bible
provides confusing itin-
eraries celebrating the
imagined "march" of the
Israelite ancestors toward
the Promised Land. One
(Num. 33:37–49) imag-
ined a northerly route,
and then along the
King's Highway through
Edom and Moab.
Another (Num. 21:4;
Judg. 11:17–18) envi-
sioned a southerly route,
which skirted east of
Edom and Moab. The
early Yahwists, who con-
sidered the oasis at
Kadesh-barnea their
home, seasonally took
their flocks and herds
through the steppeland,
sometimes arranging
grazing rights with local
groups along the way.
The so-called "conquest
of Palestine" began
when Sihon dispatched
soldiers against them.
Sihon's force was defeat-
ed and the villages east
of the Dead Sea were no
longer politically
accountable to anyone.

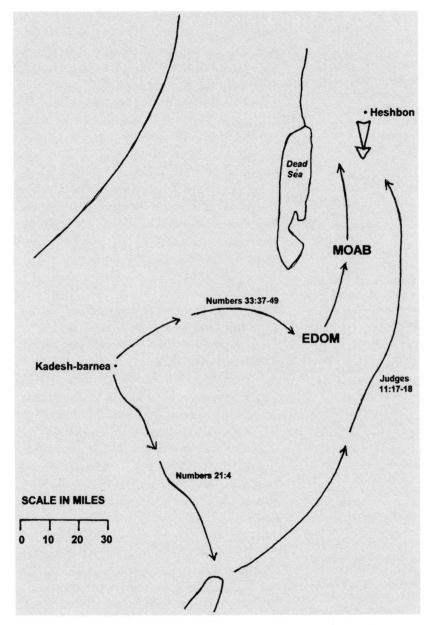

failed in their mission, and their deaths so seriously undermined Sihon's
ability to control the villages surrounding Heshbon that his "kingdom"
there collapsed.

According to the Bible, Sihon's territory was almost immediately
occupied by the tribe of Reuben. But what happened to Sihon's former
"subjects"? There is no hint in either the Bible or the archaeological
record that the Yahwist shepherds had any grievance against these vil-

lagers, much less put them to the sword or seized their houses and fields. A more plausible explanation is that the villages in this area, relieved to be rid of Sihon's regime, made a covenant (or agreement) with the Yahwist shepherds that included recognizing Yahweh now as their god, too. Again, if these villagers had originally come to Transjordan as Apiru refugees with a frontier mentality, hoping to escape an intolerable social, political, and religious situation in their native lands, the prospect of a new god appearing as an alternative to all the old (political) ones would have been quite attractive. The idea of a community based on a shared commitment to a fundamental religious ethic, rather than on centralized force, must have seemed especially appealing. In other words, these Transjordanian villagers formerly ruled by Sihon *became* the tribe of Reuben (if they were not already constituted as such in Sihon's time). Interestingly, later biblical genealogies accord to Reuben the status of "first-born of Jacob/Israel," consistent with the tradition that the Israelite federation began here with this Transjordanian tribe.

Soon thereafter, another warlord, the semilegendary Og of northern Transjordan, mustered his warriors to "pacify" these politically unclaimed Reubenite villages to his south. Like Sihon, he was probably a recent immigrant from the north, whose armed gang had taken control of the villages of Bashan. Og's warriors were routed at Edrei, and his political support collapsed. Like Sihon, he perished as his regime crumbled (Num. 21:33–35).

Vast portions of village farmland and steppeland in Transjordan were now unpatrolled and unclaimed by any political organizations, no longer appearing on any kingdom's tax rolls. Curiously, Deuteronomy 29 records a covenant being made here in the land of Moab. This serves no apparent literary purpose in the narrative and must have been mentioned because the tradition preserved historical memory of such a covenant actually being made there at the time. Historically speaking, a covenant would be necessary for large segments of the Transjordanian population to be formally incorporated into the community of Yahweh. This population comprised villages belonging to the tribes and clans of Reuben, Gad, Machir, and Gilead. A federation was beginning to form.[8]

8. The book of Judges shows that there was always some new warlord eager to impose his control over these Yahwist villages in Transjordan. The tribal structure there proved to be especially fragile, unable to withstand these warlords for very long. Within a century or so, a Moabite regime had successfully gained political control over the Reubenite villages. The ninth-century inscription of Mesha, king of Moab (see Box 5.4), implies that some people within his domain continued to identify themselves as Israelites.

Stage Two: Palestine. The Bible also provides numerous clues that many of these Transjordanian people had close social ties with people farther west, in Palestine, who had likewise fallen victim to military gangs roaming the hill country there. In addition, the various Philistine regimes on the coast were establishing their own political confederation to consolidate their hold on the southern coastal plain. The news of the demise of the Transjordanian regimes would have been welcomed by the

Palestinian villagers of the hill country, some of whom probably had kinsmen in Transjordan. But the military warlords of the hill country would have received the news with mounting concern. For example, when the people of Gibeon (who remained non-Yahwist) made a covenant with the new Yahwist federation, they were attacked by a coalition of Amorite regimes operating out of the towns of Jerusalem, Hebron, Jarmuth, Lachish, and Eglon, presumably to punish Gibeon for making peace with these Apiru/Hebrews. Apparently assisted by Yahwist volunteers from Transjordan and some kind of meteorological "miracle," the Gibeonites managed to defeat the troops dispatched by this coalition.

The nature and extent of the Yahwist appropriation of hill-country Palestine is indicated by the Joshua 12 list of conquered "kings," including the hill-country warlords based in Tirzah, Tappuah, Hepher, and Aphek (vv. 17–18, 24). Each of them, along with a couple of dozen soldiers armed with swords and spears, probably controlled the nearby villages. But several hundred local villagers emboldened by the tide of

---

Box 3.3—The Defeat of the Five Amorite Kings

And Yahweh threw them [the troops of the five Amorite warlords] into a panic before Israel, who inflicted a great slaughter on them at Gibeon, chased them by the way of the ascent of Beth-horon, and struck them down as far as Azekah and Makkedah. As they fled before Israel, while they were going down the slope of Beth-horon, Yahweh threw down huge stones from heaven on them as far as Azekah, and they died; there were more who died because of the hailstones than the Israelites killed with the sword.

On the day when Yahweh gave the Amorites over to the Israelites, Joshua spoke to Yahweh; and he said in the sight of Israel,

"Sun, stand still at Gibeon,
    and Moon, in the valley of Aijalon."
And the sun stood still, and the moon stopped,
    until the nation took vengeance on their enemies.

Is this not written in the Book of Jashar? The sun stopped in midheaven, and did not hurry to set for about a whole day. (Josh. 10:10–13)

Victory resulted from an unexpected and violent hailstorm, when the sun "went silent" (Hebrew *dwm/dmh*) and the moon "stopped" (Hebrew *'md*). The poetic snippet actually suggests that the sun and moon stopped *shining,* which later scribes misinterpreted as "stopped *moving,*" inserting the prose note about the sun refusing to set (v. 13). Thus, the actual "miracle" was probably a thick cloud cover, not an interruption of the Earth's rotational spin.

9. The stories of the Israelites destroying large fortified cities (Joshua 6–7; 10:28–11:20) are historically implausible. See also note 13. More plausible is the Judges 1 scenario showing the Israelites unable to supplant the regimes ruling in many cities. Some scholars imagine the Hebrew conquest of Canaan to have been a Marxist-style peasant revolt fueled by an egalitarian Yahwist political ideology. This misses the critical point: Yahwism was embraced only *after* the warlords had been removed, for only then was the way clear for an alternative to the seemingly endless power struggles. Yahwism was, therefore, not a political ideology justifying violence but a religious value system intending to create community and peace in the absence of political structures and compulsion.

events and armed with stones, clubs, and mattocks could have routed these soldiers without any major military planning or organization. The whole central hill country would then be unclaimed by any political organization. According to this historical reconstruction, this is all that these so-called "wars" actually involved.[9] On the other hand, some of the regimes in the lowland plains of Palestine (e.g., those controlled by the Philistine coalition) had a sufficiently strong grip on the villages there that simply could not be broken.

According to Joshua 24, a late text, these events culminated in yet another covenant being made. Joshua summoned representatives of the hill-country tribes to Shechem, where he told them:

> "Now if you are unwilling to serve Yahweh, choose this day whom you will serve, whether the gods your ancestors served . . . or the gods of the Amorites in whose land you are living; but as for me and my household, we will serve Yahweh." (24:15)

This was no metaphysical inquiry about their "belief in God." It was an utterly practical question, asking people formally to declare which value system they were going to embrace. One option was to embrace the former system of *political* domination, which lay around them in ruins, a system legitimized ideologically by the worship of Baal and the concomitant devotion to political power. There was always the possibility that this system, like the mythological Baal himself, could be revived and made operational again even after it was presumed dead.

The other option was to embrace the *religious* controls of the Yahwist covenant, with its vision of a community based on a conscientious regard for certain ethical obligations, a system defined simply as "fearing and serving Yahweh" (Josh. 24:14). Joshua warned these people that it was not easy to "serve Yahweh," to build real and lasting community on little more than voluntary compliance with a fundamental ethic. Indeed, it is always difficult, but it is also always *necessary*; even communities held together by political forces cannot survive the failure of the governed to agree on the substance of ethical conduct and to voluntarily comply with it.

Yahweh Becomes "King"

The hill-country population chose to embrace the Yahwist ethic. In the metaphor of the Bible, drawn from the familiar world of LB Age international treaties, Yahweh had become their "king" or "lord." This new community of Yahwists was eventually named "Israel," probably after one of its recently incorporated population groups—probably the same

Box 3.4—Community through Covenant

Although Joshua 1–12 depicts Israel being established in Canaan through military conquest, other traditions suggest instead that it was established as people already there voluntarily joined the Yahwist fellowship. In three distinct stages—each marked by covenant—community grew numerically and geographically as people "converted" to Yahwism:

1. **Sinai (Exodus 20; 24)**—Escaped slaves from Egypt embraced the commitments articulated in the Decalogue (ca. 1200 B.C.?), becoming the people of Yahweh (see chapter 2).
2. **Plains of Moab (Deuteronomy 29)**—Village tribes of Transjordan joined the Yahwist movement after the defeat of Sihon and Og (ca. 1175 B.C.?); they, too, become the people of Yahweh.
3. **Shechem (Joshua 24)**—Village tribes of hill-country Palestine became part of the Yahwist community after the defeat of Amorite and other regimes there (ca. 1175 B.C.?).

Although the need for three covenants makes perfect *historical* sense, the presence of the latter two is *literarily and theologically* awkward, implying that the Sinai covenant was somehow inadequate. The argument that the traditions in Deuteronomy 29 and Joshua 24 were deliberately crafted fictions is extremely weak.

10. The Mishnah, a third-century Jewish legal text, says "in every generation a person is duty-bound to regard himself as if he personally has gone forth from Egypt" (*Pesahim* 10:5). This process of subjective identification is illustrated by a well-known story told by Joseph Wood Krutch. When he was at the University of Texas, he became friends with a man who worked in the same building. While his friend was visiting New England, he sent Krutch a postcard of Plymouth Rock on which he had written, "Here is where our ancestors landed." Krutch's friend was African American. For whatever reason, he had personally claimed for himself the emblematic story of the European arrival to the New World. This did not mean that he had forgotten or rejected other traditions about how his African forebears actually arrived under very different circumstances.

one mentioned a generation earlier by Merneptah. In a relatively short time, the community of Yahweh worshipers had grown from several hundred to a quarter of a million people. All these villagers in Palestine and Transjordan would eventually attach their own distinctive tribal traditions to the story they had heard about the Apiru slaves who had been delivered out of bondage in Egypt years earlier. Thus, the experiences of the formative period became part of the experience of everyone in the community—a concept still retained in the Jewish Passover Seder.[10]

The notion that Yahweh was Israel's *king* is much harder for us to comprehend than Yahweh as Israel's *god*. How can an abstract and metaphysical god literally preside over the practical affairs of concrete human beings? Who can actually *see* Yahweh or *hear* his authoritative voice? But in virtually every political system throughout history, the head of state is rarely seen in the flesh by anyone except a relative handful of people. For example, the king of England was regarded as the source of all law, even though he never appeared in any law court. What the king therefore embodied was a *policy* that all decent subjects knew and were expected to obey, even though they never actually saw or heard the king in person. In the same way, Yahweh could preside without benefit of spectacular appearances or having masses of people hear voices.

The more practical question is not who has seen or heard the king, but who most faithfully *represents* him in policy matters. (Centuries later, this urgent question surfaced when different prophets, all claiming to speak for Yahweh, would express opposing viewpoints; see chapter 5.) The conscientious subject must balance anyone's claim to be the king's representative against what the subject knows to be the king's policies. Compliance always remains a matter of personal conscience and integrity. In Baal-worshiping communities, the head of state was depicted as the gods' representative, "chosen" by them to rule. Whatever he did was—*by definition*—always right, just, and authoritative, because the gods had designated him as their representative. There was no legitimate basis on which he could be questioned, much less challenged. The only purpose of such man-made gods was to confer authority upon the king. But to the tribes of Israel, such a political monopoly of force—and the type of religion that legitimized it—had almost nothing to do with their lives, except in the form of the much-despised tax collector. In Israel, the role of "king" was performed by Yahweh.

The Typical Functions of the King	If Yahweh indeed performed as king, exactly what did he do? How did ruling through his people's voluntary compliance with such things as the ethical commitments of the Sinai covenant find expression in the practical matters of administering the affairs of the federation community? We can answer this by focusing on three basic functions performed by kings and political states throughout history (see Box 3.5):

1. *Waging War.* Ambitious city kings and petty warlords alike sought military domination to enhance their own economic (and therefore military) power. Warfare was conducted mostly for "glory, fun, and profit." The profit motive is transparent: to control territory is to control its vital agricultural, mineral, and other resources, such as trade routes. The glory motive is also obvious: the celebration of war and military prowess is as old as Homer and the ancient Egyptians. And for certain types of persons, such as mercenaries, war can be exciting, when they are winning. Should the tide of battle turn, such soldiers-for-hire can simply surrender at the

opportune moment and pledge loyalty to the victor (so they can now fight in *his* army).[11]

2. *Administering Law.* While waging war provides a check against threats from without, the administration of law certainly provides a check against threats from within. Like war, the administration of law is based on the state's monopoly of force. It requires the existence of police, courts, jails, imposed fines, executioners, and all the other mechanisms that coerce subjects into behaving themselves. We know that some states in antiquity had prisons (see the third Mari letter excerpted in Box 1.4), but there is no evidence of them in Israel until the time of the monarchy. The same is true of the modern Syrian village, where there are usually no government officials. The only legal authority there is the village headman, who usually simply represents the village in negotiations with the central government.

3. *Ensuring Economic Well-being.* War and law are supposedly the means by which economic well-being is best assured, but apparently it cannot be assured for very long on those foundations alone. Few of these

Box 3.5—The Functions of Government

From the Code of Lipit-Ishtar, kingdom of Isin, about 1875 B.C.:

> . . . when [the gods] Anu (and) Enlil had called Lipit-Ishtar . . . to the princeship of the land in order to establish justice in the land, to banish complaints, to turn back enmity and rebellion by the force of arms, (and) to bring well-being to the Sumerians and Akkadians . . . (*ANET*[3], 159)

From the Code of Hammurapi, kingdom of Babylon, about 1750 B.C.:

> . . . [A]t that time Anum and Enlil named me to promote the welfare of the people, . . . to cause justice to prevail in the land, to destroy the wicked and the evil, that the strong might not oppress the weak. . . . Hammurabi, the shepherd, called by Enlil, am I; the one who makes affluence and plenty abound. . . . When Marduk commissioned me to guide the people aright, to direct the land, I established law and justice in the language of the land, thereby promoting the welfare of the people. (*ANET*[3], 164–165)

From the Preamble to the Constitution of the United States, 1787:

> We, the people of the United States, in order to form a more perfect union, establish justice, insure domestic tranquillity, provide for the common defense, promote the general welfare. . . .

states lasted as long as two hundred years before being destroyed, and many had considerably shorter lives. This rapid turnover in ancient empires suggests that their ability to guarantee prosperity was mostly propaganda. The *real* and operating ideology—blatantly expressed in several ancient Near Eastern myths—was that the people existed to serve the interests of the gods and those favored few to whom the gods entrusted rule. At best, the economic well-being of this elite was all that really mattered to these ancient states, and even here they enjoyed limited success in ensuring this for more than a few generations.

The Transfer of Royal Functions to Yahweh

Is economic well-being possible without political management and oversight? Can justice and military defense be achieved without the costly superstructures of political government? The ancient Near Eastern mindset would have posed such questions differently: If the king could do these things because he was chosen by the gods, then why couldn't the gods do these things themselves without these costly middlemen?

Figure 3.2

God and King. In the ancient Near East, kings were considered the "chosen" instrument through which deities govern human affairs. Adorning the top of Hammurapi's law code (*left*) is a carved relief showing the god Shamash bestowing authority on King Hammurapi, who is about to administer law on the god's behalf. Below is a scene from an Assyrian palace relief showing the god Ashur (in the winged sun-disk) accompanying King Ashurnasirpal II into battle. Their poses are identical: god and king are one, and the king wages war on the god's behalf. These scenes proclaim that there can be no disagreement between king and god.

A strong argument could be made that in the prehistoric Near East (before around 2700 B.C.) the gods *did* perform these functions themselves (albeit through temple-based religious institutions), without relying on any kings they had "chosen." Religion appears to have played a constructive, socially cohesive role. It was only 1,500 years or so before the time of Moses that these religious-based tasks began to be taken over by centralized, bureaucratized monopolies of force—the Early Dynastic III kings of Sumer and the Old Kingdom pharaohs of Egypt (see Table 1.1).

For ancient Israel, the issue was this: once ethical norms are voluntarily embraced (which is presupposed by the political state, anyway), and the citizenry more or less successfully abides by those norms, then the apparatus associated with the monopoly of force becomes unnecessary. However, in the dark ages of 1200–1000 B.C. a community could not long remain independent without some kind of militia and some rudimentary mechanism for rallying able-bodied villagers to stand together against the hostile threat posed by yet another ambitious warlord.

Yahweh's Empowerment to Rule

The kings of antiquity almost always ruled by force or conquest. Even the son who succeeded to the throne of his father required the support of the military and had to be prepared to murder sibling rivals. (See, for example, the biblical story of Solomon's accession to the throne in 1 Kings 1–2.) The king became king through his superior ability to intimidate and kill others. Overcoming all rivals was what established him as king, providing objective evidence that he had indeed been chosen by the gods.

By contrast, the rule of Yahweh was founded on the voluntary acceptance of the covenant. Wherever it was adopted, there Yahweh was empowered to rule, creating a community (or a "fellowship") where none had existed before. The oldest biblical sources say nothing at all about Israel being Yahweh's "*chosen*" people; instead, as in Exodus 15 and Deuteronomy 32, they refer to it as Yahweh's "*created*" people.[12] The rule of God over human beings was not the product of military force but arose in response to Israel's deliverance *from* those who valued and relied on such force.

Not everyone was, or wanted to be, so "delivered." Some people at least tolerated the existing social organizations and found the Yahwist alternative either unattainable or undesirable, if not downright foolish, irresponsible, or dangerous. Its covenant tradition would certainly have polarized the pre-Israelite population of Palestine and Transjordan, just as it reportedly polarized the village of Ophrah in the days of Gideon (Judg.

12. The notion that God had *chosen* Israel is comparatively late and eventually became central to the self-understanding of Judaism. Because religious community there was defined ethnically, its *creation* was attributed to natural procreation; God was believed to have subsequently *chosen* this already-created commu-

nity. The older concept—that God had *created* Israel—was revived as part of early Christian self-understanding: "But to all who received him, who believed in his name, he gave power to become children of God" (John 1:12). In both this New Testament passage and the oldest poetic fragments of the Bible, the notion that God created religious community was linked to the idea of God as "father." (See the passages excerpted in Box 2.4.)

6:25–31). For example, the Bible reports that when Moses invited his Midianite father-in-law to join the covenant community, he declined (Num. 10:29–30). For him, things probably seemed better out in the desert—and he may have been right, given the collapse of civilization that was occurring everywhere *except* in the desert.

Yahwism was necessarily voluntary, since it belonged to the realm of private values and conduct. The "public realm," as we understand the term today, did not yet exist among the Israelites. Yahweh thus symbolized a shared, religiously sanctioned value system that, in an economically simple village society, performed those functions that were usually the province of emperors, kings, and warlords. In other words, through the operation of this value system Yahweh, metaphorically speaking, owned "territory" (i.e., his people) and therein exercised the royal prerogatives of waging war, administering justice, and ensuring the community's economic well-being.

Yahweh as Landowner

These newly independent villagers, the Israelites, did not develop a concept of private ownership of land. What emerged instead was a tradition that, like themselves, their landholdings belonged to Yahweh. This was an expression of the ancient Near Eastern concept that a king "owns" the land by right of conquest. In this case, the king was Yahweh, and the "conquest" was the routing of the petty warlords previously described. The lands they had claimed by right of conquest now became the "holy land" (i.e., the property of God).

The land tenure system that arose in ancient Israel is a powerful demonstration of this concept. Leviticus 25 seems to preserve an archaic tradition that the people of Yahweh could enjoy the land, keep it within the family, and transmit it from one generation to the next, as long as they remained faithful to Yahweh, its owner. Biblical law made no provision for buying or selling land because one cannot sell what one does not own (Lev. 25:23; see also 1 Kings 21:1–4).

A rival land tenure system arose with the monarchy around 1000 B.C., when King David acquired, through military conquest, vast expanses of new territory in the lowland plains, including such recovering city-states as Megiddo, Taanach, and Beth-shean. His son and successor, Solomon, made these cities administrative centers of the Israelite empire (1 Kings 4:12). Their inhabitants were not Israelites subject to Yahweh's rule, but non-Israelites subject to David's rule. Their land *could* be bought and sold, because it was crown property officially belonging to the royal family of David and allotted as they saw fit.

Yahweh and the Waging of War

Given the number of well-armed warrior gangs roaming the countryside of Palestine and Transjordan, violence was a fact of life in the early Iron Age. Consequently, it was important to distinguish between violence that was truly "holy" (and thus a legitimate exercise of Yahweh's sovereignty) and violence that was not. War became "holy" when it was the action of deity. Most of us are understandably uncomfortable with the concept of holy war, which has been distorted through the ages by ambitious politicians eager to exploit religion in the pursuit of some allegedly national interest. Our discomfort is intensified because Joshua 1–11 misrepresents the holy war against the hill-country warlords as a fairly typical, imperialistic military invasion.

A historical reading of the biblical tradition suggests that early Israelite *holy war was entirely defensive,* in other words, fought within its own home territory, the "holy land." This criterion distinguished a holy war from those waged by warrior-politicians intent on territorial expansion. The tribal federation of Israel arose as villagers merely sought to defend their homes and livelihoods from ruthless warrior gangs.

The Israelites further distanced themselves from conventional warfare by instituting the "ban" (Hebrew *herem,* usually translated "utter destruction"): all captured property must be either completely destroyed or entrusted to religious safekeeping. *No private individual or group was permitted to profit economically from a holy war,* a criterion illustrated in the later story of Achan (Joshua 7). This precluded the profit motive that often induces kings to go to war—and that often induces soldiers to join them in dividing up the spoils afterward. The execution of captured prisoners is also mandated by the ban, and through the ages it has been horribly misinterpreted to excuse the apparent slaughter of innocent noncombatants. In the Israelite "wars" of the early Iron Age previously described, captured prisoners would have surely been mercenaries serving enemy warlords.[13] Israelites were prohibited from profiting economically from the sale of such professional soldiers as slaves, but to release trained warriors entailed the risk that they might soon return better armed. The only alternative was to execute them.

Thus, a holy war must only be fought by those who possess both the nerve to fight and an overwhelming commitment to the justness of the cause. This means that *a holy war can only be fought by a volunteer militia.* This stands in stark contrast to political wars, where government and military officials must offer all sorts of material inducements to muster the troops, even to the point of forcibly conscripting them.

Finally, *a holy war must be led by God,* which means it must be called or led only by an acknowledged prophetic spokesperson for Yahweh. For example, Barak refused to take the field of battle until Deborah the

13. The picture of the so-called Hebrew conquest contained in Joshua 1–11 misrepresents the early Israelites as xenophobic imperialists, obliging the biblical author to depict them mercilessly slaughtering foreign women and children as part of the ban (yet also taking booty!). See Deuteronomy 20:10–17; Joshua 6:21; 8:25–26; 10:28–40; 11:10–14. This is one reason why the book of Joshua is so unpalatable to most morally sensitive readers. In its chapters, the Israelites—as well as their god, Yahweh—behave in such an *un*-Yahwist manner. But these chapters are almost entirely fictitious, created by a much later scribe who could not imagine the early Yahwist federation being all that different from the politically organized, imperialistically driven Israel of his own day.

Box 3.6—The Volunteer Militia

According to biblical tradition, a holy war must be fought by volunteers. If soldiers must be drafted, the war cannot be holy. Instead of indoctrinating troops as to why they *should* go to war, volunteers in a holy war must first be reminded of all the reasons why they *should not* go to war:

> When you go out to war against your enemies, and see horses and chariots, an army larger than your own, you shall not be afraid of them; for Yahweh your God is with you, who brought you up from the land of Egypt. . . . Then the officials shall address the troops, saying, "Has anyone built a new house but not dedicated it? He should go back to his house, or he might die in the battle and another dedicate it. Has anyone planted a vineyard but not yet enjoyed its fruit? He should go back to his house, or he might die in the battle and another be first to enjoy its fruit. Has anyone become engaged to a woman but not yet married her? He should go back to his house, or he might die in the battle and another marry her." The officials shall continue to address the troops, saying, "Is anyone afraid or disheartened? He should go back to his house, or he might cause the heart of his comrades to melt like his own." When the officials have finished addressing the troops, then the commanders shall take charge of them. (Deut. 20:1, 5–9)

The soldiers who remain to fight must be more committed to the justness of the cause than to their own self-interest.

prophetess independently assured him that the troops would indeed be Yahweh's agent (Judg. 4:4–9). Because the Israelite militia was led by Yahweh, the victory and the glory belonged to him. Yahwist values would not permit or tolerate any Israelite military leader or soldier to be praised in the event of victory or even personal heroism. The celebrations of victory we find in the oldest poems in the Bible (Exodus 15; Judges 5) all extol *Yahweh* as the valiant "man of war." But the tendency to focus instead on human prowess in combat eventually tempted some Israelites. They offered the title "king" to the victorious Gideon, but he declined, reminding his fellow Israelites that they already had a king: Yahweh (Judg. 8:22–23). Gideon thus exemplified yet another criterion of holy war: *A holy war does not result in human glory or advancement*. If a war does result in such things, its holiness is compromised as it becomes apparent that the war did not actually serve the interests of God as much as those of the victorious warriors.

Genuine holy wars have always been extremely rare. By definition, they cannot be characterized by the motives and conduct that mark almost every war typically waged by warrior-politicians. As long as

Yahweh was king, war for glory, fun, and profit was absolutely excluded. But as soon as someone else became king, war motivated by such things became inevitable and, sadly, frequent.

Yahweh and the Administration of Law

Another of Yahweh's functions as king was to administer law within the community. Our main source for law at this time is the so-called Covenant Code in Exodus 21–23. It is widely regarded as archaic, and it provides for no functioning social polity to implement this law beyond the village. No tribal chiefs, national kings, or federation priests are authorized to administer this law, which fits the early Iron Age context perfectly. Its eighty-five verses deal with more than forty possible scenarios, most of which are typical disputes arising between villagers in an economy based on farming and herding.

Obviously, not every potential conflict is covered in the Covenant Code, suggesting that, in practice, the administration of law was not restricted to these forty-odd scenarios. Instead, we must regard these scenarios as guidelines, which were probably not even committed to writing at this early time. They paint a picture of what justice *could* look like, rather than setting precedents for how future courts *must* act. For example, to say that a certain person guilty of an offense "*shall* be put to death" does not mean that, in any specific case, he *must* be put to death. The famous case of the goring ox shows us that courts, especially village courts, had considerable latitude:

> When an ox gores a man or a woman to death, the ox shall be stoned, and its flesh shall not be eaten; but the owner of the ox shall not be liable. If the ox has been accustomed to gore in the past, and its owner has been warned but has not restrained it, and it kills a man or a woman, the ox shall be stoned, and its owner also shall be put to death. If a ransom is imposed on the owner, then the owner shall pay whatever is imposed for the redemption of the victim's life. (Exod. 21:28–30)

In other words, one might avoid a death sentence by providing compensation to victims and/or their families.

The similarities between the Covenant Code and law attested in the various Amorite kingdoms of Mesopotamia suggest that these particular legal customs may have entered Palestine with the Amorite migrations of the MB Age (see chapter 1). If so, this law is not particularly "Yahwist"; by the time the Israelite federation was formed in the early Iron Age, these legal customs were already centuries old, deeply embedded in the culture of at least some of those people who now embraced Yahwism. They probably knew this was not *Yahweh's* law, and it is unlikely that they regarded it as "sacred," in the sense of being God-given, immutable, and of permanent, universal value. They regarded it as *their own* law reflecting their own particular customary principles and procedures. Apparently the Israelites felt they were free to render justice according to established legal principles and customs, so long as these did not conflict with the religious ethic embedded in the Decalogue. One such ancient legal principle was the *lex talionis*.[14]

All that remained was to modify these old Amorite legal principles and customs so that they now also helped reinforce the sanctity of the Yahwist religious ethic. Only a handful of wrongdoings listed in the Covenant Code are actually capital crimes, and for the most part these are deeds that most blatantly violate specific commitments listed in the Decalogue. For example, the Covenant Code goes beyond Amorite legal customs by condemning to death anyone who sacrifices to a god other than Yahweh (Exod. 22:20) as well as anyone who strikes or curses a parent (21:15, 17). These harsh-sounding statements were almost certainly designed to underscore the urgent sanctity of the covenant ethic rather than to recommend literally the actual killing of temperamental children or people guilty of unorthodox ritual lapses.

Why is the death penalty reserved for these specific infractions? Because almost every state throughout history has imposed the death penalty for treason, it is tempting to imagine the same rationale here—violating the stipulations of the covenant was regarded by the early Israelites as an act of treason against the government, namely Yahweh. To disparage these obligations was to attack the core ethic of the Yahwist community, namely, the moral principles from which it received its life and well-being.

Curiously, stealing (a subject covered in the Decalogue) was *not* punishable by death (as it traditionally had been in Amorite law) but by twofold restitution if the stolen property could be recovered. If stolen sheep or cattle, the core of a family's livelihood, were unrecoverable, the restitution was then four- or fivefold (see the opening verses of Exodus 22). Here, two Yahwist principles apparently collide: (1) stealing warrants death not only because that is an established (Amorite) legal principle but also because it violates the (Yahwist) covenant ethic, but (2) human life is more valuable in Yahweh's eyes than property. In this particular case, the established legal tradition valuing property had to yield to the latter (Yahwist) principle valuing human life. But the most serious of all thefts was the stealing and selling of *persons*, which *was* subject to the death penalty (Exod. 21:16).

14. The *lex talionis*—or "law of retaliation" ("eye for an eye")—is perhaps the most misunderstood passage in the Bible, widely misinterpreted as a religious endorsement of personal vengeance (the law of the jungle). In fact, it was exactly the opposite: it defined the outer limit of punishment, and thereby provided a safeguard against excessively harsh sentences. It also meant that a defendant found guilty of putting out someone's eye must compensate the victim by an amount at which he valued *his own eye*: "What will the defendant give to avoid losing his own eye?" Ironically, this is actually consistent with the Golden Rule ("Do unto others as you would have them do unto you"), illustrating how that rule actually operated in court.

But how does a god carry out a death sentence? Just like the king of England, Yahweh was deemed the repository and source of all law even though his presence was never required in court. The key question then became, "To whom has Yahweh delegated the awesome task of executing those whose actions have challenged his rule?" The Yahwist federation had no law enforcement officers or even judicial authorities, nor are any presupposed in the Covenant Code. The "judges" (Hebrew *shofetim*) in early Israel were primarily military leaders, although they may have acted as mediators in legal disputes. They seem to have been highly respected by their contemporaries, at least by those who could see that "the spirit of Yahweh was upon them." They possessed the "authority of competence," or what Max Weber called "charismatic authority." This meant that heeding a judge's decision was purely voluntary: some might follow him or her (women exercised such authority in early Israel, and even later), while others might not. Regardless, it was not the judge's role to execute wrongdoers (or even to pronounce judgment); that role was delegated to the entire community.

The technique of execution was stoning to death, a *communal* act in which every adult in the village participated. Theoretically, the wrongdoer would be thrown over a precipice, and if the fall did not kill him the ensuing barrage of stones would. Yahweh entrusted capital punishment to the local community, and then only for the most flagrant challenges to Yahweh's authority. This apparently did not contradict the Decalogue's injunction against killing, since it presumed that the Israelites here would be acting as Yahweh's agents, and since Yahweh had the sovereign power of life and death.[15]

At the same time, Yahweh was regarded as a sort of "court of appeals," again consistent with the function of human kings. This role is clearly implied in Exodus 22:21–24:

> You shall not wrong or oppress a resident alien, for you were
> aliens in the land of Egypt. You shall not abuse any widow or
> orphan. If you do abuse them, when they cry out to me, I will
> surely heed their cry; my wrath will burn, and I will kill you with
> the sword, and your wives shall become widows and your children
> orphans.

Such right of appeal presumably applied to capital cases as well. There is nothing "religious" about this, in the sense of an executed criminal making a posthumous appeal for mercy to God in heaven, or of God showing mercy in the afterlife that human beings did not proffer on earth. If

15. It is tempting to denounce this as unlawful mob violence. But the willingness of otherwise decent men and women personally to get their hands bloodied suggests that painful deliberation and discussion had already occurred. This may also have worked against an overreliance on the death penalty, which was undoubtedly reserved for the most incorrigible of hardened criminals whose continued presence in the village constituted a danger to innocent people. With no central government or police, almost nothing prevented a capital offender from avoiding punishment simply by running away, never to return. In fact, it is doubtful that anyone was ever actually executed in early Israel for violations of the law. The execution of Achan (Joshua 7) and the blasphemer (Lev. 24:10–23) are widely regarded as fictional stories underscoring the seriousness of religious compliance. See also the grisly story in Judges 19–20, especially 20:12–13.

Box 3.7—God as the Court of Final Appeal

The following news story was reported by the Associated Press on August 29, 1996. This part of the Middle East has resisted Western concepts of modernization. Consequently, the legal procedures and spontaneous religiosity described here—although clearly not Yahwist—are extremely archaic, perhaps providing an analogy to the way in which "ransoms," appeals for mercy, and communal deliberations were legally implemented in early Israel, with God's will being taken very seriously.

DUBAI, United Arab Emirates (AP) — As the executioner cleaned the sword for her beheading, a condemned Saudi woman won a pardon from the father of the man she had slain, according to a dramatic Saudi account that offered a rare glimpse of crime and punishment in the Islamic nation. Tears and pleading are the only appeals criminals can make in Saudi Arabia, where only the families of their victims can grant pardons. In the woman's case, clemency came just moments before she was to die, the Al-Eqtisadia newspaper said. The newspaper gave this account:

Najah Al-Kariss was locked in a truck Sunday when she heard the roar of the crowd. She knew that meant the first execution of the day—of a Pakistani man convicted of armed robbery—had been carried out. Hers would be next. As the executioner wiped the crescent-shaped blade of his sword, Al-Kariss asked to see Dakheel Al-Luhaybi, the father of the man she killed. A guard opened the truck door, and Al-Kariss stepped into the 109-degree sun. In a tearful appeal, she begged Al-Luhaybi to spare her. Al-Luhaybi, 66, had already heard appeals from the woman's friends and family, and had even been offered $1 million to grant the pardon, he said. His wife and children, however, were opposed to it, and he had resolved to watch Al-Kariss die. But after hearing the woman's pleas—and after the intercession of police officers and others in the crowd—he consulted family members again and decided to forgive Al-Kariss in order to "gain God's blessings."

Al-Kariss wept with gratitude, and as word circulated through the square, the crowd began chanting "Allahu akbar," Arabic for "God is great." Some spectators cheered and ululated, while others fought back tears, the report said. It said Al-Kariss would be freed as soon as the family signs papers acknowledging the pardon. It did not indicate whether Al-Luhaybi would take the $1 million.

God has delegated trials, verdicts, and punishments to human beings, so has God also delegated the hearing of appeals and the showing of mercy. The community had to take appeals to Yahweh seriously and be prepared to grant mercy whenever conscience ("the fear of Yahweh") dictated. The Covenant Code is quite explicit in excluding bias or corruption (e.g., "bribes"; Exod. 23:2–3, 8) as influences in such life-and-death decisions.

Yahweh and Economic Well-being

Yahweh's third function as king was to provide for the economic well-being of the community. The idea that worshiping Yahweh may enhance the gross national product or keep the stock market healthy surely seems preposterous, but so, arguably, is the belief that we can successfully engineer (on our own) the sources of our prosperity. Farm populations harbor few such delusions. Our food supply still depends on forces of nature that we have yet to harness much beyond the irrigation strategy developed over five thousand years ago.[16]

For farmers—and for the villagers who constituted the early Yahwist federation—the unpredictability of nature was enough to deal with, not to mention a powerful urban population of consumers and armed tax collectors who produced nothing and were often insensitive toward those who did. How could Yahweh *fail* to provide economic well-being better than they?

16. The genetic manipulation of crops and beef cattle still depends on the availability of sufficient water. Such scientific breakthroughs often create the illusion that economic blessings do not ultimately depend on chance and circumstance but on technical specialists, bureaucratic planning, and (of course) sufficient funding.

The real challenge, as always, is to find a measure of satisfaction with what you have been given to meet your (and your family's) material needs. This measure of satisfaction cannot be quantified as some particular annual income or amount of money in the bank. Ethnographic literature is full of reports about "primitive" people living at a subsistence level who rate their quality of life quite highly, perhaps more highly than many modern Westerners.

With personal health and the supply of basic material goods (food, wool for clothing, resources for shelter) dictated by natural forces largely beyond one's control, one was obligated to direct attention instead to those areas where some personal influence might be effective, namely, one's own commitment to the morale of the community. And the morale of the Yahwist community was defined by the obligations of the Sinai covenant, which proscribe coveting and demand "the fear of Yahweh" (Hebrew *yir'at YHWH*), that is, a conscience not motivated by material gain or self-interest. These, in turn, can produce "love" (Hebrew *'ahabah*), a selfless concern for the well-being of others. It would not be bad to live in a community of people such as this. The stoicism of the Yahwist villager in the face of economic uncertainty, and his or her faith in the ability of the covenant ethic to yield "good fruit" within the community, is expressed in such pithy folk sayings as Proverbs 15:16–17, which can very loosely be translated:

A meager livelihood where there is also the fear of Yahweh [*yir'at YHWH*]

Figure 3.3
The Agricultural Village. If unencumbered by burdens placed on them by a central government, Near Eastern village populations rate their quality of life quite highly. The modern Near Eastern village has changed little from its ancient counterpart, as seen from this contemporary sketch of the village of Deir 'Allah in the Jordan Valley. (Drawing by Eathel Mendenhall)

> is better than a large bank account where there is fighting.
> An inexpensive meal of vegetables where there is also love
> ['*ahabah*]
> > is better than a large serving of roast beef where there is enmity.

But there is more than stoic resignation at work here. There is indeed an identifiable connection between obedience to the Yahwist covenant and economic health. Stated differently, disregard for the religious ethic exacts an economic toll. Most fundamentally, if conscience no longer inspires people to do good, an effective government organization can—but such organizations are extremely costly to establish and maintain. Other costs are more hidden, such as those associated with recovering from embezzlement and caring for the victims of crime. This and countless other things are unnecessary drains on the economy that could be minimized or redirected toward more worthy goals if human beings could simply exercise some moral restraint—if they were truly committed to ethical principles such as those of the Sinai covenant.

The curses and blessings of the covenant acknowledge this causal relationship: the best recipe for the economic success of the community—aside from a good harvest—is to be a polity where ethical considerations consistently outweigh self-interest.[17] Jesus expressed this same folk insight and linked it to the ancient Yahwist notion of Israel's God as "king" in Matthew 6:33, which can be loosely translated:

> First, strive for the kingdom of God and its resulting righteousness, and all these things [food, drink, and clothing] will be provided as well.

17. Utopian visions often underestimate the pervasiveness and intractability of human self-interest. The biblical tradition insists that nothing short of an act of God can enable people to transcend (personal or corporate) self-interest, and even then, usually after everything else they rely on is destroyed (Isa. 6:8–12).

Suggestions for Further Reading

Additional information on the topics discussed in this chapter can be found in the following sources.

Dictionary/Encyclopedia Entries

> *Anchor Bible Dictionary:* Anthropology and the OT; Family; Harvests and Harvesting; House (Israelite); Israel, History of; Judge; King, Kingship; Land; Law; Marriage; Punishments and Crimes; Palestine, Archaeology of; Shibboleth; Sociology (Ancient Israel); Wilderness Wandering
>
> *Interpreter's Dictionary of the Bible:* Jeshurun; Missions; Government, Israelite (Supplement volume); Tribe (Supplement volume)

Early Israel

> D. N. Freedman and D. Graf, eds., *Palestine in Transition: The Emergence of Ancient Israel.* Sheffield: Almond Press, 1983.
>
> G. Herion, "The Impact of Modern and Social Science Assumptions on the Reconstruction of Israelite History." *JSOT* 34 (1986): 3–33.
>
> G. Mendenhall, "The Hebrew Conquest of Palestine." *BAR* 3:100–120.
>
> M. Weippert, *The Settlement of the Israelite Tribes in Palestine.* Naperville, Ill.: Allenson, 1971.

Four

King David and the Transition to Monarchy: The Adaptive Period (II)— The Abdication of Yahweh

Suggested Reading

The Philistine Crisis: 1 Samuel 4; 8
King Saul and David: 1 Samuel 10:17–27; 18–19; 27; 31
The Davidic Covenant: 2 Samuel 5–7
David and Bathsheba: 2 Samuel 11:1–12:14

Adapting the Faith to Changing Realities

The biblical books of Joshua and Judges were compiled either during or after the reign of Josiah, one of the last Hebrew kings of Jerusalem, who ruled from 642 to 609 B.C. (see Appendix A). They reflect that era's beliefs about what happened over half a millennium earlier when Israel first appeared. The first eleven chapters of Joshua provide a glowingly triumphalistic picture of Yahweh's people gaining possession of virtually the entire land of Canaan. Its account of the early Yahwists conducting a genocidal campaign to seize other peoples' property is widely considered to be historically inaccurate, not only in its depiction of the Israelites as an invading army but also in its basic claim: in fact, significant territory in the land of Canaan remained under the control of military regimes unsympathetic toward and intolerant of Yahwism.

Ancient traditions preserved in the opening chapter of the book of Judges reinforce this more sober reality. According to Judges 1:21, Jebusites occupied Jerusalem prior to the Israelite monarchy and continued to live there alongside Benjaminites "to this day," probably referring to the time of the writer (see Table 4.1). Even after serving as Israel's capital for almost four hundred years, Jerusalem apparently still retained its Jebusite identity. Other details in Judges 1 likely reflect the actual situation at the time of King David's coronation, ca. 1000 B.C. For example, the tribe of Manasseh had been unable to "drive out" the non-Yahwists occupying cities such as Beth-shean, Taanach, Dor, Ibleam, and Megiddo, whose surrounding villages remained under their political control (v. 27).

Amorite regimes still controlled Har-heres, Aijalon, and Shaalbim (v. 35), and, of course, Philistine regimes still dominated the southern coastal plain (see Map 3.1).

Thus, at the time of David, many of the once great city-states of the LB Age were still inhabited by non-Yahwists, although the Israelite federation must have weakened them further by removing so many villagers from their tax rolls. Early in his reign, David conquered most of these cities and absorbed them into his kingdom. A generation later, his son and successor, Solomon, made some of them—notably Beth-shemesh, Taanach, Megiddo, and Beth-shean—centers for his provincial governors (1 Kings 4:7–19), effectively dismantling the old network of tribal authority.

This centralization of political control was facilitated by a process we might call "sacred politics." A change in people's sense of what is "sacred" brings about a change in the body politic. When a critical segment of the Israelite community began abandoning the religious

Table 4.1 Chronology of the Jerusalem Monarchy

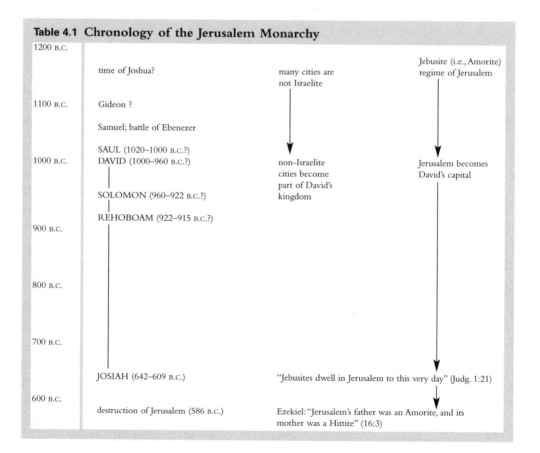

1200 B.C.	time of Joshua?	many cities are not Israelite	Jebusite (i.e., Amorite) regime of Jerusalem
1100 B.C.	Gideon ?		
	Samuel; battle of Ebenezer		
	SAUL (1020–1000 B.C.?)		
1000 B.C.	DAVID (1000–960 B.C.?)	non-Israelite cities become part of David's kingdom	Jerusalem becomes David's capital
	SOLOMON (960–922 B.C.?)		
	REHOBOAM (922–915 B.C.?)		
900 B.C.			
800 B.C.			
700 B.C.			
	JOSIAH (642–609 B.C.)	"Jebusites dwell in Jerusalem to this very day" (Judg. 1:21)	
600 B.C.	destruction of Jerusalem (586 B.C.)	Ezekiel: "Jerusalem's father was an Amorite, and its mother was a Hittite" (16:3)	

commitments of the formative period of the faith, this induced changes in their choices, patterns of relationships, and (in time) the entire social structure. The Yahwist faith entered an adaptive period in which the constitutive factors of the faith were being superseded by social and economic factors. In other words, a religious value system that had once provided a basis for unity among a large group of diverse people from different tribes and clans was disappearing, being replaced by a more cynical attitude that only the political monopoly of force could coerce people into uniformly "correct" behavior. The processes of sacred politics came full circle when the ruling elite, assisted by priestly specialists, formally redefined the essence of the sacred so that now, in an adapted form, religion legitimized the new political order.

When all was said and done, an Israelite empire (of sorts) had been formed with Yahweh, ironically, playing the role of Baal—symbolizing and justifying its exercise of coercive force.

The Philistine Military Occupation of Israel

1. The external stimulus of the Philistine threat did not set the movement toward monarchy in motion; impulses in that direction dated back earlier at least to the days of Gideon (see Judg. 8:22). But it apparently did stimulate a critical mass of Israelites to enlist Yahwist religion in the movement.

This centralization process probably was precipitated by the battle of Ebenezer around 1050 B.C. (1 Samuel 4), when the Philistines defeated an Israelite militia and captured the ark of the covenant, a sacred chest symbolizing the presence of Yahweh.[1] A Yahwist shrine at nearby Shiloh, where the young Samuel was first introduced to the teachings of Yahwism (1 Sam. 1:24–2:26), was destroyed about the same time, an event that the prophet Jeremiah (7:12) recalled four hundred years later.

The Philistines' presence this far inland suggests that they were bent on extending their rule over the weaker and less centralized Israelite federation of villages. The Yahwist ethic precluded an Israelite political monopoly of force, and the Israelite villages, with comparatively few weapons and no military specialists, represented a tempting power vacuum waiting to be filled. The presence of Philistine pottery at Beth-shean shows that Philistine influence had penetrated as far north as the fertile Esdraelon Valley. After the battle of Ebenezer, they were poised to strike at the central hill country, the heartland of the Israelite federation.

The ark of the covenant was taken to the Philistine city of Ashdod and placed in a central shrine dedicated to the god Dagon (1 Sam. 5:1–2), a north Syrian Amorite deity whose worship dated back to the Early Bronze Age. This god's enshrinement at Ashdod shows both the extent of Amorite cultural influence by the early Iron Age, and the tendency of invaders (such as the Philistines) to adopt the gods of the people they conquer.

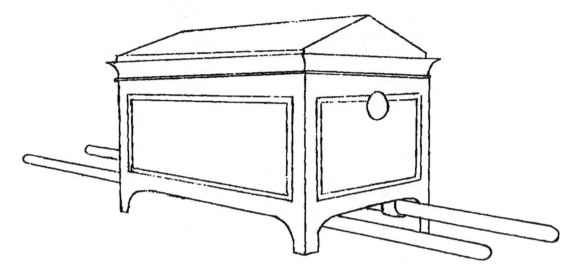

Figure 4.1
Ark of the Covenant. The biblical ark (= chest) of the covenant may have been based on Egyptian analogies, such as this chest of Pharaoh Tutankhamun (ruled 1336–1327 B.C.?). Rings mounted below made it possible to insert poles for transporting the chest. Archaic traditions state that the Israelite ark served as a repository for the tablets of the Sinai covenant; when later placed in the Jerusalem temple, it was said to serve as Yahweh's throne. Later tradition also depicted the ark as quite ornate, overlaid with gold and with a solid gold lid (the so-called "mercy seat") adorned by two cherubim facing each other.

Samuel and Deuteronomy 32

The battle of Ebenezer was an enormous blow to the morale of the Israelite federation, whose only central authority was the intangible Yahweh. If Yahweh could not protect the ark of the covenant, how could he protect the Israelites? Significantly, the very question itself assumes that issues should now be framed within the more tangible framework of material self-interest rather than within a religious framework of ethical values.

That the Yahwist religion—and community—did not collapse in the face of such a stinging question seems remarkable. William F. Albright argued that it survived largely because of Samuel, its enormously wise and insightful advocate. Samuel may well be the author of Deuteronomy 32, which seems to constitute a response to the disasters of Ebenezer and Shiloh.[2] Many scholars today follow Otto Eissfeldt in dating Deuteronomy 32 to around 1050 B.C. It is written in a more archaic form of Hebrew and takes the form of a legal indictment, beginning with the invocation of elements of nature to serve as witnesses (see Box 2.4). It links Yahweh's primary concern not with shrines and arks but with human beings who, sadly, have rejected Yahweh (vv. 15–18). The author bemoans the corrosive materialism and self-interest infesting the Yahwist community:

2. This poem is usually called the "Song of Moses," and it is truly "Mosaic" insofar as it reflects the same pattern of thought found in the Sinai covenant.

> Jacob ate his fill;
>> Jeshurun grew fat, and kicked.
>> You grew fat, bloated, and gorged!
> He abandoned God who made him,
>> and scoffed at the Rock of his salvation. (v. 15)

The priorities of the new society's early days were fading. Replacing them was the self-centered interest to guarantee the material benefits that had accrued over the past century and a half better than Yahweh could. A critical mass of Israelites began to feel that a centralized system of planning and command was needed; this was the first step that led gradually to the abandonment of the religious solidarity that, in the past, had made them the formidable foe of ambitious warlords.

This is one of the earliest expressions of a familiar biblical theme attributing religious rebellion (apostasy) to the loosening of ethical controls that often accompanies affluence. We see this same theme in Jesus' parable of the Rich Man and Lazarus (Luke 16:19–31), and in such statements as "Blessed are you who are poor, for yours is the kingdom of God" (Luke 6:20) and "It is easier for a camel to go through the eye of a needle than for someone who is rich to enter the kingdom of God" (Matt. 19:24).[3] Religious ascetics seem to be correct: it is affluence, not poverty, that human beings have the most trouble coping with spiritually. Oliver Goldsmith captured this nicely in his poem "The Deserted Village":

> Ill fares the land, to hastening ills a prey,
>> Where wealth accumulates, and men decay.

This same insight was well articulated some 2,800 years earlier in Deuteronomy 32.

3. In these and other sayings of Jesus, the phrase "kingdom of God" seems to echo and revive the premonarchic notion of "Yahweh's rule/kingship" described in the previous chapter.

An Israelite King to Wage War

The defeats at Ebenezer and Shiloh fragmented the Israelite federation, whose towns were now occupied by Philistine garrisons determined to collect ample revenues and suppress any organized resistance. Eventually, the cry went up for an Israelite king—one more tangible than Yahweh—to lead the fight against the oppressor. War is, after all, the first function of a king. Probably by 1020 B.C., toward the end of Samuel's life, Saul was selected to serve as king, primarily to wage war.

The institution of kingship in the Near East was not quite two thousand years old by the time of Saul and David. Political states with standing armies and permanent bureaucracies had already arisen in the temple-cities of Mesopotamia around 2700 B.C. (see Table 1.1), even though these cities date back as far as 5000 B.C. We have no written documents about social organization in those prehistoric times, but the archaeological record hints at a high degree of civil cooperation. For example, Tell Ghassul had a dense population and a walled city prior to 3500 B.C., but excavators there have yet to find a single object that could be interpreted as a weapon, even though there were plenty of highly skilled coppersmiths there at the time. Maintaining civility in a densely populated community apparently did not necessarily require *political* organization. However, once the growing Sumerian temple-cities began crowding each other, more and more resources were directed toward the organization of warfare. Kingship logically followed, and, when it did, the standard ancient Near Eastern practice of sacred politics depicted it as a divine institution "lowered from heaven" by the gods.

Given this standard practice, it is interesting that the biblical writers go into such detail to portray the *human* origins of Israelite kingship. It is all the more interesting because these writers actually preserve traditions critical of the rise of kingship in Israel, even though other biblical traditions, in standard Near Eastern fashion, depict God actively *endorsing* it. In 1 Samuel 8, the prophet Samuel is shown predicting that an Israelite state would eventually be indistinguishable from all the others of the time (vv. 10–18). In fact, the people are shown demanding that Samuel appoint a king precisely so they *can* be "like other nations" (Hebrew *goyim*; vv. 5, 20; contrast chapter 1, note 9).

The biblical text records the complete reversal of the Israelite religious ideology that had operated for almost two centuries. Yahweh himself is shown conceding this point to Samuel: "Listen to the voice of the people in all that they say to you; for they have not rejected you, but they have rejected me from being king over them" (v. 7). Rather than depicting Yahweh exercising supernatural power to punish these rebels or change their minds, the biblical tradition depicts Yahweh simply yielding his role as Israel's "king" to someone else. He is shown abdicating the throne. In a sense, Yahweh has now been "kicked upstairs," becoming little more than the symbolic figurehead of an authority structure now fully in the hands of human beings.

The biblical text then notes that Samuel warned the people that the short-term *material benefits* of political government also carried long-term *material costs*. The first thing Samuel predicted was growing military expenditures and the creation of a favored class of Israelites who would facilitate that: "These will be the ways of the king who will reign over you: he will take your sons and appoint them to his chariots and to be his horsemen" (v. 11). Horsemen and charioteers were the elite military aristocracy of ancient times. To this day in India, only the priestly caste is higher than the military aristocracy, and we know of at least one case at Ugarit where a member of the charioteer class—called the *maryannu*—was ordained to be priest of the goddess Ishkhara. Whether he himself ever fought in battle was probably irrelevant: he provided military hardware for the state.

Samuel's second warning was "He will appoint for himself commanders of thousands and commanders of fifties, and some to plow his ground and to reap his harvest" (v. 12). Agriculture was the economic base of these ancient kingdoms. Whenever a neighboring country was conquered, its land became crown property, and the victorious king could allocate it to whomever he wished—often to high-ranking military officials. Whether these generals ever took plow in hand and tilled the land themselves was irrelevant. What mattered was that the king entitled them to collect the revenues from the lands or villages he awarded to them. The idea that the state should own all the means of production has most recently been extolled by Marxism. Predictably, this has not resulted in a classless society but, as usual, one in which those functionaries most loyal to the state, like the ancient generals, received special entitlement to its economic resources.

Finally, Samuel foresaw that a human king "will take the best of your fields and vineyards and olive orchards and give them to his courtiers. He will take one-tenth of your grain and of your vineyards and give it to his officers and his courtiers [i.e., to the bureaucracy]" (vv. 14–15). "The tenth" was the typical tax of the LB Age political state, and it could be a daunting amount given the precarious nature of agriculture in that part of the world. As with all other political matters, the early Israelites originally entrusted taxation to Yahweh, which is how the concept of the "tithe" originated. The Israelites apparently never determined how Yahweh could collect and spend these tax revenues, although later priests were always eager to accept such revenues on behalf of Yahweh. But even as late as the time of Josiah, the laws of Deuteronomy (14:22–29) did not quite know what to do with the tithe. They recommend that it be donated to those who have no income (priests, Levites, the poor, and widows and orphans); if any was left over, the family could spend it on a pilgrimage to Jerusalem. What Samuel was predicting, however, was a revival of the old LB Age political system of tax collection, now under Israelite auspices and therefore promoted *in the name of Yahweh*.[4] Ironically, the hope of avoiding such a system—under Philistine auspices—was probably what drove the Israelites to request a king in the first place.

But the Israelites were not interested in the long-term implications of political rule. They shouted down Samuel: "No! but we are determined to have a king over us" (1 Sam. 8:19).

4. While focusing on the negative impact this will have on the Israelites, we should not ignore its potentially negative impact on Yahweh's *name*, since now Yahweh was being named in support of all sorts of things to which he had previously been opposed. A tradition eventually emerged that Yahweh was periodically compelled to punish his people for the sake of his name (i.e., their conduct was ruining the integrity and reputation of the whole religious structure).

An Israelite King to Administer Law

After anointing Saul as king, the biblical tradition recounts that Samuel told the people the *mishpat ha-meluka* (1 Sam. 10:25), which the NRSV translates as "the rights and duties of the kingship." But our modern concept of "rights" is barely four hundred years old, and it would be a mistake to apply it to biblical times, as this translation does. The most characteristic meaning of *mishpat* in biblical Hebrew is "custom." What Samuel proclaimed and *wrote down on a scroll* for Saul (v. 25) must therefore have been the "customary law" that the Israelite king was expected to uphold, since he (or his bureaucratic appointees) would inevitably be called on to arbitrate legal disputes that village courts could not resolve.

Some scholars believe that Samuel's scroll of *mishpat*—which was said to have been "laid up before Yahweh" (v. 25)—was indeed revered and eventually incorporated into scripture as part of the so-called Covenant Code (or book of the covenant) in Exodus 21–23. (The law found therein was discussed briefly in chapter 3.) If these scholars are correct, then the Israelite king was expected to abide by this collection of legal principles (mostly Amorite in origin), many of which had probably been customary for at least half a millennium among some of the groups that eventually became Israelite. Samuel wanted the monarchy's powers limited by a firmly established body of custom. This may well be the earliest record we have of a "constitutional monarchy."

The Hammurapi Code shows that the Babylonians did not believe their laws were promulgated by the gods. It simply says that the gods created the authority structure (i.e., Hammurapi and his administration), and that this structure, in turn, was responsible for the laws (see Box 3.5). Likewise, the ancient Israelites did not originally believe that their laws originated with Yahweh. Behind the Covenant Code and Samuel's *mishpat ha-meluka* was likely the notion that Yahweh created the community and that the community, in turn, was responsible not only for the laws but also for the authority structure (Saul's kingship) to enforce them. In Samuel's time, it was not the king or even Yahweh but the Israelite *community* that was considered the source of the law, and the community was free to base its law on ancient customs, as long as these did not conflict with the Yahwist ethic.[5]

5. As the Torah/Law became increasingly central to Jewish identity, Israel's God came to be viewed as its author. This view was challenged by Jesus' startling claim that the biblical law pertaining to divorce, for example, did not reflect a divine decree but a custom accommodating human social reality (Matt. 19:3–9, especially v. 8). He was saying that human factors, not divine ones, were responsible for the law (a notion that Paul of Tarsus in the New Testament also seems to embrace). As we shall see in chapter 8, in bypassing the official Jewish views of their day and embracing a more archaic Yahwist view (e.g., concerning the origins of law), Jesus and Paul resembled religious reformers.

Saul as King

There are varying accounts of Saul's selection as king. In 1 Samuel 10:1 he is anointed by Samuel, but in verses 20–21 he is selected by lot. Samuel then introduces Saul with the words "Do you see the one whom Yahweh has *chosen?*" (v. 24, emphasis added). In typical Near Eastern fashion, the word "chosen" (Hebrew *bahar*) was primarily applied to the king, who was believed to have been "chosen" or "designated" by deity. Only much later did Israelites begin extending the word to the entire religious community, characterizing Israel as God's "chosen people" (see chapter 3, note 12).

After Saul's coronation, "Samuel sent all the people back to their homes. Saul also went to his home at Gibeah" (vv. 25–26). Excavations at Gibeah uncovered the remains of an early Iron Age structure that W. F. Albright identified as Saul's "capital." Measuring perhaps 100 feet wide by 150 feet long, it could have housed little more than the king, his family, and a dozen or so loyal soldiers—more of a command headquarters than a capital city.

At least initially, participation in the Israelite monarchy seems to have been a voluntary matter, strange as that might sound. The Bible reports that Saul was followed by "warriors whose hearts God had touched" (1 Sam. 10:26). Although he was in no position to coerce anybody into recognizing his government, Saul's ability to command a loyal band of warriors (as Sihon and Og had done) was certainly a good first step toward acquiring a monopoly on political force. Those who first joined the "monarchic movement," if we can call it that, did so simply

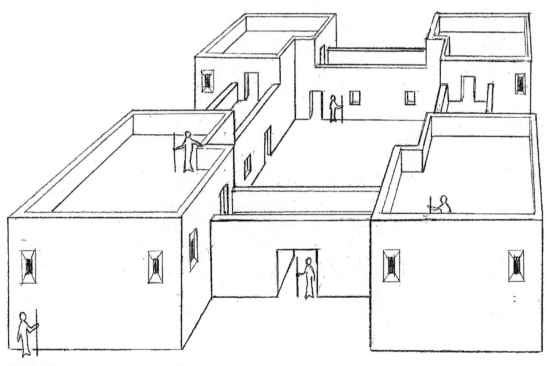

Figure 4.2
Saul at Gibeah. Reconstruction of the early Iron Age structure excavated at Tell el-Ful (i.e., Gibeah).

because they believed it was right: "God had touched their hearts." The very next verse reports that some Israelites refused to recognize Saul's legitimacy, "[saying], 'How can this man save us?' They despised [Saul] and brought him no present. But [Saul] held his peace." The characterization of these Israelites as "worthless fellows" (v. 27) reflects the bias of a later biblical writer who supported the idea of an Israelite monarchy. Otherwise, these people exhibit typical Apiru/Hebrew attitudes in their refusal to commit resources to the maintenance of the monarchy, that is, to "pay their taxes." They apparently opposed the monarchic movement, and Saul was as yet in no position to force their allegiance.

He was also trying to preside over an enormous shift from the piety and ethos of the village to an ideology that legitimized a centralized government. The scholarly consensus is that he cracked under the strain. The Bible reports numerous examples of his paranoia—his envy of successful protégés like David, his distrust of anyone (even his own children) drawn to such a protégé, and his ruthlessness in trying to eliminate those he perceived as his rivals. A war chant that had become popular among the Israelite village girls is mentioned three times in 1 Samuel:

> "Saul has killed his thousands,
>   and David his ten thousands." (18:7; also 21:11 and 29:5)

This chant is said to have triggered Saul's jealous rage. He attempted to have David killed, forcing him to flee and live as an outlaw. The chant also marks a radical departure from the older war-chant tradition of the Israelite federation, which reserved all military honor and glory exclusively for Yahweh. But within Israel's monarchic movement, an "alpha male's" superior ability to kill others is now celebrated.

The religious ethos of Yahwism was losing its grip. Gresham's law—"Bad money drives out good money"—is apparently true in the realm of social ethics as well: "Bad ethics drives out good ethics." Acts that would have been censured a couple of generations earlier (note Gideon's *rejection* of kingship in Judg. 8:22–23) were now becoming acceptable. This erosion of the Yahwist ethic was both a cause and an effect of the development of the Israelite state. Samuel clearly foresaw that by the time the Israelites realized how much they needed that ethic, it would be too late. No longer having any authority within the community, it could not provide guidance or help in time of trouble (1 Sam. 8:18).

The erosion of that ethic can be seen in the way Saul waged war, which was far from holy. In contrast to Barak, who several generations earlier would not enter battle without authorization from the religious leader Deborah (Judg. 4:8), Saul was so eager to fight that he improperly authorized himself to do so by performing a ritual sacrifice (1 Sam.

Box 4.1—Saul's Paranoia

Now the spirit of Yahweh departed from Saul, and an evil spirit from Yahweh tormented him. . . . And David came to Saul, and entered his service. Saul loved him greatly, and he became his armor-bearer. . . . And whenever the evil spirit from God came upon Saul, David took the lyre and played it with his hand, and Saul would be relieved and feel better, and the evil spirit would depart from him. (1 Sam. 16:14, 21, 23)

The next day an evil spirit from God rushed upon Saul, and he raved within his house, while David was playing the lyre, as he did day by day. Saul had his spear in his hand; and Saul threw the spear, for he thought, "I will pin David to the wall." But David eluded him twice. (1 Sam. 18:10–11)

When the new moon came, the king sat at the feast to eat. . . . Jonathan stood, while Abner [Saul's general] sat by Saul's side; but David's place was empty. . . . And Saul said to his son Jonathan, "Why has [David] the son of Jesse not come to the feast, either yesterday or today?" Jonathan answered Saul, "David earnestly asked leave of me to go to Bethlehem; . . . For this reason he has not come to the king's table."
   Then Saul's anger was kindled against Jonathan. He said to him, "You son of a perverse, rebellious woman! Do I not know that you have chosen the son of Jesse to your own shame . . . ? For as long as the son of Jesse lives upon the earth, neither you nor your kingdom shall be established. Now send and bring him to me, for he shall surely die." Then Jonathan answered his father Saul, "Why should he be put to death? What has he done?" But Saul threw his spear at him to strike him; so Jonathan knew that it was the decision of his father to put David to death. (1 Sam. 20:24–25, 27–33)

13:8–10). The politician-general had now set himself up as a religious authority. Nor did he adhere to the other principles of holy war (1 Sam. 15): Saul kept alive both the captured livestock—probably booty for his soldiers—and the captured leader, perhaps to serve as a vassal in Saul's expanding kingdom. There is also the laconic note that after one of his victories "Saul went to Carmel, where he set up a monument for himself" (1 Sam. 15:12). War in Israel was now completely political, fought essentially for profit and glory.

David Becomes King

We do not know how long David was an outlaw trying to survive outside the protections of Saul's government. David even entered the service of the Philistines as a sort of vassal of the king of Gath (1 Samuel 27). He was fairly typical of what in the LB Age would have been called "leader of Apiru" (see Box 1.9). The biblical narrative, literally translated, identifies David's followers as "everyone who was oppressed, everyone who had a creditor, and everyone who was discontented" (1 Sam. 22:2). But the Covenant Code strictly prohibited such "creditors": "If you lend money to my people, to the poor among you, you shall not deal with them as a creditor; you shall not exact interest from them" (Exod. 22:25). That people in David's gang were indebted to creditors shows that this customary law was being ignored in Israel. A man who could not pay the interest on his debts would first have to surrender to the creditor his children, then his wife, and finally himself. Having fled to avoid this, the debtor's only security lay in banding together with others in the same situation. Their economic base was extortion and plunder (1 Samuel 25 and 27).

Around the time of Saul's death, about 1000 B.C., David's gang gained control of the southern hill-country town of Hebron. Elders from David's tribe, Judah, recognized him there as king of Judah, that is, the southern part of the old twelve-tribe federation. Shortly after the death of Ishbosheth, Saul's son and successor, the northern tribes also recognized David as their king (2 Sam. 5:1–5). Assessments of David as king range from Machiavellian scoundrel to a combination of saint and political genius, and there is much to be said for both portraits. The biblical story of David is "warts-and-all" blunt, especially from 2 Samuel 11 to 1 Kings 1. His affair with Bathsheba (2 Samuel 11) was no mere peccadillo. He was guilty not only of coveting and adultery but also of committing murder to cover up his misdeeds. There is no analogy for this sort of story in ancient Near Eastern fiction, lending credibility to the claim that such traditions about David are grounded in historical memory.

Jerusalem: The "City of David"

Shortly after becoming king of all Israel, David seized Jerusalem. The city had a colorful cultural history long before David captured it. During the Bronze Age, the city was named "Urusalim," which means "city of (the god) Shalem." It was a small but well-fortified town, situated on a low hill near a subterranean spring just outside what is today called the Old City of Jerusalem. Its entire population would have fit into an area the size of a modern city block. The Amarna letters of Abdu-Hepa suggest that various north Syrian peoples (e.g., Hurrians and Kashites) were settled in the city during the LB Age.

Sometime during the turmoil at the end of the LB Age, the native Jebusite population had seized control of the city from Abdu-Hepa's successors and renamed the city after their own tribe, *Yabus* (Hebrew *yebus,* or Jebus). By the time David captured it, Jebus had another well-established name, *Mesudat Zion,* "the stronghold of Zion" (2 Sam. 5:7). "Zion" is a curious word. Even though it is clearly not a Semitic word, much less a Hebrew one, it became virtually synonymous with Jerusalem in later biblical poetry. However, it is likely related to the Hittite word, *Sius,*

Figure 4.3
Jerusalem at the Time of David. Looking west across the Kidron Valley, the City of David probably extended four hundred yards from south (*left*) to north (*right*). The palace/bureaucratic complex he inherited (A) may have sat on a terrace reinforced by the stepped stone structure (B) still visible today (see Fig. 7.2), although the date of that structure is debated. Remains of the city gate (C) are also still visible, leading to a cave (D) containing a subterranean spring. A vertical shaft provided more limited access to the spring from inside the city. King Solomon expanded the city onto the northern hill (E), building his new palace and temple there. The city later expanded onto the western hill (F). King Hezekiah, anticipating an Assyrian siege in 701 B.C., expanded the city wall to enclose a reservoir pool (G). He also had his engineers seal the cave (D) and dig a new tunnel linking its spring to this reservoir, referred to as the pool of Siloam in John 9:7. This tunnel was discovered by British officers in the 1860s. (Adapted from Lloyd K. Townsend)

6. Whenever a Hittite noun such as *Sius* is preceded by a phrase such as "city of," "stronghold of," or "mount of," it takes a suffix *-nas*. According to the rules of grammar, *Sius* becomes *Siunas*, shortened to *Siun*, which becomes "Zion" in Semitic.

"god." From this same Hittite word is derived the name of the greatest of all Greek gods, Zeus.[6]

When David conquered Jebus, he simply restored the town's original name, "Urusalim" (*yerushalayim* in Hebrew, or Jerusalem). But he could not erase the cultural stamp that the previous regimes had left on the town and its population. Indeed, even four hundred years after David the non-Israelite character of Jerusalem was still plainly visible: the prophet Ezekiel mocked the faithless Jerusalem by declaring its "father" to be an Amorite and its "mother" a Hittite (Ezek. 16:3; see Table 4.1).

What the Bible *does not* tell us about David's capture of Jerusalem is as intriguing as what it *does* say. The story focuses on how David's troops gained access to the town via a "water shaft" (2 Sam. 5:7–8), presumably an underground shaft used to bring water into the town from its subterranean spring. But the text tells us virtually nothing about what David did to the town and its residents. There is no usable archaeological evidence for the city at this time. In all likelihood, its inhabitants, most of whom were the bureaucrats of the previous king, simply shifted their allegiance to David. The change from serving the old Jebusite regime to serving the new Israelite one probably had little impact on the daily lives of these non-Yahwists.

David entrusted the military organization to the command of his cousin, Joab. He could probably ill afford to trust anyone else in this sensitive and strategic position. This army essentially comprised a corps of professional soldiers (mercenaries) who had formerly served the Jebusite king. The ethnic diversity of names among David's key soldiers (2 Sam. 23:24–39) shows that their cultural forebears had come from different parts of the Near East. These soldiers were certainly not Israelite. All that had changed for them was the source of their paychecks.

The pattern is a familiar one: as long as bureaucrats continue to receive their salaries, they care little about the religious ideology of the ruling regime. Such indifference was precisely captured in the early medieval slogan, "*cuius regio, eius religio,*" literally "whose rule, his religion." The bureaucrats of Jerusalem undoubtedly went about their business uninterested in, and perhaps even privately disdainful of, David's ancestral faith—unless it could be exploited to their advantage. They may have given a token nod to the new king's god, Yahweh, but their values—that is, what they "worshiped"—remained, for them, the old and familiar.

As described in the Bible, the political structure of the city during the reigns of David and his son Solomon mirrored that of pharaonic Egypt, perhaps because the city had been a vassal of Egypt in the Amarna period, when pro-Egyptian Abdu-Hepa had been its king. Immediately below the king was the grand vizier, a sort of secretary of state who oversaw the entire nonmilitary bureaucracy. His title was *'asher 'al ha-bayit* ("one who is over the house"), an exact, literal translation of the Egyptian title. There was also the recorder (Hebrew *mazkir*), in charge of internal affairs and probably of the secret police, because his counterpart in ancient Egypt was supposed to circulate among the markets and the populace, reporting to the king anyone particularly deserving of royal wrath or commendation. The character of "the Satan" in the book of Job—a servant of Yahweh who performs his duties by "going to and fro on the earth, walking up and down on it" (Job 1:7)—may have been based on this royal official.

By right of conquest, Jerusalem became David's personal property and took on yet another name, the "City of David." It was ideally suited to serve as his capital: its inhabitants provided the bureaucrats he needed to manage his growing kingdom, and it was situated on the border between the northern and southern tribes of the old Yahwist federation. Moving the capital here from Hebron helped ensure its neutrality, due both to its new central location and to the fact that Jerusalem had never been an Israelite town (and therefore was not associated with any particular Yahwist tribe). David thus fused two fundamentally different population groups under his rule: (1) the northern and southern Yahwists of the old Israelite federation, and (2) the pagans of the recently captured non-Israelite urban centers.

Formation of the Israelite State

There is almost no archaeological evidence to confirm the biblical account of the formation of the Israelite state. Indeed, traditions embedded in the Bible are virtually our only source for what was happening in tenth-century-B.C. Palestine, Syria, Transjordan, Anatolia, and even Egypt and Mesopotamia, whose inhabitants were all struggling to recover from the collapse of Bronze Age civilization. So-called "maximalist" interpreters of the Bible (e.g., fundamentalists) regard the biblical picture of a tenth-century-B.C. Israelite kingdom under David and Solomon to be historically correct in all its details. But this is perhaps challenged by later nonbiblical evidence, which seems to point to the ninth century B.C. as the time political states began to form in these areas (see chapter 5). From this, the so-called "minimalist" school of biblical interpreters conclude that there could not possibly have been an Israelite kingdom, much less empire, in the tenth century B.C. In their opinion, the biblical texts here are fictions about a nonexistent "golden age," while Samuel, Saul, David, and Solomon never really existed anywhere except in some fiction writer's imagination.

As is often the case, the truth lies between these extremes. David's kingdom was far more rudimentary than the grand European monarchies with which we are familiar, and in terms of which the maximalists often (incorrectly) interpret the biblical stories. However, it was also more sophisticated than Saul's rustic command headquarters at Gibeah (if that is indeed the structure Albright identified as such). What the minimalists fail to appreciate is that the formation of an Israelite monarchy as early as the tenth century B.C. is entirely plausible due to a constellation of historical factors peculiar to that time and place:

1. Most important was *the loyalty of a relatively large population base,* in the form of the twelve-tribe federation, which by then had existed for almost two centuries, and from which Saul and David could rally support. As far as we know, nothing comparable to this existed anywhere else in the Near East for any would-be ruler in the tenth century to build upon. Such a base of loyalty may have been even harder to find in the ninth and eighth centuries B.C.

2. Saul and David thus presided over *an already functioning economic organization encompassing a vast geographical area.* Consequently, they initially did not have to divert precious manpower and resources toward acquiring an economic base, as any other would-be ruler elsewhere would have had to do at this time. Even a century later, politicians struggling to build state structures in other parts of the Near East did not enjoy the strategic advantages that Saul and David seemingly enjoyed already in the tenth century B.C.

3. David's *resources, especially military, could thus be entirely deployed externally* against cities within Palestine ruled by weaker and less-popular

regimes. Not only was David strategically more fortunate than any ninth-century counterpart elsewhere, but the cities he captured were also comparatively weaker than those that kings had to conquer a century later. Nevertheless, these cities did have bureaucrats whose loyalties were for hire. We do not know how many of these cities David conquered by direct military attack, and how many fell to him as a result of *coups* by factions within them who saw the advantages of joining David. The Amarna tablets suggest this sort of thing was common (see EA 74 in Box 1.7).[7] The point is that David probably captured non-Israelite cities with significantly less effort than a king in another part of the Near East would have to expend a century or two later.

4. As centers of specialization, *these cities also gave David access to certain technological skills,* including literacy, which were essential to the maintenance of a large-scale political organization, although in tenth-century Palestine such skills must still have been somewhat rudimentary. David's son and successor Solomon later had to import some experts (mostly construction engineers) from the Phoenicians (1 Kings 5:1–6).

5. Finally, *David's bureaucrats—all pagans—practiced some sacred politics to help him adapt his old Yahwist traditions to meet the "modern" demands of statecraft.* They provided him with an ideology that, for a generation anyway, successfully transcended the divisions between the Yahwists of the tribal villages (the economic base) and the pagans of the urban centers (the organizational specialists). This reconciliation was the very essence of his kingdom. Sacred politics legitimized David's rule in the eyes of Yahwists and non-Yahwists alike, lending an enviable unity and stability to this infant social organization. His kingdom thus consolidated, David would have had relative ease extending his sovereignty into Transjordan, overpowering the petty regimes controlling Edom, Moab, Ammon, and Damascus.

The official implementation of sacred politics probably began with the recovery of the ark of the covenant and its relocation to Jerusalem (2 Samuel 6). This was a symbolically significant declaration that the old Yahwist traditions had a future here in the (non-Yahwist) city of Jerusalem. The sanctity of the ark of the covenant may have been reinforced at this time by a scribal addition to the Sinai tradition, in which Moses, Aaron, Aaron's sons, and seventy tribal elders are portrayed taking a trip up Mount Sinai to receive a divine revelation concerning the proper design and construction of this ark (see Box 2.5). Many other techniques associated with sacred politics were used not only to present the new Davidic regime of Jerusalem as legitimately authorized to wield power but also to consolidate further the unity between the Israelites and non-Israelites of the kingdom. At least three major aspects of this sacred politics have left their marks on the Hebrew Bible.

7. Note the biblical account of the Assyrian king Sennacherib's attempt to conquer Jerusalem three hundred years after David (2 Kings 18:17–37). The Assyrian Rabshakeh, a sort of propaganda minister, tried to divide the population of Jerusalem by promising them greater security and prosperity under Sennacherib's regime. How many of the cities listed in Judges 1 succumbed to David through a strategy such as this?

8. For example, see the archaic poetry of Genesis 49:2; Deuteronomy 33:28, and Numbers 23:7 and 24:5. Genesis 32:28 is part of a story that explains why "Jacob" and "Israel" are synonymous. In most tribal societies, the common ancestor symbolically fuses different groups who can all feel comfortable claiming him as their own. It has nothing to do with literal biological kinship.

9. Scholars remain divided on whether these traditions about Abraham existed prior to Moses or were later literary creations. Regardless, the Yahwist population appears to have been slow to embrace the figure of Abraham. Aside from the book of Genesis itself, and the biblical phrase "Abraham and Isaac and Jacob" that presupposes its genealogical scheme, there are almost no biblical references to Abraham except in very late passages.

10. The Old Testament word for "breast" is *shad*, the same as in Amorite. The Amorite dual suffix (used for things occurring in pairs) was -*ay*. Later Greek translators mistakenly viewed the word *shadday* as an adjective linked to the Hebrew word *shadad*, "to devastate," loosely translating El Shaddai as "God Almighty," a rendering that has today become standard, even though it is wrong.

Abraham and His God. First is the range of traditions that portray Abraham as Israel's "ancestor of note." No biblical text dated prior to the time of David even mentions Abraham. The earliest Yahwist poetry instead consistently identifies *Jacob* as the "common ancestor" of all Yahweh worshipers, whose very name was synonymous with Israel.[8] But the sudden assimilation of non-Israelites into David's kingdom meant that a more inclusive common ancestor had to be found—one acceptable to Yahwists and non-Yahwists alike.

Traditions about a man named Abraham were well suited to meet this need: in them, both Yahwists and non-Yahwists alike could recognize their common cultural forebears. This enabled *everyone* in David's kingdom to acknowledge a shared cultural heritage that was pre-Mosaic and pre-Sinai.[9] The two-century-old breach between village Israelites and urban non-Israelites was now officially portrayed as having been transcended and therefore healed. As far as the political establishment was concerned, it seems that the Abraham tradition actually took precedence over the Mosaic-Sinai tradition. (Subsequent chapters will show how the Mosaic-Sinai covenant tradition, with its emphasis on religious ethic, constantly struggled over the centuries to remain viable within an Israelite state that either ignored or abused those devoted to it.)

Abraham as a Proto-Yahwist. Second, traditions about Abraham's religion—especially the curious tradition linking Abraham to El Shaddai (NRSV "God Almighty"; Gen. 17:1–2)—now had to be recast. The name "El Shaddai" was Amorite in origin, designating a place (i.e., "the god *of* Shaddai"). The name was well-known throughout the region, being attested in Aramaic inscriptions of the seventh century B.C. and as a personal name in an unpublished Arabic inscription from the Roman period. There is an unusual archaeological site along the Euphrates River that forms twin mounds rising above the plain. Situated near the Balih River where the ancient trade route branches south toward Damascus (via Palmyra), this site already had this distinctive shape when it was occupied in the Bronze Age. Today, in Arabic, it is called Tell eth-Thadyen, literally "ruin site of the two breasts." It is almost certainly the ruins of the ancient city of Tuttul mentioned in the Mari archives, whose name means "breasts" in Sumerian (see Map 1.1). The local Amorite equivalent would have been Shaddai, "two breasts."[10]

In other words, a seemingly ancient biblical tradition recalled that Abraham worshiped the god of the city of Shaddai, a god whose worship was brought to Palestine by Amorite immigrants and adopted there by popular pagan religion (as had been done with the god Dagon mentioned above). Because this god was relatively unknown to the ancient Israelites,

Box 4.2—Abraham, El Shaddai, and Yahweh

When Abram was ninety-nine years old, Yahweh appeared to Abram, and said to him, "I am God Almighty [El Shaddai]; walk before me, and be blameless. And I will make my covenant between me and you, and will make you exceedingly numerous." Then Abram fell on his face; and God said to him, "As for me, this is my covenant with you: You shall be the ancestor of a multitude of nations. No longer shall your name be Abram, but your name shall be Abraham; for I have made you the ancestor of a multitude of nations. I will make you exceedingly fruitful; and I will make nations of you, and kings shall come from you." (Gen. 17:1–6)

God also spoke to Moses and said to him: "I am Yahweh. I appeared to Abraham, Isaac, and Jacob as God Almighty [El Shaddai], but by my name 'Yahweh' I did not make myself known to them." (Exod. 6:2–3)

11. The apocryphal book of 1 Maccabees 12 reports that centuries later, when the Judaeans were forging an alliance with the Spartans, it was "discovered" that they were "brothers" because they shared the same ancestor, Abraham (v. 21). The apostle Paul, a first-century Pharisaic Jew, likewise invoked Abraham as common ancestor to support his claim that God was now bringing non-Israelites into religious fellowship with Israel (see chapter 8). Even today, whenever Jews, Christians, and Muslims engage in ecumenical endeavors, they regularly invoke Abraham as their common ancestor.

and had no negative connotations as a parochial Baal, it was not regarded as a rival to Yahweh and was apparently considered an inoffensive deity.

Consequently, the Israelite scribes equated Abraham's god of Shaddai with the Israelite god Yahweh, a god unknown prior to the time of Moses (Exod. 6:2–3). This resulted in stories claiming that Abraham, long before Moses, had actually known and worshiped the god Yahweh (Gen. 12:8; 15:2; 24:2). In short, Abraham was depicted as a practicing Yahwist centuries before Yahwism, as such, even emerged. This blending of originally distinct deities (such as Yahweh and the god of Shaddai) was commonplace in antiquity: the non-Israelites accepted Yahweh as just another name for the Baal who served as divine patron for David's regime, while the Israelites more or less accepted "Shaddai" as a title of their one and only god, Yahweh.

The amended Abraham tradition thus provided a religious foundation for the other benefits ("blessings") of union between the mostly urban non-Israelites and the mostly village-based Israelites. In fact, this became a major theme in the Abraham tradition, judging from how often it was repeated and varied (Gen. 18:18; 22:18; 26:4; 28:14). The note is first struck in Genesis 12:3, where Yahweh's words to Abraham may be translated, "by means of you [Abraham] shall all the families of the land be blessed." Such a statement would certainly have resonated with the urban non-Israelites of David's kingdom, whose standard of living no doubt improved when they "discovered" their common ancestry with the Israelites of the economically productive countryside. After two centuries of enmity, Abraham became a powerful symbol uniting these two diverse populations.[11]

Abraham's power as a symbol was enhanced by another theme in the tradition: the divine promise that the childless Abraham and Sarah would have a royal heir who will one day rule over the land of Canaan. This, too, is reiterated in numerous passages, such as Genesis 17:16, where Yahweh says, "I will bless her [Sarah], and she shall give rise to nations; kings of peoples shall come from her." In chapter 1 we observed that this theme (the childless man destined to sire a royal heir) also appears in Bronze Age epics. This epic theme may have functioned to legitimize the king whose ancestor had received such hearty support from deity. The genealogical linking of Abraham to King David (through Jacob and his son Judah) was easily accomplished. Not only was Abraham a common ancestor to all the subjects of David's kingdom, but David himself was the royal heir in whom the divine promises to the childless Abraham were fulfilled.

The Divine Charter. The third major feature of David's sacred politics leaving its mark on the OT was the Divine Charter, also known as the Davidic covenant (2 Sam. 7; 23:1–5; Psalm 89). In fact, it seems to have been the centerpiece of David's sacred politics, directly proclaiming what was indirectly hinted at in the Abraham narrative: David was divinely chosen to rule. Such a statement was essential for both Yahwists and non-Yahwists, although for different reasons. As far as the former were concerned, Yahweh was still king, at least in theory, but the only practical way his kingship could be maintained within their community was for his authority to be delegated to a human being. The members of the twelve tribes had, in fact, already agreed that this human being was David, a fellow Yahwist (2 Sam. 5:1–3). Minimally, the Divine Charter confirmed what they already believed—Yahweh wanted David to rule. For the non-Yahwists, the identification of military conquest with the divine right to rule was customary. Since David had, in fact, conquered them and was now promising a more bountiful future, they reached the same conclusion from a different direction: David, a child of Abraham like themselves, was divinely authorized to rule.

The Divine Charter, as presented to David by the prophet Nathan, tilts toward pagan beliefs insofar as David's dynasty is unconditionally granted eternal rule (Ps. 89:19–37). The sins of his successors may incur Yahweh's wrath, but never to the point where Yahweh will terminate their kingdom. Later biblical texts try to make it appear as if the preservation of the dynasty (and kingdom) had always been dependent on the kings' submission to the Sinai covenant (e.g., 1 Kings 2:1–4; 6:12–13; 8:23–26 [especially v. 25]), but David and his heirs behaved as if they believed otherwise. Centuries after David's death, his descendant King Josiah was actually shocked to discover that submission to the Sinai covenant was indeed one of the terms of his kingdom's survival (see

Box 4.3—Yahweh's Covenant with David

Second Samuel 7 recounts the story of the revelation of the Divine Charter or Davidic covenant. The substance of Yahweh's promise to David is also recounted poetically in Psalm 89:

> I will sing of your steadfast love, O Yahweh, forever;
>   with my mouth I will proclaim your faithfulness to all generations.
> . . . .
> You said, "I have made a covenant with my chosen one,
>   I have sworn to my servant David:
> 'I will establish your descendants forever,
>   and build your throne for all generations.'
> . . . .
> I have found my servant David;
>   with my holy oil I have anointed him;
> . . . .
> I will crush his foes before him
>   and strike down those who hate him.
> . . . .
> If his children forsake my law
>   and do not walk according to my ordinances,
> . . . .
> then I will punish their transgression with the rod
>   and their iniquity with scourges;
> but I will not remove from him my steadfast love,
>   or be false to my faithfulness.
> . . . .
> His line shall continue forever,
>   and his throne endure before me like the sun." (vv. 1, 3–4, 20, 23, 30, 32–33, 36)

chapter 6). Unlike the Yahweh of Sinai, who was fiercely committed to a religious ethic, the Yahweh of the Davidic covenant was a typical ancient Near Eastern divine patron whose primary commitment to uphold the political order was so strong that he might occasionally tolerate some level of royal corruption and ruthlessness.

Almost any time a king was crowned in the ancient Near East, he received some title such as "son of God." The Egyptians sanctified political authority a bit differently, declaring the pharaoh himself to be the actual embodiment of a god. Each of David's successors would be considered God's son (2 Sam. 7:14; Ps. 89:26). Thus, Psalm 2:7 depicts the Israelite king saying,

> I will tell of the decree of Yahweh:
> He said to me, "You are my son;
>   today I have begotten you."

This feature of the Davidic covenant tradition provided the foundation for Jewish "messianism," including the Christian claim that Jesus—as scion of the house of David—was worthy to receive from both Israelites (Jews) and non-Israelites (Gentiles) the royal titles "messiah," "Son of God," and "Lord."[12]

David undoubtedly instituted this program of sacred politics with the laudable goal of healing the rift between Yahwists and non-Yahwists. Yahwism was being adapted to a new social reality. By means of the Abraham tradition and the Divine Charter, David (or his Jebusite bureaucrats) sought to establish a religious structure capable of transcending old social and religious divisions for the future benefit of all concerned. David's sacred politics transformed the "either-or" of Yahwism—choose either Yahweh or the gods of the ancestors (Josh. 24:14–15)—into the "both-and" of an emerging new religious structure, where Yahweh is identified with El-Shaddai, one of the gods of the ancestors.

But, inevitably, the Jerusalem power structure's non-Yahwist view of Yahweh (as the divine patron of the state) came to dominate the public sphere for as long as David's dynasty endured. That is why the author of Judges 1, writing in its waning days, could accurately say, "Jebusites have been living in Jerusalem right up to this very day." Certainly their pagan ways of thinking remained influential in Jerusalem affairs long after David had died.

12. The word "messiah" is a transliteration of the Hebrew word *mashiah*, which means "anointed one" and refers to the ritual of pouring holy oil over the head of (i.e., anointing) someone to whom authority has been delegated. Its Greek equivalent is *christos*, or "christ."

Solomon's Empire

Solomon's mother, Bathsheba, was the widow of Uriah the Hittite, a soldier whose north Syrian forebears two or three centuries earlier may have settled into the service of the king of Jerusalem. Uriah was certainly not a Yahwist, although in 2 Samuel 11 he is portrayed as a man of principle whose ethical standards were far superior to those of the Yahwist David. Bathsheba's name literally means "daughter of (the) Seven," suggesting that she was named in honor of the Pleiades (i.e., "Seven Sisters"), goddesses favored in north Syria. Like Uriah, Nathan the prophet, and Zadok the priest (other Jerusalem characters exercising influence over David), Bathsheba was likely a member of a prominent non-Yahwist family in Jerusalem who now "belonged" to David.

Children in the ancient Near East, such as young Solomon, had little contact with their fathers during the first five years of their lives. Their outlook on life was shaped largely by their mothers, whose cultural background and values informed their children's development. Yahweh was David's god, not Bathsheba's, and she probably felt little if any commitment to the Israelite faith.[13] The Bible portrays her scheming with Nathan to manipulate David into proclaiming her son,

13. For example, what role (if any) did she play in giving her son such a non-Israelite name as Solomon? Some scholars think this was Solomon's throne name, meaning "Devotee of (the god) Shalem," the traditional pagan deity of Jerusalem. Solomon's given Israelite name was Jedidiah, meaning "Beloved of Yahweh" (2 Sam. 12:25).

Solomon, the surprise heir to the throne (1 Kings 1). This raises intriguing questions about Bathsheba's character. What ethical principles, if any, limited her ambitions? How calculated had her actions been years earlier (2 Sam. 11:2)—with her husband off at war and David experiencing marital problems—when she undressed one afternoon in full view of the palace?

At its peak, Solomon's empire extended south to the border established by treaty with the pharaoh, whose daughter was given in marriage to Solomon (1 Kings 3:1). This means that, at least for a while, the Philistine regimes of coastal Palestine recognized Solomon as their nom-

Map 4.1

Solomon's Empire. The territory encompassed not only hill-country areas of Palestine and Transjordan but also lowland areas and rival kingdoms (Damascus, Ammon, Moab, Edom) that David had conquered as well as other politically independent areas (the Philistines) that nominally recognized Solomon as overlord. The area between Damascus and the Euphrates River was virtually unpopulated and unpatrolled.

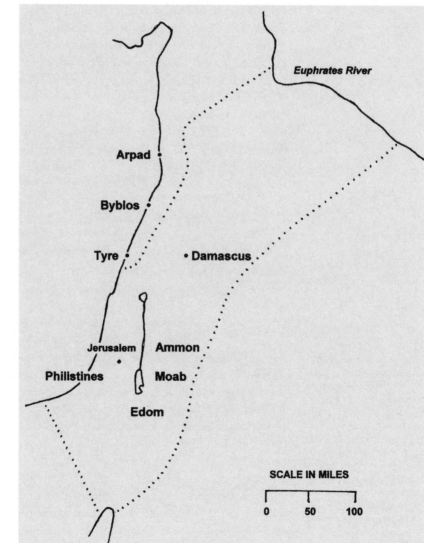

inal overlord. To the northwest, he established a border by treaty with the Phoenician king of Tyre. To the northeast, his rule extended as far as the Euphrates River, a feat that is not really as impressive as it appears on the map. Like the Philistines, the ruling family in Damascus simply recognized Solomon's nominal sovereignty. Even today, the two hundred miles of steppeland between Damascus and the Euphrates is home only to a handful of small settlements and defenseless shepherds, who can easily be "ruled" by a dozen or so policemen. There were simply no other political regimes in the area during Solomon's time that could have challenged his tax collectors.

Aided by architects and engineers supplied—for a price—by the king of Tyre, Solomon's construction projects in Jerusalem included the first temple to Yahweh, a new palace for himself, and extensive military fortifications. This ambitious program also necessitated the unpopular policy of forcibly conscripting laborers from the northern tribes of Israel (1 Kings 5:13–17), overextending both his economic and moral resources. In order to settle his debt to the Phoenician king, Solomon was forced to cede to him control of twenty Israelite villages in Galilee (1 Kings 9:10–14). Solomon also faced a rebellion of some Israelites led by one of his own bureaucrats, Jeroboam (1 Kings 11:26–40). His empire, always somewhat ephemeral and precarious, was gone within his own lifetime (1 Kings 11:14–25). Shortly after his death, around 922 B.C., his own kingdom was rent by civil war and split into two rump kingdoms, each no larger than a typical American county.

Suggestions for Further Reading

Additional information on the topics discussed in this chapter can be found in the following sources.

Dictionary/Encyclopedia Entries

> *Anchor Bible Dictionary:* Ark of the Covenant; David; Davidic Covenant; Jerusalem; Nationality and Political Identity; Sacral Kingship; Samuel; Shiloh; Jerusalem; Zion Traditions

War, Law, and Kingship in Early Israel

> M. Lind, *Yahweh Is a Warrior: The Theology of Warfare in Ancient Israel.* Scottsdale, Pa.: Herald Press, 1980.
> I. Mendelsohn, "Samuel's Denunciation of Kingship in the Light of the Akkadian Documents from Ugarit." *BASOR* 143 (1956): 17–22.
> G. Mendenhall, "Ancient Oriental and Biblical Law." *BAR* 3: 3–24.

David's Kingship

R. Clements, *Abraham and David*. Naperville, Ill.: Allenson, 1967.

G. Mendenhall, "The Monarchy." *Interpretation* 29/2 (1975): 155–170.

J. J. M. Roberts, "The Davidic Origin of the Zion Tradition." *JBL* 92 (1973): 329–344.

Five

The Legacy of King Solomon: The Traditional Period (I)— Yahwism versus Yahwisticism

Suggested Reading

Reign of Solomon: 1 Kings 1–5; 11–12
Kings and Prophets: 1 Kings 16:25–19:21; 21–22

A New Day for Israel

The Israelites had no royal traditions of their own to follow when they established their monarchy. True, Yahweh had been their "king," but this was a religious ethic inherently incompatible with the coercion of others, which is the fundamental rationale for adopting a political structure in the first place. In fact, the biblical tradition explicitly shows this religious ethic first being rejected before the political structure was created (1 Samuel 8).

People creating governments need models to guide them. This has been the case with the hundred or so states created in the latter half of the twentieth century,[1] and so it was with the Israelites. As we have seen, David inherited the non-Israelite political system that was already in place in Jerusalem. By the time of his successor, Solomon, the non-Yahwist traditions of this system—nurtured not only in Jerusalem but also in the other urban centers that served as Solomon's provincial capitals—became dominant in the state. As we shall see, the much extolled "glory of Solomon" actually entailed the revival of Bronze Age political structures and the religious systems (of Baal and Asherah) that undergirded them. Thus, Solomon's name was conspicuously absent from the list of Israel's good kings that Jesus ben-Sirach compiled around 200 B.C. for the inclusion in the apocryphal book known as Ecclesiasticus:

1. The model for many of these newly emergent states has been parliamentary democracy.

> Except for David and Hezekiah and Josiah,
>   all of them were great sinners,
> for they abandoned the law of the Most High;
>   the kings of Judah came to an end. (Ecclus. 49:4)

The Religion of Solomon's Temple

King Solomon's reign marked a systematic regression of the Israelite monarchy to LB Age pagan political traditions, which had probably continued virtually uninterrupted in Jerusalem/Jebus itself. This is clearly evident in the transformation of what it meant to worship Yahweh. Solomon exiled the old Yahwist priest Abiathar and established the Jerusalem-based Zadok as the sole priest of his regime. Solomon was also eager to replace David's tabernacle (housing the ark of the covenant) with a permanent temple, so that Yahweh would have a "house" like other ancient Near Eastern gods. But since there had never before been an *Israelite* temple, Solomon had to hire architects, building contractors, and artisans from the Phoenician king Hiram to build it for him (1 Kings 5:1–12). They constructed a temple virtually identical to pagan ones excavated in north Syria. As a concession to Yahwist attitudes about idolatry, Solomon did not erect a statue of Yahweh in the temple's inner sanctuary. Placed there instead was the ark of the covenant, flanked by two cherubim, to be regarded metaphorically, if not literally, as Yahweh's throne. Such iconography is straight from the pagan Near East.

Figure 5.1
Tell Tainat Temple. Artist's reconstruction of a ninth-century-B.C. Phoenician-style temple excavated at Tell Tainat in Syria. It has the same tripartite architectural design as Solomon's temple: a porch with two columns, a main room, and an inner sanctuary where the statue of the god was placed. In Solomon's temple, the ark of the covenant (Fig. 4.1) was placed in the inner sanctuary, flanked by two cherubim (see Fig. 5.2). (Adapted from *Great People of the Bible and How They Lived* [Pleasantville, N.Y.: The Reader's Digest Association, 1974], 181.)

Indeed, the Sinai tradition was apparently revised to validate this new emphasis on worship as ritual. Exodus 34, which many scholars believe was composed around the time of Solomon, shows Moses yet again ascending Mount Sinai to receive a second set of tablets inscribed with the obligations of the covenant. However, this time the Decalogue focuses entirely on ritual and ceremonial matters (vv. 10–28), which are depicted as replacements for the ethical commitments inscribed on the original tablets. The first seven chapters of the book of Leviticus take this historical revisionism one step further, depicting Yahweh revealing to Moses the complex system of rituals that would eventually be performed in Solomon's new temple. Most of these rituals are actually attested in earlier Canaanite sources. Many other terms and provisions for this ritual sacrifice match Bronze Age liturgical practice, again

Box 5.1—Canaanite Sacrifices in an Israelite Temple

In 1921, the French scholar René Dussaud claimed that Israelite temple sacrifice was actually Canaanite in origin. Eight years later, texts unearthed at Ugarit validated his claim. The five types of sacrifice described in Leviticus 1–7 are listed below. All except the "sin offering" have now been attested, in identical words, in Canaanite/ Phoenician sources. The Hebrews, Canaanites, and Phoenicians all used the same word for "sacrifice," *zebah*.

Term	NRSV translation	Description
'olah	"burnt offering"	voluntary; atonement for unintended sin; expression of devotion to God
minhah	"grain offering"	voluntary; recognition of God's goodness and benevolence
shelamim	"well-being offering"	voluntary; an expression of thanksgiving and fellowship that included a communal meal ("barbecue")
hatta't	"sin offering"	mandatory; atonement for specific sin, with confession, forgiveness, and atonement
'asham	"guilt offering"	mandatory; atonement for specific sin that also requires making restitution

Managing the daily slaughter of animals, the preparations of the meat, and the rituals of the altar was a full-time job involving a whole organization of priests and their assistants, including a corps of custodians responsible for keeping the facilities clean.

demonstrating Israelite borrowing. In his temple designed and built by pagans, Solomon had Zadok install a highly elaborate pagan liturgy requiring ritual specialists.

By thus expanding David's sacred politics (see chapter 4) into a full-blown ritual system, Solomon introduced so many non-Israelite features that it would be misleading for us to continue labeling it "Yahwism." True, the divine patron being honored and appeased by all this was named Yahweh, but the whole system suggests a sort of "Yahwisticism" that, at best, only faintly resembled the original faith in a few superficial features.[2] The uniqueness of Yahwism was being jeopardized by a vigorous royal policy that was successfully steering Israel along a path wherein it would indeed resemble "all the other nations" of the time. Had Solomon gone too far?

Many Yahwists were undoubtedly troubled that the substance of Israelite worship was shifting from ethical commitment to ritual ceremony, but they were powerless to oppose it. Several centuries later, the prophet Jeremiah, standing at the entrance to this temple, mocked this "Yahwistic" preoccupation with ritual, in effect claiming that such things as Exodus 34 and Leviticus 1–7 were being used to distort more authentic Yahwist notions of worship:

> Add your burnt offerings to your sacrifices, and eat the flesh. For in the day that I brought your ancestors out of the land of Egypt, I did not speak to them or command them concerning burnt offerings and sacrifices. But this command I gave them, "Obey my voice, and I will be your God, and you shall be my people." (Jer. 7:21–23)

2. This distinction between the formative "Yahwism" of Moses and the traditional "Yahwisticism" of the later Israelite monarchy has parallels in the study of ancient Persian religion: scholars distinguish the "Zarathustrianism" of the founder, Zarathustra, and the "Zoroastrianism" of later Persian monarchs who adapted the founder's religious views to serve their political goals. I owe this insight and the term to my colleague, Professor Gernot Windfuhr.

Solomon's Wives

Solomon's reliance on Bronze Age pagan models was not limited to the temple and its liturgy. The architecture of his royal palace (described in 1 Kings 7:1–12) closely resembled Hittite palace design. His conduct of statecraft and diplomacy also followed the Bronze Age pattern, expressing itself in his relationships with his wives. The Bible reports that

> King Solomon loved many foreign women along with the daughter of Pharaoh: Moabite, Ammonite, Edomite, Sidonian, and Hittite women . . . ; Solomon clung to these [women] in love. Among his wives were seven hundred princesses and three hundred concubines; and his wives turned away his heart. (1 Kings 11:1–3)

Someone unfamiliar with ancient Near Eastern statecraft might interpret this as a reference to Solomon's insatiable lust, an indication that his spiritual commitments were being replaced by his preoccupation with more carnal affairs. But the Hebrew word translated here as "love" has a specific meaning not in the context of romance and sex but of ancient diplomacy. For example, 1 Kings 5:1 reports that the Phoenician king Hiram had "always loved David" (the correct RSV rendering; i.e., he looked out for the interests of his ally, David). And in Hebrew, the "heart," *leb*, is not considered the center of one's subjective emotions and romantic feeling as in the West, but of one's rational priorities, commitments, and choices (such as strategic alliances). Solomon's "heart" (priorities) was in politics, not Yahwism. He was not being led astray by romantic feelings of passion or lust. Solomon's carefully arranged political marriages helped to solidify international relations, with the hope that a future king born from one of these unions might further strengthen those relations. So the question of the king's legal heir was fraught with significance, as different nations—and the princesses who represented them—vied with one another to have one of their own someday occupy the throne of Israel.[3] If Solomon was being "led astray," it was because he was first and foremost a political animal.

In a sense, each of these princesses was the formal head of her nation's delegation to Jerusalem. Not only would she, and any of her children sired by Solomon, be given official quarters in the king's new palace complex, but space would be set aside in the environs of the capital for her nation's "embassy." Such facilities were as protected then as they are today, and each contained many of the national symbols and emblems. In the modern world, these tend to be flags. In antiquity, they included not only statues of gods ("idols"), each of which was the divine patron of a particular nation, but also the various ritual ceremonies that showed "patriotic" loyalty to these gods. The distinction between an embassy and a temple could become very fuzzy, because the activity inside both was considered "sacred."

As a result of the political priorities and commitments that required the presence of these non-Israelite women, embassies, and gods in Jerusalem, Solomon not only introduced pagan polytheism into Israel, but he also supported it with Israelite state funds (1 Kings 11:7–8). From the standpoint of the Yahwist villager of the old twelve-tribe federation, it was unthinkable that an Israelite king should show such disregard for the first two commitments of the Yahwist Decalogue (prohibiting other gods and supporting idolatry). But from the standpoint of the Jerusalem elite, this was a necessary and normal aspect of political survival: it was simply the practical wisdom of supporting those

3. The Israeli scholar Abraham Malamat noted that, in its early days, Israelite royalty was more interested in a "blue-blooded" successor to the throne than in a "true-blooded" Israelite. They certainly had no reservations about having the next king raised by a mother who had no Yahwist commitments. Focusing on bloodline rather than religious ethic, Malamat observed that the "Jewish blood" of David's great-grandson, King Abijah, was so diluted that even by the standards of 1930s Germany he would probably have been considered "acceptable."

who support you.[4] Those eager to excuse Solomon, rationalizing that these were mere token gestures forced on him by circumstance, are missing the point: Solomon "wholeheartedly" believed in pagan polytheism (1 Kings 11:3). Besides, such respect accorded to other gods could never be merely token so long as these gods represented actual political states and so long as Solomon's respect was genuine for the power those other states wielded. He was therefore not merely tolerating these foreign gods; to a significant degree, he was actually relying on them for his own welfare and for that of his kingdom. Stated biblically, Solomon "bowed down" to these foreign gods.

Two well-known biblical stories seem to cast Solomon in more positive light, but on closer inspection they also testify to his reliance on non-Yahwist principles. Like the genie who appears when the magic lamp is rubbed, Yahweh on one occasion appears to Solomon to grant his wish, whatever it may be (1 Kings 3:4–15). The pious Solomon simply asks for "wisdom." Apparently he receives it, because in the second story, where Solomon adjudicates the case of the two women who claimed the same child (3:16–28), he is shrewd enough to detect the real mother. These stories show that the administration of justice in Solomon's kingdom was rooted not in established Yahwist legal precedents but in (presumably

Box 5.2—A Late Appraisal of Solomon and His Wives

Writing around 200 B.C., the Jewish scribe Jesus Ben-Sirach shared the overall negative appraisal of Solomon's rule. But he attributed Solomon's religious failures not to his obsession with power politics (an obsession that Ben-Sirach may have shared) but to his sexual lust. Ever since, Bible interpreters have made Solomon an object lesson of the man whose faith was undone by carnal passions.

> Solomon reigned in an age of peace,
>   because God made all his borders tranquil.
> . . . .
> How wise you were when you were young!
>   You overflowed like the Nile with understanding.
> . . . .
> But you brought in women to lie at your side,
>   and through your body you were brought into subjection.
> You stained your honor,
>   and defiled your family line,
> so that you brought wrath upon your children,
>   and they were grieved at your folly.
>   (Ecclus. 47:13–14, 19–20)

God-given) royal ingenuity or "wisdom." The Hebrew word for "wisdom," *hokmah,* actually connotes being "skilled" or "clever," and in some contexts (e.g., 2 Sam. 13:3) can even mean being sly, crafty, or devious. King Solomon determined what was just not by consulting the Covenant Code or any other collection of Israelite laws, but by relying simply on whatever skills his divine patron has bestowed on him.[5] These stories reveal that, under the Israelite monarchy, justice was no longer defined with respect to the covenant ethic, but with respect to whatever royal edicts happened to issue from the mind and mouth of the king, who was accountable to no one but the divine patron who chose him in the first place. It would surely take a very brave or a very foolish person—or a prophet—to claim that the edicts of the king were contrary to the will of the king's own god, Yahweh. This again fits the Bronze Age pattern.

The Israelites started down the road to monarchy when they demanded that Samuel give them a king so they could be like other "nations" (Hebrew *goyim;* 1 Sam. 8:5, 20). In the reign of Solomon, they got precisely what they asked for: a polity no different from any other "nation" in pagan antiquity.[6] Israel was now virtually indistinguishable from other nations with respect to the following:

- Its basic political organization as a "nation"
- Its hierarchical structure of government officials and bureaucrats
- Its military and taxation operations
- Its palace architecture
- Its dependence on alliances with other nations
- Its official ideology that the king has been "chosen" by a divine patron
- Its legal system's view that royal initiative and charisma are the repository of justice
- Its temple, designed to serve as that deity's house
- The sacrificial system at the heart of that temple's liturgy

The list goes on. In one sense, it could be argued that Solomon had *not* gone too far in instituting this new Yahwisticism: he had merely gone to the lengths necessary to consolidate the political state that the Israelites two generations earlier had demanded. And Solomon also institutionalized this new religious system, handing it over to a corps of priests and scribes responsible for maintaining the official religious rituals and doctrines. This impulse to preserve religious forms is the chief characteristic of a religion's Traditional Period (see page 6), and as long as the monarchy existed there would be powerful forces exploiting the worship of Yahweh for political ends, identifying it with the temple, the priests, the sacrificial rituals, the king, and the political state itself.

5. It is interesting that the story of Yahweh granting Solomon's wish is set not in Jerusalem but at a shrine in Gibeon, a traditionally non-Israelite town, reinforcing the impression that the "wisdom" Solomon received there was somewhat unorthodox from a purely Yahwist perspective. This gift of wisdom was apparently temporary, virtually gone by the time Solomon began enacting his foolish and destructive taxation policy (1 Kings 11).

6. Contrast this with chapter 1, note 9. This rapid transformation created many ironies. For example, just as Moses had fled into the wilderness to escape the wrath of Pharaoh, so Jeroboam several centuries later fled *to* Pharaoh to escape the wrath of Solomon (1 Kings 11:40). And several centuries after that, when threatened by the Assyrian Empire, Israelite kings dispatched ambassadors south in a desperate attempt "to take refuge in the protection of Pharaoh, and to seek shelter in the shadow of Egypt" (see Isa. 30:1–5; 31:1–3). The Israelites now saw the Egyptian pharaoh as a savior!

The Growing Obsession for Power

Nations exist because power is considered indispensable. The adage "Power corrupts" is only half-true. The other half is expressed in Jotham's fable (see Box 3.2): those who value and seek power are already prone to corruption. Once the exercise of coercive force is considered indispensable, people who want it will begin sacrificing most other ethical considerations to get it and keep it. It is not surprising that practically every member of David's family "sinned"—that is, abandoned the religious ethic of the Sinai covenant—in ways that would have subjected them to the death penalty under the Covenant Code (Exodus 21–23) of the old Yahwist federation. David himself committed adultery with Bathsheba and then engineered the murder of her husband Uriah, one of his own high-ranking officers (2 Samuel 11). David's son Amnon raped his half sister, Tamar; David's other son Absalom then murdered Amnon (2 Samuel 13). Absalom's subsequent rebellion against David (2 Samuel 15–18) was an attempt to dishonor and even kill his father. All these stories are recounted with astonishing candor in the Bible, probably because the writer adhered to the traditional Yahwist morality.

As soon as a power structure is established, those who hold power tend to regard themselves as immune from the ethical obligations that apply to those they govern. Keenly aware of this, the old Yahwist morality insisted that the ethical commitments of the Sinai covenant equally applied to any king who claimed legitimacy from Yahweh. No one was above its religious ethic. But the kings themselves, claiming direct divine appointment and support, did not concede this, nor were the Yahwists in any position to compel them. The stories of the Israelite monarchs in 1–2 Kings are almost universally condemnatory. A few kings are praised for their halfhearted attempts at reform, but all the rest are reviled.[7]

7. So far, this is unprecedented in the annals of any ancient Near Eastern people, demonstrating the degree to which the Hebrew scriptures reflects the religious and ethical perspective of grassroots Yahwism, and not the sociopolitical one of the official Yahwisticism.

The story of the kings after Solomon's death—more so in the northern kingdom than in the southern kingdom—is the story of a constant power struggle, foreshadowed by the one that brought Solomon himself to power (1 Kings 1–2). Adonijah, probably the oldest surviving son of David, had presumed that he was entitled to the throne. He was supported by David's cousin Joab as well as Abiathar, a descendant of the Yahwist priesthood at Shiloh. Both men had been with David since his days as an Apiru fleeing from Saul. With such military and religious support, Adonijah had every reason to expect that his claim would prevail. But Bathsheba's son Solomon was supported by Zadok and Nathan, two men who first appear at David's side only after the capture of Jerusalem and who, like Bathsheba herself, probably came from the non-Israelite aristocracy of the city. Unfortunately, Adonijah had not reckoned with the intrigues of the Jebusite bureaucracy interested in supporting the child of one of their own. Benaiah, the commander of the army, along with David's personal bodyguards, also supported Solomon, who not only won the throne but also later had Abiathar banished and Adonijah and Joab executed.

Prophetic Involvement in Political Power Struggles

The struggles that followed the reign of Solomon were not only between different factions within the army and bureaucracy over power; they also surfaced between the politically dominant Yahwisticism and the village-based Yahwism over the actual content of the culture, specifically its religious values. Often the village perspective was articulated by individuals called "prophets." Conflicts between a Yahwist prophet and the ruling dynasty usually arose because the priorities needed to maintain the political state were incompatible both with Yahwism (which had now been thoroughly adapted to *legitimize* the state) and with the actual well-being of the people. A prime example is Solomon's extravagant expenditures for both military and public construction projects, which so drained the northern tribes' economies that a civil war erupted when Solomon's son and successor Rehoboam refused to pursue a less onerous policy. His refusal is portrayed in the Bible as yet one more example of the arrogance of power and its indifference to ethical concerns (1 Kings 12). The northern tribes split with Rehoboam, creating their own kingdom called "Israel" (or "Ephraim"). The southern tribe of Judah, which remained loyal to Rehoboam, lent its name to the Jerusalem regime of David's dynasty.

Toward the end of Solomon's reign, the prophet Ahijah from Shiloh predicted that his kingdom would soon be torn apart. This prophecy was realized when Jeroboam, a former bureaucrat who had earlier led an unsuccessful revolt against Solomon, returned from exile in Egypt to be crowned the first king of the north (1 Kings 12:20). About twenty years later, the prophet Ahijah reappeared, old and half-blind, with another prediction: because Jeroboam had also strayed from Yahweh's mandate, Yahweh—working through the normal unfolding of historical processes—would soon bring Jeroboam and his dynasty to an end (1 Kings 14).

Jeroboam died a natural death, but his son Nadab was assassinated after ruling only two years. The new king, Baasha, promptly exterminated the rest of Jeroboam's family (1 Kings 15:25–30). He also went on to rule for more than twenty years only to be condemned by a prophet, Jehu son of Hanani, also for departing from the ways of Yahweh. Baasha's son then ruled only two years before being assassinated at a dinner party (1 Kings 16:8–11), and in the week that followed every male in Baasha's family was executed. Out of this political chaos emerged a powerful military leader named Omri (1 Kings 16:15–28). He built a splendid new

Table 5.1 Chronology of the Early Kings and Prophets of Northern Israel

date	archaeology	kings and dynasties of northern Israel	prophets
930 B.C.			
920	IRON AGE I C	Jeroboam I (922–901)	Ahijah of Shiloh
910			
900 B.C.		Nadab (901–900)	
890	IRON AGE II A	Baasha (900–877)	Jehu son of Hanani
880		Elah (877–876) Ethbaal of Sidon	
870		Zimri (7 days) Omri (876–869) Ahab (869–850)——Jezebel	
860			Elijah of Tishbe
850		Ahaziah (850–849)	Micaiah son of Imla
840		Jehoram (849–842) Jehu (842–815)	Elisha of Abel-meholah
830			
820		Jehoahaz (815–801)	
810			
800 B.C.		Jehoash (801–786)	
790	IRON AGE II B	Jeroboam II (786–746)	

city, Samaria, to serve as the new capital of northern Israel (v. 24). His dynasty became so powerful that a century later foreigners referred to northern Israel as the "house of Omri." However, once again prophets such as Elijah of Tishbe were on hand to condemn the Omride kings for betraying Yahweh. And when yet another coup eventually swept away Omri's dynasty, the Yahwist prophet Elisha of Abel-meholah was there to declare this the will of Yahweh.

From the death of Solomon (922 B.C.) to the time of the prophet Amos (about 740 B.C.), the Yahwist prophets tended to blame *the king* for all of society's problems, implying that the social malaise arose from the sins of the rulers, who "went after the Baals and the Asherahs" (i.e., "worshiped" power and wealth), made graven images, and thus caused the nation to sin (e.g., 1 Kings 14:15–16; 15:26, 30). The prophet would then pronounce a divine curse upon the king, depriving him of any further religious legitimacy and invalidating his claim to rule as Yahweh's "chosen one." Of course, not everyone believed the prophet's curse, and ruling kings continued to enjoy varying levels of popularity and support. Whenever a new king would be anointed by a Yahwist prophet, many

8. U.S. Supreme Court justice Benjamin Cardozo noted that "justice" has always been an irrational ideal ("a yearning for what is fine or high"), and that legal procedures inevitably entail compromises to this ideal (*Selected Writings* [1947], 224, 254). Years ago a law student was quoted in the university newspaper as saying, "Justice is a topic for meditation in a monastery." If the political and legal systems with their instruments of coercion are incapable of producing justice, much less love and mercy (i.e., kindness), then people must either learn to live without these things, or else produce and nurture them somewhere else other than government.

Yahwists naively expected that national "sinning" would end now that the right man was in power. Some argue that this prophetic dabbling in politics effectively gave religious license and justification to any political rival who wanted to murder the king; and some kings felt sufficiently threatened by a prophet's ranting to want the prophet dead.

Most of these Yahwist prophets came from rural villages, and as far as they were concerned, a Yahweh who did little more than sanction the political state was clearly not the Yahweh of the Sinai covenant. It would be a mistake to view all this as a clash between religion and politics, when it is actually a clash between two radically different value systems (both of which persist in different forms to this day) surrounded by different types of religious auras. One essentially deifies coercive force, promoting the belief that the ultimate source of prosperity and security is political government (the state). This is what the biblical tradition decries as "Baal worship." The other promotes a faith that is fixed on something transcending social control interests altogether: while refusing to be itself coercive, this faith attempts to create something that governmental power characteristically cannot—love, justice, and mercy.[8] This was the Yahwism of Sinai, which the monarchy had transformed into a Yahwisticism designed to make its underlying worship of Baal less obvious and therefore less offensive to its Yahwist subjects.

Religion in the Northern Kingdom

After he split with the Jerusalem regime in 922 B.C., Jeroboam established cult centers at Dan and Bethel, where he set up "golden calves" (1 Kings 12:25–33). The pro-Jerusalem biblical narrator condemns these golden bulls as the idolatrous "sin of Jeroboam," but they most likely represented Jeroboam's attempt to be multicultural. The Yahwists in his kingdom, and perhaps Jeroboam himself, probably did not regard these as gods in their own right but as cherubim, similar to those that flanked the ark of the covenant in the Jerusalem temple. The non-Yahwists, on the other hand, may well have viewed them in the familiar context of pagan fertility religion, where the bull symbolized the power and affluence guaranteed by the political economy of the state (see Fig. 5.2).

Within two generations of Jeroboam's death, King Omri's regime in Samaria attempted to change divine patrons, substituting Melqart, a Phoenician name for Baal, in place of Yahweh. Omri had made a treaty alliance with the Phoenician king Ethbaal who, according to the first-century-A.D. Jewish historian Josephus, was also the high priest of Melqart. Ethbaal gave his daughter Jezebel in marriage to Omri's son Ahab, who soon thereafter built not only a temple (embassy?) and altar to Baal (Melqart) in Samaria, but also an *'asherah* (1 Kings 16:31–33).[9]

9. We do not know precisely what an *'asherah* was. Some biblical passages suggest it was a pole or a sacred tree or grove of trees, while others present it simply as the name of the Canaanite goddess Asherah.

Figure 5.2

Cherubim. In the ancient world, cherubim were mythological winged bulls ("calves") or winged lions (sphinxes), such as this one that guarded the throne room of the Assyrian king Ashurnasirpal. The Jerusalem temple was adorned with images of such creatures, as were the temples at Dan and Bethel established by King Jeroboam. The modern notion of a cherub (singular) as an angel is post–New Testament.

10. This being the case, *not* to choose either was, in fact, submitting to Baal: people's fears about coming forward reflected, in part, their prior decision to defer to power rather than to ethic. Of course, some people will occasionally risk their necks for a principle, thereby testifying that they defer to ethic rather than power, to what seems right rather than to what best guarantees their own tangible well-being. In the biblical tradition, such people are called "martyrs" (from the Greek word for "witness," i.e., one who attests to the truth).

Jezebel placed 450 prophets of Baal and 400 prophets of Asherah on the royal payroll (1 Kings 18:19).

The Bible recounts that, after several years of drought, the Yahwist prophet Elijah forced a showdown at Mount Carmel between himself, representing Yahweh, and Jezebel's prophets, representing the new order. Elijah challenged those in the assembled crowd to come forward and publicly declare themselves, one way or the other:

> "How long will you go limping with two different opinions? If Yahweh is God, follow him; but if Baal, then follow him." The people did not answer him a word. (1 Kings 18:21)

Apparently no one was going to stick out his neck until it was clear who the "winner" would be.[10] The confrontation ended in a violent thunderstorm and driving rain, which persuaded the euphoric masses to choose Yahweh—and to slaughter the 450 prophets of Baal. The fate of the 400 prophets of Asherah is not mentioned. The Bible reports, rather curious-

Box 5.3—Prophecy at Mari

Prophets were regarded as spokespersons for God. Among the many Amorite cultural traits preserved in ancient Israel was the phenomenon of prophecy. Different types of prophets are attested in the Mari letters, either upbraiding kings for neglecting social justice or reassuring them with politically upbeat predictions (excerpted from *OTPar,* 320):

> To: Zimri-Lim, king of Mari
> From: Nur-Sin, official of Mari
>   ...An apilum prophet of Addu, divine patron of Halab, told me: "I am Addu, your divine patron. I am the divine patron of Halab ... who helped you regain your father's throne. Have I ever asked too much of you? Hear the cry of your people when they suffer injustice. Give them justice. . . . Obey my word. Protect the land. Defend the state."

> To: Zimri-Lim, ruler of Mari
> From: Mukannisum, official of Mari
>   After I offered the sacrifice to Dagan for the king's health, an apilum prophet of Dagan in Tuttul stood up and told me: "Babylon, what do you think you are doing? I will bring you down like a bird with a net. . . . I will give you, your seven covenant partners and all their land to Zimri-Lim."

These prophets (and gods) shared the king's interest in the welfare of the political organization. The second prophecy above proved completely false: Babylon actually defeated Zimri-Lim and destroyed Mari. The Bible mentions similar prophets in Israel giving politically upbeat but false predictions (e.g., Jeremiah 27–28; 1 Kings 22; see also Box 6.4) and parading their own partisan interests as if they were Yahweh's interests.

ly, that Elijah himself ran in front of the chariot of Ahab, all the way back to Jezreel (1 Kings 18:46). This can only mean that, despite fearing a death sentence from Ahab, Elijah was willing to act as Ahab's personal bodyguard.

If true, this episode may attest to a dawning awareness in the prophetic movement that *nations* per se do not sin; consequently, it would be wrong to attribute religious apostasy to royal policy and to hope that apostasy might be abolished either by a new king with different policies or by a bloodbath of apostate prophets. Government inquisitions would solve nothing. Up to this point, the prophetic movement had apparently not appreciated this, naively hoping that a Yahwist religious ethic from village life (where political power is either irrelevant or nonexistent) could be simply transferred to the public domain (which is necessarily characterized by such power). But the episode at Mount Carmel showed that as long as there was private ambivalence about the Yahwist ethic at the grassroots level, it was impractical to hope that it could function publicly at the level of state policy. By running in front of Ahab's chariot, Elijah was saying, in effect, that Ahab could not be blamed or harmed for deferring to Baal when the people themselves shared the same inclination. Because it is *people* (not nations) who sin, the solution cannot be simply a change of regimes at the public level; what was needed was a change of heart at the private level.

Yahweh and the Asherah

Elijah's victory at Mount Carmel hardly meant that the Yahwist faith would now be embraced by a people who so recently had been unwilling to stand up for it. What was won was essentially the guarantee that *the name* of the divine patron of northern Israel would continue to be Yahweh, not Melqart. Otherwise, politics as usual continued in the northern kingdom.

The story of the prophet Micaiah in 1 Kings 22 is illustrative. Late in his reign, Ahab decided to go to war. At the request of his ally, the king of southern Judah, Ahab produced 400 prophets declaring this to be a holy war in which Ahab's forces would prevail. Some scholars have speculated that these may have been the same 400 prophets of Asherah that Jezebel had earlier placed on the royal payroll. The king of Judah, no doubt familiar with the ways of such yes-men, asked for a second opinion. Ahab then grudgingly summoned Micaiah, who was known for his harsh criticisms of the king. The biblical narrator is careful to portray the *social* pressure that was brought to bear on the prophet to deliver a message in the name of Yahweh supporting the interests of the powerful: "The messenger who had gone to summon Micaiah said to him, 'Look, the words of the prophets with one accord are favorable to the king; let your word be like the word of one of them, and speak favorably'" (v. 13). But Micaiah accused the other 400 prophets of speaking under delusions inspired by the spirit of lying, and predicted Ahab's death in battle. Micaiah was then imprisoned until Ahab's triumphant return; but Ahab did not return alive, and we hear no more of Micaiah.

Historical or not, this story reveals the deep divisions between two prophetic parties in ancient Israel, each claiming to speak for Yahweh. One, in fact, deferred to the social, economic, and political interests of the powerful, valuing the social rewards and fearing the legal penalties they dispense. The other—in typical Apiru/Hebrew fashion—essentially discounted the social system altogether, neither desiring its rewards nor fearing its penalties. Instead, it deferred to the ancient Yahwist ethic regardless of its personal cost, holding a bleak vision of what the future would hold if the Israelites' covenant with Yahweh continued to be perverted by the powerful. The guiding ideology of the powerful—and of the government—was Baal worship, except that Baal now happened to be named Yahweh.

A large storage jar uncovered in the ruins of a caravan station at Kuntillet Ajrud in the southern Negeb desert indicates how interchangeable the two deities had become. The site dates to around 800 B.C., about a generation or two after Ahab. The storage jar is covered with drawings and graffiti. One is a blessing invoked in the name of "Yahweh of Samaria and his Asherah." Another conveys a blessing in the name of "Yahweh of Teman and his Asherah." This is completely unexpected. In the Bible, *Baal* (not Yahweh) was the god typically linked to different places (e.g., Baal of Peor, Baal of Hazor) and characteristically paired with Asherah (Judg. 3:7; 2 Kings 23:4; and, of course, 1 Kings 18:19). These inscriptions show that, in the minds of many people, Yahweh had simply become a surrogate Baal.

With the support of Elijah's successor Elisha, an Israelite military commander named Jehu led a coup wiping out the Omri/Ahab dynasty,

Figure 5.3
Drawings and Graffiti from Kuntillet Ajrud.
The inscription invokes blessings in the name of "Yahweh of Samaria and his Asherah." It is unclear whether the three figures are related to the inscription and, if so, whether they are crude attempts to depict these gods.

including Jezebel (2 Kings 9–10). Jehu also massacred all the remaining devotees of Baal/Melqart. He destroyed the graven image of Baal and the temple of Baal that Ahab built in Samaria, converting its ruins into a public latrine. But apparently Jehu did not touch the Asherah that had been erected by Ahab, because we learn (2 Kings 13:6) that it was still standing in Samaria a generation later when Jehu's son Jehoahaz was king there (ca. 815–801 B.C.). In the eyes of this new Israelite regime, Yahweh and Baal could not possibly coexist, but Yahweh and Asherah apparently could, because Yahweh had essentially *become* Baal—a mere symbol of political legitimacy, a "divine patron."

The Iron II Period

11. There are no remains of Solomon's palace complex or his temple to Yahweh, which, if they exist, probably lie buried beneath the inaccessible Haram esh-Sharif (or "Temple Mount") in Jerusalem. Nor is there yet any evidence of the foreign embassies/temples reportedly built in Jerusalem. If Solomon's "Millo" in Jerusalem (1 Kings 9:24) refers to the stepped stone structure archaeologists discovered there (see Fig. 4.3), then its date is debated. The dates of the fortified gates of Hazor, Megiddo, and Gezer—often attributed to Solomon (1 Kings 9:15)—are also being debated by archaeologists. Some scholars interpret this absence of evidence as "evidence of absence," insisting that David and Solomon were fictional characters invented by later scribes.

David's kingdom and Solomon's empire date to the end of the Iron I period (tenth century B.C.), a time for which we have limited archaeological evidence and no evidence at all of Solomon's grandeur or his major building projects reported in the Bible.[11] Jerusalem in the days of David was little more than a fortified town roughly the size of a city block. There were probably only a few observable differences between tenth-century David and Solomon and twelfth-century military dictators such as the Amorite "king" Sihon: (1) David's regime did not arise in the immediate aftermath of the collapsing LB Age; (2) it initially made a token effort to respect regional village interests and traditions; and (3) it lasted longer than Sihon's. Nevertheless, one could view David and especially Solomon—and the subsequent regimes of Jerusalem and Samaria—as just part of a series of urban warlords who, using Bronze Age patterns, were trying to establish petty states in the power vacuum resulting from the absence of large empires.

In the Iron II period (900–586 B.C.), specifically in the century beginning with the establishment of the Omri dynasty (ca. 850 B.C.), inscriptions suddenly begin appearing all across the Near East. This apparent revival of literacy is sometimes linked to the rise of fully mature states, including the so-called Neo-Hittite kingdoms of south-central Turkey (mentioned at the conclusion of chapter 1). Consequently, many historians suggest that Near Eastern civilization began recovering from the collapse of the Bronze Age not in the tenth century B.C. (the time of David and Solomon) but in the ninth century B.C. From this, some claim that the stories of David and Solomon are pure fiction, even though almost all these ninth-century inscriptions allude to preexisting political institutions closer to the times of David and Solomon.

Box 5.4—The Revival of Mature States in the Ninth Century B.C.

The relatively sudden appearance of ninth-century-B.C. inscriptions has led some scholars to conclude that political states reappeared then, and not earlier in the tenth century as the Bible suggests. As in the Israelite kingdoms, the chief god in these inscriptions is regarded as a "divine patron," that is, the supernatural counterpart to the king himself (excerpted from *OTPar,* 158, 161–163).

Stela of Mesha, king of Moab:
> I am Mesha, ruler of Moab from Dibon. My father was the ruler of Moab for thirty years, and I became king after him. . . . Omri, ruler of Israel, invaded Moab year after year because Chemosh, the divine patron of Moab, was angry with his people. When the son of Omri succeeded him during my reign, he bragged: "I too will invade Moab." However, I defeated the son of Omri and drove Israel out of our land forever.

Annals of Hazael of Aram-Damascus:
> [T]he father of my household, invaded Israel. . . . Then the king of Israel invaded the land of my father, and Hadad, my divine patron, made me king. With Hadad riding before me, I marched out of my land and destroyed seventy rulers with their corps of chariots and horsemen. I put [Jehoram], son of [Ahab] and ruler of Israel, and [Ahaz]iahu, son of [Jehoram] and ruler of the house of David, to death.

Annals of Azitiwada of Adana:
> I am Azitiwada, the steward of Baal. I have been raised to my position of authority by my father, Awariku, king of Adana. . . . I filled the temple storehouses of Pa'ar, and greatly increased the supplies of arms and the size of the army at the command of Ba'al and the divine assembly. I dealt harshly with traitors, expelling all troublemakers from the kingdom.

12. In villages, large families are essential to agricultural productivity, and children are seen as valuable assets. In urban centers, however, many children tend to diminish each one's share of the parents' estate and are seen as economic liabilities. This may help explain why child sacrifice was practiced at certain times in the ancient Near East.

The recovery of civilization also resulted in economic surplus, which unfortunately tended to divide urban and village populations further. The latter tends to invest a surplus in having more children and larger families,[12] while the former tends to spend it on public works, chief of which is often the military, which soon must be deployed if for no other reason than to justify its expense. It did not take long before the nascent states of Syria-Palestine began pitting their armies against one another. The Assyrians of northern Iraq soon deployed their impressive military apparatus in a westward expansion that was resisted by coalitions of smaller states, each with its own imposing army. For example, the advance of the Assyrian king Shalmaneser III in 853 B.C. was halted by a bloc of states including Ahab's Israel, which reportedly supplied two thousand chariots and ten thousand soldiers. Shalmaneser III proved to be more formidable when he returned about ten years later, extracting taxes from most of these states, including the Israel of King Jehu (see Fig. 6.3).

As soon as the Assyrian threat began to wane after 800 B.C., the states of Syria and Palestine again went to war with each other. But the eighth century B.C. also seems to have been a time of some prosperity, due in part to the restoration of international trade routes, including the incense route of western Arabia. Economic surplus not directed toward the military now went to personal indulgence. The archaeological record confirms the proliferation of luxury goods among the wealthy of Samaria.

By 745 B.C., the Assyrian Empire had resumed its southward push toward the states of Syria and Palestine, who once again desperately dispatched ambassadors to each other's capitals in the hopes of forging alliances that would save them from the invaders.

Figure 5.4

Samaria Ivory. Luxury goods such as this were unearthed in the ruins of Samaria. The person who purchased this cherub carved out of imported ivory had expensive tastes in art. The eighth-century-B.C. Israelite prophets denounced the moral indifference of the wealthy aristocrats of Samaria.

Box 5.5—Affluence, Corruption, and the Plight of the Poor

The eighth-century-B.C. biblical prophets note the conspicuous consumption among affluent Israelites. In the first passage, "Joseph" metaphorically represents the people of the northern kingdom of Israel.

> Alas for those who lie on beds of ivory,
>   and lounge on their couches,
> and eat lambs from the flock,
>   and calves from the stall;
> who sing idle songs to the sound of the harp,
>   and like David improvise on instruments of music;
> who drink wine from bowls,
>   and anoint themselves with the finest oils,
>   but are not grieved over the ruin of Joseph! (Amos 6:4–6)

> Ah, you who rise early in the morning
>   in pursuit of strong drink,
> who linger in the evening
>   to be inflamed by wine,
> whose feasts consist of lyre and harp,
>   tambourine and flute and wine,
> but who do not regard the deeds of Yahweh,
>   or see the work of his hands! (Isa. 5:11–12)

These prophets also show how economic profit motives induced many Israelites to ignore the basic ethical thrust of the Yahwist covenant:

> Hear this, you that trample on the needy,
>   and bring to ruin the poor of the land,
> saying, "When will the new moon be over
>   so that we may sell grain;
> and the sabbath,
>   so that we may offer wheat for sale?
> We will make the ephah [i.e., value] small and the shekel [i.e., price] great,
>   and practice deceit with false balances,
> buying the poor for silver
>   and the needy for a pair of sandals." (Amos 8:4–6)

> Alas for those who devise wickedness
>   and evil deeds on their beds!
> When the morning dawns, they perform it,
>   because it is in their power.
> They covet fields, and seize them;
>   houses, and take them away;
> they oppress householder and house,
>   people and their inheritance. (Mic. 2:1–2)

> Ah, you who make iniquitous decrees,
>   who write oppressive statutes,
> to turn aside the needy from justice
>   and to rob the poor of my people of their right,
> that widows may be your spoil,
>   and that you may make orphans your prey!
> What will you do on the day of punishment,
>   in the calamity that will come from far away? (Isa. 10:1–3)

The First "Canonical" Prophets

13. This insight is actually embedded in the story of the rise of Israelite kingship (1 Samuel 8). The popular demand for a human king was a *consequence* of the fact that the people had already rejected the authority of Yahweh. They were looking for some principles to govern their communal life other than the religious ethic of the Sinai covenant. Religious problems are thus ultimately rooted in the *values and choices of the people*, not in the *policies of the king*.

14. Interestingly, this heterogeneous mix of foreigners eventually became united by their embrace of the god Yahweh, to whom they built a temple not far from Samaria. By New Testament times they were called "Samaritans" (e.g., John 4), many of whom apparently embraced the early Christian movement (Acts 8:1–25; 9:31; 15:3). From the outset, southern Judaeans considered their Yahwism unorthodox because it rejected the sanctity of Jerusalem (see Luke 9:51–53; the Judaean disdain for them is obvious in 2 Kings 17:29–41). On the other hand, Samaritans always considered their form of Yahwism more authentic than the Judaean form. The few surviving Samaritans today still use an ancient text of the Pentateuch that has some noticeable differences from the text used by Jews and Christians.

The Yahwist prophets after about 740 B.C., beginning with Amos and Hosea, are called "canonical" prophets because their words have been preserved in Old Testament books bearing their names. They are part of the "sacred canon" (see Appendix A).

These prophets exhibit a much greater maturity of thought than did earlier prophets such as Ahijah of Shiloh, Jehu son of Hanani, Elijah, and Elisha. They understood that the king was a *symptom*, not a *cause* of the problem.[13] They leveled no divine curses against kings, nor were they political activists seeking to install a better government and to deploy its power against apostates. They recognized that the king usually did whatever was demanded or expected of him by the most influential members of society and that he would, in turn, be imitated by others seeking to curry royal favor. This is why these prophetic oracles were directed against *the people*. Amos and Hosea (and those who followed them) were adamant that the political sector was beyond redemption, meaning that it was incapable of effecting the urgently needed changes in people's ethical and spiritual commitments. Viewing the state as religiously irrelevant, they predicted its destruction—both in Israel and in Judah. Their predictions began coming true in 722 B.C., when the Assyrians captured and destroyed Samaria. The Assyrians deported large numbers of the Yahwist and non-Yahwist population of northern Israel to distant parts of the Assyrian Empire, resettling in Samaria various other conquered peoples from distant parts of their empire (2 Kings 17:24).[14]

A major reason the words of these prophets were remembered and eventually preserved in biblical books was that their prophecies came true. Another reason was that their oracles and sermons relied heavily on the old Sinai covenant tradition and its ethic. Prophetic utterances—often in poetry—were thus both a vindication and a preservation of the old Yahwism that had been largely eclipsed by the official Yahwisticisms of Jerusalem and Samaria. It is hardly a surprise that most of these prophets came from small villages such as Tekoa (Amos), Moresheth (Micah), and Anathoth (Jeremiah).

The canonical prophets consistently condemned the political corruption of the influential elite and their disregard for the poor and defenseless, including widows and orphans. These prophets saw a society increasingly stratified and class-bound, whose citizens were self-centered and heartless. It was a society marked by conspicuous consumption on the part of the wealthy, the use of law for profit at the expense of the weak, the ruthless acquisition of land by certain prominent families, and the use of ritual for self-congratulation and status. The prophets also condemned the intrigues and compromises of international power politics, which eventually destroyed both Israel and Judah.

Sinai Covenant Traditions in Amos and Hosea

One need not read much of Amos and Hosea to see how deeply these prophets adhered to the essence of the Sinai covenant. Its importance is invoked in the very words with which Amos hears Yahweh address Israel: "You only have I *known* of all the families of the earth" (3:2). The Hebrew word *yada'*, translated as "know," is a covenant term with parallels in LB Age Hittite treaties. It refers to the establishment of a direct covenant relationship. Israel is the only people yet to have enjoyed a covenant relationship with Yahweh. Various specific elements of the Sinai covenant tradition, which have parallels in LB treaties (cf. Box 2.3), appear throughout their oracles:

Historical Foundation. Israel's covenant relationship with Yahweh had been based on *past blessings* received, a notion these (and other) prophets affirmed. They "heard" Yahweh constantly reminding the Israelites of the benefits they had received from Yahweh, who says,

> . . . I brought you up out of the land of Egypt,
>   and led you forty years in the wilderness,
>   to possess the land of the Amorite. (Amos 2:10)

> Yet I have been Yahweh your God
>   ever since the land of Egypt;
> you know [*yada'*] no God but me,
>   and besides me there is no savior.
> It was I who fed you in the wilderness,
>   in the land of drought. (Hos. 13:4–5)

Obligations. The prophets contrast these (and other) benefits the Israelites have received from Yahweh with their current neglect of their *covenant commitments and responsibilities*. As above, the speaker here is Yahweh:

> For I know how many are your transgressions,
>   and how great are your sins—
> you who afflict the righteous, who take a bribe,
>   and push aside the needy in the gate. (Amos 5:12)

> There is no faithfulness or loyalty,
>   and no knowledge of God in the land.
> Swearing, lying, and murder,
>   and stealing and adultery break out;
>   bloodshed follows bloodshed. (Hos. 4:1–2)

These neglected obligations have to do with the *dynamic* sense of what it meant to worship Yahweh (i.e., an operating commitment to a religious ethic and value system that transcends self-interest). As far as these divine spokesmen were concerned, this had nothing to do with the *formal* sense of what it meant to worship Yahweh (i.e., participating in ritual ceremonies). Again, the speaker is Yahweh:

> I hate, I despise your festivals,
>> and I take no delight in your solemn assemblies.
> Even though you offer me your burnt offerings and grain
>> offerings,
>> I will not accept them;
> and the offerings of well-being of your fatted animals
>> I will not look upon.
> Take away from me the noise of your songs;
>> I will not listen to the melody of your harps.
> But let justice roll down like waters,
>> and righteousness like an ever-flowing stream. (Amos 5:21–24)

15. Hosea's word for "knowledge" here (and also in 4:1, previously cited) is a form of the Hebrew *yada'*. The prophet declares that a covenant relationship with Yahweh, marked by "steadfast love" (Hebrew *hesed,* selflessly "doing good"), is better than participation in liturgical ceremonies.

> . . . I desire steadfast love and not sacrifice,
>> the knowledge of God rather than burnt offerings. (Hos. 6:6)[15]

This displacement of the Yahwism of Sinai by a different religious value system ("Yahwisticism") is deemed as scandalous as the abandonment of a legitimate marriage in order to spend time in "whoredom" with illicit lovers (Hos. 4:12; 9:1; see also Jer. 3:1–10; Ezekiel 16).

Witnesses. These prophets frequently made appeals to nature itself as a *witness* to Israel's sworn obligation to abide by its covenant commitments. Earlier we noted the parallels to the archaic treaty tradition (see Box 2.4).

Curses. Given the popular disregard for these Yahwist commitments, the prophets regarded the future as grim: *curses* (i.e., historical calamities) will soon befall the entire community, not just the political leadership. The language depicting the "wrath of God" tried, albeit in vain, to show the entire population the grave danger of continuing to embrace the "Baalist" veneration of power and affluence that was now inducing them to take up arms against the powerful Assyrian Empire:

I saw Yahweh standing beside the altar, and he said:
Strike the capitals until the thresholds shake,
    and shatter them on the heads of all the people;
and those who are left I will kill with the sword;
    not one of them shall flee away,
    not one of them shall escape.
. . . .
And though they go into captivity in front of their enemies,
    there I will command the sword, and it shall kill them;
and I will fix my eyes on them
    for harm and not for good. (Amos 9:1, 4)

So I will become like a lion to them,
    like a leopard I will lurk beside the way.
I will fall upon them like a bear robbed of her cubs,
    and will tear open the covering of their heart.
. . . .
I will destroy you, O Israel,
    who can help you?
. . . .
they shall fall by the sword,
    their little ones shall be dashed in pieces,
    and their pregnant women ripped open. (Hos. 13:7–9, 16)

The Wrath of God

16. Many people feel that a religion dwelling on divine anger and vengeance loses some of its power to uplift and inspire its followers. This was essentially the argument that Marcion gave in the second century A.D. for severing Christianity from the Old Testament. For him, the God who, in Christ, lovingly forgives

Because such passages are usually regarded as religious, it is tempting to suppose that the language here provides a glimpse into the author's understanding of the nature and temperament of God. Assuming that the role of religion is to inform us of otherworldly realities, such passages portraying an intolerant and murderously angry Yahweh are disturbing. Indeed, many people through the ages have often disparaged this biblical image of a violent and vengeful God, as if human beings were not violent, and as if history itself were not full of cruel and devastating vengeance.[16]

In one sense, these "wrath of God" passages are not even about God, much less God's temperament. A second reading shows that they are about the actual historical consequences of the collapse of social order. They are about refugees, about human violence, about humanity's unspeakable capacity for cruelty, and about a widespread disregard for human life. They concern not realities in heaven but those here on earth. Linking these terrible things to an angry God was merely the Hebrew way of saying that human beings inevitably pay a terribly high—and terribly real—price when they neglect their fundamental ethical commitments.

sins could not be the same as the one who, in the Old Testament, angrily punishes sinners. Marcion's fellow Christians in Rome considered his views heretical and dropped all religious fellowship with him. Nevertheless, Marcion's "heretical" views seem to be accepted by many Christians today.

In other words, the God who works through the processes of history simply does not tolerate such persistent contempt for the principles that dignify human life: Yahweh "gets angry" when human beings "sin."

Under these circumstances, an uplifting and inspiring picture of a more benign Yahweh presents an ethical problem. Is the alternative to the picture of an angry God at war against human ruthlessness indeed the picture of a smiling God unaffected by it? Is the price for this picture of a good-tempered God to be paid by the innocent who must, as a result of this picture, continue to suffer at the hands of the wicked, whose ruthlessness now constitutes no offense against the sacred? From the perspective of the innocent—and it is their perspective to which the biblical prophets were especially attuned—there is nothing attractive about such a God. On the contrary, there is something cruel about such cosmic indifference. In the Bible, it is Yahweh's wrath that brings about salvation by finally destroying the source of injustice and suffering. A god who cannot get angry is a god who cannot "save" anyone.

Complaining that the Old Testament does not provide a more uplifting picture of God, history, and human nature misses a central aspect of Hebrew faith, which is to engage human beings meaningfully with the shared realities they experience, in the hope that genuine community can result.

"Repentance"

17. Those who insist that Israelite religion (or the ethical thrust of Yahwism) originated here with these prophets have not yet explained why the biblical tradition does not cast them as religious innovators. If they were indeed the founders of this faith, it is curious that the tradition does not celebrate them as such; instead, it depicts them advocating a return to an older, preexisting faith.

The benefits of political power, regarded as the source of all blessings (such as peace and prosperity), had become the "ultimate concern" many Israelites were most afraid to be without. The prophets were trying desperately to find a transcendent position by which, with the grace of God, this might somehow change. "Repentance"—literally "returning" to Yahwism (and therefore to the Yahweh of the Sinai covenant)—is a reorientation *away from* this reliance on political coercion *toward* another, more transcendent perspective eliciting different choices and more constructive patterns of living.[17] A major theme of the biblical prophets is that such repentance might well forestall historical calamity (i.e., the wrath of Yahweh):

> Seek good and not evil,
>   that you may live;
> and so Yahweh, the God of hosts, will be with you,
>   just as you have said.
> Hate evil and love good,
>   and establish justice in the gate;
> it may be that Yahweh, the God of hosts,
>   will be gracious to the remnant of Joseph. (Amos 5:14–15)

> Sow for yourselves righteousness;
>> reap steadfast love;
>> break up your fallow ground;
> for it is time to seek Yahweh,
>> that he may come and rain righteousness upon you. (Hos. 10:12)

> But as for you, return to your God,
>> hold fast to love and justice,
>> and wait continually for your God. (Hos. 12:6)

All such hopes aside, Hosea was also realistic about the chances of such repentance actually occurring. Yahweh speaks:

> I know Ephraim,
>> and Israel is not hidden from me;
> for now, O Ephraim, you have played the whore;
>> Israel is defiled.
> Their deeds do not permit them
>> to return to their God.
> For the spirit of whoredom is within them,
>> and they do not know Yahweh. (Hos. 5:3–4)

> You have plowed wickedness,
>> you have reaped injustice,
>> you have eaten the fruit of lies.
> Because you have trusted in your power
>> and in the multitude of your warriors,
> therefore the tumult of war shall rise against your people,
>> and all your fortresses shall be destroyed. (Hos. 10:13–14)

The frightening prospect is that the people of Yahweh must soon learn to live without the one thing they have become most afraid to lose—the benefits of political power.

Yahwism as a Universal Religion

The kingdom of Israel—and eventually Judah also—was apparently beyond redemption. But the prophets also provided a hopeful analysis: the violence to come would not destroy or undermine the religious ethic embedded in the Sinai covenant tradition. In other words, to lose the benefits of political power was not to lose the favor of Yahweh, who refuses to be identified with it. In this regard, the prophet who articulated Yahweh's wrath so starkly also articulated Yahweh's compassion for Israel:

> How can I give you up, Ephraim?
>   How can I hand you over, O Israel?
> . . . .
> My heart recoils within me;
>   my compassion grows warm and tender.
> I will not execute my fierce anger;
>   I will not again destroy Ephraim;
> for I am God and no mortal,
>   the Holy One in your midst,
>   and I will not come in wrath. (Hos. 11:8–9)

Furthermore, the Sinai covenant was a set of commitments that transcended the specifics of culture; therefore, anyone—hence, everyone—could potentially embrace it. Yahweh was the God of any person who was willing to be ruled by him, not just Judaeans and Israelites. This inclusivism later became extremely important, especially for Christianity. It is already implicit in the Sinai covenant tradition itself (see chapter 2) and is demonstrated in its early capacity to serve as the sole bond unifying the diverse population of early Iron Age Palestine and Transjordan prior to the monarchy of David and Solomon (see chapter 3). The prophet Amos was one of the first to develop this universalism further:

> Cross over to Calneh, and see;
>   from there go to Hamath the great;
>   then go down to Gath of the Philistines.
> Are you better than these kingdoms?
>   Or is your territory greater than their territory? (Amos 6:2)

> Are you not like the Ethiopians to me,
>   O people of Israel? says Yahweh.
> Did I not bring Israel up from the land of Egypt,
>   and the Philistines from Caphtor
>   and the Arameans from Kir? (Amos 9:7)

Yahweh is not merely the validating symbol of ancient Samaria or Judah, or of the United States, or of any nation. His interests and welfare are not linked to theirs. Yahweh has nothing to do with parochial political power, authority, or legitimacy. The Bible presents Yahweh instead as an impartial "god of history" whose rule is identified not in the religious systems of particular groups (he is *no one*'s "divine patron") but in the historical processes that enmesh all peoples and nations, processes that sometimes leave great devastation in their wake. In this sense, Yahweh shows no partiality to any culture, nation, or ethnic group, a point later emphasized by

Paul (Rom. 2:11). If the historical process itself is the exercise of divine governance, then Yahweh is free to use these pagan nations to "punish" *anyone* who has rejected the ethic that constitutes the divine will (see Appendix B).

But only true prophets could ascertain God's presence and purposeful activity within the observable processes of history, rather than within the partisan politics of those who were superficially God's most ardent cheerleaders. For the rest, the so-called false prophets, Yahweh was a divine patron of the political state and its leading citizens, first in the monarchy of David and Solomon (tenth century B.C.) and then in the kingdoms of Israel and Judah (ninth–sixth centuries B.C.).

Usually, when ancient Near Eastern states ceased to exist, so did the religious systems that had upheld them. Archaeologists must literally dig them up out of the dirt in which they were so long ago buried. But this was not the case with the biblical tradition. This is because the religious faith of Israel (Yahwism) had existed for centuries prior to the Israelite state, and within the prophetic movement it survived in a grassroots form quite distinct from the official Yahwisticism linking Yahweh to this or that temple, or this or that political regime, or this or that Asherah. Even after northern Israel had been destroyed by the Assyrians in 722 B.C., and southern Judah (Jerusalem) by the Babylonians in 586 B.C., the religion of Yahweh persisted because something within it was intrinsically valuable *to human beings* regardless of their cultural and ethnic backgrounds, and independent of the political regimes and social institutions that exploited and distorted the religion in the guise of promoting it.

The faith remained viable even though the political state did not, something else the prophets correctly predicted—a surviving remnant would remain to keep it alive:

> The eyes of the Lord Yahweh are upon the sinful kingdom,
>   and I will destroy it from the face of the earth
>   —except that I will not utterly destroy the house of Jacob,
>   says Yahweh. (Amos 9:8)

Suggestions for Further Reading

Additional information on the topics discussed in this chapter can be found in the following sources.

Dictionary/Encyclopedia Entries

Anchor Bible Dictionary: Ahab; Jezebel; Kuntillet Ajrud; Levites and Priests; Phoenicia, History of; Phoenician Religion; Propaganda;

Prophecy; Sacrifice and Sacrificial Offerings; Samaritans; Solomon; Temple, Jerusalem; Wrath of God (OT); Zadok

Solomon and Religious Institutions

L. Grabbe, *Priests, Prophets, Sages: A Socio-Historical Study of Religious Specialists in Ancient Israel.* Valley Forge, Pa.: Trinity Press, 1995.

E. W. Heaton, *Solomon's New Men: The Emergence of Ancient Israel as a National State.* New York: Pica, 1974.

T. Mullen, "The Sins of Jeroboam." *CBQ* 49 (1987): 212–232.

The Hebrew Prophets

J. Bright, *Covenant and Promise: The Prophetic Understanding of the Future in Pre-Exilic Israel.* Philadelphia: Fortress Press, 1976.

A. Heschel, *The Prophets.* 2 vols. New York: Harper & Row, 1963.

H. Huffmon, "The Covenant Lawsuit in the Prophets." *JBL* 78 (1959): 285–295.

P. J. King, *Amos, Hosea, Micah—An Archaeological Commentary.* Philadelphia: Westminster Press, 1988.

Six

Josiah Reforms the Imperial Religion: The Traditional Period(II)—The Troubling Legacy of the Monarchy

Suggested Reading

Isaiah and Ahaz: Isaiah 6–7
Ahaz and Hezekiah: 2 Kings 16–20

Southern Judah after Solomon

Despite his military buildup, Solomon failed to maintain much control over such outlying territories as Aram/Damascus and Edom. The financial setback caused by the loss of their tax revenues was probably a major reason for the disastrous policies of his son and successor, Rehoboam (see 1 Kings 12). Rehoboam's senior advisers recognized—and he clearly did *not*—that these were desperate times: the issue was not *whether* the Jerusalem bureaucracy would have to be more frugal, but rather *how much* more frugal it would now have to be. The refusal of Rehoboam and his junior advisers to deal with this reality triggered the secession of the more affluent and populous northern tribes, further depleting the tax revenues and royal treasury of Jerusalem.

In chapter 5 we focused on the challenges the Yahwist faith encountered in the secessionist northern kingdom of Israel. Now we will focus on how it fared in the southern kingdom of Judah. At the official level, this faith—what we have called Yahwisticism—was now the purview of conservative priestly and scribal specialists whose first priority, in typical ancient Near Eastern fashion, was to assist government leaders in preserving social order. This required that the worship of Yahweh become formally identifiable and institutionally fixed; consequently, under the auspices of these religious specialists from the time of Solomon on, it entered what we call a traditional period. Most of the traditions concerning the faith's early days—its formative and adaptive periods—were solidified in official ways that accommodated post-Solomonic realities. Committed to writing, this Jerusalem-based perspective on Israel's faith would eventually characterize much of the biblical literature. From this point on, any changes or adaptations to the tenets of Yahweh worship would encounter stiff resistance from the Jerusalem authorities.

The loss of its northern territories meant that the Jerusalem regime was comparatively slow to recover economically. By the eighth century B.C. some prosperity had returned to Jerusalem, suggested by the expansion of the city to the hill west of the City of David (see Fig. 4.3). The incessant rivalries among Judah, Israel, and their neighboring states played into the hands of the Assyrians to the east. Although a coalition of these states had managed to slow the Assyrian advance in 853 B.C., they were less successful when the Assyrians returned a century later.

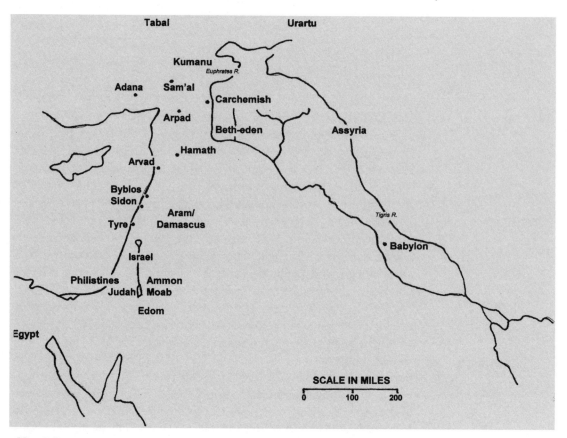

Map 6.1
Political States in the Iron II Period. By 850 B.C. the dark age following the LB Age had ended as new states appeared. These included the so-called Neo-Hittite kingdoms of the Tabal federation, Kumanu, and the city-states of Adana, Sam'al (capital of Ya'diya), Carchemish, and Arpad. The kingdoms surrounding Israel and Judah are all listed in Amos 1–2. The Assyrians and Babylonians to the east eventually developed powerful empires.

King Ahaz and "Immanuel"

1. We have observed that some prophets were harshly critical of those who regarded the welfare of the state as essential to the well-being of the people.

The westward expansion of the Assyrian Empire intensified after 745 B.C. The smaller states of Syria, Palestine, and Transjordan scrambled to forge coalitions, hoping that treaties and alliances could save the state.[1] Two of these states—Aram (or Syria), led by King Rezin of Damascus, and Israel, led by King Pekah of Samaria—tried unsuccessfully to draw Ahaz, the recently crowned king of Judah (ruled ca. 735–715 B.C.), into their anti-Assyrian coalition. The two then began plotting against him, hoping to topple Ahaz and replace him with a king more committed to war against Assyria (2 Kings 16:5; Isaiah 7). These international tensions are referred to as the Syro-Ephraimite War of 734 B.C.

The prophet Isaiah appeared in the midst of this crisis, eager to give Ahaz a sign that Yahweh would not abandon him. Referring to a well-known woman who was at the time pregnant, Isaiah reassured Ahaz that Yahweh would honor the covenant with David, in which Yahweh pledged that the throne would always remain with David's descendants:

> "Therefore the Lord himself will give you a sign. Look, the young woman is with child and shall bear a son, and shall name him Immanuel. . . . For before the child knows how to refuse the evil and choose the good, the land before whose two kings you are in dread will be deserted." (Isa. 7:14, 16)

In other words, within a few years the crisis will have passed, those who conspire against Ahaz will be gone, and the throne of Judah will remain securely with the dynasty of David. The name of the child to be born was symbolic: "Immanuel" means "God (is) with us."

There are numerous problems of interpretation associated with the significance and context of this prediction, particularly concerning the identity of the pregnant woman in question. But whoever she was, Isaiah's prediction turned out to be more or less accurate: within twelve years both Damascus and Samaria (the northern kingdom of Israel) lay in ruins.

But the pragmatic Ahaz had apparently doubted Isaiah's prophecy and had chosen to respond less as a Yahwist and more as a politician, trusting in political alliances rather than Yahweh's movement in history. He had offered tribute to the Assyrian king as a token of his submission, thus guaranteeing that the Assyrians would help rescue him from his foes in Damascus and northern Israel. At the same time this action demonstrated Ahaz's commitment to a *political* definition of the Israelite community as opposed to a *religious* one; in biblical parlance, he had trusted Assyria rather than Yahweh. Ironically, his submission to the Assyrians exposed

Table 6.1 Chronology of Southern Judah

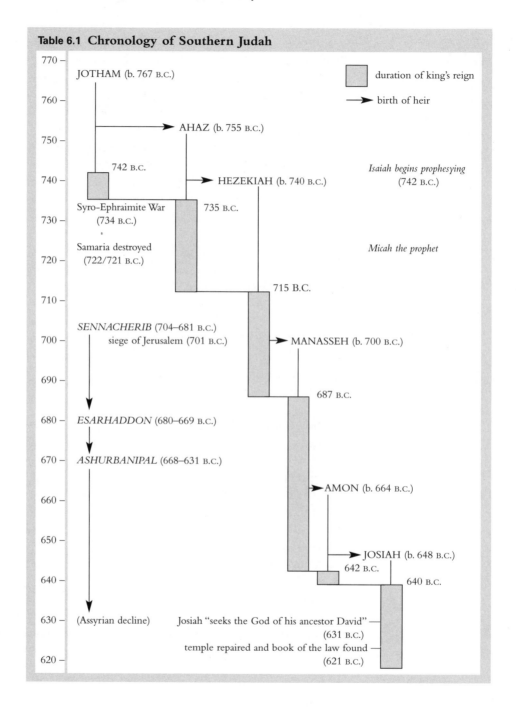

770 —

JOTHAM (b. 767 B.C.)

760 —

AHAZ (b. 755 B.C.)

750 —

742 B.C.

Isaiah begins prophesying
(742 B.C.)

740 —

HEZEKIAH (b. 740 B.C.)

Syro-Ephraimite War
(734 B.C.)   735 B.C.

730 —

Samaria destroyed   *Micah the prophet*
(722/721 B.C.)

720 —

715 B.C.

710 —

SENNACHERIB (704–681 B.C.)
siege of Jerusalem (701 B.C.)

700 —   MANASSEH (b. 700 B.C.)

690 —

687 B.C.

ESARHADDON (680–669 B.C.)

680 —

670 —   *ASHURBANIPAL* (668–631 B.C.)

660 —   AMON (b. 664 B.C.)

650 —   JOSIAH (b. 648 B.C.)

642 B.C.

640 —   640 B.C.

(Assyrian decline)   Josiah "seeks the God of his ancestor David"
(631 B.C.)

630 —

temple repaired and book of the law found
(621 B.C.)

620 —

duration of king's reign

→ birth of heir

Box 6.1 Assyrian Influence on Deuteronomy?

Ahaz's eighth-century-B.C. vassal treaty with the Assyrians would not have followed the covenant form of the Bronze Age (see Box 2.3) but would probably have taken the form of an eighth-century-B.C. Assyrian loyalty oath. Like covenants, loyalty oaths contained curses against any disloyal vassal, curses that were presumably well known throughout the Assyrian Empire. Some scholars believe that Deuteronomy 28 was written by a Judaean scribe copying directly from the Assyrian vassal treaties, such as those of Esarhaddon, who ruled 680–669 B.C. (excerpted from *ANET*[3], 538–39).

Covenant Curses in Deuteronomy 28	*Curses in Esarhaddon's Vassal Treaties*
The sky over your head shall be bronze, and the earth under you iron. Yahweh will change the rain of your land into powder, and only dust shall come down upon you from the sky until you are destroyed. (vv. 23–24)	May all the gods who are named in this treaty . . . turn your soil into iron. . . . Just as rain does not fall from a copper sky, so . . . let it rain burning coals in your land instead of dew. (nos. 63–64)
Your corpses shall be food for every bird of the air and animal of the earth, and there shall be no one to frighten them away. (v. 26)	May Ninurta, leader of the gods, . . . give your flesh to eagles and vultures to feed upon. May Palil, lord of first rank, let eagles and vultures eat your flesh. (nos. 41, 59)
Yahweh will afflict you with madness, blindness, and confusion of mind; you shall grope about at noon as blind people grope in darkness, but you shall be unable to find your way. (vv. 28–29)	[Y]our days should be somber, your years dark, may [the great gods of heaven and earth] decree for you an unrelieved darkness, your lives should end in sighs and sleeplessness. (no. 56)
You shall become engaged to a woman, but another man shall lie with her. (v. 30)	May Venus, the brightest among the stars, let your wives lie in the embrace of your enemy before your very eyes. (no. 42)
In the desperate straits to which the enemy siege reduces you, you will eat the fruit of your womb, the flesh of your own sons and daughters whom Yahweh your God has given you. (v. 53)	[M]ay you eat in your hunger the flesh of your children. . . . so may he [the god Shamash?] make you eat in your hunger the flesh of your brothers, your sons, and your daughters. (nos. 47, 69)

Judah to all sorts of Assyrian cultural influences, including the Assyrian-style altar that Ahaz constructed in the Jerusalem temple (2 Kings 16:10–18). Although it is impossible to say precisely which of them were due to Assyrian influences, it is clear that there were important cultural changes in Judah in the eighth century B.C., especially in religious ideology and cultic practice. It is possible that the Yahwistic priests in Jerusalem considered this a threat to the established religious order in Jerusalem they had helped to create.

Hezekiah, Sennacherib, and Zion

Ahaz's son and successor, Hezekiah (ruled 715–687 B.C.), soon began to test the resolve of his Assyrian overlords. Jerusalem now became the center of a new coalition seeking independence from Assyrian control. Believing an eventual Assyrian siege to be inevitable, Hezekiah had his engineers construct a winding tunnel, redirecting the waters of the city's subterranean spring to a reservoir pool now safely inside the walls of the city (see Fig. 4.3).

The Assyrian response to the rebels was King Sennacherib's ruthless "scorched earth" policy of 701 B.C. His forces demolished town after town. Even fortified cities such as Lachish were leveled by the Assyrian siege engines. Isaiah predicted and lamented the devastation:

> Your country lies desolate,
>   your cities are burned with fire;
> in your very presence
>   aliens devour your land;
>   it is desolate, as overthrown by foreigners.
> And daughter Zion is left
>   like a booth in a vineyard,
> like a shelter in a cucumber field,
>   like a besieged city. (Isa. 1:7–8)

The Assyrian siege of Jerusalem began. Some prophets, such as Micah, not only felt that Jerusalem would be destroyed but that it *should* be destroyed for its perverse twisting of authentic Yahwism:

> Its rulers give judgment for a bribe,
>   its priests teach for a price,
>   its prophets give oracles for money;
> yet they lean upon Yahweh and say,
>   "Surely Yahweh is with us!
>   No harm shall come upon us."
> Therefore because of you
>   Zion shall be plowed as a field;
> Jerusalem shall become a heap of ruins,
>   and the mountain of the house a wooded height.
>   (Mic. 3.11–12)

Others, such as Isaiah, felt that (for the moment) Yahweh still had a commitment to the welfare of Jerusalem, and that consequently the Assyrian siege would fail:

> "Therefore thus says Yahweh concerning the king of Assyria: He shall not come into this city, shoot an arrow there, come before it with a shield, or cast up a siege ramp against it. . . . For I will defend this city to save it, for my own sake and for the sake of my servant David." (Isa. 37:33, 35)

Figure 6.1
Siege of Lachish. The palace reliefs discovered at Nineveh included scenes of the 701 B.C. Assyrian siege and capture of Lachish, thirty miles southwest of Jerusalem. Battering rams approach the city up paved earth-ramps, while Judaean defenders throw torches from the parapets hoping to set the battering rams afire. Refugees or prisoners are shown leaving the city (*bottom right*). The Assyrian siege of Lachish is alluded to in 2 Kings 17:13–17. See also Fig. 7.1.

What became important to later generations of Judaeans, however, was not that Sennacherib's forces cut a swath of death and destruction across the Judaean countryside, but that the residents of Jerusalem narrowly escaped it, just as Isaiah had predicted:

> Like birds hovering overhead, so Yahweh of hosts
>   will protect Jerusalem;
> he will protect and deliver it,
>   he will spare and rescue it. (Isa. 31:5)

A deadly epidemic in the Assyrian camps, depicted in the Bible as an "act of God" (2 Kings 19:35), had forced Sennacherib to end the siege, but he had exacted a heavy fine from Hezekiah for his disloyalty (2 Kings 18:13–15). While Sennacherib's annals refer to this siege, they understandably include no reference to any Assyrian setback:

> But as for Hezekiah, the Jew, who did not bow in submission to my yoke, forty-six of his strong walled towns and innumerable smaller villages in their neighbourhood I besieged and conquered by stamping down earth-ramps and then bringing up battering rams. . . . He himself I shut up like a caged bird within Jerusalem, his royal city. . . . the awful splendour of my lordship overwhelmed him, and . . . together with 30 talents of gold, 300 talents of silver, precious stones, . . . all kinds of valuable treasures, . . . he sent me later to Nineveh, my lordly city. (*DOTT*, 67; compare 2 Kings 18:13–15)

The inability of the Assyrians to capture Jerusalem gave rise to an idea with far-reaching consequences: that Yahweh would *never* under any circumstances permit the destruction of Jerusalem and its temple. This doctrine of the inviolability of Zion—already implicit within the Davidic covenant—lulled the politicians and aristocrats of Jerusalem into a false confidence and sense of security, at a time when clerical leaders were eager to win their favor by promoting an upbeat religion of peace and prosperity (Mic. 2:6, 11; 3:5–6; Isa. 30:9–11). This triumphalistic posturing powerfully reinforced the notion that Yahweh was indeed the divine patron—or Baal-protector—of the state, a notion that actually found expression in a number of biblical psalms apparently written at this time. This Judaean Yahwisticism depicted a Yahweh who, when tested, would always protect his anointed king (Davidic dynasty) and holy city (Jerusalem).[2] The military defense of the Jerusalem state was Yahweh's highest priority—according to government officials.

2. Jesus' statement that one should not put God to the test (Matt. 4:7; quoting Deut. 6:16) meant that one should not view God as a divine patron bound to protect the material welfare and interests of his devotees.

Box 6.2—Songs of Zion

It is extremely difficult to determine when and by whom individual psalms were actually written. The opening verse attributing authorship of a psalm was usually added much later, presenting a meaningful context for the psalm but not necessarily its actual historical origin. Consequently, scholars have studied the psalms in terms of their purported "genres," one such genre being the so-called Songs of Zion alluded to in Psalm 137 (see Box 7.1). These psalms celebrate the splendor and strength of Jerusalem, confident that its defense is a divine priority. Such psalms were composed before Jerusalem was destroyed in 586 B.C. Psalms 46 and 48 were probably two such Songs of Zion:

> God is our refuge and strength,
> a very present help in trouble.
> Therefore we will not fear, though the earth should change,
> . . . .
> God is in the midst of the city; it shall not be moved;
> God will help it when the morning dawns.
> . . . .
> Yahweh of hosts is with us;
> the God of Jacob is our refuge. (Ps. 46: 1–2, 5, 7)

> Great is Yahweh and greatly to be praised
> in the city of our God.
> . . . .
> Mount Zion, in the far north,
> the city of the great King.
> Within its citadels God
> has shown himself a sure defense.
> . . . .
> [God's] right hand is filled with victory.
> Let Mount Zion be glad,
> let the towns of Judah rejoice
> because of [God's] judgments. (Ps. 48:1–2, 10–11)

Manasseh's Policies

The birth of Hezekiah's eventual heir around 700 B.C.—a generation after the Assyrian destruction of the northern kingdom of Israel and soon after Jerusalem's deliverance from Sennacherib's siege—occasioned much public rejoicing:

> For unto us a child is born,
> unto us a son is given. (Isa. 9:6, KJV)

Isaiah saw this as a moment fraught with potential blessings for the people of Yahweh:

> His authority shall grow continually,
>> and there shall be endless peace
> for the throne of David and his kingdom.
>> He will establish and uphold it
> with justice and with righteousness
>> from this time onward and forevermore.
> The zeal of Yahweh of hosts will do this. (Isa. 9:7)

But Hezekiah's heir, Manasseh (ruled 687–642 B.C.), proved to be one of the worst of all Judaean kings (according to the Israelite scribes who wrote the Bible). His mother, Hephzibah, was probably very slightly, if at all, "Israelite," and the only Israelite religious tradition that would have meant anything to her would likely have been the Davidic covenant promising that her son would one day rule. When Jerusalem was finally destroyed about a half century after Manasseh's reign, it was said that all the good done by all the other kings failed to outweigh the evil he had wrought (2 Kings 23:26).

The author of 2 Kings tended to focus on the religious dimension of royal policies, as opposed to their economic or even political dimensions. In treating Manasseh, he lists the religious policies of a king who had clearly departed radically not only from the ancient Yahwist faith but also from the hybrid Yahwisticism that had been cultivated in Jerusalem for the previous three hundred years. Instead, he fostered such things as Baal worship, child sacrifice, astrology, and divination.

"He erected altars for Baal, made an Asherah, as King Ahab of Israel had done" (2 Kings 21:3). One of the major problems in biblical studies is that we know so little about what this ancient paganism ritually involved. There are hints that the cult of Asherah may have involved sexual intercourse that was regarded as sacred. There are references to a "sacred marriage" ritual in third-millennium-B.C. Mesopotamia, in which a priestess would engage in sexual intercourse while assuming the role of a goddess. Two thousand years later, Herodotus penned a matter-of-fact description of women serving as prostitutes in Babylonian temples. But to reconstruct Judaean phenomena on the basis of this evidence is problematic. However, it is safe to say that when Manasseh built altars for Baal and made an Asherah, he was following some fairly typical procedure for the pagan religions of the time, something not even the Jerusalem priests of Yahweh would have endorsed.

"He made his son pass through fire" (2 Kings 21:6). In an age when there were no safe or reliable methods of birth control or abortion, child sacrifice was probably an acceptable means of eliminating unwanted children and the associated financial burdens. Aristocratic families in particular would not want large families because that would only divide and

Figure 6.2
Child Sacrifice at Carthage. A limestone obelisk from
the fourth century B.C., discovered in the sacred precinct
of the goddess Tanit at Carthage, shows a Phoenician
priest holding a child, probably preparing it for sacrifice.

diminish the family's economic status. Human lives were therefore sacrificed for economic goals, with the added bonus of appearing to be religiously "pious" at the same time.

"[*He*] *worshiped all the host of heaven, and served them*" (2 Kings 21:3).
The verse here may allude to new ways of thinking about the universe and
about celestial bodies. Some scholars believe Manasseh's policy here reflects
Assyrian and Babylonian influences, while others suggest this reverence
for stars and constellations goes back to second-millennium-B.C. Syria-
Palestine. Interest in what the Greeks would later organize as the "zodiac"
was spreading across the Mediterranean world at this time, laying the foundation for what would later be called astrology. Whatever else it tells us
here, the biblical text makes it clear that Manasseh was trying to keep up
with what was most fashionable. Furthermore, if the terms had been available to them, Manasseh's bureaucrats would probably have labeled this new
religion not only "modern" but also "scientific" and "empirical."

The text says "he worshiped and served them." The Hebrew verb
translated here as "worshiped" actually designates the physical act of
"bowing down," not an internal spiritual attitude of devotional reverence.
This act was identical to the Muslim prayer posture. These were the
visible gestures of submission, obeisance, dependence, and obedience.
Such worship by Manasseh was a highly public endorsement of a rival
religious system. Originally a demonstration of political submission, as to
an overlord like the Egyptian pharaoh, "bowing down" was transferred to
the religious realm (Law of Transference, p. 3). For Muslims, it indicates
the complete "submission" (Arabic *islam*) to Allah. Muslims, Jews, and

Christians believe that to bow down to a political power structure is incompatible with the worship of the one God, and both Jewish and Christian history is replete with martyrs who refused to bow down to symbols of political authority.

The next verb in this passage is "serve," which is understood to be the logical consequence of bowing down. Once you have formally signaled your submission to a superior force or being, then your choices and behavior must henceforth defer to *its* will, not your own (the point of Jesus' troubling statement in Luke 17:7–10). That is what it means to "serve." Even though we do not know exactly what is meant by the "host of heaven," it is clear that Manasseh was bowing down to something that had nothing to do either with Yahwism or with the official Yahwisticism of Jerusalem. His choices and policies were concretely shaped by some alternative set of values.

"*He practiced soothsaying and augury, and dealt with mediums and with wizards*" (2 Kings 21:6). This refers to omenology and divination, for which there is abundant evidence going back to third-millennium-B.C. Mesopotamia. Divination is the prediction of the future by reading and interpreting such "signs" as the flight patterns of birds or markings on sheep livers. It was an empirical body of knowledge and data collection— the domain of a specialized class of priestly experts—and at this time was probably regarded as "scientific." But although these predictions were surrounded by an aura of "truth" due to their empirical methodologies, they were largely devoid of value considerations. When the king sent his priest

Figure 6.3
"Bowing Down" Equals Worship. "Bowing down" was a universal political act of submission transferred to the religious realm. A fifteenth-century-B.C. painting from the tomb of Sebek-hotep (in Thebes) shows Syrian tribute bearers prostrating themselves before Pharaoh (*left*). The Black Obelisk of Shalmaneser III depicts the Israelite king Jehu in the same posture as he brings tribute to the king in 841 B.C. (*right*). The winged sun-disk above the king is the artistic equivalent to a halo, indicating that the king is invested with the sanctity of Ashur, divine patron of the Assyrians.

3. The question of whether a policy was good or bad was answered at the outset by the fact that the king desired it. Morality was only introduced later to justify this desire.

to consult the omens, the only thing that concerned him was the technical or "scientific" validity of a desired course of action. The question was not whether the desired action was "good" or "bad" but whether it would succeed.[3] In the biblical tradition, practices such as astrology and palm reading are considered wrong not because they are intrinsically "evil" but because they are relativistic, glossing over questions of right or wrong. Because traditional Yahwism always expected that choices and decisions would defer to ethical considerations rather than to favorable or unfavorable omens, it was sharply opposed to any kind of divination. When such considerations are waived, the possible becomes the obligatory, regardless of its merits or wisdom: people begin to think that certain things *should* be done simply because they *can* be done.

But did anyone raise such value questions during Manasseh's forty-five-year-long reign? We are not given the name of one single prophet who spoke out.[4] Of course, this does not mean that no one dared publicly to question or oppose Manasseh. That none are named may mean that they were quickly disposed of at the first hint of opposition. The biblical text supports this conclusion, informing us that "Manasseh shed very much innocent blood, until he had filled Jerusalem [with blood] from one end to another" (2 Kings 21:16). In a political state where value questions are suppressed and decisions are almost never based on a religiously grounded ethic such as the commitments of the Yahwist Decalogue, the powerful can easily justify the extermination of anyone who disagrees with them.

4. The Talmud and several ancient pseudepigraphic books not included in the Bible contain a legend that Isaiah criticized Manasseh and was subsequently executed for it by being sawn in half (see also Heb. 11:37).

The Legacy of Manasseh

The summary of Manasseh's reign in 2 Kings does, however, hint that some prophetic individuals may have been active:

> Yahweh said by his servants the prophets, "Because King Manasseh of Judah has committed these abominations, . . . and has caused Judah also to sin with his idols; therefore thus says Yahweh, the God of Israel, . . . I will wipe Jerusalem as one wipes a dish, wiping it and turning it upside down. I will cast off the remnant of my heritage, and give them into the hand of their enemies; they shall become a prey and a spoil to all their enemies, because they have done what is evil in my sight and have provoked me to anger, since the day their ancestors came out of Egypt, even to this day." (2 Kings 21:10–15)

Manasseh's legacy is complicated by the claim in the later biblical book of 2 Chronicles (33:10–13) that he converted to Yahwism late in life. An even later apocryphal book, the Prayer of Manasseh, details the extent of his contrition and repentance. The historicity of this curious tradition is undermined both by the fact that it first appears two hundred and fifty years after Manasseh's death, and by earlier biblical traditions that Manasseh's son, Amon, "did what was evil in the sight of Yahweh, as his father Manasseh had done. He walked in all the way in which his father walked, served the idols that his father served, and worshiped them" (2 Kings 21:20–21). Written only a generation after Manasseh's death, this text implies that Manasseh was an apostate to the end. We cannot currently explain how and why the tradition of his conversion arose.

Within two years of ascending the throne, Amon was murdered by his own servants, the Jerusalem bureaucrats (2 Kings 21:23). We are not told what motivated them, perhaps a power struggle over continuing to recognize Assyrian hegemony, or a conservative backlash to restore some semblance of the old Yahwisticism to the capital. Whatever the reason, Judah began to change dramatically with Amon's death, as did the international scene.

Josiah and the "People of the Land"

5. The term 'am ha'arets appears frequently in Rabbinic Jewish sources of the post-Christian era as an uncomplimentary label. Present-day Orthodox Jews still use it to mean "ignoramus," applied to secular Jews unconcerned with the religious Torah (law).

After the assassination of Amon "the people of the land killed all those who had conspired against King Amon, and the people of the land made his son Josiah king in place of him" (2 Kings 21:24). Part of the problem in understanding the historical event reported here is uncertainty over the meaning of the phrase "people of the land" (Hebrew 'am ha'arets)[5]; however, the only thing clear here is that it designates the opponents of those bureaucrats who assassinated Amon. They might well have been residents or representatives of the outlying towns and villages. In any event, the text suggests there was an uprising by people who ordinarily had little or nothing to do with government affairs. Only if we assume that there was a popular commitment to the Davidic dynasty can we make sense, first, of their placing Josiah on the throne (reigned 640–609 B.C.) and, second, of this dynasty's endurance for nearly four hundred years.

Because Josiah was only eight years old at the time, affairs of state were initially run by a regent, probably one of his uncles. All the biblical traditions credit Josiah with sweeping religious and cultural reforms, although the books of 2 Kings and 2 Chronicles disagree on the actual chronology and sequence of the reforms. Second Kings focuses on Josiah's eighteenth year as king (621 B.C.), reporting that his reforms were precipitated by an unexpected event that occurred that year while the Jerusalem temple was being repaired (see below). Second Chronicles, however, emphasizes the eighth year of his reign (around 631 B.C.) as the time Josiah began to "seek the God of his ancestor David," noting that he launched his reforms shortly afterward (in 628 B.C.; 2 Chron. 34:3–35:19). In the Chronicles account, the repair of the temple in 621 B.C. was one of the *concluding* elements of his reform (see Table 6.1).

Josiah and the Collapse of Assyria

By placing the beginning of Josiah's reforms at around 631 B.C., 2 Chronicles makes it roughly contemporaneous with the death of Ashurbanipal, the last great king of Assyria. The Assyrian Empire collapsed soon thereafter and, as Assyrian governors and armies became preoccupied with urgent crises in their homeland, its vassals quickly began reclaiming their independence. The Babylonians gained autonomy around 626 B.C., and by 612 B.C. they had captured the Assyrian capital of Nineveh, although an Assyrian government-in-exile held out for a few more years at Haran in north Syria. Also, by linking Josiah's reforms to his "seeking after the God of his ancestor David," 2 Chronicles may imply that Judah's royal policy was now directed toward reestablishing the "golden age" of King David, both culturally and geopolitically. The collapse of the Assyrian Empire meant that the time was right to recapture not only those nostalgic glories of the past but also that former territorial empire.

In fact, a wave of antiquarianism was beginning to sweep across most of the ancient Near Eastern world at this time and would persist for well over a century. Egyptian pharaohs were trying to recapture the nostalgic glories of the Pyramid Age: they revived ancient gods and cults; they imitated ancient prototypes in their royal inscriptions; and they superimposed grids on ancient murals so they could more easily duplicate, mass-produce, and sell these popular imitation antiques. Some ancient Egyptian sculptures were copied so precisely that even the most skilled art historians have difficulty distinguishing a twenty-seventh-century-B.C. original from a seventh-century-B.C. replica. At the other end of the Fertile Crescent, King Ashurbanipal established a library in Assyria to collect, copy, and preserve the myths and legends of ancient Mesopotamia, many of which were then already two thousand years old. A similar antiquarian nostalgia for the past surfaced in Babylonia and Phoenicia at this time.

A series of imperial wars in the following century (between 630 and 530 B.C.) would leave most of these societies exhausted and impoverished and many regions nearly depopulated. While it cannot be demonstrated, one suspects that the Near Eastern peoples of the seventh century B.C. sensed the approaching end of their civilization, and their response was to retreat into their respective pasts.[6] This nostalgic longing for the reassurances of the past occurs so frequently, in almost all cultures and historical periods, that one scholar observed that there is nothing quite so conventional as a restored convention.

The "Book of the Law"

According to 2 Kings, Josiah's reforms did not begin in earnest until around 621 B.C., when he was having Solomon's temple refurbished, a project which itself may have begun as a yearning for the old Yahwisticism of David and Solomon. Then, as we are told in 2 Kings 22, the project uncovered something unexpected:

> The high priest Hilkiah said to Shaphan the secretary, "I have found the book of the law in the house of Yahweh." When Hilkiah gave the book to Shaphan, he read it. Then Shaphan the secretary came to the king, and reported to the king, . . . "The priest Hilkiah has given me a book." Shaphan then read it aloud to the king.
>
> When the king heard the words of the book of the law, he tore his clothes. (vv. 8–11)

The tearing of garments was a sign of grief and shock, a deep reaction of utter dismay. Something in the "book of the law" clearly unsettled Josiah.

Ensuing events suggest that he perceived an enormous gap between the operating ideology of his kingdom and the contents of this book, which almost all scholars today believe was the core of the biblical book of Deuteronomy (see Box 6.3). Josiah's first step was to try to authenticate its contents, so he commanded his bureaucrats:

> "Go, inquire of Yahweh for me, for the people, and for all Judah, concerning the words of this book that has been found; for great is the wrath of Yahweh that is kindled against us, because our ancestors did not obey the words of this book, to do according to all that is written concerning us." (2 Kings 22:13)

Josiah had been exposed to a previously unknown principle of cause and effect to which his kingdom was subject, a principle emphasizing not divine patronage but the "wrath of God." For the first time, he was encountering a more authentic Yahwism. None of his predecessors had

6. Anthropologists studying such "nativist movements" note that archaic indigenous traditions and national cultures are often enthusiastically revived whenever foreign domination weakens, or whenever the native groups sense their own culture's impending demise. As we shall see in chapter 7, the Persian emperors actually nurtured these native enthusiasms, encouraging conquered peoples to embrace and "canonize" their respective archaic traditions.

ever shown much regard for it. At best, they were familiar only with the official Yahwisticism naming Yahweh as the divine patron of Jerusalem who had promised unconditionally to protect the Davidic monarchy and to defend Jerusalem against all enemies. Josiah began to sense impending doom, suggesting that this book of the law originally included the curses in Deuteronomy 28 (see Box 6.1). Such doom was precisely what the prophets had repeatedly predicted.

Their search for authentication led Josiah's officials to Huldah the prophetess,[7] who (presumably) read the scroll, and told them,

> "Thus says Yahweh, the God of Israel: Tell the man who sent you to me, Thus says Yahweh, I will indeed bring disaster on this place and on its inhabitants—all the words of the book that the king of Judah has read." (2 Kings 22:15–16)

By affirming the validity of the curses, she also affirmed the entire Sinai covenant tradition behind them.[8] This meant that Yahweh's support of the state, the king, the city, and the people had never been absolute, as stated in the Davidic covenant tradition, but had always been contingent on submission to the will of Yahweh, as described in the Sinai covenant tradition. Huldah then described the pagan religious activities that would justify the oncoming doom, concluding with a personal message to Josiah:

> "[B]ecause your heart was penitent, and you humbled yourself before Yahweh, . . . and because you have torn your clothes and wept before me, I also have heard you, says Yahweh. Therefore, I will gather you to your ancestors, and you shall be gathered to your grave in peace." (2 Kings 22:19–20)

In fact, Josiah did not go to his grave "in peace"; he was killed in battle about twelve years later. That Huldah's failed prophecy is retained in the biblical record illustrates the Israelites' abiding respect for the historical facts, even the unpleasant and embarrassing ones.

7. The prophet Jeremiah was a teenager and still relatively unknown. Josiah's bureaucrats needed to consult an older and more reputable authority on the Yahwism contained in the "book of the law."

8. Indeed, the very next reference to the book no longer labels it the "book of the law" but the "book of the covenant" (2 Kings 23:2, 21).

The Reforms of Josiah

When Huldah observed that Josiah's "heart was penitent" (2 Kings 22:19) she was acknowledging that Josiah was committed to a change of policy. "Repentance" means a reorientation of a value system and a redirection of choices and actions consistent with those values. This is precisely what the biblical narrative goes on to depict:

The king went up to the house of Yahweh, and with him went all the people of Judah, all the inhabitants of Jerusalem, the priests, the prophets, and all the people, both small and great; he read in their hearing all the words of the book of the covenant that had been found in the house of Yahweh. The king stood by the pillar and *yikrot 'et-habberit* before Yahweh, to follow Yahweh, keeping his commandments, his decrees, and his statutes, with all his heart and all his soul, to perform the words of this covenant that were written in this book. All the people *ya'amod babberit*. (2 Kings 23:2–3)

The Hebrew phrase *yikrot 'et-habberit* (NRSV "he made a covenant") actually has nothing to do with a "covenant" in the usual sense of two parties forming a pact through an oath made binding by some solemn religious or symbolic act. Josiah simply "made a vow" to abide by the words of the book discovered in the temple.[9] Likewise, the people were *not* entering into a covenant: the phrase *ya'amod babberit* (the NRSV "[they] joined in the covenant" is misleading) literally means "they stood by the vow"; in other words, they signaled approval of Josiah's avowed intention to implement the policies outlined in the recently discovered book. In fact, Josiah probably convened the people precisely to gauge the level of their support for this change in policy, a change that would affect the "official" way Yahweh was viewed. After all, the people (*'am ha'arets*) had helped bring him to power.

According to 2 Kings 23, Josiah's reforms began in Jerusalem and Judah proper. After destroying the religious paraphernalia of Baal, Asherah, and the host of heaven that had been placed in the temple of Yahweh, he "deposed the idolatrous priests [Hebrew *kemarim*] whom the kings of Judah had ordained to make offerings in the high places at the cities of Judah and around Jerusalem" (v. 5). This was a well-established class of Canaanite priests, mentioned in the LB Age Amarna letters, endorsed by the Israelite royal establishment in Jerusalem, but condemned by Israelite prophets such as Hosea (10:5) and Zephaniah (1:4) as a threat to Yahwist values. Under the circumstances, one can understand why Josiah had to ascertain the level of support for their removal before actually deposing them. Fortunately for the *kemarim* of Judah there was little support for their outright execution, even though the book of the law apparently mandated it.

The cleansing of the Jerusalem temple involved not only the removal of all the pagan ritual paraphernalia that had accumulated over the centuries, much of which was probably a vestige of Manasseh's policy of "cultural modernization." It also included the dismantling of "the houses of the *qedeshim* that were in the house of Yahweh, where the women did weaving for Asherah" (2 Kings 23:7). Evidence from Mari

9. That the word *berit* had come to mean "vow" or "oath" by the time of King Josiah illustrates linguistic change from the early days of Israel, when it referred to the whole pact itself and not just the solemn oath. It also helps us to appreciate how the original covenant ideal in Israel could be so grossly misunderstood and distorted by the scribes and bureaucrats of later kings.

Box 6.3—Josiah and Deuteronomy

Each aspect of Josiah's reform corresponded to a command in Deuteronomy, prompting scholars to conclude that the book of the law discovered in the Jerusalem temple contained at least some portions of Deuteronomy. Note that although Deuteronomy specifies death for those who worship the sun, moon, and host of heaven, 2 Kings suggests that, at least in southern Judah, Josiah merely deposed (removed) them.

Aspects of Josiah's Reform (2 Kings)	Command in Deuteronomy
He deposed the idolatrous priests who had made offerings to the sun, the moon, and the host of heaven. (23:5)	You shall not worship the sun, the moon, or the hosts of heaven (4:19), and you shall put to death all who do. (17:2–5)
He demolished the houses belonging to the male cult prostitutes. (23:7)	There shall be no male cult prostitutes in Israel. (23:18)
He defiled Topheth, where child sacrifice had been practiced. (23:10)	No one shall practice child sacrifice. (18:10) (See also Deuteronomy 12:31.)
He broke the pillars in pieces and cut down the sacred Asherim poles. (23:14)	Break down their (pagan) altars, smash their pillars, and burn their sacred Asherim poles with fire (12:3). You shall not plant a sacred Asherim pole, nor set up a stone pillar (16:21). (See also Deuteronomy 7:5.)
He removed all the shrines of the high places. (23:19)	You must completely demolish all high places. (12:2)
He executed all the priests of the high places of Samaria. (23:20)	You must execute anyone who worships pagan gods. (12:2)
He reinstituted the Passover in Jerusalem, which had not been celebrated for centuries. (23:21–22)	You shall perform the Passover sacrifice in the one place where Yahweh chooses to make his name dwell. (16:1–8)
He put away the mediums and wizards. (23:24)	No one shall practice divination, or be a soothsayer, augur, or sorcerer. (18:11)

(see Fig. 1.4) and from as far away as India suggests that weaving women were often closely linked with prostitution. Not only are the nature and function of these *qedeshim* debated, but the very translation of the word is problematic. Since the word is the masculine plural form of *qedeshah*, "female cult prostitute," it ought to be translated "male cult prostitutes," which perhaps suggests some kind of ritual homosexual practices. Josiah also "defiled" the Topheth, where the aristocrats of Jerusalem sacrificed their surplus infants to Molech (v. 10). And there is an intriguing reference to the removal of the horses that had been dedicated to the (deified) sun and to the destruction of the "chariots of the sun" (v. 11), recalling the Greek myths about the sun god Helios.

All this is dramatic testimony to the fact that, over the centuries, the policies, traditions, and value system of the royal court in Jerusalem had become utterly estranged from the official Yahwisticism of David and Solomon, not to mention the more archaic Yahwism associated with the exodus and Mount Sinai. According to 2 Kings 23, even the Passover—a festival celebrating the exodus from Egypt—had not been celebrated there in the capital for almost four hundred years (2 Kings 23:21–23).

New Directions in Foreign Policy

There were also international geopolitical ramifications to these reforms. Josiah "defiled the high places that were east of Jerusalem, . . . which King Solomon of Israel had built for Astarte the abomination of the Sidonians, for Chemosh the abomination of Moab, and for Milcom the abomination of the Ammonites" (v. 13). This was "embassy row" in ancient Judah. The destruction of these shrines/embassies constituted a severing of the network of political alliances that had previously constituted Judaean foreign policy. The kingdom of Judah repudiated all international obligations and commitments. A new political day was dawning.

Josiah then ventured north into the territory of the old kingdom of Israel, which had been an Assyrian province since its destruction a hundred years earlier. But the weakened Assyrians had now withdrawn, creating a power vacuum that Josiah sought to fill. He reserved his most savage acts for the priests he found there: they were slaughtered on their own altars. This was Josiah's double standard at work: the pagan priests of Judah, who enjoyed some popular support, were not only spared but perhaps reemployed in other official capacities in Jerusalem, while the priests of Israel, who enjoyed no such support in the south, were exterminated.

The slaughter of these priests and the centralization of ritual worship in the Jerusalem temple make it clear that Josiah's so-called reforms were actually little more than a typical exploitation of religious tradition to consolidate political control. His destruction of northern shrines ended all rituals that might serve to solidify rival communities and solidarities. This was politically crucial: the people of northern Israel had not recognized the legitimacy of the Jerusalem regime since the days of Solomon, and lingering northern solidarities would have interfered with Josiah's ambition to restore the golden age of David and Solomon. The only acceptable rituals were those in Jerusalem that solidified the national solidarity over which Josiah presided.

Josiah's Legacy

10. Note the massive expense of time, energy, and human victims the Soviet Union devoted in its futile attempt to "re-educate" the Russian masses toward Marxist values. Despite its bureaucratic centralization, modern modes of mass communication, technological sophistication, unparalleled police surveillance, closely monitored judicial system, and unprecedented military strength, all deployed to inculcate Marxist values, few actually embraced this value system or rose to defend it when it crumbled in the late 1980s.

Political reforms can only establish sanctions to alter external behavior. Because they cannot penetrate the heart, they never really create new value systems among the citizenry. Consequently, they are usually superficial and short-lived.[10] So it was with Josiah. Unfortunately for him, his own value system—imperial expansion—was shared by his neighbors, notably Pharaoh Necho II of Egypt. In 609 B.C., Necho was moving his troops through Palestine, apparently en route to confront the Babylonians. Perhaps perceiving Necho to be a threat to Judaean imperial interests, Josiah mobilized his army against him but was himself killed in battle. Within a few years, all commitment to his reform program had collapsed. Many of the citizens who "stood in the covenant" with Josiah had apparently done so halfheartedly. Josiah's premature death on the battlefield probably convinced some of them that his zeal for Yahweh worship, however it was defined, had been misplaced.

Josiah's reform was not—and given his ambitions, could not be—a creative reform drawing on the actual religious values of the premonarchic period. It was merely imitative, and even then only of the monarchy of David and Solomon. Thus, Josiah was hardly the first king in Jerusalem (or anywhere else) to be guilty of identifying political ambition and imperialism with the worship of Yahweh. But his actions, coupled with a thoroughgoing imitative reform, had particularly lasting repercussions because it spawned a burst of history writing in Jerusalem. Busy scribes collected memories of ancient heroes and events, and recast everything—including the picture of premonarchic Israelite society and religious values—to make the past support Josiah's vision of the ideal Israel. The result was the sweeping narrative found in the books of Joshua, Judges, 1–2 Samuel, and 1–2 Kings (see Appendix A).

This blending of the premonarchic faith of Sinai with narrow, ambitious nationalism and imperialism introduced terrible and tragic religious confusion into the biblical tradition, permanently etching in many people's minds the notion that Yahweh was, from the beginning, the god of one particular nation and one group of people. Perhaps nowhere is its unhappy effect more evident than in Joshua 1–11, where the early Yahwists are inaccurately depicted along the lines of Josiah's ideal—as an army invading Canaan in a genocidal campaign to gain control of territory promised them by their god. More tragically, this identification of political ambition with biblical faith would set a precedent for countless Western imperialists, who often wrapped their ruthless conquests, crusades, inquisitions, and pogroms in the splendid garments of biblical piety and rectitude. These echoes of Josiah's reforms still reverberate today.

Jeremiah and Jerusalem's Destruction

11. Despite one complimentary remark about Josiah's commitment to justice (Jer. 22:15–16), Jeremiah would likely have been as unimpressed with Josiah's imperialistic ambitions as he was with those of the other kings of Jerusalem. He may also have been upset with the literary output of Josiah's scribes, judging from his remarks about the "false pen of the scribes" (8:8). Excerpts from the book of the law—such as Deuteronomy 20:10–17 ("put all its males to the sword . . . you must not let anything that breathes remain alive")—were used not only to justify Josiah's bloodbath in the north but also to shape that literary output, inspiring the view that faithful Yahweh worshipers throughout history have always been prepared to kill foreigners in the name of religion.

If the biblical prophet Jeremiah was impressed with Josiah's religious reforms, he never let it show.[11] Many Judaeans undoubtedly congratulated themselves that there was no longer any traffic for the likes of the *kemarim* and the *qedeshim,* but they failed to understand that Yahwism had never been about such superficial ritual matters per se. It had always been about *transcendent ethical values,* and the way in which religious systems promote either those values or something inferior (Jer. 7:21–23). Like prophets before him, Jeremiah noted the widespread neglect of the old Yahwist religious ethic, while many of his contemporaries countered that things were not all that bad. Had not all the pagan religious influences been removed? Had not Yahweh demonstrated a century earlier, during the siege of Sennacherib, that his highest priority was the military defense of the kingdom, especially Jerusalem? Were not people worshiping in the temple of Yahweh? The good feelings all this generated became "proof" for many people that at last the true faith had triumphed.

As a prophet, Jeremiah was unconcerned with people's "good feelings." He was more concerned with truth, which he sought in the observation of historical processes. On the horizon were the Babylonian armies. Why should anyone think that prayers and rituals in the temple would charm them all away? Why should anyone think that Yahweh would defend Jerusalem and its temple when, almost five hundred years earlier, Yahweh had permitted the Philistines to overrun Shiloh and capture the ark of the covenant? Speaking as Yahweh, Jeremiah addressed this very question before worshipers at the temple:

Do not trust in these deceptive words: "This is the temple of Yahweh, the temple of Yahweh, the temple of Yahweh."

For if you truly amend your ways and your doings, if you truly act justly one with another, if you do not oppress the alien, the orphan, and the widow, or shed innocent blood in this place, and if you do not go after other gods to your own hurt, then I will dwell with you in this place. . . .

Here you are, trusting in deceptive words to no avail. Will you steal, murder, commit adultery, swear falsely, make offerings to Baal, and go after other gods that you have not known, and then come and stand before me in this house, which is called by my name, and say, "We are safe!"—only to go on doing all these abominations? . . . Go now to my place that was in Shiloh, where I made my name dwell at first, and see what I did to it for the wickedness of my people Israel. And now, because you have done all these things, . . . I will do to the house that is called by my name, in which you trust, . . . just what I did to Shiloh. And I will

Box 6.4—A Jeremiah Sampler

Like other prophets, Jeremiah criticized international alliances concerned only with rescuing the political organization. He was also sharply critical of the official Yahwisticism that declared the social order to be healthy and secure. He lamented the fact that too many of his contemporaries viewed their religious obligations as ritual, not ethical, in nature.

> What then do you gain by going to Egypt,
>   to drink the waters of the Nile?
> Or what do you gain by going to Assyria,
>   to drink the waters of the Euphrates?
> . . . .
> You shall be put to shame by Egypt
>   as you were put to shame by Assyria.
> . . . .
> for Yahweh has rejected those in whom you trust,
>   and you will not prosper through them. (2:18, 36–37)
>
> For the house of Israel and the house of Judah
>   have been utterly faithless to me,
>   says Yahweh.
> They have spoken falsely of Yahweh,
>   and have said, "He will do nothing.
> No evil shall come upon us,
>   and we will not see sword or famine."
> The [false] prophets are nothing but wind,
>   for the word is not in them. (5:11–13)
>
> For scoundrels are found among my people;
>   they take over the goods of others.
> . . . .
> They know no limits in deeds of wickedness;
>   they do not judge with justice
> the cause of the orphan, to make it prosper,
>   and they do not defend the rights of the needy.
> Shall I not punish them for these things?
>   says Yahweh,
>   and shall I not bring retribution
>   on a nation such as this? (5:26, 28–29)

cast you out of my sight, just as I cast out all your kinsfolk, all the offspring of Ephraim. (Jer. 7:4–10, 12–15)

Truth, revealed in the unfolding processes of history, won out. In 586 B.C., the Babylonians demolished the city of Jerusalem.

Yahweh did nothing to stop them (Jer. 21:1–10).

Suggestions for Further Reading

Additional information on the topics discussed in this chapter can be found in the following sources.

Dictionary/Encyclopedia Entries

Anchor Bible Dictionary: Deuteronomistic History; Fertility Cults; Hezekiah; Historiography (Israelite); Jeremiah; Josiah; Magic; Manasseh; Omens in the Ancient Near East
Encyclopedia Britannica (14th rev. ed., 1964): Hezekiah
Interpreter's Dictionary of the Bible: 'Am Ha'arez

Jeremiah

P. J. King, *Jeremiah: An Archaeological Companion.* Louisville, Ky.: Westminster John Knox Press, 1993.

Deuteronomy

E. W. Nicholson, *Deuteronomy and Tradition.* Philadelphia: Fortress Press, 1967.
M. Weinfeld, *Deuteronomy and the Deuteronomic School.* Oxford: Clarendon Press, 1972.

Seven

Destruction and Exile: The Creative Reform of Yahwism

Suggested Reading

Jerusalem Destroyed: 2 Kings 25; Ezekiel 16; 23
Second Isaiah: Isaiah 40; 42; 44:1–8; 49–50; 52:13–53:12
Reviving Religious Institutions: Ezra 3:1–4:5; Nehemiah
    9–10; 13

Introductory Overview

The simple fact that we do not have to dig up Israelite religion from the ruins of the ancient world is nothing short of remarkable: from 1200 B.C. to the present day there has been an unbroken line of different communities reflecting continuity with that faith.

This is a stunning contrast to the historical norm. Like the worship of the Canaanite, Assyrian, Babylonian, Egyptian, and Hittite gods—to name only a few—the worship of Yahweh, a god closely linked to the fortunes of a petty state in backwater Palestine, should have ended around 586 B.C. with the destruction of Jerusalem. We should today be excavating its remains, along with those of other religions, from the ruins where its disillusioned practitioners left it millennia ago. Instead, this faith endured, and living expressions of it today are no farther away than the neighborhood church, synagogue, or mosque.

Why did this religion survive when the others did not? We cannot attribute it to some mystical tenacity of the so-called "Hebrew people": the biblical record clearly shows that, like anyone else, the Israelites were individuals who could be firm or wavering in their faith. And the events of 586 B.C. were certainly potentially faith-shattering. After Jerusalem and its temple were destroyed, many of these Yahweh worshipers—referred to now as "Judaeans"—were forcibly resettled in and around Babylon (southern Mesopotamia), leaving only the poorest villagers in Judah. In fact, some of these exiled Judaeans embraced the religion of their

Babylonian captors. For them, Yahweh had probably never been much more than the divine patron of the Judaean state. Its destruction proved either Yahweh's weakness, or his unreliability, or perhaps even his nonexistence or death: they turned to other gods more capable of displaying the power they could respect.

However, the two generations following the destruction of Jerusalem were also some of the most creative and impressive in Yahwist religious thought since the time of Moses or Samuel. No longer distracted by an official Yahwisticism treating Yahweh as the divine patron of the Jerusalem regime, some exiled Judaeans were able to rediscover the old Yahwism of Mosaic times and readapt it to their new circumstances. Such a reinvigoration of faith had been foreseen over a century earlier by Isaiah. When he realized that his own prophecies were having almost no impact on his contemporaries, Isaiah began to wonder what would per-

Box 7.1—Psalm 137

The disillusionment of the exiled Judaeans was compounded by Babylonian taunts reminding them of their now-discredited belief in Jerusalem's invincibility. The author of Psalm 137—probably an exiled Jerusalem bureaucrat—was resolved not to abandon the Israelite religious heritage.

> By the rivers of Babylon—
>   there we sat down and there we wept
>   when we remembered Zion.
> On the willows there
>   we hung up our harps.
> For there our captors
>   asked us for songs,
> and our tormentors asked for mirth, saying,
>   "Sing us one of the songs of Zion!"
>
> How could we sing Yahweh's song
>   in a foreign land?
> If I forget you, O Jerusalem,
>   let my right hand wither!
> Let my tongue cling to the roof of my mouth,
>   if I do not remember you,
> if I do not set Jerusalem
>   above my highest joy. (vv. 1–6)

Excerpts from possible Songs of Zion are provided in Box 6.2.

suade his fellow Israelites to appreciate the things ultimately necessary for their own well-being (Isa. 6:9–10). His bleak but hopeful realization was that historical forces must first play themselves out and that true religious insight will only emerge after all the false religious notions have been discredited and destroyed:

> "Until cities lie waste
> without inhabitant,
> and houses without people,
> and the land is utterly desolate;
> until Yahweh sends everyone far away,
> and vast is the emptiness in the midst of the land."
>
> (Isa. 6:11–12)

The Israelite state had become completely incompatible with the religious purposes for which the Israelite community had originally been created (chapters 2 and 3). It had not even been capable of acting competently enough to ensure its own political survival. It is not surprising that most of the preexilic biblical prophets predicted its destruction. Once the Israelites dropped the illusion that their state and its divine patron would protect them, they were free to inquire into the religious source of real and lasting security, such as represented by the Yahweh of the Sinai covenant.[1]

1. In fact, there is evidence that Yahwism actually attracted converts in Mesopotamia and elsewhere during the exile. Ezra 2:59 notes that when the Judaeans began returning to Jerusalem, there came with them certain families who could not prove genealogically that their families "belonged to Israel." See also Isaiah 63:16.

The Broader Historical Picture

2. This conflict between East and West (Iran and Greece) would endure for the next thousand years—until the East was conquered and became Muslim (seventh century A.D.). Yet this hardly ended the East-West conflict; as the Western imperial power base shifted from Byzantium farther west into Europe, it was manifest in the numerous Crusades of 1096–1270.

Between 586 B.C. and 330 B.C.—from the Babylonian destruction of Jerusalem to the time of Alexander the Great—the center of imperial power shifted from the north-south axis of the LB Age (when the Hittites and Egyptians competed for dominance) to an east-west axis, with power first emerging in the East (what is now Iran) and subsequently in the West (Greece and, later, Rome).[2]

Although political power emerged quite late in the West, it changed the world radically. The classical civilizations of Egypt and Mesopotamia essentially disappeared over the course of four centuries (between 300 B.C. and A.D. 100). It is difficult for us to imagine what it was like for the whole complex of ancient Near Eastern cultures to die out so rapidly, including the most enduring and conservative aspect of culture—namely, language. Three-thousand-year-old languages ceased to be spoken or written. If one can imagine a four-hundred-year-long period in which the English, Russian, and Chinese languages all became extinct, then one might begin to grasp the enormity of the

3. The last known cuneiform text—an astronomical almanac—was written around A.D. 75 by some member of an ancient priestly family. In all likelihood, the writer's children, enamored of the opportunities afforded by their modern world, found better things to do than learn their father's arcane language and perpetuate his old-fashioned worldview. And so the language became extinct, completely unknown until the middle of the nineteenth century, when archaeologists first began digging up these relics of a long-dead civilization.

4. Indeed, large portions of the Old Testament are similarly incomprehensible to many modern readers. The intellectual shortcut taken by fundamentalists is to regard it mainly as a godly book of rules dictating how people should live their lives. However, this shortcut fails to do justice to the full range of material in the Hebrew Bible and its vision of what a meaningful life in covenant with God actually entails.

cultural changes taking place in the Near East after the conquests of Alexander the Great.[3]

Particularly in Greece, new social organizations (protodemocracies) and new ways of thinking (the "philosophical revolution") arose. Alfred North Whitehead exaggerated only slightly when he said that all of Western civilization is a series of footnotes to Plato and Aristotle. A Westerner of today, equipped with good translations, need only contrast the intelligibility of almost anything written by Plato or Aristotle with the frustratingly incomprehensible myths of ancient Sumer, Babylon, and Egypt.[4] Even indigenous Near Easterners began losing both the ability and the desire to grasp the ancient elements of their own dying cultures. In the third century B.C. some Phoenicians still preserved ancient Canaanite myths, but by then they were garbled distortions of the fourteenth-century-B.C. "originals" unearthed at Ugarit. The Phoenicians apparently did not have the slightest idea what their own myths meant and in fact were becoming quite attached to the Greco-Roman ones.

The Assyrian and Babylonian empires left vast regions severely depopulated, especially the Euphrates River valley and Transjordan. This is silent but powerful testimony to the suffering of the civilian population during the death throes of these empires. Although they were not the primary target of imperial attack, they became the primary victims, simply

Box 7.2—The Four Horsemen of the Apocalypse

Ancient peoples understood the cause-and-effect relationship between war and economic collapse (where a day's wages might buy a piece of bread), famine, and epidemic disease. It found expression in many apocalyptic visions of the end of the world, including this one from the New Testament:

> Then I saw the Lamb open one of the seven seals. . . . I looked, and there was a white horse! Its rider had a bow; a crown was given to him, and he came out conquering and to conquer.
> When he opened the second seal, . . . out came another horse, bright red; its rider was permitted to take peace from the earth, so that people would slaughter one another; and he was given a great sword.
> When he opened the third seal, . . . I looked, and there was a black horse! Its rider held a pair of scales . . . and I heard . . . a voice . . . saying, "A quart of wheat for a day's pay, and three quarts of barley for a day's pay. . . ."
> When he opened the fourth seal, . . . I looked and there was a pale green horse! Its rider's name was Death, and Hades followed with him; they were given authority . . . to kill with sword, famine, and pestilence. . . . (Rev. 6:1–8)

5. The Bible notes that spring is "the time when kings go out to battle" (2 Sam. 11:1). The grain is being harvested, the summer vegetables are ripening, and (if the rains have been good) food is everywhere for the taking.

6. Interestingly, it was in this relatively isolated corner of the Near East that ancient cultural features continued to be preserved. For example, even as archaic Semitic languages began to die out elsewhere, Arabic not only persisted but also retained many linguistic features dating back to the Bronze Age.

because these ancient armies lived off the land. Instead of carrying their own supplies, they forcibly confiscated whatever was available locally, with no regard for whether the indigenous population would even have seed for the next planting season.[5] Economic collapse, famine, and disease inevitably followed war.

But farther south in the Arabian peninsula, prosperity and population were both increasing, due to rapid economic growth fueled by the exploitation of natural resources such as gold and incense. Because these were luxury goods, trade in them was extremely profitable. The towns and states along the incense route of western Arabia formed the Ishma-elite confederation, whose members also traditionally claimed Abraham as a common ancestor.[6] Gaining control of this remote but profitable trade route had been a cornerstone of Assyrian imperial policy in the seventh century B.C., and it is only at this comparatively late phase of biblical history that we first begin to see in these desert caravaneers anything resembling bedouin nomads. The last Babylonian king, Nabonidams (ruled 556–538 B.C.), moved his capital to the remote oasis of Tema, where he could more closely supervise the flow of this wealth out of Arabia.

Assyrian and Babylonian Imperial Policies

Some scholars have applauded the Assyrians and their empire, noting that they had maintained international order. Indeed, they had. But at what cost? A recent survey of the Euphrates River valley showed that the whole area was virtually depopulated by the end of the Assyrian period, undoubtedly as a direct result of the very policies that some scholars now find so admirable. There are people today who, like the pagans of antiquity, regard the political monopoly of force as the source of peace, order, prosperity, and security. Catastrophes such as those wrought by the Assyrians begin innocently enough when good people start to place a high value on power and affluence, and support the sort of politics that seem (in the short term) to guarantee them—at least for some. What eventually results is a social and political organization that increasingly defines itself by its ability to control others through coercion.

At the beginning of World War II, Winston Churchill remarked that he had no intention of presiding over the dissolution of the British Empire. No imperial leader ever does. But history does not respect their political agendas for very long, a point well understood by the Hebrew prophets (see Appendix B). The Assyrian Empire succumbed to the Babylonian Empire beginning around 620 B.C. The Babylonians reached their zenith around 605 B.C., but by 539 B.C. had themselves fallen victim to the expanding Persian Empire.

The cornerstone of imperial policy—then as now—was economics. The Assyrians and Babylonians were generally intolerant of the local cultures, religions, and social institutions of the peoples they conquered, especially if these things fostered competing loyalties that might fuel rebellion against the empire. Rebellion was defined as the withholding of tribute (taxes). Any small state that did so surely realized that it had no chance of success unless it obtained the wholehearted cooperation of other states (such as Egypt), and at a cost less than the original tribute itself. Not surprisingly, key government officials were often murderously divided over just such questions of foreign policy. Because it sometimes took as long as a year for an imperial power to mobilize its resources and move against a rebellious state, those in revolt usually had time to organize their neighbors against the alleged common enemy.

After suppressing a rebellion, the victorious empire would almost always execute the leader (usually the king), although occasionally he would be taken prisoner and kept in protective custody. Babylonian records confirm the biblical account (2 Kings 25:27–30) that such was the fate of Jehoiachin, king of Judah. The tribute imposed on the "pacified" population would then be increased, both to punish the rebels and to help the empire recover the costs of crushing the uprising. Sometimes the victorious empire would deport any personnel who were essential to a military buildup—particularly specialized craftsmen such as smiths—in the hopes of disarming the state and forestalling future insurrections. A state whose rebellion failed could expect the dismantling of its political apparatus, the physical destruction of the capital itself (along with its temples and palaces), the execution of its leaders, and the relocation of everyone except the most insignificant villagers.

Figure 7.1

Assyrian State Terrorism. Assyrian palace reliefs contained graphic scenes, such as this from the siege of Lachish (Fig. 6.1) showing defeated Judaean rebels being impaled. By displaying such art publicly in government buildings, the Assyrians attempted to intimidate vassals and foreign ambassadors by showing how they dealt with rebels.

7. Nationalism—the ideological impulse to identify one's self with the political state—hardly existed in the ancient world. Most people's affairs centered around their village, their family, and their private lives. For them, the political state was, at best, a hardship to be endured.

These methods date back to the Egyptian Empire of the fifteenth century B.C. (see Box 2.1), so everyone must have known what punishment awaited defeated rebels. But these methods had an enormous and unintended side effect: by resettling conquered peoples in the imperial homeland (whether in Assyria or Babylonia), the indigenous population there became so diluted that there was insufficient solidarity to maintain the empire itself, which increasingly comprised only the king and his bureaucracy.[7]

Judaean Writers in Exile

8. If these writers were creating traditions on the spot, we would expect these traditions to be handled with greater skill and competency. As it is, biblical writers often appear to have had little, if any, understanding of many features of the traditions they were recording, such as (for example) proper names, old poems, the meaning of actual words (e.g., '*elef* as "military unit"; see chapter 2), and above all the covenant itself, which constituted Israel as a religious community. This is another way of saying that a great deal of biblical literature lacks real literary polish, even by ancient Near Eastern standards.

We know almost nothing about the living conditions endured by those who were forcibly resettled in Babylon. As state slaves, they undoubtedly were forced into the lowest menial labor with virtually no compensation. One scholar has suggested that they were employed dredging the canals in and around Babylon, which were constantly silting up and jeopardizing the entire economy of southern Mesopotamia. Yet in the midst of this apparent squalor, the Judaeans in exile produced an extraordinary body of religious literature, ranging from Ezekiel's breathtaking description of the valley of dry bones (Ezekiel 37) to the compiling of the Former Prophets (see Appendix A). Most of this writing, in one way or another, dealt with the urgently relevant question "Why has this disaster happened?"

In fact, by the 1930s most biblical scholars assumed that 90 percent of the Old Testament text was organized and written down around this time as a response to the crisis of exile. Of course, even if this is true, it does not follow that the Old Testament traditions about the past were necessarily created or invented at this time, a distinction that some biblical scholars today seem unable to grasp. Often referred to as historical "minimalists," some of them go so far as to claim that prior to the Babylonian exile there was no Israelite or Judaean community, religion, or history. They regard biblical traditions about Abraham, Moses, and later judges, kings, and prophets all to be sixth-century-B.C. (or later) fictions artificially created to provide those in exile with a common identity and heritage. However, it is doubtful that even the best literature has ever had the power to create a real-life community from scratch. Furthermore, these traditions simply contain too much accurate historical knowledge of ancient Egypt and Mesopotamia (corroborated by ancient sources outside the Bible) to be dismissed as mere fiction. It seems unreasonable to assume that these sixth-century-B.C. Judaean fiction writers, who knew so much about life and history elsewhere, knew nothing at all about their own roots, heritage, or past.[8]

But it was consistent with the spirit of the times for sixth-century-B.C. Judaean writers to have preserved (in "relevant" form) the ancient traditions that were uniquely their own. As noted earlier, this was an era when people all over the Near East, perhaps sensing the exhaustion of their indigenous cultures, were nostalgically returning to their respective ancient traditions and heritages. Assuming the Judaeans were like their contemporaries in this regard, the impulse to preserve (and, of course, to make meaningful) archaic traditions about the past would have been far more powerful than any desire to fabricate a fictional past out of thin air.

Making Sense of the Disaster of 586 B.C.

The destruction of Jerusalem and history's apparent invalidation of its religion and its god, had a polarizing effect. As previously mentioned, some Judaeans were so devastated by the experience that they surrendered all Yahwist convictions. But wrestling with the question "Why did this disaster happen?" led to a variety of answers and insights. Some were rather simplistic explanations designed to fix blame. For example, some Judaeans apparently made a dogmatic, literalist appeal to an old formula embedded in the Decalogue:

> "I Yahweh your God am a jealous God, punishing children for the iniquity of parents, to the third and fourth generation of those who reject me." (Exod. 20:5)

Thus, it became fashionable to say, "This disaster is not our fault, but the fault of those earlier scoundrels." In fact, both Jeremiah (31:29) and Ezekiel (18:2) mention (disapprovingly) a popular saying at the time:

> "The parents have eaten sour grapes,
>   and the children's teeth are set on edge."

Each condemned this tendency to blame today's suffering on the sins of one's forebears, no matter how much that might be true. For them, a text such as Exodus 20:5 simply describes a broad pattern of historical cause and effect and does not absolve individuals of moral culpability. Or, as Jeremiah would say, "the teeth of everyone who eats sour grapes shall be set on edge" (31:30).

Another simplistic explanation for the disaster came from some of the Judaeans who fled to Egypt at the time, taking the aged prophet Jeremiah with them. Although Jeremiah had blamed the destruction, in part, on apostasies such as the cult of the "queen of heaven" (7:18), some of his fellow Judaeans—who formerly had been devoted to this cult and now wanted to revive it—turned Jeremiah's explanation against him, saying,

"[W]e are not going to listen to you. . . . We used to have plenty of food, and prospered, and saw no misfortune. But from the time we stopped making offerings to the queen of heaven and pouring out libations to her, we have lacked everything and have perished by the sword and by famine." (Jer. 44:16–18)

In other words, the blame lay earlier in Josiah's reform outlawing these non-Yahwist cults. Ironically, Jeremiah's adversaries were interpreting their own Israelite history within the framework of ancient superstition and polytheism![9]

But not all efforts to make religious sense of destruction and exile led to such simplistic answers. In fact, four writers at this time expressed religious insights that were deeper and more profound: Jeremiah, Ezekiel, the author of the book of Job, and the anonymous biblical poet known simply as "Second Isaiah."

9. Something similar happened after Emperor Theodosius I made Christianity the official religion of the Roman Empire in 392, less than twenty years before the city of Rome fell to the barbarians. The pagans of Rome blamed Christianity for this, saying that everything had been fine until the empire rejected the traditional Roman gods.

Jeremiah and the New Covenant

One example of deepened religious insight during the exile is Jeremiah's "new covenant" prophecy. The content and context of this oracle suggest that it came shortly after the destruction of Jerusalem. This was when Jeremiah, who had been vigorously denouncing Judaean apostasy, immediately changed his tone and spoke optimistically of a new covenant between Yahweh and his people:

The days are surely coming, says Yahweh, when I will make a new covenant with the house of Israel and the house of Judah. It will not be like the covenant that I made with their ancestors when I took them by the hand to bring them out of the land of Egypt—a covenant that they broke, even though I was their husband, says Yahweh. But this is the covenant that I will make with the house of Israel after those days, says Yahweh: I will put my law within them, and I will write it on their hearts; and I will be their God, and they shall be my people. No longer shall they teach one another, or say to each other, "Know Yahweh," for they shall all know me, from the least of them to the greatest, says Yahweh; for I will forgive their iniquity, and remember their sin no more. (Jer. 31:31–34)

The very phrase "new covenant" presupposes that the "old" one is no longer operative. In other words, in typical Near Eastern fashion it presumes that the original covenant had been abrogated by its violation: after all, the ultimate penalty for breaching ancient covenants was always political destruction and the scattering of the population, such as had befallen the Israelites in 586 B.C.

There was no longer any corporate body with whom Yahweh could make a new covenant, a reality also reflected in the wording of this passage. The phrases "house of Israel" and "house of Judah" sound archaic, suggesting that Jeremiah (and Yahweh) had in mind some covenant partner other than those who identified themselves with the former political organization. "Kingdom"-language is completely absent here. The new covenant presumes conditions much like those at the end of the LB Age, the time of the old Sinai covenant, when there was likewise no existing corporate body with whom Yahweh could make a covenant. Indeed, as we saw, the oldest poetry praises Yahweh for having *created* the community (see chapter 3, especially note 12). Now, too, it would be *persons—individuals*, not some preexisting social organization or corporate body—who would embrace the commitments and receive the benefits of the covenant relationship with Yahweh.

This focus on persons above corporate bodies is seen in the assertion that this covenant's law would be "written on the heart," and would involve the forgiveness of sin. Neither of these benefits would mean much to a collective body or social organization, which has no "heart" (or "conscience") and therefore cannot "sin" in the first place. Both are aimed at private individuals, and are framed in such a way as to preclude the use of religion to consolidate an already existing community (something religion had been doing in Israel since the establishment of the monarchy).

For example, because the law of the new covenant is "written on the heart," the undelegated will of Yahweh is once again regarded as the actual determinant of behavior. As in the formative period of the faith, the internalization of Yahweh's will makes unnecessary the entire machinery of external enforcement and religious indoctrination. The "knowledge of Yahweh" does not reside in an accumulated written corpus of religious traditions or doctrines, maintained by scribes and theologians. Instead, it is an aspect of personal character; as such, it exists irrespective of social distinctions altogether, whether class rank ("from the least of them to the greatest") or moral reputation (no one is more privileged than another to pass judgment on personal character).

The Prophet Ezekiel

The work of Ezekiel is a second example of deepened religious insight. In 597 B.C. he was one of the first Judaeans taken in captivity to Babylon, eleven years before Jerusalem was finally destroyed. Among his oracles are some of the harshest condemnations of the corruption of the Judaean state and society. A few, such as Ezekiel 16 and 23, are so obscene that literal translations would be X-rated, a powerful illustration of his extreme bitterness, and of his desperate desire to shock his contemporaries out of their complacency.

But as soon as Jerusalem was destroyed, Ezekiel's tone—like Jeremiah's—changed dramatically. Even though he might have been entitled to gloat, Ezekiel refused to do so. Instead, in chapters 47–48 he described what is sometimes called "the first utopia"—an idealized description of the restoration of Israelite community. While this vision

Map 7.1
Ezekiel's Vision of the Restored Twelve Tribes. (Adapted from *The Macmillan Bible Atlas,* ed. Y. Aharoni and M. Avi-Yonah. 3d ed. [New York: Macmillan, 1993], 126.)

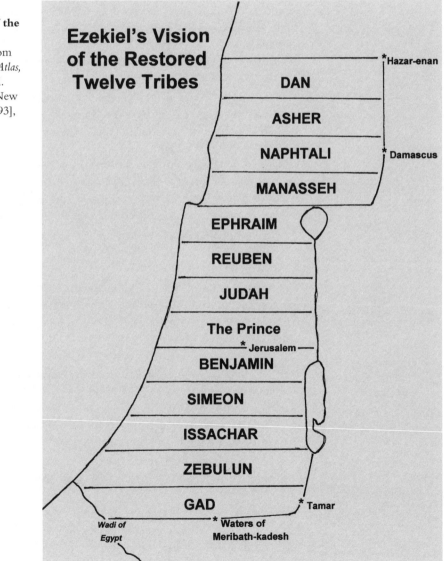

accommodates a Judaean government, it does not simply envision the return of the political state. Instead, Ezekiel imagined the revival of the whole twelve-tribe federation in the Promised Land, the entire length of which would be divided neatly into thirteen east-west strips. One tribe would occupy each strip, with the central one, in and around Jerusalem, reserved for the support of the temple and the Davidic prince. Since the royal bureaucrats and priests would derive their income from this central strip, the other Israelites would not be required to pay taxes.

Ezekiel's understanding of the actual role of the ideal king is consistent with this. Experience no doubt showed him that political leaders rarely do much good for anyone but themselves. His tirade against the shepherds (i.e., the Jerusalem kings) can be compared to Samuel's description of "the ways of the king" discussed in chapter 5:

> Thus says the Lord Yahweh: Ah, you shepherds of Israel who have been feeding yourselves! Should not shepherds feed the sheep? You eat the fat, you clothe yourselves with the wool, you slaughter the fatlings; but you do not feed the sheep. You have not strengthened the weak, you have not healed the sick, you have not bound up the injured, you have not brought back the strayed, you have not sought the lost, but with force and harshness you have ruled them. So they were scattered, because there was no shepherd; and scattered, they became food for all the wild animals. (Ezek. 34:2–5)

It is noteworthy that this oracle ends with Ezekiel's embrace of the pre-monarchic tradition that Israel's only shepherd (i.e., king) is Yahweh, whose rule is characterized by a selfless concern for the well-being of others.

> For thus says the Lord Yahweh: I myself will search for my sheep, and will seek them out. . . . I will bring them out from the peoples and gather them from the countries, and will bring them into their own land. . . . I will feed them with good pasture, and the mountain heights of Israel shall be their pasture; . . . I will seek the lost, and I will bring back the strayed, and I will bind up the injured, and I will strengthen the weak. (vv. 11, 13, 14, 16)

Interestingly, Ezekiel also identified Yahweh's "servant" David as the shepherd (vv. 23–24). Centuries later the notion of God's sovereignty blending into that of an ideal David would help shape the Christian notion that God's kingdom and Christ's rule were one and the same.

The Book of Job

A third example of deepened religious insight is the biblical book of Job, which was most likely written at this time. The vocabulary and imagery of the book suggest that its anonymous author must have been a highly educated man now forced by circumstances to endure a life of great hardship. Indeed, the bitter tone he confers on the main character, Job, reinforces the suspicion that the author had formerly been accustomed to a relatively secure and comfortable life. But the disasters and dislocations of 586 B.C. seem to have radically shaken his outlook on life.

The book of Job has been widely misunderstood.[10] Its main concern is not theodicy—the eternal and fruitless attempt to justify why God allows injustice to prevail and righteous people to suffer. Instead, the central problem with which it wrestles was a set of questions of more urgent relevance to the Judaeans: What is the point of continuing to worship Yahweh? Where does one find religious meaning in it? These are questions for which the book of Job eventually provides an answer.

The author began by creating a brief narrative that sets the stage for an extended discussion between Job, one of the most righteous men of all, and three of his friends.[11] Here at the outset, the central problem is introduced in stark terms: Should Judaeans even bother to continue clinging to a religion that has apparently been discredited by the calamitous turn of events? In fact, this is precisely the question posed by Job's wife after all their children had been killed, after their property had been carried off (by Babylonians, no less!), and after Job's body had been wracked by disfiguring disease: "Do you still hold fast your integrity? Curse God, and die" (2:9, RSV). If God is supposed to support the righteous, hasn't he somehow failed Job? In other words, is not Yahweh unreliable, and therefore unworthy of worship?

Instead of providing comfort, Job's three friends (joined later by a certain Elihu) then spend almost three dozen chapters arguing about the cause of Job's misfortune. It is this long-winded argument that gives readers the (mistaken) impression that the book is a theodicy. Clearly, Job—who is not yet willing to abandon Yahweh—personifies the Judaean community in exile.[12] His demand for an explanation parallels their search for religious meaning. The significance of his three friends can be understood in two different ways. First, when viewed as part of the theodicy debate, they unquestionably represent the rather conventional (and unsatisfactory) view that God rewards the righteous and makes the wicked to suffer, a view that the author, from beginning to end, repeatedly rejects: in truth, the suffering Job happens to be righteous.

But second, when viewed in terms of the exilic Judaean search for a meaningful foundation for the future of the faith, the three friends signify something broader and deeper—namely, the tendency to find

10. Part of the problem is that the book of Job is notoriously difficult to translate. W. F. Albright once remarked that an academically honest translation would leave one-third of it blank.

11. Even here, at the height of biblical fiction writing, the impulse was still strong not to create out of thin air but to draw on archaic traditions. Traditions about an ancient and legendary Job were well known at the time (see Ezek. 14:14, 20). Whatever those archaic traditions might have been, they were probably thoroughly recast by the author to address the urgent predicament of the Judaean exile.

12. The notion that Job is a representative character is reinforced by a tradition in the Babylonian Talmud that the book was a parable and that the biblical Job was not a historical person.

religious meaning by returning to traditional doctrines and teachings. They insist that Job's (i.e., Israel's) future alongside Yahweh can best be secured by actively embracing established religious forms and doctrines (such as, in this particular case, conventional teachings about the suffering of the wicked). Job's three friends simply recommend that he "repent"—in other words, return to the traditions, acquiesce to their authority, accept the validity of their conventional teachings, and thereby guarantee a bright future of religious fellowship with Yahweh. Because they believe religious meaning resides in established traditions, they assume that Job's future (and that of the religious community) depends on embracing those traditions.

Throughout the (intentionally?) long-winded arguments, Job refuses to follow the recommendation of the three friends—whether rightly or wrongly, he simply has no confidence in conventional religious teachings. Instead, he repeatedly demands from Yahweh a face-to-face explanation for his current suffering. When Yahweh finally appears in a theophany (chapters 38–41), it is not to offer any such explanation but rather to extol his own magnificence. Job then realizes that explanations for present suffering are irrelevant as far as the future is concerned. Yahweh himself confirms that the strategy recommended by the three friends (i.e., more firmly embrace established doctrines) is all wrong. Here, at the end of the book, the author returns to the central problem with which the book wrestles: What must be the basis for the continuity of the religious community? The book's climax provides the answer: religious meaning—the foundation for the future—does not lie in established religious traditions (what "the ear had heard") but in a dynamic encounter with the reality of God (what "the eye now sees"), even in the midst of suffering:

> "I had heard of thee by the hearing of the ear,
>   but now my eye sees thee;
> therefore I recant
>   and I am comforted in dust and ashes."
> (Job 42:5–6, author's translation)[13]

In other words, Job's future with Yahweh—and Israel's—does not require deference to established religious teachings or systems. This remarkable work illuminates a unique concept of the Yahwist faith: that the preservation of familiar traditions, doctrines, and forms alone cannot ensure a religion's future. Furthermore, in another stroke of profundity it insists that a commitment to this particular God—Yahweh—must not be based on the expectation of reward. It must be grounded in the perceived intrinsic value of something else. The role of faith is to affirm that value, not to seek any reward.

13. Following an ancient Greek version, this last line is almost always translated, "I *repent* in dust and ashes," even though Job has consistently and correctly insisted that he has done nothing wrong. The key word is the Hebrew *nhm;* this word appears in Isaiah 40:1, where it is correctly translated "comfort." The use of this word in Job 42:6 brings the book to an apt conclusion: Job's longed-for "comfort" is finally found, not in his embrace of traditional religious teachings but in his dynamic experience of the reality of Yahweh. But the Greek translators had little grasp of what the book was actually about; consequently, they considered Job's contrition as loosely analogous to an act of repentance and translated accordingly. This illustrates the extent to which ancient traditions—even biblical ones—were being misunderstood by later scribes.

"Second Isaiah"   The fourth example of deepened religious insight during the exile is the poetry contained in chapters 40–55 of the book of Isaiah. Their author cannot have been the eighth-century-B.C. prophet Isaiah associated with the first thirty-nine chapters of that book; instead, this poet lived in the sixth century B.C. and witnessed firsthand the fall of the Babylonian Empire to Cyrus, king of Persia. Scholars refer to the anonymous author (or authors) of these poems simply as "Second Isaiah."

In one key aspect, Cyrus's political policy was quite different from that of his Assyrian and Babylonian predecessors: whereas they were generally intolerant of the indigenous cultures, religions, and social institutions of the peoples they conquered, Cyrus chose to exploit the popular nostalgia for these things. He and his successors actually encouraged the distinctive religions and customs of their subject peoples to flourish, hoping that by directing their energies inward to the cultivation of their respective cultures, they would accept Persian control of the political arena. This strategy appears to have been largely successful.

Cyrus's triumph was the historical moment when Second Isaiah heard Yahweh command the heavenly courtiers to go to Babylon to comfort and console the Judaeans with the good news that the period of exile is over:

Box 7.3—The Edict of Cyrus

This ancient text, commissioned by the Persian king Cyrus, portrays the Babylonian god Marduk having rejected the Babylonian kings. It also foreshadows Cyrus's policy of fostering the traditional cultural and religious life of the various conquered peoples:

> [The god Marduk] scoured all the lands for a friend. . . . He called Cyrus, king of Anshan. He nominated him to be ruler over all. . . . At my deeds Marduk, the great lord, rejoiced, and to me, Cyrus, the king who worshiped him, . . . he graciously gave his blessing. . . . All the kings who sat in throne rooms . . . brought me their heavy tribute and kissed my feet in Babylon. . . . [T]he holy cities beyond the Tigris whose sanctuaries had been in ruins over a long period, the gods whose abode is in the midst of them, I returned to their places and housed them in lasting abodes. . . . May all the gods whom I have placed within their sanctuaries address a daily prayer in my favour before Bel and Nabu, that my days be long. (*DOTT,* 92–94)

The Old Testament preserves independent memory of Cyrus's support of his subjects' native customs and traditions. He is shown addressing the exiled Judaeans in Babylon, giving them permission to return (or "go up") to Jerusalem:

> "Thus says King Cyrus of Persia: Yahweh, the God of heaven, has given me all the kingdoms of the earth, and he has charged me to build him a house in Jerusalem, which is in Judah. Whoever is among you of all his people, may Yahweh his God be with him! Let him go up." (2 Chron. 36:23)

> Speak tenderly to Jerusalem,
>   and cry to her
> that her warfare is ended,
>   that her iniquity is pardoned. (Isa. 40:2, RSV)

Yahweh will now lead the people back to their ancestral land. The poet portrays the creation of a highway for God:

> Every valley shall be exalted,
>   and every mountain and hill shall be made low:
> and the crooked shall be made straight,
>   and the rough places plain:
> And the glory of the LORD shall be revealed,
>   and all flesh shall see it together:
>   for the mouth of the LORD hath spoken it. (Isa. 40:4–5, KJV)

The beauty of this passage can only be adequately rendered in something as majestic as Handel's · oratorio *Messiah*—nothing but music can approach what is achieved in this beautiful lyric poetry.

Just as other prophets had seen Yahweh's hand in the unfolding of human historical processes (see Appendix B), so did Second Isaiah. Yet with one bold stroke of the pen, he also attempted to invalidate the Israelite exercise of political power that had become normative during the monarchy: he declared Yahweh's "messiah," to whom political authority and power were delegated, to be a *non*-Israelite, Cyrus:

> Thus says Yahweh to his anointed [i.e., to his messiah], to Cyrus,
> . . . .
> I will go before you
>   and level the mountains,
> I will break in pieces the doors of bronze
>   and cut through the bars of iron,
> . . . .
> so that you may know that it is I, Yahweh,
>   the God of Israel, who call you by your name.
> For the sake of my servant Jacob,
>   and Israel my chosen,
> I call you by your name,
>   I surname you, though you do not know me. (Isa. 45:1–4)

This prophet is also known for the four so-called "Servant Songs" (Isa. 42:1–9; 49:1–7; 50:4–9; 52:13–53:12). In these songs (as in the passage just quoted) the poet transferred some of the traditional titles of kingship—"chosen one" and "servant"—to the eponymous ancestor of Israel, Jacob (not Abraham!). The legitimate titles and duties of Israelite kingship have now been delegated to the entire community. At the same time, the royal duties have been radically redefined in nonpolitical terms. For example, whereas kings and states usually maintain (even by force) the boundary that separates "us" from "them," the Servant is commanded by Yahweh to seek fellowship with foreigners:

> "It is too light a thing that you should be my servant
>> to raise up the tribes of Jacob
>> and to restore the survivors of Israel;
> I will give you as a light to the nations,
>> that my salvation may reach to the end of the earth." (Isa. 49:6)

The Hebrew word here translated "nations" is also often translated "Gentiles"; it refers to those peoples whose religious and traditional heritage heretofore has not been Israelite (see note 1, this chapter). Furthermore, the servant Israel is said to *be* the covenant (42:6) in the archaic sense of the word—the instrument by which these non-Israelites are drawn into fellowship with Yahweh. But whereas kings and states characteristically exercise coercive force, the servant Israel must not, even to the point of submitting to others' attacks (50:6). The hope is that the servant Israel's example will show the Gentile world something more noble and inspiring than "politics as usual."

14. The creation story in Genesis 1–3, which also may have been penned during the exile, promotes a similar vision by asserting the common ancestry of all human beings. The myth of common ancestry may be closer to the biological truth than most people realize. Every one of us has two biological parents, four grandparents, eight great-grandparents, etc. If we were to go back twenty-four more generations—only seven hundred years at most—every one of us would have the same number of forebears as populated the entire planet at the time (approximately 300 million people in A.D. 1300).

Thus, in a sense, the Servant's mission subverts the policies of the Persian emperors, which rewarded subject peoples for retrenching within their respective parochial boundaries and traditions. Like Job's rejection of the advice of his three friends, Second Isaiah's so-called universalism sees the Israelite community existing for some purpose other than preserving its own cultural traditions within its own traditional boundaries. Its purpose is frankly "missionary": enlightening the whole world to those ethical principles that transcend particular social and cultural differences. This is a vision of the unity of all humanity that draws deeply on religious emphases found in premonarchic Yahwism. Second Isaiah thus foresees the worship of Yahweh accomplishing religiously and substantively what the Persian Empire could only do politically and superficially.[14]

The insights each of these four writers acquired during the exile each answered one of the vital questions confronting the Judaeans at the time:

1. Would there be a future for any religious community associated with the god Yahweh? (Jeremiah's new covenant says "Yes.")

2. What form will the future community take, or not take? (Ezekiel's utopian vision says it will not be political in nature.)

3. Where can one find the meaning necessary for sustaining the religious character of this community? (The author of Job finds it in a dynamic encounter with the reality of God, not in traditional doctrines and teachings.)

4. Who—or what—will constitute an authoritative mission for this religious community? (Second Isaiah says it will be the apolitical "outreach" mission of the Servant of Yahweh.)

These writers and their answers, each in their own ways, expressed a vision of Yahweh very different from the image of the divine patron affirmed by the now-defunct Yahwisticism of Jerusalem. After the disaster of 586 B.C., this vision inspired sufficient commitment to the worship of Yahweh that many Judaeans resisted the temptation to defect to other religions and gods.

Revived Loyalty to Parochial Traditions

15. This tendency is exemplified by the book of Esther, which contains no reference to God or to Israel's religious character. Ethnicity is not the same as race. Ethnic groups are fundamentally concerned with maintaining a social boundary distinguishing their members from outsiders (Law of Contrast). Members subordinate their personal identities and behavior to the collective norm, signaling their affiliation through symbolic and visible actions such as how they dress, what they eat, whom they marry (and how), what names they give their children, what ritual ceremonies they perform (and when), how they speak, whom they consider a "brother," etc.

In the century or so following the triumph of Cyrus and the end of the exile in 538 B.C., a different kind of religious impulse arose and soon became prominently associated with Israel's god. This was the tendency to view religion as somewhat peripheral in a Judaean culture whose core was becoming defined increasingly in terms of distinctive ethnic traits.[15] Persian policy supported and encouraged this sort of preoccupation among subject peoples. It was reinforced by the wave of cultural nostalgia still sweeping across the Near East—many peoples sought to nurture and develop the indigenous cultural traits, social institutions, and traditions that apparently made them distinctive. For example, Persian "underwriting" may well have facilitated the compiling and canonizing of the Pentateuch, the first five books of the Hebrew Bible, or Old Testament (see Appendix A). Israelite religion became a useful tool helping to enhance Judaean distinctiveness. Ironically, this Persian goodwill reinforced the very tendency that the author of Job had criticized: many Judaeans now considered the essence and the future of their religion to be the preservation of sacred traditions and doctrines.

For example, on returning from exile in Babylon, some Judaeans began rebuilding the Jerusalem temple, reviving the parochial association of Yahweh with a particular sacred place and formal set of rituals. A rift soon developed between them and the existing population to the north, who initially volunteered to share in the rebuilding effort, citing their shared religious beliefs ("we worship your God as you do"; Ezra 4:2). Zerubbabel, a descendant of the house of David, rebuffed this request on

16. Apparently, the Judaeans themselves lacked the will and the resources to finish the temple (see Haggai 1). Work resumed only after the Persian emperor Darius (ruled 521–485 B.C.) pledged imperial funds to underwrite its construction and upkeep (see Ezra 6).

behalf of the returnees, subordinating these religious considerations to a seemingly sacrosanct social and cultural boundary separating "us" from "you." He said to them, "You shall have no part with us in building a house to our God" (Ezra 4:3). Work on the temple ground to a halt.[16]

When Cyrus's successor Cambyses died in 522 B.C., revolts erupted across the empire, destabilizing the early years of Darius's rule. Judaean leaders apparently thought the time was right to reestablish yet another aspect of past traditions: the political glories of the Davidic dynasty. The prophet Haggai, speaking on behalf of Yahweh and alluding to the political turmoil of the time, proclaimed Zerubbabel the "chosen one" and the "servant" of Yahweh, endorsing Zerubbabel's monarchic (if not imperial) pretensions:

> I am about to destroy the strength of the kingdoms of the nations, and overthrow the chariots and their riders; and the horses and their riders shall fall, every one by the sword of a comrade. On that day, says Yahweh of hosts, I will take you, O Zerubbabel my servant, son of Shealtiel, says Yahweh, and make you like a signet ring; for I have chosen you, says Yahweh of hosts. (Hag. 2:22–23)

The normally tolerant Persians drew the line at the revival of parochial *political* traditions such as the Davidic covenant. Darius quelled the revolts; the predicted overthrow of kingdoms never occurred; and Zerubbabel was never heard from again, his political ambitions apparently unfulfilled.

In stark contrast to the earlier prophets (see chapters 5 and 6), those of the postexilic period (such as Haggai) tended to link religion with parochial social, cultural, and political traditions. As Haggai's misguided oracle about Zerubbabel demonstrates, these later prophets had little insight into the events of their own day and were incompetent when it came to foreseeing the future ramifications of current priorities and choices. It is not surprising that the phenomenon of prophecy soon died out.

Over the next century, other Judaean traditionalists would seek to establish additional formal criteria to define social and cultural boundaries increasingly considered sacrosanct. Among these were commitments to temple ritual and the Jerusalem priesthood, to dietary laws, to circumcision, to Hebrew names and language, to Sabbath observance and other sacred holidays, to the avoidance of pronouncing the name "Yahweh," and to the social application of the Torah as enforced law. They were so successful in this endeavor that by the first century A.D. these traits had become part of the distinctive hallmark of Judaean religion (i.e., Judaism) and among the most tangible emblems of Judaean identity. Even today, Orthodox Jews identify most of these traits as part of the core of Judaism. Israel's God, who had previously been associated with a religious community and then a political regime, was now being associated with an emerging ethnic group.

Ezra and Nehemiah

Around 445 B.C., Nehemiah, a Judaean, was appointed by the Persian king to serve as governor of Judaea, administering civil affairs on behalf of the empire. The book of Nehemiah clearly indicates that he arrived in Jerusalem from Persia not only with a royal mandate but also with lavish funding from the Persian king. Jerusalem remained in ruins, with only temple personnel and a few bureaucrats living there (Neh. 11:1–2). Rebuilding the city had apparently been such a low priority for the Judaean population that individuals had to be coerced or induced to abandon their farms, relocate there, and participate in urban renewal projects.

The rapid rebuilding of the city's walls and gates provoked intense opposition from neighboring social groups (Nehemiah 6), who apparently saw this project as part of Jerusalem's bid to establish regional political control. At best, this would alter the balance of regional political interests; at worst, it might be a prelude to rebellion against the empire, threatening the peace and economic stability of Palestine and Transjordan. A power struggle raged within the city, with various members of the Judaean aristocracy and priestly class developing close ties with other regional "strong men" such as Sanballat of Samaria and Tobiah the Ammonite (Neh. 6:17–19; 13:4–9). The Judaean community was thus divided not only along political lines but also along economic ones. Nehemiah implemented strict measures attempting to control the greed of the wealthy

Figure 7.2

Nehemiah Rebuilds Jerusalem. Remains of the corner of a second-century-B.C. tower (*top left*) were discovered in Jerusalem abutting the older stepped stone structure (*top right*). Most scholars believe that this tower was built on the foundation of Nehemiah's rapidly constructed eastern wall, a wall that may have reused the stepped stone structure for defensive purposes. Situated higher up the slope than the old Jebusite-Davidic wall (Fig. 4.3), Jerusalem in Nehemiah's time must have been extremely small. (Courtesy Gary A. Herion)

in the Judaean community, who were seizing the children and the property of poor people unable to pay the interest on their loans (Nehemiah 5).

Nehemiah also mandated Sabbath observance, threatening to "lay hands" on anyone who violated it (Neh. 13:21). Whereas the old Jerusalem kings had used a religious tradition (the Divine Charter) to consolidate and support their use of coercive force, Nehemiah used coercive force to consolidate and support a religious tradition ("proper" Sabbath observance). Either way, religion was employed as an official instrument of social control, and the God of Israel was again being invoked to legitimize the wielding of power over other human beings.

At some point, Nehemiah was joined by Ezra, a Judaean priest and scribe appointed by the Persian king to administer Judaean religious affairs. Together, the two sponsored a reform whose centerpiece was a "covenant" (actually a vow or pledge) to observe the "law of Moses, which Yahweh had given to Israel" (Nehemiah 8–9). The community's religious standard of behavior had now become some sort of written document. Opinions are divided over what actually comprised this written "law of Moses": some feel that it may have been the book of the law discovered in the temple during the reign of King Josiah; others believe it was the law code contained in Leviticus; and some argue that it may even have been the first five books of the Bible, now completed. Since the Judaeans viewed their subjugation to the Persian Empire as punishment for their apostasy (Neh. 9:32–38), they may have believed that obedience to this law of Moses would result in a reversal of fortune, restoring Judaean political power and economic prosperity. If so, this "vow" constituted a blatant identification of a religious tradition with purely political ambitions and economic interests.

But even the stipulations of this code fell short of meeting society's needs, at least as these needs were defined by Ezra and Nehemiah. For example, ancient and generalized warnings about the dangers of covenant alliances with non-Israelites were now interpreted by them as strict prohibitions against marrying Gentiles. Ezra and Nehemiah even took the additional step of requiring, and enforcing, the divorcing of non-Judaean wives (Ezra 9–10). In time, endogamy (marriage only within the group) would also constitute part of the core of Judaism.[17]

From this time on, there was a persistent tendency, especially among the Jerusalem elite, to identify the proper or "orthodox" religious community with formal patterns of ritual and economic behavior sanctioned by specific interpretations of scriptural laws. The problem was that the religious authorities themselves could not agree about what specifically constituted orthodox religious belief and practice. Nor could they agree about who was authorized by God to receive the privileges and responsibilities of leadership. The first-century Jewish historian Josephus notes

17. This prohibition against intermarriage remains official dogma throughout much of Judaism, although it has often been ignored in the modern Western world. Such prohibitions would have been counterproductive to the original Yahwists of the early Iron Age, who were inclined to extend their community to include anyone from any "tribe" who was committed to the religious ethic of Yahweh. See the book of Ruth.

Box 7.4—Ezra and the Law of Moses

Although no one knows what constituted Ezra's "book of the law of Moses," it clearly established binding standards of Jewish life and conduct. (Regulations pertaining to the festivals of booths [or Sukkoth] are found in Leviticus 23:33–43.) The following passage from Nehemiah describes the Judaeans' response to Ezra's reading from this book of the law.

> [A]ll the people gathered together into the square before the Water Gate. They told the scribe Ezra to bring the book of the law of Moses, which Yahweh had given to Israel. . . . This was on the first day of the seventh month. He read from it facing the square before the Water Gate from early morning until midday, . . . and the ears of all the people were attentive to the book of the law. . . .
>
> On the second day the heads of ancestral houses of all the people, with the priests and the Levites, came together to the scribe Ezra in order to study the words of the law. And they found it written in the law, which Yahweh had commanded by Moses, that the people of Israel should live in booths during the festival of the seventh month. . . . So the people went out . . . and made booths for themselves. . . . And there was very great rejoicing. And day by day, from the first day to the last day, he read from the book of the law of God. (Neh. 8:1–3, 13–14, 16–18)

This is a classsic description of an imitative reform, where people restore what they believe to be an ancient religious form or ritual practice, whose meaning may be entirely lost or unknown.

that shortly after the time of Ezra, such internecine disagreements could even reach fratricidal proportion, as when the high priest John murdered his own scheming brother, Joshua (*Jewish Antiquities* 11.7.1). Joshua had apparently bribed the Persian governor to support his bid to replace John as high priest. One day, their argument grew violent, and John brazenly killed Joshua right on the spot—within the sacred precincts of the Jerusalem temple.

A class of scribes (or "teachers of the law") arose to ensure that particular scriptural interpretations did not deviate from the party line of the various sects that soon began to form.[18] In 1941, Ralph Marcus described the diversity of these Judaean sects, observing that they ranged from extremist right-wing reactionary groups to lunatic revolutionaries of the far left. Not surprisingly, most Judaeans busily engaged in the daily routines of village life undoubtedly had little interest in the hairsplitting arguments of the scribes. The latter responded in kind, disparaging these folks as "ignoramuses" and "bumpkins" (*'am ha'arets*).

18. The NT Gospels contain abundant references to these scribes, and in the first several centuries of the Christian era many of their most memorable legal interpretations were collected and preserved in the Mishnah and Talmud, books that are today considered quasi-sacred by Orthodox Jews.

Box 7.5—Arguing Over the Purity of Vessels

If a liquid is poured from a ceremonially clean vessel (A) into an unclean one (B), does the clean vessel now become unclean? In other words, does ritual "contamination" flow upstream? Such questions could be extremely divisive within early Judaism, as entire sects identified themselves in terms of their positions not only on ritual matters such as this but also on certain doctrines (Are angels real? Do the dead get raised to life again?).

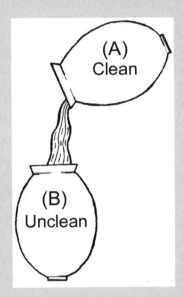

The author of one of the Dead Sea Scrolls (the so-called "Halakhic Letter"), probably the leader of the Essene sect, claimed that the clean vessel (A) *did* become unclean because the stream of liquid had become impure and had contaminated it:

> [And even] regarding [poured out] liquid streams, we sa[y] that they do not have [pu]rity. (*RDSS*, 86)

According to the Mishnah (*Yadaim* 4:7), the Pharisees believed otherwise, claiming that the stream remained pure and the clean vessel (A) remained clean, a view which the Sadducees disputed:

> Say Sadducees: "We complain against you, Pharisees. For you declare clean an unbroken stream of liquid."

Such disputes over seemingly irrelevant matters are an excellent illustration of the Law of Elaboration (see p. 4): *Religious specialists with nothing better to do will produce elaborate refinements on minor esoteric points*. In the villages, most Jews ignored such hairsplitting as a waste of religious energy, further discrediting the religious authorities in their eyes. Many of them would have endorsed Jesus' criticism of sectarian Jews more preoccupied with the ceremonial purity of vessels than with the weightier issue of the religious ethic (Matthew 23, especially vv. 23–26).

The End of the Old Testament Period

19. This has also altered the way historians view the rise of Christianity. Prior to the twentieth century, early Christianity was viewed as a sect deviating or branching off from a more normative or traditional Judaism. Since there now appears to have been no "normative Judaism" at this time, the notion of Christianity being an "aberration" has lost its appeal. Early Christianity was no more deviant than any other Jewish sect at the time, and its claim to constitute the true Israel was no less valid.

20. Ironically, apocalypticism and dualism were not Israelite in origin but were major elements in the Persian religion, Zoroastrianism. The Persian emperors promoted a politicized version of Zoroastrianism, in which the god Ahuru-Mazda functioned as the divine patron of the empire. The Jews embraced some elements of this religion, so that within a few centuries these elements found natural expression in Jewish literature.

Many cracks began to appear within the Judaean community after the conquests of Alexander the Great (around 330 B.C.) brought aspects of Greek culture to the Near East (Hellenism). Once the idea had become established in principle that a legitimate role of Judaism (i.e., the Judaean religion) was to maintain the social boundaries that preserved Judaean ethnic distinctiveness, it was inevitable that the Judaeans, or Jews, would begin quarreling over the details. Was it essential to perform sacrifice in the Jerusalem temple, or not? What sort of behavior could "defile" a person? How fully could a Jew participate in Hellenistic culture? What exactly did it mean to "keep the Sabbath day holy"? Even circumcision proved divisive. The result was a tragic expenditure of religious energy, spent on differentiating not just Jews from non-Jews but also "good" Jews from "bad" ones. Schisms were so rampant at the time that scholars are now reluctant to speak of one single Judaism, referring instead to multiple—and competing—Judaisms, none being "normative" and each claiming to be the legitimate heir of the "Israel" described in Hebrew scriptures (the Law and the Prophets).[19]

Around 170 B.C., the Greek king Antiochus Epiphanes IV dispatched his soldiers to aid Jewish aristocrats in Jerusalem who were eager to embrace Hellenism, the international culture of the Greeks. With Antiochus's support, the pro-Hellenistic factions became sufficiently powerful to begin ruthlessly persecuting other Jews who clung to traditional modes of Judaean identity. Tradition recalls that they went so far as to publicly execute Jewish mothers whose infant sons had been circumcised. Antiochus's troops gained control of the Jerusalem temple, sacrificing swine on its altar and erecting a statue of the god Zeus within its precincts in open contempt for Jewish tradition (see the apocryphal book of 2 Maccabees 3–6).

Some Jewish traditionalists apparently felt that the world, as they knew it, was about to come to a violent end. This notion finds expression in the book of Daniel, which was written at this time. Unlike the Israelite prophets of old, Daniel's predictions about the future were *apocalyptic*, using cryptic symbols and bizarre visions to describe violence unfolding according to some divinely predetermined timetable. These predictions were also *dualistic*, envisioning humanity caught between clearly defined forces of good and evil.[20] Believing themselves to be participating in an end-times struggle against evil, many Jews found their resolve strengthened in the face of this persecution. Eventually, they recaptured and "purified" the temple, expelling Antiochus's troops. Over the next several centuries, Jews would write numerous other apocalyptic books. In their dualistic frameworks, Jews belonging to rival sects were sometimes listed among the "wicked" slated for destruction.

By 140 B.C., a politically ambitious Jewish family could position its members to serve not only as priests in the Jerusalem temple but also as kings over a newly independent Jewish state. Ironically, this Hasmonean Dynasty—known popularly as the Maccabees—embraced Hellenistic culture. For a variety of very different reasons, many Jews refused to identify with this regime, which lacked traditional legitimacy: its kings were not of the house of David, and its priests were not from the appropriate families. One group, the Essenes, abandoned Jerusalem in disgust over the Hasmoneans and established its own sectarian enclave along the Dead Sea. Other opponents actually invited the Roman general Pompey to come to Jerusalem and put an end to the Hasmonean regime.

The famous Dead Sea Scrolls, discovered in the mid-twentieth century, contain a remarkably vivid picture of this Jewish factionalism. Each sect—such as the Essenes who likely wrote these scrolls—produced religious literature to promote its own view of the essence of Israel's faith. As various of these sects disappeared (either through dwindling popularity or violent suppression at the hands of Roman soldiers or even fellow Jews), their literature fell into disuse. However, sometime around A.D. 100 Jews sympathetic to the scribes and Pharisees collected the additional writings they preferred to include as scriptural supplements to the Law and the Prophets (see Appendix A). The result was the completion, and effectively the creation, of what is today called the Hebrew Bible or Old Testament.

Suggestions for Further Reading

Additional information on the topics discussed in this chapter can be found in the following sources.

Dictionary/Encyclopedia Entries

Anchor Bible Dictionary: Bedouin and Bedouin States; Dead Sea Scrolls; Essenes; Ezra; Hasmonean Dynasty; Ishmaelites; Josephus; Judaism; Maccabean Revolt; Nehemiah; New Covenant; Persian Empire; Pharisees; Queen of Heaven; Sabbath; Sadducees; Scribes; Unclean and Clean

The Exile

B. Anderson, "Exodus and Covenant in Second Isaiah and the Prophetic Tradition." In *Magnalia Dei, the Mighty Acts of God,* edited by F. M. Cross et al., 339–360. Garden City, N.Y.: Doubleday, 1976.

_____,"The New Covenant and the Old." In *The Old Testament and Christian Faith,* 225–242. New York: Herder & Herder, 1969.

D. N. Freedman, "'Son of Man, Can These Bones Live?' The Exile." *Interpretation* 29 (1975): 171–186.

C. North, *The Suffering Servant in Deutero-Isaiah*. 2d ed. New York: Oxford University Press, 1956.

Postexilic and Greco-Roman Times

E. Bickerman, *From Ezra to the Last of the Maccabees*. New York: Schocken Books, 1962.

M. Hengel, *Judaism and Hellenism*. 2 vols. London: SCM Press, 1974.

Sectarian Judaism and Literature

S. Cohen, *From the Maccabees to the Mishnah*. Philadelphia: Westminster Press, 1987.

L. Finkelstein, *The Pharisees*. 2 vols. Philadelphia: Jewish Publication Society, 1962.

J. Neusner, *From Politics to Piety: The Emergence of Pharisaic Judaism*. Englewood Cliffs, N.J.: Prentice-Hall, 1973.

G. Nickelsburg, *Jewish Literature Between the Bible and the Mishnah*. Philadelphia: Fortress Press, 1981.

D.S. Russell, *The Old Testament Pseudepigrapha*. Philadelphia: Fortress Press, 1987.

E. P. Sanders, *Judaism: Practice and Belief 63 B.C.E. to 66 C.E.* Harrisburg, Pa.: Trinity Press, 1992.

M. Stone, *Scriptures, Sects, and Visions: A Profile of Judaism from Ezra to the Jewish Revolts.* Philadelphia: Fortress Press, 1980.

Eight

Jesus and the New Testament Reformation: The Renewal of an Old Faith

Suggested Reading
The Teachings of Jesus: Matthew 5–7; 18:23–35; 21:33–46
The Final Days of Jesus: Luke 19–24
The Early Church: Acts 1–4
Christian Community and Traditional Judaism: Romans 1–4; 9–11

Introduction

Even before the 1947 discovery of the Dead Sea Scrolls, Ralph Marcus, writing in the *Journal for Near Eastern Studies,* had described the Jewish world of Jesus in terms of the American political scene: He characterized the Essenes as right-wing, separatist fundamentalists, who lost in their bid to control the Jerusalem temple, then withdrew to a community house on the shores of the Dead Sea. The Sadducees were extremely wealthy and conservative, their power consolidated in the Jerusalem temple. The Pharisees were centrists who were themselves divided into the conservative-leaning Shammaites and the more liberal Hillelites.[1] On the radical left was what Josephus termed "the fourth philosophy," the Zealots and Sicarii. The latter were revolutionary terrorists, publicly assassinating fellow Jews in the name of God. According to Josephus, the revolutionary fanaticism of the Zealots prompted Roman legions to mobilize against the Jews in A.D. 66, and to destroy the city of Jerusalem four years later.

From the ruins of the first century A.D. emerged Rabbinic Judaism, in some respects an extension of the centrist-learning Pharisees. It cultivated a strong sense of Jewish "peoplehood" as well as a devout commitment to obeying the Torah as a way of serving God and of consolidating and preserving Jewish ethnic identity. At the same time it gave rabbinic officials significant control and influence over the Jewish community, at least locally at the subpolitical level. Rabbinic Judaism succeeded in preserving many forms of Jewish life that had emerged in the postexilic

1. The centrist position of the Pharisees may explain why the Romans entrusted them to define Judaism after the Jewish War of A.D. 66–70. Pharisaic rabbis established an academy of Jewish life and culture in the coastal town of Jamnia, becoming the officially recognized leaders of the Jewish community. Their religious vision would eventually be canonized in the Mishnah and Talmud.

period—particularly dietary laws, circumcision, and avoidance of inter-marriage with non-Jews—and it is still alive today in the Orthodox Judaism it spawned.

But here we turn our attention to another religious movement that arose out of the ruins of first-century Judaism, one whose dependency on the Hebrew religious tradition may not seem so obvious. This was early Christianity. In fact, because it soon rejected most of the Jewish religious forms that had emerged in the postexilic period, almost everything about it seems "new." Yet it would be a mistake to caricature early Christianity as representing a complete or even a significant break from the Israelite religious past. For example, the early Christians' concern for and adherence to the ongoing Yahwist tradition is attested, among other things, by the fact that one out of three NT verses contains an OT reference or allusion, intentionally directing readers back to the biblical religious tradition. It is often assumed that these early Christian writers were more or less struggling to create a formal (and somewhat contrived) link between something possessing religious "authority" (the OT) and some-

Figure 8.1

Isis and Madonna. A popular mystery cult in the Roman Empire was associated with the Egyptian goddess Isis (*left*), often depicted with son Horus on her lap. This cult promised worldly success and the reassurance of resurrection. Some Christian depictions of Mary and Jesus adopted this classic pose (*right*), suggesting that they gave Christian content to a popular Greco-Roman artistic motif.

thing needing religious credibility—namely, Jesus and the newly emerging religious fellowship of his disciples and followers. But the issue is hardly this simple, if for no other reason than that the non-Jewish world at large offered many other techniques for establishing religious credibility and authority. Why would the adherents of an ostensibly new and universal religion such as Christianity stake their credibility on something considered *old* and parochially *Jewish?*[2]

These writers appealed to the OT as a means of understanding and explaining their faith—and they understood their "founder," Jesus of Nazareth, to have done the same. Yet they saw their fellowship not as just another sect of Judaism but as God's true "Israel," which was open to all, Jews and non-Jews. And although they believed that ancient Yahwism provided genuine religious *substance* for their faith, they did not believe it was necessary for their fellowship to preserve the Jewish *forms* commonly used to express and convey that tradition. They even had a proverb (attributed to Jesus himself) acknowledging this paradoxical embrace-yet-rejection of tradition: "No one puts new wine into old wineskins" (Mark 2:22).

This final chapter offers a preliminary exploration into what the early Christians embraced from the Israelite heritage, what they rejected, and why. The guiding question is a fairly simple one: How "new" was this religious substance—the proverbial "wine" of Christianity? Here we propose a fresh approach for answering this question and for placing the NT in historical perspective by viewing the NT as *a witness to a religious reform movement within first-century Judaism.* Typically, such reform movements—disenchanted with the prevailing religious norms, priorities, and traditions of the day—discover religious meaning in the distant past and reach back there for a fresh perspective on the troubled present. Something old can suddenly seem quite "new." In other words, the early Christian community, probably beginning with Jesus himself, had an understanding of scripture that was not only *different* from the Jewish religious establishment of the time but also based on *older* Israelite understandings of the religious tradition.

2. The prevalence of pagan mystery cults shows that popular messages of salvation hardly required a Jewish foundation. Around A.D. 150, a man named Marcion agreed and began expunging all New Testament references to the Old Testament. His fellow Christians in Rome were so appalled that they dropped all religious fellowship with him, forcing him to establish his own church. Ironically, Marcion's lingering influence on orthodox Christianity is reflected in the comparative neglect given to the Old Testament in Christian sermons and adult education programs.

Examples of the Archaic Nature of "New" Teachings

Many readers will understandably be skeptical about the claim that a Testament called "New" retains and promotes a religious tradition that is actually quite *old.* But two examples may be cited to demonstrate that this is precisely what we encounter time and again in the NT.

1. *Paul's Treatment of Abraham.* In many of the extrabiblical Jewish writings at that time, the patriarch Abraham was treated as if he was the

3. In earlier times that role had been given to the patriarch Jacob (see chapter 4, note 8). Although Jacob's very name was synonymous with Israel, first-century writers observed that the hallmark sign of Jewish ethnicity—circumcision—had been associated with *Abraham* (Genesis 17). And unlike Jacob, Abraham had been explicitly identified as a "Hebrew" (Gen. 14:13). Originally this text probably identified Abraham *socially* as an Apiru; but by the first century it was believed and used to identify him *ethnically* as a Jew. Thus Abraham—not Jacob—became emphasized as the emblematic ancestor particularly of the Jews. Jacob apparently remained an adequate symbolic ancestor as long as the name "Israel" designated a religious community; but once it came to designate an ethnic group, Abraham replaced him in this capacity.

4. By the first century, the Torah presumably revealed at Mount Sinai functioned to define Jewish ethnicity (Law of Contrast). Increasingly, the Sinai covenant was regarded as merely another particular feature of a tradition now considered exclusively "Jewish." Curiously, it was often referred to by the Greek loanword *diatheke,* which did not mean "covenant" or "pact" but "last will and testament." Did this word

ancestor exclusive to the Jews.[3] But the apostle Paul treated Abraham differently, not parochially as the forefather only of the Jews but universally as an ancestor shared by all people of faith (see Romans 4; Galatians 3). In Galatians 4:21–31 he even drew a sharp contrast between the Sinai covenant, another parochial emblem of Judaism at the time,[4] and God's promise to Abraham, whose "purpose was to make [Abraham] the ancestor of all who believe" (Rom. 4:11)—Jews and non-Jews.

It is commonly assumed that the inspiration behind Paul's "unusual" treatment of Abraham was something "new" and unprecedented; but in fact, a thousand years earlier, at the time of King David, Abraham had been similarly invoked as a common ancestor uniting village Israelites and urban pagans (or "Gentiles"; see chapter 4). Thus, Paul was employing neither a novel Christian view nor a contemporary Jewish view of Abraham; he was employing a much more archaic Israelite view of Abraham—and for the same reason as the ancient Israelites: to transcend the traditional boundary separating them, as Yahweh's people, from "outsiders" (see also Eph. 2:11–16). The Gospels likewise follow Paul, disparaging the exclusivistic way in which Abraham was usually invoked within first-century Judaism (see Matt. 3:7–9 and John 8). The point is that this critique was not grounded in subjective religious sentiment; it was grounded in ancient biblical tradition.

2. Stephen's Reference to the Angel. The early Christian recovery of more archaic aspects of the biblical tradition is also evident in the final speech Stephen delivered just before his execution (Acts 7). In it he notes that

> "[Moses] was there [in the desert] with our ancestors and with the angel who spoke to him on Mount Sinai, and he received God's living messages to pass on to us." (v. 38, TEV)

In this same speech he also refers to "God's law, that was handed down by angels" (v. 53, TEV). However, the notion of an angel (Greek *angelos;* Hebrew *mal'ak*) being the agent through which God delivered the law or spoke to Moses is not attested either in the Old Testament or in the extrabiblical Jewish writings at the time. Instead, these all associate the giving of the law at Mount Sinai with the *'anan,* an archaic Hebrew word that later biblical writers imagined to be a thick "cloud." The Old Testament story thus says a lot about a "cloud" at Mount Sinai, but nothing about an "angel." As with the apostle Paul, Stephen (or Luke, who put this speech on Stephen's lips) diverged from the prevailing tendency of his day. Where did he get this seemingly "novel" idea?

Box 8.1—The Angel and the Cloud

Even though later biblical writers misunderstood Yahweh's *'anan* at Sinai to be a "cloud" rather than a direct divine manifestation, the tradition still preserved faint memories about the presence of a sacred manifestation of Yahweh—what later generations called a *mal'ak,* "angel." The Bible shows this *mal'ak* behaving exactly like the *'anan,* although it does not portray this "angel" delivering the law to Moses.

> The angel [*mal'ak*] of God who was going before the Israelite army moved and went behind them; and the pillar of cloud [*'anan*] moved from in front of them and took its place behind them. It came between the army of Egypt and the army of Israel. And so the cloud [*'anan*] was there with the darkness, and it lit up the night; one did not come near the other all night. (Exod. 14:19–20)

This verse probably contains two variant forms of the same tradition about a supernatural manifestation of Yahweh positioning itself between the Egyptian soldiers and the escaping Apiru/Hebrew slaves (here anachronistically depicted as a full-blown Israelite army). The archaic form of the tradition labeled this manifestation *'anan,* while the later one labeled it *mal'ak.* This supports the conclusion that *'anan* and *mal'ak* were basically synonymous with one another.

foster the view that the Sinai covenant was something God had bequeathed exclusively to the Jewish people as part of their distinctive heritage or cultural legacy? Did it foster the view that God had somehow "retired" or retreated from active involvement in his people's affairs?

As we saw in chapter 2, the word *'anan* did not originally mean "cloud"; already in Canaanite myth centuries before the time of Moses it designated a supernatural, divine emanation. It was the powerful, sacred manifestation that simultaneously reveals and masks deity—exactly what later generations of Israelites would call *mal'ak,* "angel." This archaic sense is still retained today in the Arabic use of the word *'anan.* Consequently, far from being a "novel" view, Stephen's reference to the "angel" preserved the archaic sense of the biblical tradition, untainted by later misunderstandings of *'anan* as a mere "cloud." This more authentic understanding of the Sinai tradition had been forgotten in official Jerusalem circles, as bureaucratic scribes over the centuries revised and updated the Sinai tradition to make it more relevant, intelligible, and meaningful to themselves and to later audiences.

The Grassroots Preservation of Archaic Traditions

Thus, the original meaning of such things as the *'anan* of Yahweh and the role of Abraham was apparently not forgotten everywhere. But why did some people remember and preserve such aspects of the tradition's remote past while others—particularly the religious authorities—did not?

For most historical periods, we know almost nothing about the lives of 80 percent of the people, mainly the village populations. This is true of ancient China and medieval Europe, as well as of ancient Israel and the

5. This attitude is perfectly expressed in the words of Nathanael: "Can anything good come out of Nazareth?" (John 1:46). In Roman Palestine, the Jewish religious elite often dismissed the Jewish peasantry as "ignoramuses" (Hebrew 'am ha'arets).

6. Ironically, whereas maintaining the status quo in the village requires constancy, in the centers of political power and wealth it requires change. In the book *1984*, George Orwell satirized this in his portrait of the bureaucrats of Oceania, who maintain the Party's political control by regularly rewriting history to conform to the changes made by the politicians.

7. This is so prevalent in peasant-type societies that social scientists have a name for it: the social organization of tradition. It holds that in such societies there are two streams of religious tradition: (1) the thought and character of religious specialists and influential elites find expression in a prestigious "Great Tradition," while (2) those of nonspecialists and common folk constitute a sort of "Little Tradition."

Roman Empire. The little we do know is found in texts written by urban sophisticates who usually viewed rural folk with disdain, if not contempt.[5] It is easy for modern historians unwittingly to absorb the elitist biases woven into these ancient texts. For example, if a text presents Abraham as the exclusive forefather of the Jews, some historians may assume either that rural villagers agreed, or else that their differing views were historically inconsequential.

But such an assumption would be wrong. Archaic traditions, ideas, figures of speech, and customs are *always* much more likely to be preserved intact and unchanged in remote villages than in cosmopolitan urban centers.[6] For example, even today some villagers in southeastern Italy continue to speak an ancient dialect of Greek, while some villagers north of Damascus (and also in Turkey and Iraq) still speak Aramaic. Extremely archaic Bronze Age structures of law and religious thought are still preserved today in Saudi Arabia and Yemen. Under the circumstances, it is not difficult to imagine that village populations in Roman Palestine could still remember such things as the original meaning of 'anan. Indeed, that archaic meaning of 'anan is still preserved in the Arabic-speaking world today, as in such age-old folk sayings describing the origin of the camel's notoriously bad temper: "The camel was created from the 'anan (spiritual emanations) of the *jinn* (demons)." Villagers preserve ancient traditions because change of any kind—new ideas, new social patterns, even new technologies—entails too much risk for too little potential return. As anthropologists have observed, it is not such *continuity* that needs to be explained, but rather *change*. Thus, what requires explanation is not Paul's treatment of Abraham or Stephen's reference to an "angel" at Mount Sinai, but rather the early Jewish tendency to treat Abraham as the exclusive ancestor of the Jews and 'anan as if it were a "cloud."

Also, the submerged 80 percent of the population tend to be concerned mainly with *private* affairs—their own families and the network of neighboring families that constitute their primary communities. This is part of why they are "submerged"—that is, unnoticed by the urban elite who manage the *public* affairs and institutions of social control. Rural villagers are also typically concerned with that conservative body of customs and beliefs that effectively maintains peace and security within the local community. They are also pragmatic, and evaluate ideas, institutions, and innovations—including religious ones—in terms of their practical value for daily life. Consequently, their religious priorities tend to differ sharply from those of the religious elites. Official religious symbols, rituals, and doctrines that help sanctify the public realm are much less meaningful to—and often resented by—simple folk whose experiences of public institutions and urban elites are often negative.[7]

Figure 8.2

The Changeless Countryside. The *shaduf* is used today by Egyptian *fellahin* (peasants) to raise irrigation water out of the Nile (*right*). It is identical to that depicted in a thirteenth-century-B.C. painting in the tomb of Ipui at Thebes (*left*).

The religious teachings of Jesus of Nazareth seem to reflect such a conservative, village-based, grassroots understanding of religion. His criticisms of religious elites were obvious (Matt. 21:45–46): while these teachings may have placed him at risk with the religious leaders, "the common people heard him gladly" (Mark 12:37, KJV). All this explains why the earliest followers of Jesus were not drawn from official religious circles or from the ranks of those sectarian Jews eager to gain control of the public realm; they were drawn from among the submerged Jewish population of Jewish Galilee and Judaea—in other words, from among the *'am ha'arets* (or "people of the land").

New Testament Writings as Popular Religion

8. Paul was trained as a Pharisee, and the author of Matthew's Gospel may have been a Jewish scribe. But both eventually

Although most of the New Testament books appear to have been written in more cosmopolitan settings, they differ conspicuously from other religious writings of the time. For example, unlike the Mishnah and Talmud, they were not the product of technically trained scribes ("lawyers") plying their specialization.[8] Unlike the Dead Sea Scrolls or most of the Pseudepigrapha (see Appendix A), they were not written by religious sectarians eager to define and control the public institutions of religion. Unlike the first-century Jewish writer Josephus and the authors

repudiated their training
and employed their tal-
ents at promoting some-
thing other than parochial
religious traditions.

of 1 and 2 Maccabees, the New Testament writers were restrained in their use of sophisticated Hellenistic literary conventions. And unlike the first-century Jewish philosopher Philo of Alexandria or later Gnostic Christians, the New Testament authors showed little interest in doctrinal or philosophical minutiae. In other words, this literature was not the product of religious elites, as Paul of Tarsus observed (1 Cor. 1:26–29). The early New Testament community itself was not elitist.

Box 8.2—Sophisticated Disdain for New Testament Writings

In the second century, Gnostic Christians began producing their own scriptures portraying human beings as divine "souls" trapped within an evil physical world, requiring the liberating self-knowledge (*gnosis*) of their own divinity that only the spiritual Christ could provide. They regarded as simpletons other Christians who preferred the New Testament scriptures. In the *Gospel of Philip* excerpted below, Gnostic believers are praised for being more mature than other Christians because they understand the true (i.e., Gnostic) meaning of Christian concepts and rites. In fact, they are said to have achieved more than mere Christianity—they have achieved Christhood itself. The excerpt below begins by listing some of the ways New Testament readers fail to grasp the deeper truths of the faith:

> The names which are given to worldly things contain a great occasion for error. For they twist our considerations from the right meaning to the wrong meaning. For whoever hears (the word) "God" does not know the right meaning but the wrong meaning. It is the same with (such words as) "the Father" and "the Son" and "the Holy Spirit" and "the life" and "the light" and "the resurrection" and "the Church" and all the other names. Folk do not know the right meaning. . . . Some say Mary was impregnated by the Holy Spirit. They err. They do not know what they say. When did a woman become pregnant by a woman? [Gnostics considered the Holy Spirit to be a feminine entity.] They err who say, "The Lord first died and then he arose." First he arose, then he died [i.e., Jesus achieved *gnosis* before he died]. . . . No one can see anything of created things unless he becomes as they. It is not thus with the man who is in the world. He sees the sun and he is not a sun, and he sees the heaven and the earth and all other things, and he is not these—it is this way with the truth. But you (singular) saw something of that place and you became these: you saw the Spirit and became Spirit; you saw the Christ and became Christ. . . . It is necessary not only that those who have it [i.e., who are baptized] received the name of the Father and the Son and the Holy Spirit, but that they took it themselves. If someone does not take it himself, the name also will be taken away from him. . . . For this reason one is no longer a Christian, but a Christ. (*DocStGos*, 57–59, 62, 66)

Many scholars today still have difficulty understanding esoteric Gnostic phrases and ideas precisely because these texts are the product of specialists engaging in unbounded elaboration of their (philosophical) specialty—the Law of Elaboration. Some New Testament texts warned early Christians not to be seduced by such sophisticated religious systems promising salvation through *gnosis*, (self-)knowledge (1 Cor. 8:1; 1 Tim. 4:1–5; 6:20–21). Some scholars feel that Johannine Christianity arose, in part, to persuade Gnostic Christians of the superiority of John's Gospel testimony (John 1:1–18 refutes basic Gnostic claims about the relationship between the spiritual Christ and the physical world; see also 1 John 2:4; 4:1–3; 2 John 7).

Written in koine (common) Greek, the lingua franca of the eastern Mediterranean world, the New Testament is actually quite pedestrian as literature. But it was accessible, arising from and speaking to the submerged masses disillusioned by the available religious options, none of which seemed capable of providing a meaningful basis of civilized community in an increasingly diverse and fragmented Roman world. Was there any basis for civilization other than Roman power—or any other political power, for that matter? The answer provided in the various New Testament books proved attractive to people of different ethnic and cultural backgrounds. Within its first generation, the Jesus movement already included men and women from all social classes and many different nationalities, from earthy Corinthian sailors to some more-cultured Orthodox Jews. A few generations later, these so-called Christians (Greek *christianoi*) could be found almost anywhere, from the borders of India to the Strait of Gibraltar.

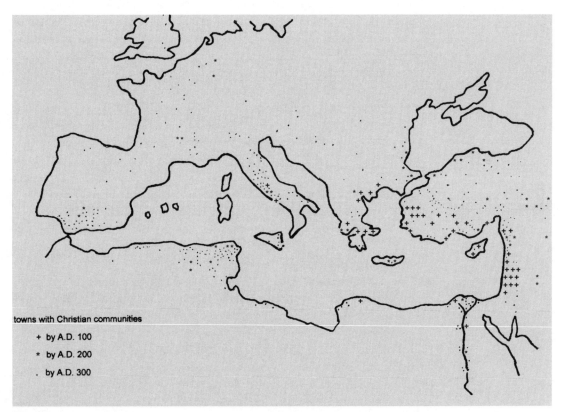

towns with Christian communities

+ by A.D. 100

* by A.D. 200

. by A.D. 300

Map 8.1
The Spread of Early Christianity. Well before Emperor Constantine legalized Christianity in A.D. 313, the religion had cut across the pronounced ethnic and cultural divisions of the Roman Empire. Christian communities could be found in towns from northern Europe to North Africa, from Spain to Syria and beyond.

Early Christianity as a Religious Reform

But the New Testament is not only the literary repository of a *popular* movement. Its frequent allusions to the Old Testament suggest that it is also the "library" of a *reform* movement within first-century Judaism. It was clearly not a *political* reform movement bent on changing the social, political, or economic order. This is reflected in the social and political conservatism of passages such as Matthew 22:21 ("Render therefore unto Caesar the things that are Caesar's," RSV); Romans 13:1 ("Let every person be subject to the governing authorities"); and 1 Peter 2:13 ("accept the authority of every human institution"). Rather, as a *religious* reform movement its immediate concern was for the integrity of a religious community and tradition, not the civil order per se (although religious reformers usually believe that positive social and political changes will result). The strategy of religious reformers is not to effect change by forcibly ousting the religious authorities who have a vested interest in the status quo, but rather to withdraw and simply create (or *become*) the desired religious alternative. This repudiation of political power is the hallmark of a genuinely "religious" reform. In other words, the use of coercion would constitute sufficient proof that the movement is motivated primarily by *political interests,* not *religious values.* Coerced acts have no religious value (see the Sermon on the Mount).

Most important, reform movements often turn to the remote past for guidance and inspiration. To some extent, this means they must also turn to the conservative countryside where archaic traditions still have meaning. Thus, it is probably no coincidence that many religious reformers throughout history—from the preexilic biblical prophets to Jesus to Martin Luther—came from small and comparatively remote villages. The recovery of ancient perspectives and frameworks of meaning provides a new way not only of addressing the current religious crisis but also of understanding the developments that led up to it. Encountering an ancient value system and ethic that has lain dormant for centuries can be religiously revitalizing.

Some reformational appeals to the remote past are truly *creative* in the sense that they recover a long-lost religious perspective or framework of values. The classic example is the Protestant movement of the sixteenth century: an encounter with the first-century teachings of the apostle Paul led to massive defections from the Roman church, most of whose doctrines and structures arose after the fourth century. Other reformational appeals to the past are merely *imitative,* designed to revive or preserve those religious forms, structures, and institutions from the past that continue to have meaning.

In part, the Old Testament itself is a collection of writings from various Israelite reform movements. On one hand, creative reform inspired

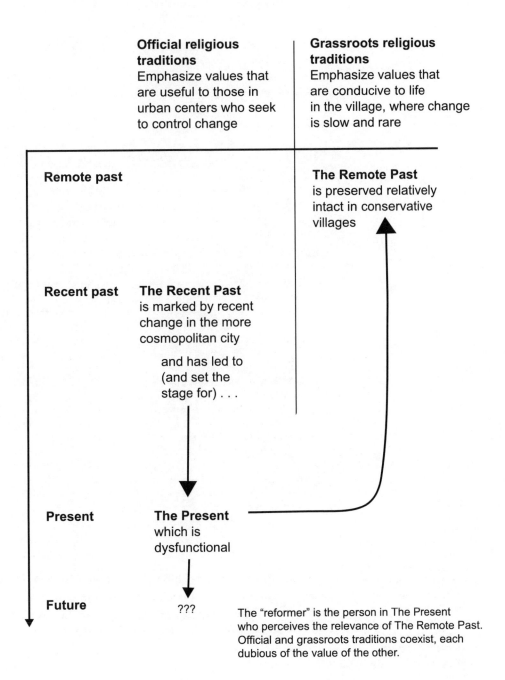

Official religious traditions
Emphasize values that are useful to those in urban centers who seek to control change

Grassroots religious traditions
Emphasize values that are conducive to life in the village, where change is slow and rare

Remote past

The Remote Past is preserved relatively intact in conservative villages

Recent past

The Recent Past is marked by recent change in the more cosmopolitan city

and has led to (and set the stage for) . . .

Present

The Present which is dysfunctional

Future

???

The "reformer" is the person in The Present who perceives the relevance of The Remote Past. Official and grassroots traditions coexist, each dubious of the value of the other.

Figure 8.3
Dynamics of Religious Reform

Box 8.3—A Reformer Reappraises the Past

Martin Luther's 1520 treatise "To the German Nobility" illustrates how religious reformers can use the *remote* past—sometimes quite accurately—to challenge erroneous religious views that have arisen in the *recent* past. Luther appealed to the Bible (a pre-second-century text) over against Roman tradition and canon law that had arisen after the fourth century. He had an affection for Augustine (fourth century), but hardly ever cites Aquinas (thirteenth century) who laid the foundation for Roman Catholic theology.

Claiming that the pope had inherited the authority and prerogatives of the apostle Peter, Roman Catholic officials (the "Romanists") insisted that only the pope could summon a church council to correct abuses or mistakes in the church. Luther responded,

> The Romanists have no basis for their claim that the pope alone has the right to call or confirm a council. This is just their own ruling, and it is valid as long as it is not harmful to Christendom or contrary to the laws of God. Now when the pope deserves punishment, this ruling no longer obtains, for not to punish him by authority of a council is harmful to Christendom. Thus we read in Acts 15 that it was not St. Peter who called the Apostolic Council [in the first century] but the apostles and elders. If then that right had belonged to St. Peter alone, the council would not have been a Christian council, but a heretical *conciliabulum* [i.e., a mere gathering of people]. Even the Council of Nicea [in the fourth century], the most famous of all councils, was neither called nor confirmed by the bishop of Rome, but by the emperor Constantine. Many other emperors after him have done the same, and yet these councils [the first seven "Ecumenical Councils" prior to the ninth century] were the most Christian of all. But if the pope alone has the right to convene councils, then these councils would all have been heretical [i.e., in violation of church doctrine].
>
> —from J. Potter, *Luther: Selected Political Writings* (1974), 47

9. It is noteworthy that Josiah's operating value system—which was largely imperialistic—prevented him from reaching as far back as premonarchic times. Many of the remaining Old Testament writings come not from reformational periods in Israel's past but from traditional periods, in which Israelite or later Judaean scribes were intent on preserving the rituals and doctrines of the institutions to which they were loyal.

the oracles of the preexilic biblical prophets who preserved the Sinai covenant tradition of premonarchic Yahwism, using it to decry the Yahwisticism of their own day. Likewise, during the exile—when enthusiasm was at an all-time low for the Yahwisticism of the now-defunct monarchy—Jeremiah, Ezekiel, Second Isaiah, and the author of Job promoted an understanding of Israelite faith that presumed a framework of meaning and values derived from premonarchic Yahwism. On the other hand, Josiah's imitative reform, hoping to recover the political glories of David and Solomon, has also left its mark on the Old Testament; it spawned the particular interpretation of Israel's past (as a "national history") canonized in the books of Joshua, Judges, Samuel, and Kings.[9]

Ezra and Nehemiah also launched an imitative reform designed to consolidate Jewish ethnicity in terms of specific forms, structures, and institutions they and their followers considered sacred.

The Jewish World of Jesus

First-century Judaism, as depicted in the writings of Josephus, was ripe for reform. In fact, Josephus describes "prophetic" leaders who made appeals to Israel's remote past. John the Baptist, who evoked the image of the prophet Elijah, was one; another was the otherwise unknown "Egyptian" who led Jews on an exodus into the wilderness (although he was a political opportunist hoping to exploit the mass appeal of religious reform). In little over two centuries—between the time of Alexander Jannaeus (ca. 94 B.C.) and the Bar Kokhba revolt (A.D. 132)—three bloody civil wars were fought by Jews within the city of Jerusalem, even while foreign armies were outside laying siege to it.

This is powerful testimony to the deep divisions within Judaean society, as competing factions increasingly resorted to violence in their struggle for power. Because they all invoked religion in this struggle, the whole religious system fell into disrepute. Jewish peasants, who typically had little interest in politics or power struggles, probably did not identify themselves with any of the sectarian forms of Judaism. Besides, by the first century the twin pillars of Judaism—temple sacrifice and obedience to Torah (or law)—were largely irrelevant and widely ignored by them.

The Irrelevance of the Temple

10. The rationale underlying animal sacrifice was the age-old pagan notion of bribing the gods: by ritually demonstrating how much you were devoted to the god, you might entice the god to do you a favor (or forgive your sins). Pagan temples also served as meat markets. This is why the propriety of eat-

Josephus makes it clear that the masses had no confidence in the temple priests and their Sadducean supporters, who were the aristocratic descendants of priestly families dating back to the time of Solomon. The Jerusalem temple was their power base. In the first place, it was the national meat market. Because the priests and their families could not eat all the sheep and oxen regularly sacrificed there, they sold the surplus mutton and beef on the open market.[10] Besides, temple sacrifice was impractical for most villagers, who could rarely afford to travel to Jerusalem, buy meat on a regular basis, or bring an animal for sacrifice. An ox cost the equivalent of ten months' wages for an agricultural worker. For them, the temple cult continued to be peripheral at best, as it had been in premonarchic Israel (Jer. 7:22).

In the second place, the sacred precincts of the Jerusalem temple—as with temples across the eastern Mediterranean world—housed the national treasury, which received gifts from the wealthy. As such, it was a source of great wealth for the priests who controlled and protected it. In

Table 8.1 Chronology of the Postexilic Period

date	event	literature
	Cyrus the Great—the exile ends (538 B.C.)	*Second Isaiah*
500 B.C. —	Jerusalem temple rebuilt (515 B.C.)	
450 B.C. —		
	Nehemiah is governor of Judaea	
400 B.C. —	Ezra ?	*Pentateuch canonized ?*
350 B.C. —		
	Alexander the Great defeats Persians	
300 B.C. —		
250 B.C. —		*Greek translations of Hebrew Scriptures begun*
200 B.C. —		*Wisdom of Ben-Sirach*
	Antiochus IV Epiphanes - persecution of Jewish traditionalists	*book of Daniel*
150 B.C. —	HASMONEAN DYNASTY Essenes at Qumran	
100 B.C. —	Alexander Jannaeus	
	Roman general Pompey	
50 B.C. —	Herod the Great	
0 —	Philo of Alexandria	*Dead Sea Scrolls*
A.D. 50—	Jesus of Nazareth the apostle Paul the Jewish War (A.D. 66–70)	*Paul's epistles*
A.D. 100—	Josephus the Jamnia Academy	*NT Gospels*
A.D. 150 —	the Bar Kokhba Revolt (A.D. 132–135)	

ing meat sacrificed to a pagan god concerned some early Christians (1 Corinthians 8): by patronizing a particular temple's meat market, was a Christian publicly signaling devotion to that particular temple's god?

exchange for a cut of the profits, the priests granted licenses not only to various merchants selling sacrificial animals to prospective worshipers but also to other businessmen who could change foreign currency into acceptable local coinage. With picturesque imagery, Jesus apparently referred to the temple coffers as the "carcass" around which "buzzards"—foreign and domestic—flock (Matt. 24:28 = Luke 17:37). His disgust with this whole system is reflected in the story of his tirade in the temple (Mark 11:15–18; John 2:13–16). His lament was literally true: the temple had become a "den of robbers" who had compromised the integrity of the religion. The priests and their Sadducean cohorts were little more than corruptible businessmen and bankers who cloaked their economic activity in the official garb of religious piety.

The Irrelevance of Religious Law

11. The cultural elevation of ceremonial matters to the detriment of the covenant tradition may well be illustrated by the fate of the Hebrew word *berit*, "covenant." By the first century even its corrupted meaning as "vow" had been forgotten. In postbiblical Hebrew it meant "circumcision," merely designating another feature marking one's ethnic identity. This is a classic illustration of the Laws of Finality (concerning rituals) and of Functional Shift (concerning the meaning of the word *berit*) at work during a religion's traditional period.

It is equally unlikely that the Jewish masses identified very closely with the major proponents of Torah—the Rabbis and their scribal and Pharisaic forerunners. Village pragmatists would have been unimpressed by any of them whose preoccupation with ceremonial matters was accompanied by a general neglect of the age-old ethic of the Yahwist covenant.[11] Sayings such as Matthew 23:23–24 would have struck a responsive chord among them:

> "Woe to you, scribes and Pharisees, hypocrites! For you tithe mint, dill, and cummin, and have neglected the weightier matters of the law: justice and mercy and faith. It is these you ought to have practiced without neglecting the others. You blind guides! You strain out a gnat but swallow a camel!"

Even scribes, Pharisees, and Rabbis obstensibly sensitive to ethical matters became increasingly removed from the Jewish population. For example, they were increasingly resorting to Greek methods of logic and philosophy when interpreting Old Testament laws. In fact, the Talmud—that great compendium of rabbinic legal interpretations written in Hebrew—utilizes almost two thousand Greek loanwords to express the meaning of Hebrew laws. Even the name of the central religious institution within Pharisaic-rabbinic circles—*synagogue*—was Greek.

Their specific interpretations of biblical laws would have found few adherents in Jewish villages. For example, the old law of firstfruits (Exod. 23:19)—probably originally an ancient village custom modified to promote the ancient Yahwist ethic—had been reinterpreted to mean that fields could not be harvested until after the firstfruits had been offered in Jerusalem (Neh. 10:35). But it would be foolish for Jewish farmers in the

Figure 8.4
"Firstfruits" Custom
in Modern Syria. The
age-old custom of burning
the first grain harvested is
still practiced in villages
today. This produces
parched grain such as that
which Boaz offered to
Ruth (Ruth 2:14). The
biblical firstfruits injunctions attributed religious
significance to this cus-
tom. (Photograph by
Eathel Mendenhall)

Jordan Valley to delay their harvests for this ceremony to take place. If
enforced, such a religious law would require them to watch their crops
wither and rot. Similarly irrelevant would have been most of the purity
laws that, if followed strictly, would have driven wedges between neighbors now afraid of ritually defiling one another, paralyzing the daily
affairs of village life. Many Jews surely questioned whether the scribes
and Pharisees, as well as the priests and Sadducees, had any meaningful
understanding of the Israelite religious heritage. Someone like John the
Baptist or Jesus of Nazareth would have provided a welcomed alternative
(Matt. 7:28–29).

The Historical Jesus as Reformer

The New Testament contains the historically reliable tradition that Jesus'
contemporaries likewise viewed him as a throwback to an earlier age:

> [Jesus] asked his disciples, "Who do people say that I am?" And
> they answered him, "John the Baptist; and others, Elijah; and still
> others, one of the prophets." (Mark 8:27–28)

Might Jesus himself have been a reformer reaching into the remote past
to find something of religious meaning for the present?

The question is fraught with difficulties. First, the Christian tendency to classify Jesus not as a reformer but as the founder of a new religion is deeply entrenched. Christian doctrine asserts that he gathered disciples to establish a new religious fellowship, the church, and therefore
treats Jesus, his disciples, and especially the apostle Paul as innovators. This
approach handles the Israelite religious tradition much the same way the
Bronze Age was handled in chapter 1 of this book—as background "pro-

logue" to the emergence of a new religion. Its coverage of the Old Testament sometimes seems little more than a token nod to the fact that Jesus happened to be Jewish (see Appendix C).

Second, Jesus left no writings. Everything we know about him comes from devoted followers passionately committed to proclaiming him as Savior (see John 20:31). It is extremely difficult to reconstruct the historical facts about him from these glorifying proclamations, especially when Gospel narratives often disagree on crucial details. Thus, a saying or episode that casts Jesus as a reformer may not necessarily be rooted in historical fact.[12] However, at least three aspects of Jesus' teaching are widely regarded as historically reliable. Each supports the claim that Jesus himself was a reformer who found religious meaning in the remote Israelite past:

1. *God as "Father."* The historical Jesus characteristically referred to God as *Abba*, "father," complete with filial connotations, and he encouraged other Jews to do the same. This practice was virtually unheard of in the Judaism of Jesus' day, even though it had precedent in the preexilic period (see Hos. 11:1–11; also chapter 3, note 12). This seems to be a clear instance of the historical Jesus retrieving a long-lost religious perspective from early Yahwism.

2. *Ethic and Ritual.* Jesus' remark in Mark 7:15 is virtually unparalleled in the Judaism of his day: "There is nothing outside a person that by going in can defile, but the things that come out are what defile." With remarks like this, Jesus challenged the religious system's legal distinctions between "clean and unclean" that provided the criteria for distinguishing Jews qualified for religious fellowship from those who were not. This helps explain many other passages in the Gospels where Jesus tried (and failed) to prohibit the use of such distinctions as instruments of social control.[13]

Jews in the postexilic period could certainly distinguish between "meaningful" ethnic norms such as dietary laws ("exterior things that are internalized") and ethical values that inspire deeds ("interior things that manifest themselves externally"). However, it is hard to find Jewish literature of the time exalting the latter (righteous integrity) to the point of virtually eliminating the former (ceremonial customs). Instead, the best analogies come from the much earlier preexilic prophets. Jesus revived an archaic Yahwist perspective that religious leaders, interested in defining Jewish identity formally and ceremonially, had lost. In such an environment, Jesus must have indeed seemed old-fashioned.

3. *Parables of the Kingdom of God.* Both the form and the content of Jesus' parables are those of a reformer. The historical Jesus undoubtedly used the parable *form,* an apparent throwback to the age of the preexilic prophets (see 2 Sam. 12:1–9; Isa. 5:1–7). It was certainly not a commonly

12. For example, John's Gospel shows Jesus consistently preaching about the sacred significance of himself, while the Synoptic Gospels (Matthew, Mark, and Luke) have him characteristically avoiding this. In the Synoptic Gospels, a major theme of Jesus' preaching is "the kingdom of God," but John's Jesus hardly ever mentions it. Since the middle of the twentieth century scholars have proposed numerous criteria to help "objectively" determine whether a saying or episode pertaining to Jesus is likely to be historical, although the usefulness of individual criteria has often been debated.

13. Jesus also challenged the social exploitation of "clean/unclean" by deliberately keeping scandalous company, including tax collectors, known "sinners," and women. His willingness to touch and declare healed "unclean" people with various skin diseases (Greek *lepra*, erroneously translated "leprosy") overtly usurped the prerogatives of the priests, who reserved for themselves the right to determine who was (or was not) religiously, and therefore socially, "clean."

used teaching technique in Jesus' day. Moreover, the actual *content* of many of these parables also seems to draw upon archaic religious themes. His use of the phrase "kingdom of God"—unusual for the times—was itself religious shorthand for the premonarchic understanding of the rule or kingship of Yahweh (see chapter 3).

Several of Jesus' parables seem to allude deliberately to the reform dynamic itself as described above (see Matt. 18:23–35; Matt. 21:33–41; Luke 14:16–25; and Luke 19:11–27 = Matt. 25:14–30). They share a similar plot: A protagonist (God), before withdrawing from the scene, entrusts the care of some property (his people? their religion?) to certain stewards or caretakers (the religious authorities of Jerusalem). In the years that follow, the stewards not only fail to discharge their duties consistent with the protagonist's will but also arrogantly assume that they enjoy complete autonomy, so that now the situation has become intolerable. When the protagonist returns, these stewards will lose all their privileges, and worse.

These parables are about the coming kingdom of God, the time when the protagonist will return to manage his property directly. This notion of God's direct rule unmediated by costly institutional middlemen seems not only to describe the formative period of the Israelite religious tradition (1200–1000 B.C.) but also to advocate its vision of religious community (see chapter 3). Through the centuries, this ancient vision was probably preserved by villagers long after it had been forgotten and replaced in Jerusalem by more modern visions of religious community accommodating the institutional middlemen (kings and priests) and their scribes. The tradition of God's rule could be just as critical of postexilic religious officials as it had been of preexilic ones:

> When the chief priests and the Pharisees heard his parables, they realized that he was speaking about them. They wanted to arrest him, but they feared the crowds, because they regarded him as a prophet. (Matt. 21:45–46)

Many other aspects of the Jesus tradition apparently presumed archaic (i.e., preexilic) religious content. The Sermon on the Mount was, in some ways, an update of the Covenant Code (Exodus 21–23). The Beatitudes and the story of Jesus' temptation restated claims made time and again by the Israelite prophets. His teaching about the Good Shepherd was basically a homily on Ezekiel 34 (see chapter 7). At the same time, virtually no aspect of the Jesus tradition hints that he had any appreciation of more recent (postexilic or even first-century) modes of Jewish religious interpretation.

Calling Himself "Messiah/ Christ"

Jewish sectarians and the common people apparently also held diverging views about the Messiah (or Anointed One; Greek *christos*). The views of the various sectarian groups, whose scribes wrote extensively on the subject, are well known to historians: the Messiah was widely regarded as a warrior-king who would expel the hated Romans. As late as A.D. 130 the great Rabbi Akiba hailed the revolutionary leader Simon Bar Kokhba as just such a messiah. This view was deeply rooted in antiquity, where the ritual of anointing (pouring oil on someone's head) indicated the delegation of political authority and the transfer of power. Thus, like the phrase "son of God," Messiah/Christ was an honorific title for a king authorized to exercise political power and authority. The Israelites had had such messiahs from Saul to Zerubbabel.

Box 8.4—Expecting the Messianic Warrior-King

The royal Messiah, identified variously as the Anointed One, Son of God, Son of David, and Prince of the Congregation, was widely regarded in first-century Judaism as a warrior-king who would institute an era of unending peace.

[God said:] "And as for the lion whom you saw rousing up out of the forest and roaring and speaking to the eagle [i.e., to the Roman authorities] and reproving him for his unrighteousness, . . . this is the Messiah whom the Most High has kept until the end of days, who will arise from the offspring of David. . . . He will denounce them for their ungodliness and for their wickedness. . . . For first he will bring them alive before his judgment seat, and when he has reproved them, then he will destroy them." (2 Esd. 12:31–33)

[God said:] "And it will happen when the time of its fulfillment is approaching in which it [the Roman Empire] will fall, that at that time the dominion of my Anointed One . . . will be revealed. . . . The last ruler who is left alive at that time will be bound, whereas the entire host will be destroyed. And they will carry him on Mount Zion, and my Anointed One will convict him of all his wicked deeds. . . . And after these things he will kill him, . . . he will call all nations, and some of them he will spare, and others he will kill." (*2 Baruch* 39:7; 40:1–2; 72:2, in *OTP* 1:633, 645)

See, Lord, and raise up for them their king,
    the son of David, to rule over your servant Israel
    in the time known to you, O God.
Undergird him with the strength to destroy the unrighteous rulers,
    to purge Jerusalem from gentiles
    who trample her to destruction.
                  (*Psalms of Solomon* 17:21–22, in *OTP* 2:667)

He shall be called the Son of God. . . . With God's help he will make war, and God will give all the peoples into his power. (4Q246, a Dead Sea Scroll)

14. This would have been Pontius Pilate's main concern about Jesus. If the Gospels are historically accurate, Pilate was convinced that Jesus was not competing for the monopoly of force and therefore posed no direct threat to Roman interests. He is shown consenting to Jesus' execution only after being persuaded that Jesus was undermining confidence in the Jewish religious authorities, whose interests Pilate had to respect, if not support.

The historical Jesus could not have publicly accepted the label "Messiah." To have done so would have entangled him in other people's expectations that he was just another ambitious warrior-politician hoping to rule through a legal monopoly of force.[14] It is unlikely that all of the Jewish masses shared the view that the Jewish messiah must be such a warrior-politician. In fact, half a millennium earlier Second Isaiah had rejected that notion by identifying Yahweh's messiah (in the political, military sense) as a Gentile—Cyrus, King of Persia (Isa. 45:1). The insistence that Israelite religious leaders should not be competing for political power would have resonated among villagers much more than among ambitious sectarians.

Because the king was anointed, any biblical text treating the Israelite king would be relevant to the topic of the Messiah, even if the word "messiah" did not appear in that text. Numerous biblical texts from extremely different historical contexts describe an alternative view of the nature and role of Israel's anointed king. Three in particular suggest that Israel's Messiah must be a humble king: Deuteronomy 17; 1 Kings 12; and Zechariah 9.

Deuteronomy 17: The "Messianic" Ideal in Deuteronomy

"Who ever heard of a humble king?" With this wry question Moshe Greenberg, a leading Israeli biblical scholar, once concluded a discussion of Deuteronomy 17, the law of the king. It says the following of the Israelite king:

> [H]e must not acquire many horses for himself. . . . And he must not acquire many wives for himself, or else his heart will turn away; also silver and gold he must not acquire in great quantity for himself. When he has taken the throne of his kingdom, he shall have a copy of this law written for him . . . and he shall read in it all the days of his life, so that he may learn to fear Yahweh his God, . . . neither exalting himself above other members of the community nor turning aside from the commandment. (vv. 16–20)

The "ideal king" is one who devotes his time to sharpening his commitment to the Yahwist ethic. This is hardly what one would expect, given the three functions of political government. Deuteronomy—itself the result of a reform movement (see chapter 6)—views the anointed king as something very different from a warrior-politician:

- There is nothing about the king's role in *administering law.*
- The references to "horses"—the ancient equivalent of tanks and jet bombers—show that the Israelite king has no role to play in *waging war.*

- The references to "silver and gold" suggest that he performs no role in *managing the economy*.

In fact, it is pointless even to think of such a "king" in the usual political terms. This mirrors the popular attitude toward political leadership expressed as early as the parable of Jotham (see Box 3.2). The religious authorities and sectarians of Jesus' day who were busily writing about the coming Messiah essentially ignored Deuteronomy 17, even though it was a part of the sacred and authoritative Torah; it simply did not support their objectives or fit into their worldview.[15]

Villagers typically have little use for warrior-politicians, and a messiah who is seen as one is unlikely to find much support among them. We should avoid the assumption that most Jews, even in the days of Jesus, necessarily regarded Israel's anointed "king" as a political office-holder. Deuteronomy 17 shows us that other "messianic" associations were possible. Its description of the humble Israelite king who shall not exalt himself above other members of the community recalls a teaching of Jesus:

> "You know that among the Gentiles those whom they recognize as their rulers lord it over them, and their great ones are tyrants over them. But it is not so among you; but whoever wishes to become great among you must be your servant." (Mark 10:42–43)

15. One should never underestimate scribal ingenuity in explaining away discrepancies between the sacred scriptures they claim to follow and their actual operating value system. Religious specialists have always been able to concoct opaque interpretations (moralistic, allegorical, etc.) of sacred texts whose obvious meaning undermines their beliefs and values. Jesus' comments on hypocrisy addressed this phenomenon directly.

1 Kings 12: The Negative Model of "Messiah"

Jesus' comment here about "servant leadership" recalls 1 Kings 12, the account of Rehoboam going to Shechem "for all Israel had come to Shechem to make him king" (v. 1). The northern tribes had suffered mightily under the policies of Rehoboam's father Solomon, and now they wanted some relief: "Your father made our yoke heavy. Now therefore lighten the hard service of your father and his heavy yoke that he placed on us" (v. 4). Here the king is likened to the farmer who puts a yoke on a beast of burden, that is, on his subjects. In this case, the subjects are seeking relief from taxation and conscription. The advice of Rehoboam's senior advisers is illuminating: "If you will be a servant to this people today and serve them, . . . then they will be your servants forever" (v. 7). Their counsel presents the notion of the humble king who serves his people rather than dominates them, a concept these advisers knew would resonate well among the people. But Rehoboam and his junior advisers were of a different mind, and their decision to "make the yoke even heavier" resulted in a civil war that reduced the Davidic kingdom to a fraction of its former size.

In the early Israelite monarchy, both Saul and David likely had to defer repeatedly to the servant-king concept. So, too, would any political leader in a fledgling political state: something analogous to the humble king ideal probably existed in the early stages of every kingdom. Over time, the king as "servant" or "shepherd" of the people survived more in words than in deeds, expressed in the royal propaganda of even the most brutal of tyrants. But apparently this ancient understanding of the servant-king continued to define the ideal messiah for many people in the conservative countryside.

Matthew's Gospel contains a saying of Jesus that also appears in the second-century Gnostic *Gospel of Thomas* (saying no. 90), which, for some, confirms its authenticity: "Take my yoke upon you, and learn

Box 8.5—"Yokes" Belong to Kings

The Bible refers to the "yokes" of the kings of Egypt, Assyria, and Babylonia:

> I am Yahweh your God who brought you out of the land of Egypt, to be their slaves no more; I have broken the bars of your yoke and made you walk erect. (Lev. 26:13)

> I will break the Assyrian in my land,
>   and on my mountains trample him under foot;
> his yoke shall be removed from them,
>   and his burden from their shoulders. (Isa. 14:25)

> But if any nation or kingdom will not serve this king, Nebuchadnezzar of Babylon, and put its neck under the yoke of the king of Babylon, then I will punish that nation with the sword, with famine, and with pestilence. . . . But any nation that will bring its neck under the yoke of the king of Babylon and serve him, I will leave on its own land, says Yahweh, to till it and live there. (Jer. 27:8, 11)

The later rabbinic notion of Law/Torah as a "yoke" is probably based on the notion that God, as king, is entitled to place obligations and requirements on his people:

> R[abbi] Nehunya b[en] Ha-Kanah said: He that takes upon himself the yoke of the Law, from him shall be taken away the yoke of the kingdom and the yoke of worldly care; but he that throws off the yoke of the Law, upon him shall be laid the yoke of the kingdom and the yoke of worldly care. (Mishnah *'Abot* 3:5)

Acts 15:9–10 uses "yoke" in this sense of obeying Torah obligations:

> [I]n cleansing their hearts by faith he [God] has made no distinction between them [Gentiles] and us [Jews]. Now therefore why are you putting God to the test by placing on the neck of the [Gentile] disciples a yoke that neither our ancestors nor we have been able to bear?

from me; for I am gentle and humble in heart. . . . For my yoke is easy, and my burden is light" (Matt. 11:29–30). Those who regard the historical Jesus exclusively as a product of his times often assume that such words were inspired either by postexilic sectarian literature or by first-century Pharisaic disputes over Torah obedience, both of which include metaphorical references to "yokes." But it is equally plausible that Jesus (and/or Matthew) was alluding to something as old as Solomon's unbearable "yoke" of 1 Kings 12, thus inviting Jesus' audience (and/or Matthew's readers) to contrast Solomon's and Rehoboam's examples of messianic kingship with the example of Jesus. Although the word "messiah" is not used, Jesus' claim to possess a "yoke" is a royal (and therefore messianic) claim, albeit that of the humble servant-king.

It is doubtful that the first-century religious authorities and sectarians writing about the coming Messiah would have taken the humble-king notion very seriously. Given their framework of values and expectations, it is more likely that they would have sympathized with Rehoboam's junior advisers (and not with the author of 1 Kings 12), assuming the "proper" Messiah to be a warrior king entitled to conscript and to tax—to impose on the people a "yoke" of political obligations. This is yet another example of first-century religious leaders rejecting, in practice, one of their own religious traditions that the common people still may have taken very seriously.

Zechariah 9: The Humble "Messiah"

This idea of the humble king resurfaced in the sixth century B.C., when the Jerusalem state was in ruins. Ezekiel's contrast of the "good" and "bad" shepherds (read "kings") is one clear example (see chapter 7). This idea also appeared many decades later in the prophecy of Zechariah:

> Rejoice greatly, O daughter Zion!
>   Shout aloud, O daughter Jerusalem!
> Lo, your king comes to you;
>   triumphant and victorious is he,
> humble and riding on a donkey,
>   on a colt, the foal of a donkey.
> He will cut off the chariot from Ephraim
>   and the war horse from Jerusalem;
> and the battle bow shall be cut off,
>   and he shall command peace to the nations;
> his dominion shall be from sea to sea,
>   and from the River to the ends of the earth. (Zech. 9:9–10)

The messianic king envisioned here is perhaps the exact opposite of the Israelite warrior-politicians responsible for the devastation, humiliation, and suffering of 586 B.C. This king's policy seems to be disarmament ("he will cut off chariot, war horse, and battle bow").

Zechariah's description of the humble king/messiah itself draws on extremely archaic, pre-Israelite imagery. For example, a memo to one of the Mari kings around 1760 B.C. reminded him that even though he was king of the Akkadians he was also the king of the Amorites, and as such it would be more appropriate for him to be seen publicly riding a donkey rather than a horse (ARM 4:76). In other words, while the Akkadians—the urban sophisticates in and around Mari—would expect a king riding on a glorious and expensive war animal, the Amorites—the folk in the outlying villages—would prefer a king who rides a humble beast of burden. Images matter. The New Testament preserves the tradition that Jesus rode a donkey into Jerusalem as the crowds chanted, "Hosanna, O Son of David."[16] It is often assumed that Jesus (or the early church) was drawing on imagery from the fairly recent Judaean past (the postexilic book of Zechariah). But the Mari text above suggests that this episode was also evoking an enduring image of the humble king that was much older than Zechariah and much more widespread than Jewish culture.

This strongly suggests that the early church's "Christology" (i.e., its exalted view of Jesus as messiah) sprang not from official or sectarian Jewish sources but from beliefs that, by the first century, were already a thousand years old. But the most important historical question pertaining to Jesus currently remains unanswerable: To what extent did the historical Jesus himself invite followers to look to him as an alternative model of royal authority? Even if he did not publicly identify himself as the Messiah, did he still regard himself as the humble king of ancient Israelite tradition?

16. The usual translation, "Hosanna *to* the Son of David" (Matt. 21:9) is incorrect. The chant not only addressed Jesus as royalty ("O Son of David") but also appealed to him for deliverance (Hebrew *hosha'-na'*, "Save, I pray"). Here in Jerusalem, the expectation seems to have been that, as the Davidic Messiah, he would be a warrior-politician. The donkey-riding, conjuring images of a humble king would have impressed many cynical politicians as an effective propaganda stunt.

The Eucharist as an Oath

We conclude this chapter by examining one more feature of the early Christian tradition in light of the thesis that the NT writings attest to a religious reform movement recovering ancient traditions. This is the account of Jesus' Last Supper, which provides the foundation for the Christian rite of the Lord's Supper, also known as the Eucharist, the Sacrament of the Altar, the Mass, or Holy Communion. It ranks alongside the crucifixion and resurrection as one of the most important elements of the Jesus tradition. Some scholars have recently claimed that both the biblical story and the Christian rite were inventions of the early church, even though the account of the Last Supper rite is described in one of the earliest New Testament documents written (1 Corinthians). If a "reformational" dynamic also underlies this element of the NT tradition, then we can examine the recent scholarly claim in an entirely new light.

The Synoptic Gospels (Matthew, Mark, and Luke) present the Last Supper as a Passover meal. During it, Jesus distributes bread and wine, characterizing this part of the meal as "the covenant" (Mark 14:24; Matt. 26:28) or "the new covenant" (1 Cor. 11:25; Luke 22:20). As described in previous chapters, a covenant is a formal act (not a mere written document) establishing a new relationship between two parties, accompanied by a promise to meet certain specified obligations. It was enforced not by threats of human retaliation or of institutionalized punitive force, but entirely by acts of God—in other words, by circumstances that human effort can neither bring about nor prevent. The covenant relationship was made binding by an oath making the covenant a historical reality, something *enacted* rather than simply spoken.

At first glance there seems to be no oath involved in Jesus' Last Supper with his disciples, and therefore his characterization of the meal as a "(new) covenant" seems strange. Actually, it presumes archaic patterns of thought and behavior that have been unattested now for several millennia. But these patterns were apparently known to Jesus, his disciples, and the early church, suggesting that the eucharistic meal of bread/body and wine/blood in "remembrance" of Jesus was itself the oath of a (new) covenant that was then being made. This is strongly reinforced by the following:

First, as early as the eighteenth century B.C. the *ritual consumption of bread and wine* served as an instrument ratifying a binding agreement. A number of legal documents from Mari record important legal agreements between two parties (e.g., the transfer of real estate or ownership of slaves), often concluding with the note that "they have eaten the bread, they have drunk the cup, they have anointed themselves with oil" (ARM 8:13). The Amarna letters show political covenants being ratified by two parties ceremonially eating and drinking together (EA 162). And centuries later, the Assyrian king Esarhaddon noted that treaties were sworn before the gods "by [means of eating at] the laden table, by [means of] drinking from the cup," hoping that the gods would inspire covenant sincerity in the hearts of vassals the same way vassals let the "bread and wine enter [their] intestines" (*ANET*[3], 536, 539). Thus, oaths need not be spoken—sometimes they took the form of nonverbal gestures.

Second, some *act of ritual identification* often accompanied ancient covenant oath taking. This is present in the Lord's Supper tradition, where Jesus identifies the bread and wine with his body and blood. Similar instances of the ritual identification of persons with the sacrifice itself appear in treaties (i.e., covenants) centuries earlier:

> If Mati'ilu [the vassal] sins against (this) treaty . . . then, just as this spring lamb, brought from its fold, will not behold its fold again, alas, Mati'ilu . . . together with the people of his land [will be ousted] from his country . . . and not behold his country again. This head is not the head of a lamb, it is the head of Mati'ilu. . . . If Mati'ilu sins against this treaty, so may, just as the head of this spring lamb is torn off, . . . the head of Mati'ilu be torn off. (*ANET*³, 532)

Thus, in this very complex Last Supper narrative we see an age-old binding ritual (an enacted oath) combined with the age-old practice of identification: the bread and wine was identified with the person of Jesus. By eating and drinking, early Christians were identifying themselves with the person of Jesus, taking Jesus' body and blood into their own bodies.

Third, the earliest account of the Last Supper (1 Cor. 11:23–25; see also Luke 22:19) says that Jesus distributed the bread and wine with the words, "Do this in *remembrance* of me." It seems curious for Jesus to label the rite a "remembrance" (Greek *anamnesis*), and over the centuries his use of this word has provoked much theological debate over whether the Eucharist is a sacrifice, or a memorial, or a "means of grace," or something else. However, scholars agree that if Jesus had said something like this, he would have expressed it in his native tongue, using some form of the Semitic word *zakar* (Aramaic *dakar*). Although *zakar* in Hebrew usually means "to remember," it can sometimes mean "to swear an oath."

This is illustrated in the Old Testament story of the wise woman from the village of Tekoa who begged King David to spare her only son from the death penalty (2 Samuel 14). Dissatisfied with David's vague reassurances, she finally says, "Let the king remember (*zakar*) Yahweh his God" (v. 11). Because David immediately responds by swearing a formal oath ("As Yahweh lives . . . "), her use of the word *zakar* must have meant, "*Swear an oath* (that you will spare my son)." This meaning of *zakar* has parallels elsewhere in the Hebrew Bible, and in East Semitic languages the word *zakar* normally means "to swear an oath." If Jesus also used the root *zakar* in this archaic sense, then he was telling the disciples that the covenant oath—an *enacted* oath (the ritual eating and drinking) rather than a spoken one—involved swearing loyalty to him.[17]

Fourth, this interpretation of the Last Supper—and therefore of the Eucharist—as an oath-taking rite is dramatically confirmed three generations later in a letter Pliny the Younger wrote to the Roman emperor Trajan concerning the interrogation of alleged Christians:

> They insisted that their fault or error amounted to this: they would meet before sunrise on a certain day, taking turns singing

17. Not only would an *enacted* oath be consistent with Jeremiah's "new covenant" prediction ("written on the heart"; 31:33), but it would not violate Jesus' injunction against *spoken* oaths (Matt. 5:33–37). When a recent seminar at Yarmouk University in Jordan was discussing the use of *zakar* in a Phoenician inscription (and its Arabic cognate, *dhakar*), a student from a remote mountain village remarked, "In our village, when we want someone to swear by Allah that they are telling the truth, we say *udhkur*, 'remember.'" (*Udhkur* is the imperative form of *dhakar*.) Although this archaic usage of the verb is not attested in Lane's eight-volume *Arabic-English Lexicon*, it apparently survives to the present day in village Arabic.

hymns to Christ as a god, and then they bound themselves with
an oath [Latin *se sacramento obstringere*]. But this was not a pledge
to stick together when committing crimes, but rather to abstain
from stealing, robbing, committing adultery, breaking promises, or
refusing to pay back money when called upon to do so. Later they
departed, only to return later to share a meal, but an ordinary and
harmless meal. (Pliny, *Letters* 10.96–97)

There is general agreement that *se sacramento obstringere* refers to the
Eucharist (as opposed to a typical and insignificant meal shared later that
day). Pliny's use of the word *sacramentum* is noteworthy, since normally it
referred to the Roman soldiers' oath of loyalty to the emperor. In other
words, Pliny and the early Christians themselves correctly understood the
Eucharist to be an oath of allegiance, with implicit obligations defining
personal integrity (and therefore including stipulations overlapping those
of the Decalogue). But the actual substance of the oath is expressed not
in words but in the act itself: the early Christians were swearing to *embody*
Christ.[18]

Because it was treason to swear an oath to anyone but the Roman
emperor, the Christian Eucharist could easily be interpreted as an act of
rebellion. Perhaps this explains why Mark and Matthew omit "do this in
remembrance of me"—a feature of the Last Supper that underscored its
true "sacramental" (i.e., oath swearing) character—and why John's Gospel
omits the whole story of the rite entirely.

Finally, Paul seems to remind the Corinthians that the Eucharist is
indeed a sworn oath of allegiance:

> For all who eat and drink without discerning the body, eat and
> drink judgment against themselves. For this reason many of you
> are weak and ill, and some have died. (1 Cor. 11:29–30)

Almost from the dawn of written history, sickness and death have
been considered typical punishments for breach of covenant. It was
unworthy to participate in the sacrament and then ignore or refuse the
obligations that result from identifying one's self with Jesus. Stated
bluntly, it is wrong to swear an oath and then fail to do what you have
promised.

Because all these archaic oath-taking features are present in the earliest Christian account of the Last Supper (1 Corinthians 11), and because
the peculiar meaning of "remembrance" as "swearing" is characteristic
only of the Semitic languages (and not of Greek), it is difficult to imagine the Last Supper story and the Lord's Supper rite being fabricated by
the early church. If anything, the early Christians had to expurgate the

18. The stipulation of the eucharistic oath (i.e., the new covenant) is something to be demonstrated (i.e., lived out), not spoken about. As the apostle Paul described it, "[We are] always carrying in the body the death of Jesus, so that the life of Jesus may also be made visible in our bodies" (2 Cor. 4:10) and "Do you not know that your bodies are members of Christ? . . . But anyone united to the Lord becomes one spirit with him" (1 Cor. 6:15, 17). See also the New Testament admonitions to "put on Christ" and "imitate Christ." The reference in John's Gospel to the "new commandment" of love may illustrate one way of putting the stipulation of Jesus' new covenant into words, although even here the key word "love" is defined not in words but by example: "just as I have loved you" (John 13:34).

Last Supper tradition establishing their *sacramentum,* toning down its potentially subversive character as a covenant oath.

Within a century or two the original character of the Eucharist was forgotten, as Christians no longer viewed it in the ethical context of an oath of allegiance but now in the mystical context of a supernatural "elixir of immortality" (as one church father called it). The function of this rite shifted as Christianity, like so many other religions before and since, adapted and eventually entered a traditional period.

Suggestions for Further Reading

Additional information on the topics discussed in this chapter can be found in the following sources.

Dictionary/Encyclopedia Entries

> *Anchor Bible Dictionary:* Gnosticism; Hellenism; Jesus, Quest of the Historical; Jesus, Teaching of; Jewish-Christian Relations 70–170 C.E.; Kingdom of God; Last Supper; Leprosy; Lord's Supper; Marcion; Meal Customs (Jewish); Messianic Movements in Judaism; Mystery Religions; New Testament, OT Quotations in the; Parable; Persecution of the Early Church; Philo of Alexandria; Roman Imperial Cult; Rome, Early Christian Attitudes to; Sanhedrin; Semiticisms in the NT; Synagogue; Zealots

Jewish Messianism

> J. J. Collins, *The Scepter and the Star: The Messiahs of the Dead Sea Scrolls and Other Ancient Literature.* New York: Doubleday, 1996.
>
> R. Horsley and J. Hanson, *Bandits, Prophets, and Messiahs: Popular Movements at the Time of Jesus.* Minneapolis: Winston Press, 1985.

Guides to Historical Jesus Studies

> J. D. G. Dunn, *The Evidence for Jesus.* Philadelphia: Westminster Press, 1985.
>
> M. Powell, *Jesus as a Figure in History: How Modern Historians View the Man from Galilee.* Louisville, Ky.: Westminster John Knox Press, 1998.
>
> B. Witherington, *The Jesus Quest: The Third Search for the Jew of Nazareth.* Downers Grove, Ill.: Intervarsity Press, 1995.

The Apostle Paul

W. Meeks, *The Moral World of the First Christians*. Philadelphia: Westminster Press, 1986.

E. P. Sanders, *Paul, the Law, and the Jewish People*. Philadelphia: Fortress Press, 1983.

A. Segal, *Paul the Convert: The Apostolate and Apostasy of Saul the Pharisee*. New Haven, Conn.: Yale University Press, 1990.

G. Theissen, *The Social Setting of Pauline Christianity*. Philadelphia: Fortress Press, 1982.

Early Christian Writings

J. D. G. Dunn, *Unity and Diversity in the New Testament*. 2d ed. London and Philadelphia: SCM Press/Trinity International, 1990.

E. Pagels, *The Gnostic Gospels*. New York: Random House, 1979.

D. R. Cartledge and D. L. Dungan, eds., *Documents for the Study of the Gospels*. Rev. and enl. ed. Minneapolis: Fortress Press, 1994.

Christianity in the Roman World

R. L. Fox, *Pagans and Christians.* New York: Knopf, 1986.

R. MacMullen, *Christianizing the Roman Empire, A.D. 100–400.* New Haven, Conn.: Yale University Press, 1984.

R. L. Wilken, *The Christians as the Romans Saw Them*. New Haven, Conn.: Yale University Press, 1984.

Afterword

The history of the biblical tradition is a history of constant adaptation and readaptation to the ever-changing circumstances of human life and history. As Paul of Tarsus observed about Christianity, "we have this treasure in earthen vessels, to show that the transcendent power belongs to God and not to us" (2 Cor. 4:7, RSV). Here Paul may be acknowledging that the substance of the faith (treasure) is always constrained by the forms used to communicate it (vessels). Indeed, the treasure—the religious truth concerning the rule of God—endures unchanging, while the vessels—human religious systems, whether good or bad—wear out and must be periodically replaced by new ones to ensure that the truth is always accessible and comprehensible to the hearers.

Unfortunately, the failure or unwillingness to distinguish the treasure from the vessel (i.e., the message from the medium), especially in traditional periods, has often led to conflicts both within and outside religious communities, as inherited ways of "being religious" themselves become ultimate concerns and sacred preoccupations (Law of Finality). And when the practical concern of individuals and groups becomes controlling other people, then what is involved is no longer an issue of faith but an increasingly destructive power struggle. Religion ought to transcend petty fights over dominion, power, and glory. This is precisely why the early church appended to the Lord's Prayer the words "For *thine* is the kingdom, the power, and the glory for ever and ever." These things were the great ambitions of the Roman aristrocracy in early Christian times, and by ascribing these exclusively to God, the Christians renounced them as human aspirations in favor of what they believed to be "a more excellent way" (1 Cor. 12:31–13:7).

That "Way"—the actual term by which the early Christians identified themselves (Acts 9:2)—did not consist of a set of defined rules and laws, for such collections by nature must be parochial and culturally bound, viable only within the limited sphere governed by political force. In such settings, "God" would once again amount to little more than the divine patron of a self-made segment of humanity. The Christian alternative was to describe the Way in the form of a human being, and thus the great scandal of Christianity—still considered preposterious by many non-Christians today—was to describe God in purely human terms, in the person of Christ. The pagans were inspired to deify human beings (kings and Caesars) precisely because these human beings had power. Yet Jesus possessed none. By deifying him the early Christians were elevating those traits proclaimed in his teachings and exemplified by his life: principally self-sacrificial love and compassion for others. This is what the NT calls *agape,* which is not merely something God "shows"; it is something God "is" (1 John 4:16).

The ultimate rejection of Baal worship is seen in the submission of Jesus to the fate of crucifixion: politically organized force can (and often does) destroy human beings. Regardless, their transcendent value—and that of self-sacrificial love—still rises from the dead.

In Christianity's early centuries, it was loyalty to Christ that created the martyrs. The underlying issue was a fairly simple one, the same one that has run throughout the biblical tradition: whether the well-being of persons ultimately depends on political power or on something that transcends that—not the rule of law but the rule of God. What is at stake is the whole concept of human beings: are they—as pharaohs, Caesars, and governments have always claimed—like the ass, to be beaten with a stick when they stray and seduced with a carrot to do good? Such are the punishments and rewards that imperfect society uses to maintain control. Or does the value of persons transcend this, even though their pettiness often leads them to crave the carrot and avoid the stick?

The Caesars of the world have always answered, "No," for in that answer lies the justification for their existence. The ancient claim that "Caesar is Lord" was nothing less than the claim that human well-being is truly and ultimately contingent on political controls. And this claim continues to have many modern adherents. By claiming, "Jesus is Lord," the early Christians refuted this claim. In spite of all their cultural diversity, they equated their covenant loyalty to Jesus with ancient Israel's covenant loyalty to Yahweh.

What unites the Yahwist covenant with the Christian gospel is belief in the reality of the rule of God, not as an intangible religious idea one may happen to believe (or not) but as a tangible historical reality one can experience and in which one can participate. As in early Israel, so in the early church, God's rule was linked to human integrity and to those motivating forces that transcend the natural human desire for power, wealth, and glory—or even for their milder manifestations: control, comfort, and social acceptance. At the heart of the biblical tradition is the claim that the welfare of the human race is ultimately contingent on the nurturing of human integrity.

It follows from this that religion has better things to do than to define and impose uniform standards of correct behavior. That the early church, in fact, included people with diverse traditions, mores, and standards of behavior shows that this vision of religion's proper role was held across cultures. What was also cross-cultural, in the early church as in early Yahwism, was the ability to identify and agree on the content of human integrity. In ancient Yahwism, it was defined in terms of ten basic commitments held by people "in covenant" with God. The New Testament calls it the "fruit of the spirit" (Gal. 5:22–23), which actually amounts to little more than a list of desirable human character traits: love, joy, peace, patience, kindness, goodness, faithfulness, gentleness, and self-control. These things are genuinely transcendent: they have been recognized and valued by ordinary people in every age and every culture. They are manifestations of *agape* that the Caesars of the world can neither elicit nor prohibit.

But most fundamental of all, these—not governments—are also the things on which human well-being absolutely and ultimately depends, because without them there is not likely to be any civilization.

Appendix A

The Judeo-Christian Scriptures

The books of the Hebrew Bible (or Old Testament) were composed over the course of a thousand-year period marked by significant change. The oldest parts may include archaic poetry, such as Exodus 15 (composed around 1200 B.C.); the last Old Testament text to be written was probably the book of Daniel (around 165 B.C.). It is highly doubtful that Israelite writers living in later times had much real understanding of the historical contexts from which earlier Israelite traditions emerged. They preserved early traditions in forms that seemed relevant and meaningful to them. In contrast, the New Testament books were written over the course of less than a century: the earliest were Paul's epistles (written around A.D. 50–60) and, according to some scholars, the latest may have been 2 Peter (written a century later).

The Old Testament

The Jewish tradition divides the Hebrew Bible into three parts: Law, Prophets, and Writings. The fact that Jesus alluded to the Law and the Prophets (e.g., Matt. 5:17; 7:12; 22:40) suggests that no final decision about the third division had yet been made. Rabbinic Jewish sources confirm that the third division, the Writings, became finalized around a century or so after the time of Jesus, although individual books within that division were considered authoritative well before that time (see Luke 24:44).

The Law, or Pentateuch (or Torah). During the fifth century B.C., the Persian Empire encouraged its subject peoples to consolidate and preserve their respective religious traditions and customs (see chapter 7). This helped stimulate the canonization of the Pentateuch (or "five scrolls"), the first five books of the Old Testament:

Genesis
Exodus
Leviticus
Numbers
Deuteronomy

Beginning with an account of creation (Genesis 1) and ending with the story of Moses' death (Deuteronomy 34), these books preserve and update traditions about Israel's earliest days. Because the centerpiece of these books is the story of the exodus and the Sinai covenant (supplemented by various law codes), the tradition soon arose that these five books were written by the protagonist of that story, Moses himself. Since the early 1800s biblical scholars have effectively challenged this tradition, believing instead that these five books were actually formed by the "weaving together" of four post-Moses sources, conventionally labeled J, E, D, and P. "D" refers to Deuteronomy, published at the time of King Josiah's reforms in 621 B.C. (see chapter 6), and "P" designates the priestly and ritual strand that is especially prevalent in the latter half of Exodus, Leviticus, and most of Numbers (but also found in Genesis). Opinions are divided as to when each source was first compiled, but probably by the time of Ezra they had been finally combined to form the Torah (see chapter 7).

The Prophets. This second division of the Hebrew Bible is subdivided into two parts. The **Former Prophets** provide a sweeping account of the history of Israel, beginning with the death of Moses and ending with the destruction of the Jerusalem monarchy six hundred years later. It includes these books:

Joshua
Judges
1–2 Samuel
1–2 Kings

Because this history was deliberately recounted to illustrate the religious maxims of the book of Deuteronomy, scholars sometimes refer to it as the "Deuteronomistic History." It was probably compiled shortly after the discovery of Deuteronomy during the reign of King Josiah. (Christian

Bibles often insert the book of Ruth right after Judges, since Ruth is set in the period of the Judges.)

The other subdivision is called the **Latter Prophets,** largely because these books have been placed *after* the Former Prophets. For the most part, these books contain poetic oracles associated with great prophets who lived between the eighth and sixth centuries B.C. These books are subdivided, in turn, into *Major Prophets* (so designated because the books are lengthy) and *Minor Prophets* (which are much shorter):

> *Major Prophets*
>   Isaiah
>   Jeremiah
>   Ezekiel
> *The Twelve Minor Prophets*
>   Hosea
>   Joel
>   Amos
>   Obadiah
>   Jonah
>   Micah
>   Nahum
>   Habakkuk
>   Zephaniah
>   Haggai
>   Zechariah
>   Malachi

Scholars are divided on the extent to which these books contain "transcripts" of the prophets' actual words. Christian Bibles insert Lamentations after Jeremiah, and Daniel after Ezekiel.

The Writings. Sometime in the first century or so after Christ, Jewish scribes and Rabbis collected additional writings to be included in scripture alongside the Law and the Prophets. Some of these (e.g., some Psalms, sections of Proverbs) contain ancient material dating back perhaps to the time of David and Solomon, while others (e.g., Daniel) can be dated to only a century or two before Christ. The traditional Jewish order of these books is as follows:

> Psalms
> Job
> Proverbs

Ruth
Song of Songs (or Song of Solomon)
Ecclesiastes (also known as Qoheleth)
Lamentations
Esther
Daniel
Ezra
Nehemiah
1–2 Chronicles

Christian Bibles rearrange these books in a radically different order.

The Apocrypha. The Roman Catholic and various Orthodox churches use a form of the Old Testament based on an ancient Greek arrangement of the Jewish scriptures (called the Septuagint) begun sometime before 200 B.C. That arrangement included additional books that these Christian bodies consider "deuterocanonical" (or a "second part" of the OT canon). These additional books include, but are not limited to, the following:

Judith
Tobit
Wisdom of Solomon
Wisdom of Ben-Sirach (or Ecclesiaticus)
Prayer of Manasseh
1 Maccabees
2 Maccabees
2 Esdras (or "4 Ezra")

Most appear to have been written during the so-called "Intertestamental Period" (200 B.C. and A.D. 200). Protestants and Jews do not ascribe religious authority to these books and usually refer to them as the "Apocrypha," a word that means "hidden" and may mean either that these books contain secret, esoteric teachings (with "hidden" meanings) or that they contain false teachings that deserve to be removed from public circulation (and "hidden" away).

Other Nonbiblical Jewish Writings

Between 200 B.C. and the first century A.D. Jewish scribes produced a wealth of other religious writings. Although never included in the Hebrew Bible, these writings provide valuable testimony to the diversity within Judaism at the time. The **Pseudepigrapha** is the name given to many of the books, mostly written in Greek, which purport to have been written by famous OT characters. Although probably Jewish in origin, the existing editions of some of these books were apparently prepared by Christians who modified the Jewish content to underscore Christian themes. Some of these books include the following:

1 Enoch	*Testaments of the Twelve Patriarchs*
2 Enoch	*Testament of Moses*
Sibylline Oracles	*Testament of Solomon*
2 Baruch	*Jubilees*
Apocalypse of Adam	*Life of Adam and Eve*
Apocalypse of Abraham	*Lives of the Prophets*
3 Maccabees	*Psalms of Solomon*
4 Maccabees	*Hellenistic Synagogal Prayers*

"Pseudepigrapha" literally means "false books" and probably refers to the growing awareness that they could not possibly have been written by the OT characters as claimed. Many of these books are *apocalyptic,* using cryptic language and symbolic imagery (popular in the Hellenistic and Roman periods) to depict the end of the cosmos, when Good finally triumphs over Evil.

Another noteworthy collection of Jewish religious writings not included in the Bible is the **Dead Sea Scrolls,** first-century (and earlier) manuscripts discovered in the late 1940s and early 1950s in caves near the Dead Sea. This collection contained literature revered by a particular Jewish sect, the Essenes. It included manuscripts of every OT book (except Esther), as well as other major works that seem to reflect this sect's own particular expression of Judaism. Some select titles include:

Rule of the Community	*Commentary on Habakkuk*
The War Scroll	*Thanksgiving Hymns*
Melchizedek	*Prayer of Nabonidus*
The Temple Scroll	*Copper Scroll*

The New Testament

Within a century after the time of Christ, Christians had already begun to supplement the Hebrew Bible with some of their own scriptures. By the end of the 4th century A.D. these additional books had become firmly set in Christian tradition as a "*New* Testament" to be read alongside the Hebrew Bible, or "*Old* Testament." Generally speaking, the New Testament contains three different types of writings: Gospels, Epistles, and an apocalypse.

The Gospels. The word "gospel" comes from *gōdspell,* an Old English word meaning "good news," which is equivalent to the Greek word designating the first four books of the NT: *euangelion.* These books selectively recount the life, teachings, death, and resurrection of Jesus in such a way as to extol and proclaim him as the Christ (or Jewish Messiah), the son of God (see John 20:31). These books are

> Matthew
> Mark
> Luke–Acts
> John

The Gospel of Luke is actually the first part of a two-volume work: the book of Acts (or Acts of the Apostles) is the second part of this work (compare Acts 1:1 with Luke 1:1–4). Christian arrangements of the NT always place the Gospel of John (or "the Fourth Gospel") between Luke and Acts, so that traditions concerning Jesus can be read *before* traditions about his followers.

Although Christian tradition attributes each of these Gospels either to an eyewitness disciple (Matthew, John) or to a protégé of one of the apostles (Mark, Luke), scholars have found reasons to question this tradition. The first three Gospels share a large quantity of material in common. They are called the **Synoptic Gospels** because their texts can be viewed together alongside one another ("synoptic" means "viewed with one eye"). Today most scholars explain these marked similarities by theorizing that the authors of Matthew and Luke, working independently, used Mark's Gospel as the basis for theirs. Mark may have been written as early as A.D. 65–70. According to many scholars, the author of the Fourth Gospel wrote around A.D. 100, as early Christianity was becoming visibly distinct from Rabbinic Judaism and developing its own traditional vocabulary for talking about the divine Jesus.

The Epistles. The word "epistle" basically means "letter" and refers to those NT books that were originally correspondence "mailed" to different Christian communities. These twenty-one books are arranged as follows:

> Romans
> 1–2 Corinthians
> Galatians
> Ephesians
> Philippians
> Colossians

> 1–2 Thessalonians
> 1–2 Timothy
> Titus
> Philemon
> Hebrews
> James
> 1–2 Peter
> 1–3 John
> Jude

The apostle Paul (died around A.D. 64) is identified as the author of Romans through Philemon (the **Pauline Epistles**), letters addressed to specific Christian communities at a time when Christian faith was still widely regarded as an expression of early Judaism. According to many scholars, the so-called **Pastoral Epistles** (1–2 Timothy and Titus), as well as Ephesians and Colossians, may actually have been written by one of Paul's disciples around A.D. 100.

The book of Hebrews is more of a treatise than a letter, and its author and date of composition remain unknown. The remaining **Catholic Epistles** are addressed more generally to Christians at large (the word "catholic" means general or universal). Even though they are attributed to various of Jesus' disciples, many scholars believe they were composed much later by anonymous Christians writing pseudonymously (i.e., writing *as if* they were one of these original disciples). The thought, style, and vocabulary of 1–3 John bear striking resemblance to those of the Gospel of John.

The Apocalypse. We noted previously that many nonbiblical Jewish books were *apocalyptic,* envisioning the final, cosmic clash between Good and Evil. The last book of the NT is such a book:

> The Revelation (or Apocalypse) to John

The author of the book of Revelation was named John. Some early traditions identify this John as the author also of the Fourth Gospel and of the epistles of John, asserting that he was either Jesus' disciple (John son of Zebedee) or a well-known elder of the church at Ephesus. However, most scholars today suggest that the author may have been a Christian mystic living during emperor Domitian's persecutions of the church (around A.D. 95–96) and that he had no connection whatsoever with these other "Johannine" scriptures.

Appendix B

Yahweh as Lord of History

What, or who, shapes historical events? Many people naturally assume that powerful human actors and forces—such as political leaders, imperialist policies, international diplomatic initiatives, and armies and generals—exert influence to make events unfold in ways consistent with their interests. In a certain limited sense this is true.

But the great Israelite prophets of the eighth century B.C. saw a larger dynamic at work in history, which they connected with Yahweh. They understood that these human actors and forces are themselves also caught up in forces that they rarely appreciate and can never really control. Great empires rise and fall; the tide of battle may turn unexpectedly; unforeseen complications and obstacles may arise to frustrate political agendas; etc. In other words, the prophets believed that history unfolds to serve purposes of which the historical actors themselves are unaware. In this irony, they saw Yahweh at work. It was clear to them that the foreign armies being deployed against Israel had been summoned there for historical purposes ultimately determined by Yahweh himself, not by foreign kings and generals.

> Proclaim to the strongholds of Ashdod,
>   and to the strongholds in the land of Egypt,
> and say, "Assemble yourselves on Mount Samaria
>   and see what great tumults are within it,
>   and what oppressions are in its midst."
> . . . .
> Therefore thus says the Lord Yahweh:

An adversary shall surround the land,
    and strip you of your defense;
    and your strongholds shall be plundered. (Amos 3:9–11)

He [Yahweh] will raise a signal for a nation far away,
    and whistle for a people at the ends of the earth;
Here they come, swiftly, speedily!
None of them is weary, none stumbles,
    none slumbers or sleeps,
not a loincloth is loose,
    not a sandal-thong broken;
their arrows are sharp;
    all their bows bent,
their horses' hoofs seem like flint,
    and their wheels like the whirlwind.
Their roaring is like a lion,
    like young lions they roar;
they growl and seize their prey,
    they carry it off, and no one can rescue. (Isa. 5:26–29)

Ah, Assyria, the rod of my anger—
    the club in their hands is my [i.e., Yahweh's] fury!
Against a godless nation I [Yahweh] send him,
    and against the people of my wrath I command him,
to take spoil and seize plunder,
    and to tread them down like the mire of the streets. (Isa. 10:5–6)

In other words, empires—such as the Assyrians and the Chaldean Babylonians—existed to serve Yahweh's transcending purpose. Just as history does not ultimately respect their political agendas, so does Yahweh not give them complete autonomy. They are merely tools in his hands, to be disposed of when they have outlived their usefulness:

When the Lord has finished all his work on Mount Zion and on Jerusalem, he will punish the arrogant boasting of the king of Assyria and his haughty pride. For he says:
    "By the strength of my hand I have done it,

    . . . .

    I have removed the boundaries of peoples,
        and have plundered their treasures."

    . . . .

    Shall the ax vaunt itself over the one who wields it,
        or the saw magnify itself against the one who handles it?

. . . .
Therefore the Sovereign, Yahweh of hosts,
    will send wasting sickness among his stout warriors.
(Isa. 10:12–13, 15–16)

[Yahweh says:] Sit on the ground without a throne,
    daughter Chaldea!
. . . .
For you shall no more be called
    the mistress of kingdoms.
I was angry with my people,
    I profaned my heritage;
I gave them into your hand,
    you showed them no mercy.
. . . .
You felt secure in your wickedness;
    you said, "No one sees me."
. . . .
and you said in your heart,
    "I am, and there is no one besides me."
But evil shall come upon you,
    which you cannot charm away;
disaster shall fall upon you,
    which you will not be able to ward off.
(Isa. 47:1, 5–6, 10–11)

Israel is a hunted sheep driven away by lions. First the king of
Assyria devoured it, and now at the end King Nebuchadrezzar
of Babylon has gnawed its bones. Therefore, thus says Yahweh
of hosts, the God of Israel: I am going to punish the king
of Babylon and his land, as I punished the king of
Assyria. . . .

    You set a snare for yourself and you were caught, O Babylon,
        but you did not know it;
. . . .
    Yahweh has opened his armory,
        and brought out the weapons of his wrath,
    for the Lord Yahweh of hosts has a task to do
        in the land of the Chaldeans.
    Come against her from every quarter;
. . . .
        let nothing be left of her.

. . . .
Alas for them, their day has come,
the time of their punishment!
(Jer. 50:17–18, 24–27)

The New Testament in Israelite Perspective

Viewing Jesus solely as a product of his times is vastly preferable historically to viewing him through the dogmatic lens of later Christian confessions. But it prevents us from appreciating the significant ways in which both he and his followers were *out of step* with their times.

When dealing with matters of historical background, virtually every introductory textbook on the NT focuses narrowly on the Greco-Roman and first-century context. A random sampling of textbooks shows this pattern of disproportionate coverage (determined by number of words) given to different biblical periods, ranging from premonarchic Israel (1200–1000 B.C.) to the Jewish world of the first and second centuries A.D.

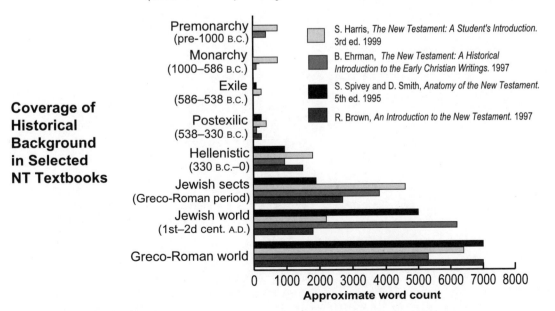

Coverage of Historical Background in Selected NT Textbooks

S. Harris, *The New Testament: A Student's Introduction.* 3rd ed. 1999

B. Ehrman, *The New Testament: A Historical Introduction to the Early Christian Writings.* 1997

S. Spivey and D. Smith, *Anatomy of the New Testament.* 5th ed. 1995

R. Brown, *An Introduction to the New Testament.* 1997

Premonarchy (pre-1000 B.C.)
Monarchy (1000–586 B.C.)
Exile (586–538 B.C.)
Postexilic (538–330 B.C.)
Hellenistic (330 B.C.–0)
Jewish sects (Greco-Roman period)
Jewish world (1st–2d cent. A.D.)
Greco-Roman world

0   1000 2000 3000 4000 5000 6000 7000 8000
Approximate word count

The word count shows that virtually no attention is given to the more remote Israelite past (Premonarchy, Monarchy, and Exile). The overwhelming attention given to Judaism in the more recent Hellenistic and Roman periods—and to the non-Jewish world in general—does not prepare students to see the many ways in which Jesus and the early church were more than mere products of their times, and prevents them from recognizing possible reformational dynamics at work in early Christianity. Worse yet, it fails to do justice to the New Testament material itself, where a third of the verses clearly allude to the Israelite religious tradition.

Glossary

Abdu-Hepa. Hurrian soldier appointed by the Egyptians as governor or king of Jerusalem during the Amarna period (ca. 1350 B.C.).

Abiathar. Yahwist priest who accompanied David from his early days; he was later exiled to Anathoth by David's son, King Solomon (1 Kings 2:27).

Abraham. A central character in the book of Genesis; father of Ishmael by Hagar and husband of Sarah and grandfather of Jacob/Israel. The historicity of Abraham is debated; he may have been an Amorite who immigrated to the land of Canaan early in the second millennium B.C. Although originally treated as an ancestor shared by Israelites and non-Israelites, later Jewish tradition often regarded him as the representative ancestor exclusively of the Jews.

Absalom. King David's son, killed in battle after leading a rebellion against his father (2 Samuel 13–19).

"act of God." An event that no human being could have caused or prevented. There is no need to posit supernatural causes. The point in labeling something an "act of God" is not so much to identify any divine intent, purpose, or reason behind the event as to prevent people from taking credit or receiving blame for the event.

Adonijah. The oldest surviving son and heir apparent of King David; however, palace intrigue involving key figures in the Jerusalem regime supported Solomon instead. As king, Solomon later had Adonijah put to death (1 Kings 1:5; 2:24, 25).

Aegean Sea. The northern extension of the Mediterranean Sea separating Asia Minor from the Greek peninsula. Several Bronze Age cultures developed in this region; when those cultures collapsed, many so-called "Sea Peoples" migrated from this area.

Ahab. King of northern Israel (869–850 B.C.). The Bible portrays him as a wicked king who was unduly influenced by his wife Jezebel (1 Kings 16:30–31).

Ahaz. Idolatrous king of southern Judah (ruled 735–715 B.C.), who made a treaty with the Assyrian king to rescue him from the kings of Israel and Damascus (2 Kings 16:7).

Ahijah. A tenth-century-B.C. Israelite prophet from the village of Shiloh, who predicted the civil war splitting Solomon's kingdom into two kingdoms, north and south (1 Kings 11:29–40). He reappeared a decade later to pronounce doom upon Jeroboam, the first king of the secessionist north (1 Kings 14:1–14).

Akhenaten. Egyptian pharaoh during the Amarna period. Also known as Amenophis IV, his idiosyncratic devotion to the sun-disk Aten has frequently been mistaken for monotheism. His inattention to political affairs in Syria and Palestine helped precipitate the crises of the Amarna Age.

Akkadian. The name given to the East Semitic languages of ancient Mesopotamia, prevalent from 2400–500 B.C. The languages of the Assyrians and Babylonians represent later dialects of Akkadian.

Alexander the Great. The young Greek king (lived 356–323 B.C.) who conquered the Persian Empire and Egypt, stimulating the spread of Hellenism into these areas.

Amarna Age. A period of political turmoil in Syria-Palestine (ca. 1380–1340 B.C.), precipitated by Egyptian weakness and Hittite expansionism. Among and within the city-states of Syria-Palestine, it was a time of shifting loyalties and political disaffection (see "Apiru").

Amarna letters. A collection of about 380 LB Age letters written by kings and governors of the Near East and Canaan to the Egyptian pharaoh, attesting to the political chaos of the time.

'am ha'arets. Literally "people of the land," this word originally designated the "common people" and village peasants who normally lacked any influence over political affairs in Jerusalem. Josiah was a king of Jerusalem apparently brought to power with the support of the 'am ha'arets. Later Jewish religious leaders used the term (in the sense of "ignoramuses") to disparage Jews not committed to the strict observance of Jewish laws and customs.

Amnon. Oldest son of King David who raped his half sister Tamar and was then murdered by her brother Absalom (2 Sam. 13:14, 28–29).

Amorite. The designation of the people of northeast Syria, or Amurru. Early in the Bronze Age, this was the name of the people of northeast Syria. As some of these Amorites migrated south and west, the name traveled with them, so that by the LB Age an "Amorite" kingdom was located in northern Lebanon. When it was destroyed in the thirteenth century B.C., some of its displaced soldiers set up military regimes farther south, so that by biblical times portions of Palestine and Transjordan were said to be "Amorite" territory (Num. 21:31; Deut. 1:7).

Amos. Yahwist prophet of the eighth century B.C. from the village of Tekoa, whose religious indictments of the northern Israelites have been preserved in the biblical book bearing his name.

Amurru. Akkadian term meaning "West," originally designating the region of northeast Syria. In the LB Age it also designated a kingdom in Lebanon (see Table 1.2). The biblical form of the word is "Amorite."

'anan. The supernatural "glory" by which gods appeared to and communicated with people, as Yahweh did at Mount Sinai. Later biblical scribes understood it in a more restricted sense as a "cloud."

Anatolia. Asia Minor, including most of modern Turkey. This was the homeland of the ancient Hittite Empire.

Antiochus Epiphanes. The Greek king of Syria (ruled 175–164 B.C.) who violently persecuted Jews committed to traditional forms of Jewish culture, while supporting those Jews who embraced Hellenistic cultural forms. Opposition to him took the form of the Maccabean revolt.

Apiru. A label (also spelled "Habiru") applied across the ancient Near East to disaffected groups and individuals who were no longer considered loyal subjects of any political organization or state. Scholars are divided on whether the biblical word "Hebrew" derived from this word.

Arabian Desert. The Arabian peninsula (see Map 1.1), erroneously considered the place of origin of waves of Semitic nomads who effected cultural change by invading the settled states of the Fertile Crescent. In fact, the Arabian peninsula has been a place of *destination* for refugees fleeing the Fertile Crescent at times of cultural collapse. Consequently, to this day vestiges of archaic Bronze Age culture can still be seen among the peoples of Saudi Arabia and Yemen.

Aram. The ancient name for Syria, the territory controlled by regimes based in the city of Damascus (see Map 6.1).

Aramaeans. People of Iron Age Syria who spoke a West Semitic language known as Aramaic.

Aramaic. Originally the West Semitic language used in Iron Age Syria. Because the Persian Empire adopted it as the official state language in the fifth and fourth centuries B.C., it became a sort of lingua franca across the Near East. Even after many Near Eastern peoples later adopted the more cosmopolitan Greek language, Aramaic persisted in the villages and was probably the language of Jesus and his disciples. Later dialects of this language are called Syriac.

ark of the covenant. A chest in which the early Israelites kept the text of the Decalogue, their covenant with Yahweh. During the monarchy, an elaborate ark was placed within the Jerusalem temple, where it served symbolically as Yahweh's throne.

Asherah. Bronze Age goddess conventionally associated with fertility. Actually, as the deification of productivity, Asherah symbolized the value of wealth, prosperity, good fortune, and happiness.

Ashurbanipal. Last great king of Assyria (ruled 668–631 B.C.). The decline of the Assyrian Empire following his death prompted many local rulers, such as the biblical king Josiah, to begin expanding to fill the political void.

Assyria. Powerful Iron Age empire of northern Mesopotamia (see Map 6.1). Beginning in 745 B.C. the Assyrians began a successful campaign conquering rival kingdoms to the west, including northern Israel in 721 B.C. They were eventually defeated by the Babylonian Empire around 609 B.C.

Astarte. A Canaanite goddess considered the consort of Baal in the LB Age Ugaritic texts, and frequently paired with Baal in Iron Age Phoenicia. Wayward Israelites are said to have worshiped the Baals and the Astartes (Judg. 10:6); the plural form may refer either to specific local manifestations of these deities, or simply mean "Canaanite gods and goddesses" in general. While the distinction between Astarte and Asherah was clear in the LB Age, by biblical times it was not (compare Judg. 3:7).

Baal. A label for any ancient Near Eastern god associated with power and manifested in storm, war, and kingship. Actually, as the deification of the state, a Baal symbolized the value of coercive force and political control. The early Israelites opposed the revival of Baal worship because it promoted power considerations above ethical ones.

Babylonia. A powerful kingdom of southern

Mesopotamia (capital Babylon) during the MB Age, that regained political prominence briefly around 621–539 B.C. before being defeated by the Persian Empire. The MB regime, whose most famous king was Hammurapi, was culturally Amorite.

Barak. The man who led the early Israelite tribal militias against the oppressive King Jabin. Consistent with principles of holy war, he refused to go to war without the authorization of an acknowledged religious leader, such as Deborah (Judg. 4:4–8).

Bar Kokhba Revolt. The name given to a Jewish revolt against the Romans in Palestine (A.D. 132–135), led by Simon bar-Kosibah. The great rabbi Akiba, a contemporary, considered Simon to be the royal messiah of the Jews, a warrior-king who would establish Jewish political autonomy from Rome. He was also called Bar Kokhba, "son of the star," following a messianic interpretation of Numbers 24:17.

Bathsheba. A native Jebusite who became King David's wife in Jerusalem after David had her husband killed (2 Samuel 11). She later gave birth to Solomon, conspiring with Nathan and Zadok—probably two other Jebusite holdovers from pre-Davidic Jerusalem—to ensure that Solomon succeed David as king (1 Kings 1).

Benjamin. The name of one of the tribes that joined the Yahwist federation of Israel. As such, Benjamin was identified as one of the "sons" of Jacob/Israel (Gen. 49:1, 27). See Maps 3.1 and 7.1. The Mari texts mention an Amorite tribe by the name of Benjamin (*banu-yamina*).

Beth-shean. A non-Israelite town in Palestine that King Solomon designated as a provincial capital. Its bureaucrats managed Israelite affairs in place of the old tribal system that had existed a generation earlier (Judg. 1:27; 1 Kings 4:12). See Map 3.1.

book of the law. A scroll discovered while repairs were being made to the Jerusalem temple in 621 B.C. (2 Kings 22:8). Scholars believe this was the core of the book of Deuteronomy, which inspired a major revision of Israelite history during the reign of King Josiah.

Bronze Age. Archaeological designation for the pre-Israelite period (3200–1200 B.C.) characterized by a technology increasingly using bronze. The period is subdivided into Early (EB), Middle (MB), Late (LB) periods.

Byblos. A cosmopolitan urban center on the Lebanese coast (modern Jbail), also known as Gebal in the Amarna Age (see Maps 1.1, 4.1, and 6.1). MB Age kings there had Amorite names, and MB Age copper tablets excavated there contained a language that appears to be a forerunner of the Arabic language.

Byzantine. The name given to the eastern part of the Roman Empire, founded by Constantine in A.D. 324 with its capital at Constantinople (Byzantium). The name also designates the period A.D. 324–640, when the Christian rulers of Constantinople governed Syria and Palestine during a time of unparalleled prosperity.

Canaanite. Name given to the culture (and thus to the people and land) of LB Age Palestine and Lebanon (i.e., Canaan). In the Iron Age, the Greeks referred to these people and their culture as "Phoenician." The early Israelites, in some respects, were culturally Canaanite/Phoenician, indistinguishable in terms of their language and material culture, although their Yahwism constituted a sharp repudiation of Canaanite religion.

Chemosh. Patron deity of the kingdom of Moab (Judg. 11:24).

cherubim. Mythological winged beings that were often regarded as composite creatures (e.g., head of a human, body of a lion or bull). Various depictions of cherubim adorned the temple of Solomon, as well as the elaborate ark of the covenant placed therein. Jeroboam's "golden calves" may have originally been cherubim, rather than actual idols to be worshiped (1 Kings 12:28).

Christianity. The name given to a religion that began in the first century as a reform movement within early Judaism, focusing on the ancient Yahwist notion of God's rule or kingdom and on Jesus' role as messiah and Son of God in that kingdom. As a creative religious reform, it stressed the ancient *substance* of Yahwist faith more than the subsequent *forms* of Israelite and Jewish religion, rejecting the value of Jewish law and ethnicity.

Christology. Religious interpretation of the transcendent identity and significance of Jesus, including notions about his divine nature, his redeeming death, etc.

covenant. A binding promise voluntarily made and sealed by an oath. Covenants provide a framework of values and obligations that bind diverse people or groups into one larger body or community. Marriages are covenants that operate privately to unite families, while treaties are covenants that operate publicly to unite nations or states. Oaths play essential roles in activating covenants, as various parties formally pledge to abide by the terms of the covenant. The early Israelites considered their relationship to Yahweh as analogous to a covenant, not as something that results "naturally" but rather as something to which people freely commit and pledge themselves.

Covenant Code. The ancient collection of law preserved in Exodus 21–23. These laws have a distinctively

Amorite character and were probably adapted to serve Yahwist ends during the premonarchic period.

Cyrus. Founder of the Persian Empire (ruled 550–529 B.C.) who accommodated his subjects' nostalgic interest in their respective and distinctive cultures, religions, customs, and traditions. Identified as Yahweh's Messiah in Isaiah 45:1, Cyrus in 538 B.C. permitted the Judaeans in exile to return to Jerusalem to revive their traditional way of life (but not their political autonomy).

Dagon. A god of the ancient Philistines and Phoenicians, this deity was originally Amorite, perhaps brought from north Syria by Amorite immigrants during the MB Age.

Damascus. See "Aram."

Daniel. The last Old Testament book to be written, probably during the persecutions of Antiochus Epiphanes (second century B.C.). The book inspires hope for divine salvation, first by telling stories of God protecting Daniel during the Babylonian exile (as when Daniel was thrown into the lions' den). The book also purports to record Daniel's (sixth-century-B.C.) visions of God rescuing faithful Jews from Antiochus's persecution.

Dan'il. A legendary Canaanite king who, according to Ugaritic legend, was imperiled by his lack of an heir. A thousand years later this legendary figure was still remembered by some Judaeans (Ezek. 14:14, 20).

Darius. King of Persia (ruled 521–486 B.C.) who supported the revival of Judaean traditions, including the rebuilding of the Jerusalem temple.

David. Israelite king from the tribe of Judah who succeeded Saul around 1000 B.C. and introduced political stability to the newly emergent Israelite state. David made Jerusalem his capital city (2 Sam. 5:3, 7) and founded a dynasty that would rule for over four hundred years. Jewish messianic hopes anticipated that an ideal king would one day return from his family line.

Davidic covenant. The Divine Charter delivered to David by the prophet Nathan in which God promised to keep the Israelite throne within David's family forever (2 Samuel 7).

Dead Sea Scrolls. Manuscripts discovered in the 1940s and 1950s in caves near Qumran, on the northwest shore of the Dead Sea. They contain biblical and other manuscripts dating from the second century B.C. to the first century A.D., most likely reflecting an Essene perspective and demonstrating the diversity and tensions within Judaism around the time of Christ.

Deborah. A Yahwist judge and prophet during the early days of the twelve-tribe federation. She gave reli-

gious sanction to the battle against King Jabin, reminding Barak that, as a holy war, the victory could not result in glory accruing to him (Judg. 4:4–10). One of the oldest portions of the Old Testament, Judges 5, may have been composed by her.

Decalogue. Literally, "ten words," that is, the ten statements that express the heart of the Yahwist religious ethic. These statements are often mistakenly viewed as commandments; in fact, they lack command language and simply list the conduct and values necessary to a covenant relationship with the god Yahweh, and violation of which would result in divine punishment.

Deuteronomistic History. A scholarly term for the biblical books of Joshua, Judges, 1–2 Samuel, and 1–2 Kings, written during the reign of King Josiah and inspired by the teachings of Deuteronomy. In the opening chapters of Joshua this history presents an idealized (and largely unhistorical) picture of the early Israelites as a political nation bent on military conquest and political expansion. In reality, this was the Israel of Josiah's day. Other parts of this history seem to contain authentic traditions about the early days, traditions that scribes in Josiah's time did not always fully understand.

Diaspora. The scattering of Judaeans geographically outside Palestine, particularly in the Near East and eastern Mediterranean lands after the destruction of Jerusalem in 586 B.C.

divination. Techniques for predicting the future by collecting and interpreting omens and signs (such as markings on sheep livers or flight patterns of birds). Today this strikes us as superstitious, but in antiquity it was esteemed for its seemingly "objective" character.

Divine Charter. See "Davidic covenant."

Edom. A state south of the Dead Sea area attested in the Iron II period (see Map 6.1), although the Bible preserves a tradition that its monarchy actually appeared before the Israelite monarchy (Gen. 36:31). The non-Israelite Edomites considered themselves descendants of Abraham through Esau, Jacob's twin brother.

'elef. An archaic Hebrew word designating a military unit comprised of six to twenty men. Later scribes knew it only as the number "thousand," yielding an inordinately inflated image of the number of slaves who fled Egypt with Moses (Exod. 12:37).

Elijah. Hebrew prophet of the ninth century B.C., from the village of Tishbe. He was an opponent of Jezebel and Ahab, perhaps best remembered for his contest with the prophets of Baal at Mount Carmel (1 Kings 18; see Table 5.1).

Elisha. Hebrew prophet of the ninth century B.C., from the village of Abel-meholah, who anointed Jehu to destroy the Omride dynasty of Ahab and Jezebel and to become Israel's next king (2 Kings 9; see Table 5.1)

El Shaddai. Name of the god of Abraham, usually translated God Almighty. Literally "the god of Shaddai," probably the Amorite patron deity of the town of Shaddai, ancient Tuttul in north Syria.

Ephraim. The name of one of the tribes that joined the Yahwist federation of Israel. As such, Ephraim, identified as a son of Joseph, was also placed alongside the other "sons" of Jacob/Israel (Genesis 49). See Maps 3.1 and 7.1. It was one of the larger and more powerful tribes, and after the civil war of 922 B.C. its name became virtually synonymous with the northern kingdom of Israel.

Essenes. Jewish sect in ancient Palestine at the time of Christ, usually associated with the Dead Sea Scrolls. In the matter of interpreting and applying the law to Jewish life, they had sharp disagreements with the Pharisees. Because they considered the Jerusalem priests to be illegitimate, they also had sharp differences with the Sadducees.

Eucharist. The Christian ceremony of consecrated bread and wine that, according to NT sources, Jesus instituted during his last meal with his disciples.

exodus. A word designating the Hebrew slaves' escape from bondage in Egypt around 1200 B.C., and (capitalized) the name of the second book of the Bible that recounts that story.

Ezekiel. The name of a Judaean priest-prophet taken into exile in Babylon in 597 B.C. (eleven years before Jerusalem was destroyed), and of the biblical book preserving accounts of his life and teachings.

Ezra. Hebrew priest of the fifth century B.C. who promoted written scripture as the religious centerpiece of the Judaean community. He helped ensure that civil power was used to support compliance with scriptural law. Later generations regarded him as a second Moses, the prototypical Pharisee. His activities are recounted in the biblical books of Ezra and Nehemiah.

Gentiles. Non-Jews. In the early Christian church it could also mean non-Christians (1 Pet. 2:12; 3:3). See "Goyim."

Gibeon. A non-Israelite village that made a covenant with the Yahwist federation of tribes (Joshua 9–10). Over two centuries later, Solomon had a religious experience at Gibeon, from which he received divine authorization to administer law in Israel not according to Yahwist traditions but according to royal wisdom (1 Kings 3:5–28).

Gnosticism. An ancient religious philosophy encouraging people to find their true self-identity in the metaphysical *soul* rather than in their physical *personhood*. Beginning around the second century A.D., this esoteric philosophy found "Christian" forms of expression: Christ raises the Self to new life by giving it the knowledge (*gnosis*) of its true identity, so that Christians "die" to the old ignorance of viewing themselves merely as persons.

Goyim. A term originally designating a collective body characterized by a politically organized chain of command, such as a "nation." The early Yahwists were remembered as being radically different from this (Num. 23:9). Over the centuries, as the Israelites became "like the other nations" (1 Sam. 8:19–20), *goyim* began to designate people affiliated with *other* political organizations, that is, foreigners. Later, as Jewish ethnicity became increasingly emphasized, *goyim* came to mean "Gentiles," that is, everyone ethnically non-Jewish.

Habiru. See "Apiru."

Habur River. A tributary to the Euphrates River in northeast Syria (see Map 1.1). The Habur River ran through the heart of ancient Amurru.

Haggai. Hebrew prophet of sixth century B.C. who advocated the rebuilding of the Jerusalem temple and mistakenly predicted the revival of the Davidic dynasty under Zerubbabel; also, the biblical book preserving his oracles.

Hammurapi. King of Babylon (1792–1750 B.C.) whose famous law code preserved Amorite legal traditions that were considered normative in Babylon at the time. Hammurapi also destroyed the city of Mari in 1760 B.C.

Haran. Important Amorite city that flourished during the MB Age (see Map 1.1). Biblical tradition recalls that the patriarch left this city to migrate to Palestine (Gen. 11:31; 12:4).

Hasmoneans. The Maccabean family who came to power in Judaea after the defeat of Antiochus Epiphanes. Although originally anti–Hellenistic, these Jewish priest-kings (ruled around 142–63 B.C.) eventually embraced Greek culture. They were so unpopular that a Jewish delegation invited the Roman general Pompey to bring their rule to an end.

Hatti. Ancient designation for the land of the Hittites (central Anatolia).

Hebrew. A biblical word originally used to label disaffected groups and people no longer considered loyal subjects of any political organization or state. See "Apiru." Because this label had been applied to the early Israelites, later generations misconstrued it as an ethnic term synonymous with "Jew."

Hebron. A town within the region of the tribe of Judah, where David ruled as king of Judah before moving his capital farther north to Jerusalem.

Hejaz. Name for the northwest part of the Arabian peninsula, between the modern Jordan border and Mecca (see Map 1.1).

Hellenism. Name given generally to the forms Greek civilization and culture took in the lands of the Near East after the conquests of Alexander the Great around 330 B.C.

Herod. King of the Jews (ruled 37–4 B.C.) appointed by the Romans to protect their interests in Palestine.

Hezekiah. King of southern Judah (ruled 715–687 B.C.) who defied the Assyrian king Sennacherib (2 Kings 18:13). While most of his kingdom's villages were decimated by Sennacherib's invasion of 701 B.C., the city of Jerusalem miraculously survived the siege.

Hillelites. A school within the sect of Pharisees that followed the more liberal legal interpretations of Rabbi Hillel (late first century B.C.).

Hiram. The Phoenician king of Tyre (ruled 969–936 B.C.?) who had a treaty with David and Solomon, and who supplied architects, engineers, laborers, and material to build the temple to Yahweh in Jerusalem (2 Sam. 5:11; 2 Kings 5:1–12).

Hittites. The Bronze Age people and kingdom in Asia Minor (2000–1200 B.C.) whose capital, Hattusas, has been excavated at modern Boghaz-koy (see Map 1.1). The word "Hittite" also designates their Indo-European language, attested in texts excavated there. Because Hittite traits continued in some of the kingdoms that arose in north Syria after 900 B.C., scholars label these kingdoms as "Neo-Hittite" (see Map 6.1).

Hobab. See "Jethro."

Horites. The biblical name for Hurrians, a non-Semitic-speaking people of north Syria and eastern Anatolia during the LB Age. Some of them migrated to Palestine and Transjordan (such as Abdu-Hepa in fourteenth-century-B.C. Jerusalem) and left such a distinctive mark on the culture that the Egyptians sometimes referred to Palestine as "Hurru-land." See also "Mitanni."

Hosea. Yahwist prophet of the eighth century B.C., whose religious indictments of the northern Israelites have been preserved in the biblical book bearing his name.

Huldah. A respected prophet and authority on matters pertaining to ancient Yahwism in the days of King Josiah. She was consulted about the validity of the book of the law discovered in the Jerusalem temple in 621 B.C. (2 Kings 22:14–20).

Hurrians. See "Horites."

Hyksos. The name (*heqaw khasut*) given to West Asian rulers who ruled portions of the Nile Delta during a period of Egyptian weakness (1750–1550 B.C.). Many scholars believe the story of Joseph (Genesis 37–50) contains traditions from this period of Egyptian history. Later generations of Egyptians remembered this as a period of national humiliation, leading them to more closely monitor the activities of Asian peoples residing in Egypt.

Indo-European. The language group to which belong Germanic, Greek, Hittite, Iranian, Indic, Italic, and Celtic languages, among others.

Iron Age. Archaeological designation of the Old Testament period (1200–330 B.C.), characterized by a technology increasingly using iron. The period is subdivided into Iron I (a dark age), Iron II (the age of recovering political states, including the Assyrian Empire), Iron III (the Babylonian Empire), and the Persian period.

Isaiah. Yahwist prophet of the eighth century B.C., whose religious indictments of the Israelites and Judaeans have been preserved in the first thirty-nine chapters of the biblical book bearing his name.

Ishmaelites. A confederation of Arab tribes, towns, and states that controlled the lucrative trade route in western Arabia in the eighth through the sixth centuries B.C. The members of this confederation considered themselves descendants of Abraham through Ishmael, Abraham's firstborn son (see Genesis 16; 25:12–16).

Israel. The name traditionally given to the community of Yahweh worshipers. The name originally belonged to some (nonreligious) social organization or tribe in the LB Age, and then was transferred to the federation of Yahwist tribes when the members of this tribe joined the federation (1200–1020 B.C.). When the federation structure was replaced with a monarchic one, "Israel" became the name of a political kingdom, first of David and Solomon (1000–922 B.C.), and then of the splinter northern kingdom (922–722 B.C.).

Jacob. The grandson of Abraham, whose second name, "Israel," properly identifies Jacob as the common ancestor distinctive to all Israelites (Gen. 32:28), the symbolic "father" of the tribes of the early Israelite federation (Genesis 49).

Jamnia. A town on the coast of Palestine where Pharisaic Rabbis and sages established an academy to consolidate Judaean religion and culture in the aftermath of the Jewish War of A.D. 66–70.

Jebus. The pre-Davidic name of Jerusalem, whose inhabitants were called Jebusites. The name is Amorite (*yabus*), suggesting that this population group was Amorite in origin. Four hundred years after David Jebusites were still resident in Jerusalem (Judg. 1:21), giving the city a distinctively Amorite character (Ezek. 16:3).

Jehoiachin. King of southern Judah who ruled for several months in 598 B.C. before being taken prisoner to Babylon (2 Kings 24:10). Babylonian archives preserve a text mentioning provisions being allocated for him.

Jehu. (1) A ninth-century-B.C. prophet who predicted the destruction of Baasha's dynasty in northern Israel (1 Kings 16:1; see Table 5.1); **(2)** king of northern Israel (ruled 842–815 B.C.) who destroyed Omri's dynasty and executed Jezebel, removing all formal elements of Baal worship from Samaria (2 Kings 10; see Table 5.1 and Fig. 6.3).

Jeremiah. Yahwist prophet of the seventh century B.C. from the village of Anathoth, whose religious indictments of the people of Judah and Jerusalem have been preserved in the biblical book bearing his name. One of his more well-known oracles envisions Yahweh establishing a "new covenant" with his people (31:31–34).

Jeroboam. The name of two kings of the secessionist northern kingdom of Israel: **(1)** its first king (ruled 922–901 B.C.), remembered for setting up "golden calves" in the northern sanctuaries of Dan and Bethel (1 Kings 12:); **(2)** one of its last kings (ruled 786–746 B.C.; 2 Kings 14:23–29; see Table 5.1).

Jerusalem. The biblical name for the non-Israelite city that David selected as his political capital. Originally called Urusalim ("city of the god Salim"), for a while its name was Jebus until David restored the original. This non-Israelite city became the center promoting the official Yahwistic religion and producing its religious texts; it eventually became so closely identified with the biblical tradition that today the city remains sacred to Jews, Christians, and Muslims.

Jesus of Nazareth. First-century Jewish prophet and miracle-worker whom Christians believe to be the Son of God and Israel's messiah (or Christ). The description of his life, teachings, death, and resurrection has been significantly shaped by the Gospel writers' Christian confession, making it difficult for modern historians to grasp the historical man, who appears to have resembled a religious reformer.

Jethro. One of the three names (along with Hobab and Reuel) that biblical tradition recalls as the name of Moses' father-in-law, a prosperous herdsman and Midianite priest (Exod. 2:15–22). All three names occur in later pre-Islamic Arabic inscriptions, and all three are probably Amorite in origin.

Jew. Or "Judaean," originally a member of the tribe of Judah. In later times, as ethnicity became increasingly central to Judaean identity, the term became synonymous with those who, by birth or conversion, claimed the biblical tradition as part of their ethnic heritage.

Jezebel. Daughter of King Ethbaal of Tyre and wife of the northern Israelite king Ahab, who promoted the official worship of her native deity, Baal, in Samaria, the capital of northern Israel. She personally sponsored 450 prophets of Baal and 400 prophets of Asherah (1 Kings 18:19).

Joab. The cousin of King David personally placed in command of the Jerusalem soldiers serving David.

John the Baptist. First-century ascetic Jewish prophet who reached God's impending judgment and baptized the repentant in the Jordan River. The Gospel writers depict him as an Elijah figure preparing the way for Jesus.

Joseph. The father of Manasseh and Ephraim (Gen. 41:50–52), whose exploits in Egypt are recounted in Genesis 37–50. After 922 B.C. the name "Joseph" became synonymous with the northern kingdom of Israel (Amos 6:6), that is, the territory of the old Yahwist tribes of Ephraim and Manasseh.

Josephus. Jewish historian (A.D. 37–100) who was taken as prisoner to Rome, where he won the friendship of the emperor's family. He wrote two lengthy books, one describing the political chaos leading up to the Jewish War of A.D. 66–70, the other an overview of Jewish history. These books provide detailed information about the period between the Old and New Testaments, as well as about the time of Christ.

Joshua. The name of Moses' associate, and of the biblical book describing his leadership in the years after Moses' death. The Deuteronomistic author of the book of Joshua had very little understanding of the historical Joshua and imagined him to be a royal warrior like King Josiah, intent on military conquest (Joshua 1–11).

Josiah. King of Judah (ruled 642–609 B.C.) who "sought the God of his ancestor David" as the Assyrian Empire collapsed. Josiah's attempt to recover the great empire of David and Solomon was given religious legitimacy by the "book of the law" discovered in the Jerusalem temple in 621 B.C.

Jotham. The youngest son of the judge Gideon. During the premonarchic period, when Abimelech promoted himself as the first Israelite king, Jotham ridiculed Abimelech by telling a parable (or fable) suggesting that only a worthless person would want to be king (Judg. 9:1–21).

Judaeans. Members of the tribe of Judah, later called Jews.

Judah. The name of one of the tribes that joined the Yahwist federation of Israel. As such, Judah was identified as one of the "sons" of Jacob/Israel (Gen. 49:1, 8–12). See Maps 3.1 and 7.1. It was one of the larger and more powerful tribes, and after the civil war of 922 B.C. its name became the name of the kingdom ruled from Jerusalem by David's dynasty, that is, the southern kingdom of Judah. David and his family were members of this tribe.

Judaism. The name given to a postexilic religion that preserved many of the forms of earlier Israelite religion. It combined the ethical thrust of Yahwism with Yahwisticism's more parochial tendency to view Yahweh as a patron deity of an established group, and defined the group in increasingly ethnic (rather than religious or political) terms.

Judas Maccabeus. See "Maccabees."

judge. An early Yahwist, male or female, who possessed sufficient religious charisma or "authority of competency" to inspire a loyal following. Judges were individuals who acted on their personal commitments rather than in any official capacity and who were joined by others who shared those commitments and who felt that Yahweh's leadership (especially in war and the administration of law) was most transparently displayed through the judge.

Kadesh. An ancient city on the Orontes River near the Lebanon-Syria border, associated with the LB Age kingdom of Amurru (see Map 1.1). The plain outside the city was the site of a major battle between the Hittites and Egyptians around 1274 B.C. (see Table 1.2).

Kadesh-barnea. Oasis site in the northeastern Sinai desert where the slaves who escaped from Egypt settled with their flocks and herds (see Map 3.2).

Kashites. A LB Age Hittite people of south-central Turkey living on the border of the Mitanni Empire. Some Kashites were settled in Jerusalem during the Amarna Age and attempted to assassinate the Hurrian king Abdu-Hepa, appointed by Egypt. As LB civilization collapsed, other Kashites migrated to the Hejaz and joined the Midianite confederation. Moses married a Kashite woman, but since later scribes had no memory of the Kashites, they mistakenly identified her as a Cushite, or Ethiopian (Num. 12:1).

Keret. A legendary Canaanite king who, according to Ugaritic legend, was imperiled by his lack of an heir. Many scholars today render the name Kirta, but the name actually seems to be a Hurrianized form of the Canaanite name Qarrad ("Warrior")—which was pronounced Karrate(n)—a name that actually occurs in LB Age texts.

Kingdom of God. The rule or governing influence of God in the lives of individuals and, more generally, in human affairs. It is associated with the conviction that human community is ultimately grounded not in a political monopoly of force but in people's voluntary commitment to a system of values transcending their own self-interest.

Kuntillet Ajrud. A site in northeast Sinai desert about forty miles south of Kadesh-barnea (Map 3.2), where inscriptions dating to around 800 B.C. invoke blessings in the name of "Yahweh of Samaria and his Asherah."

Lachish. A city of southern Judah destroyed by the Assyrians in 701 B.C. (see Fig. 6.1).

Levirate marriage. An inheritance custom followed by some Israelites. In essence, it was a form of "surrogate fatherhood," requiring a man to marry his brother's widow and sire children through her so that his deceased brother may have descendants (Deut. 5:5–10). Genesis 38 and Ruth 4 suggest that the custom may have been peculiar to the tribe of Judah.

Levites. Members of the tribe of Levi, who entered the Yahwist federation as a different type of "tribe," associated not with the geographic interests of specific villages but with religious responsibilities. Later Levites assisted the priests in the Jerusalem temple. Levi was identified as one of the "sons" of Jacob/Israel (Gen. 49:5–7).

Maccabees. A term designating a group of Jewish fighters, led by Judas, who defeated Antiochus Epiphanes' forces attempting to eradicate traditional Jewish culture. Members of Judas's family set themselves up as independent Jewish kings (see "Hasmoneans").

Manasseh. (1) The name of one of the tribes that joined the Yahwist federation of Israel. As such, Manasseh—identified as a son of Joseph—was also placed alongside the others as one of the "sons" of Jacob/Israel. See Maps 3.1 and 7.1. **(2)** King of Judah (ruled 687–642 B.C.) who sponsored the introduction of religious phenomena considered repugnant by village Yahwists and by the Yahwistic officials of Jerusalem. Biblical tradition remembers him as one of the worst of the Jerusalem kings.

Marcion. A Christian in Rome who, around A.D. 150, was labeled a heretic because he insisted that Christians had no business reading or using the Old Testament.

Mari. Bronze Age city and kingdom along the Euphrates River where many Amorite and Akkadian cultural traits blended (see Map 1.1). Twenty thousand clay tablets excavated there attest to Amorite personal names, tribal names, and cultural phenomena such as prophecy and pastoralism.

maryannu. A name (meaning "charioteer") designating a military class of aristocrats within Hurrian society and in various Syrian city-states. The title became honorific and was not always held by people who actually owned chariots or fought in battle.

maximalist. A name sometimes used to designate fundamentalist and conservative biblical scholars who believe that the biblical accounts of history are largely (if not literally) true, containing a *maximum* amount of straightforward historical information.

Megiddo. A non-Israelite town in Palestine that King Solomon designated as a provincial capital. Its bureaucrats managed Israelite affairs in place of the old tribal system that had existed a generation earlier (Judg. 1:27; 1 Kings 4:12). See Map 3.1.

Melqart. The name of the Baal serving as patron deity of Tyre. The Phoenicians associated him with navigation and the establishment of Phoenician colonies. This was probably the "Baal" that Jezebel, the Phoenician princess of Tyre and wife of Ahab, introduced to Samaria.

Merneptah. The pharaoh (ruled 1213–1203 B.C.?) during the declining days of the Egyptian Empire. A coalition of Libyans and Sea Peoples attacked Egyptian-controlled lands during his reign. A stela celebrating his victory over them provides the earliest reference to a social group in Palestine named "Israel."

Mesopotamia. Literally "between the rivers," this term designates the region along and between the Tigris and Euphrates rivers in Iraq, from the shores of the Persian Gulf in the south up to the Habur River area (north Syria) in the north (see Map 1.1). In the Israelite period, Babylon was the principal power in southern Mesopotamia, while Assyria was the principal power in the north (see Map 6.1).

messiah. Literally "anointed one," a person who has been authorized by God to serve in an official capacity and has had holy oil poured upon his head as a sign of divine selection. Israel's kings were all messiahs in this sense, as was the Persian king Cyrus (according to Second Isaiah).

Micah. Yahwist prophet of the eighth century B.C. from the village of Moresheth-gath, whose religious indictments of Jerusalem officials and southern Judaeans have been preserved in the biblical book bearing his name.

Micaiah. Yahwist prophet of the ninth century B.C. who predicted the death of Ahab, king of northern Israel (2 Kings 22; see Table 5.1)

Midianite. A member of the confederation of Midian, which comprised largely Arabian peoples residing in the Arabian Hejaz at the end of the LB Age. Moses married a Kashite woman whose tribe was part of this confederation. Midianite leaders served as vassals to King Sihon of Amurru (Josh. 13:21) and King Balak of Moab (Numbers 22). Later Midianite

warriors found the defenseless Yahwist villages to be easy prey for plunder (Judges 6).

Milcom. The patron deity of the kingdom of Ammon (1 Kings 11:5). Molech may be a variant form of this god's name.

minimalist. A term coined in the 1990s to designate those biblical scholars who believe that the biblical stories are largely fictitious, containing *minimal* historical information. Often the term is applied only to the most radical of these scholars, who claim that there was no "Israelite" identity or religion prior to the exile, and therefore none of the cultures, religions, peoples, or history prior to that time can be labeled "Israelite." For them, the biblical history was essentially fabricated to forge a meaningful identity for the Jews of the Persian-Hellenistic periods.

Miriam. The sister of Moses, who may have composed one of the oldest portions of the Old Testament (Exod. 15:1–18; see v. 21) and who complained that Moses had married a Kashite woman (Num. 12:1).

Mishnah. Literary forerunner to the Talmud, comprising a collection of early rabbinic interpretations of biblical laws as compiled about A.D. 200.

Mitanni. The name given to a LB Age confederation of Hurrian states, whose empire rivaled that of the Hittites before it was destroyed in 1350 B.C. Its capital, Washukanni, was located in north Syria along the upper Habur River (Map 1.1).

Moab. A kingdom east of the Dead Sea area that emerged in the Iron II period (see Map 6.1), although the Bible contains traditions that Moabite kings ruled contemporaneous with the twelve-tribe federation (Numbers 22–24). The non-Israelite Moabites were related to Abraham through Lot, although they are maligned in the Bible as the offspring of Lot's incest (Gen. 19:30–38).

Molech. God of the Ammonites (a variant of Milcom?) to whom children in Jerusalem were sacrificially killed and burned (2 Kings 23:10).

Mosaic-Sinai tradition. A term scholars use to designate the covenant at Mount Sinai (Exodus 19–20) and later events associated with it (e.g., the Shechem covenant ceremony in Joshua 24). The centerpiece of this covenant tradition is the tenet that Israel is under sworn obligation to Yahweh to perform the stipulations (or "commandments") of the covenant. This term is often used in contrast with the Davidic-Zion tradition or with the Abrahamic tradition, both of which emphasize not Israel's obligations to Yahweh but rather Yahweh's obligation to keep promises he makes on Israel's behalf.

Moses. The man who helped a heterogeneous group ("mixed multitude") of Hebrew slaves escape into the

Sinai desert sometime during the political and social chaos in Egypt around 1200 B.C. Moses was later inspired to present them with a covenant providing a religious identity and ethic binding them together as the people of Yahweh.

Mycenaean. Name given to the Aegean civilization that spread from Mycenae (Greece) to many parts of the Mediterranean (1400–1200 B.C.). Mycenaean merchants and trade delegations were frequently entertained at the royal courts of Canaanite cities such as Ugarit.

mystery religions. Secret religious cults flourishing in the Greco-Roman period, offering salvation and close-knit fellowship to individuals initiated into its secret rites. Participants often shared a sacred meal and had emotionally gripping experiences of death and rebirth. Scholars note some formal parallels between the early church and some mystery cults.

Nabonidus. The last king of Babylon (ruled 556–539 B.C.), conquered by Cyrus, king of Persia.

Nathan. Court prophet to kings David and Solomon (2 Sam. 12:1–15). He was inspired with the vision of the Davidic covenant (2 Sam. 7:4–17), and he later engineered the selection of Solomon, Bathsheba's son, to be David's successor (1 Kings 1:11–27). He may have been a holdover from the Jebusite regime of pre-Davidic Jerusalem, who pledged loyalty to David and David's god Yahweh.

Necho. The Egyptian pharaoh (ruled 610–595 B.C.) who exploited the decline of Assyrian influence in Palestine by apparently trying to extend his control there. This brought him into conflict with the Judaean king Josiah, who was killed (2 Kings 23:28–30).

Negeb. Wilderness steppeland in southern Palestine; adjacent to the Sinai desert (see Map 1.1).

Nehemiah. The name of the Jewish governor of Judaea, appointed by the Persian government to administer civil affairs in and around Jerusalem around 445 B.C. (see Table 8.1), and of the biblical book recounting his activities. His decision to refortify Jerusalem aroused regional suspicion and hostility (Nehemiah 2). Because civil and religious affairs overlapped, Nehemiah threatened civil punishment against Jews who did not properly observe the Sabbath (Neh. 13:15–22) and, like Ezra, enforced religious laws forbidding intermarriage (Neh. 13:23–27).

Og. A warlord who controlled the villages of Bashan in northern Transjordan during the chaotic years after the collapse of the LB Age. His forces were defeated when he tried to expand his control south into the Israelite villages previously controlled by King Sihon of Heshbon (Num. 21:33–35).

Omri. King of northern Israel (ruled 876–869 B.C.),

who made Samaria its capital and arranged for his son Ahab to marry Jezebel (1 Kings 16:24–28).

pagan, paganism. Traditionally, the worship of false gods. As such, these terms have been used pejoratively to disparage religions other than Judaism, Christianity, or Islam. These terms can also be used technically to designate the practice of associating religion with coercive institutions of social control, that is, paganism as the veneration of social control. As such, "pagan" tendencies surface among Jews, Christians, and Muslims.

Palestine. A conventional name (derived from "Philistine" and going back to Roman times) for the area west of the Jordan River, between Lebanon in the north and the Sinai desert in the south (see Map 1.1).

parochial, parochialism. Words used to describe a narrowness of interests or views, or the religious tendency to treat the peculiar specifics of one's own limited culture or society as if they were of ultimate and universal significance.

Paul. A Pharisaic Jew of the first century who became a proponent of the early Christian movement; also known as Saul of Tarsus (Acts 13:9). His letters (or epistles) constitute the earliest New Testament writings. His belief that the age of the new covenant had dawned with Jesus led him to reject the Jewish law and ethnocentrism conventionally associated with Pharisaic interpretations of the Sinai covenant.

Pax Romana. Literally, the "Roman Peace," a term used to describe the two centuries of relative political stability beginning with the reign of Augustus Caesar in 27 B.C. and drawing to a close after Marcus Aurelius became emperor in A.D. 161. Christianity spread rapidly during this period, providing a religious (as opposed to a political) framework for grounding civilization across cultures.

Pharisees. A Jewish sect in ancient Palestine at the time of Christ, primarily concerned for the proper interpretation and observance of the Jewish law and frequently depicted as bitter rivals of the Sadducees. The Romans privileged the Pharisees by permitting them to reconstitute Judaism along Pharisaic lines after the Jewish War of A.D. 66–70. Pharisaic sages and rabbis eventually assembled the Mishnah and Torah, making the Pharisees the "fathers" of Orthodox Judaism.

Philistines. An Anatolian population group constituting a segment of the Sea Peoples who were dispersed throughout the Mediterranean at the end of the Bronze Age. Some Philistines gained control of towns along the southern Palestinian coastal plain. Philistine regimes continued to rule there throughout most of the Iron Age.

Philo of Alexandria. A first-century Jew of Alexandria, Egypt, who interpreted the history, culture, and religion of the Jews—as well as the Jewish scriptures—in terms of philosophical systems derived from the Greek world. He wrote several dozen works attesting to some of the ways that some Jewish elites at the time of Christ understood their Jewish culture, history, and religion.

Phoenicians. Greek term given to the Canaanites of the Iron Age. Much of their economy was derived from maritime commerce, and Phoenician colonies such as Carthage survived well into the Roman period, preserving archaic traits of Canaanite culture (including religion and language). Many aspects of Israelite culture were essentially Phoenician.

Pliny. Roman governor of Asia Minor (early second century A.D.) whose imperial correspondences provide a valuable "outsider's perspective" on the Christian movement of that early time and place.

polytheism. The belief in many gods. Because gods are usually associated with social values, complex and pluralistic societies are frequently polytheistic: many different (and competing) values and interests find expression in the form of many different (and competing) gods. Polytheism must take other forms in societies that have historically thought of themselves as being monotheistic (believing in only one god) or secular (detached from gods and religion altogether).

Pontius Pilate. Roman procurator (or prefect) of Judaea (A.D. 26–36), who presided over the trial of Jesus and sentenced him to death by crucifixion.

postexilic period. The term conventionally used to designate the time of the Persian Empire (538–330 B.C.), *after* the Babylonian exile had ended (see Table 8.1).

preexilic period. The term referring to the time *before* Jerusalem was destroyed and before the Babylonian exile began (i.e., the time before 586 B.C.).

premonarchic period. The term referring to the time when ancient Israel was constituted as a twelve-tribe federation before the establishment of the Israelite monarchy of Saul and David (i.e., the period 1200–1020 B.C.).

prophet. A spokesperson for God. The Yahwist prophets of the monarchic period condemned the popular disregard for the ethical nature of the Israelite faith and predicted the eventual collapse of the Israelite social order. The Old Testament contains many oracles of such prophets. So-called "false prophets" also existed, insisting that the society's well-being was not dependent on the people enacting any religious ethic.

Pseudepigrapha. A term (literally meaning "false writings") applied loosely to various Jewish writings—dating roughly 200 B.C.–A.D. 200—that were not included in the Bible. Most of this literature reflects the religious perspective and interests of specific Jewish sects at the time.

qedeshim. Males employed by the Jerusalem temple prior to the reforms of King Josiah in the late seventh century B.C. Because the feminine form of the word usually means "prostitute," the *qedeshim* are often regarded as male prostitutes perhaps involved in homosexual rituals, but this is far from certain.

Rabshakeh. Literally, "chief cupbearer," an important court official of the Assyrian Empire, who appears to have been a propaganda minister who tried to demoralize the people of Jerusalem into surrendering and accepting Assyrian rule (2 Kings 18:13–37).

Ramesses II. The Egyptian pharaoh (ruled 1279–1213 B.C.?) who was defeated by the Hittites at the battle of Kadesh (1274 B.C.), setting the stage for the decline of the Egyptian Empire and the accompanying political instability and immigration of various refugee peoples south into Palestine, Transjordan, and the Hejaz (see Table 2.1). Contrary to popular belief, he was probably not the pharaoh of the exodus.

reformer. In the technical sense, a person who finds in the remote past models to help address the present social, political, or religious malaise. In religiously *imitative* reforms, those past models tend to be mainly *formal* (e.g., rituals, nomenclature, social structures, doctrinal ideas, etc.) and the break with the present is largely formal, providing nostalgic reassurances that the troubled present has been corrected. In religiously *creative* reforms, the models tend to be more *substantive* (ethical values and priorities, qualitative choices, etc.), as is the break with the present, establishing an alternative basis and pattern of relationships for society.

Rehoboam. Solomon's son and successor (ruled 922–915 B.C.) whose decision to continue his father's taxation policies resulted in a civil war. The northern tribes no longer recognized the legitimacy of the Jerusalem establishment, of the Davidic dynasty, or of the temple, and formed their own independent kingdom called "Israel." The southerners who remained loyal to Jerusalem called their kingdom "Judah."

Reuben. The name of one of the tribes that joined the Yahwist federation of Israel, and therefore of one of the "sons" of Jacob/Israel (Gen. 49:1–4). See Maps 3.1 and 7.1. This tribe existed among the villages of central Transjordan; because they were among the first to embrace Yahweh, the god of the escaped slaves, the tribe of Reuben was remembered as the "firstborn" of Jacob/Israel.

Reuel. See "Jethro."

Sadducees. A Jewish sect in ancient Palestine at the time of Christ, usually associated with the priests, providing support for the Jerusalem temple. They were members of the Jewish aristocracy, tracing their ancestry back to Zadok, the high priest at the time of King Solomon. The name "Sadducee" may represent the word "Zadokite."

Samaria. The capital city of the northern kingdom of Israel from the reign of Omri (ca. 870 B.C.) to the Assyrian destruction of the kingdom (in 721 B.C.) (1 Kings 16:24; 2 Kings 17:5–6).

Samaritans. The name given to people who lived within the territory of the old northern kingdom after the Assyrian destructions of 721 B.C. Although they, too, worshiped the god Yahweh, the Jewish leaders of Jerusalem considered them unorthodox and unfit for religious fellowship (Ezra 4:1–3; John 4:7–9).

Samuel. Hebrew judge and prophet of the eleventh century B.C., who initially opposed the movement toward an Israelite monarchy, but reluctantly accepted it as inevitable (1 Samuel 8) and anointed Saul as the first king (1 Samuel 9–10). The biblical books of 1 and 2 Samuel describe this movement toward monarchy, beginning with the birth of Samuel and ending with the reign of King David.

Sanhedrin. The supreme council of the Jews, from the third century B.C. to A.D. 70, presided over by the high priest. Various sects competed vigorously to exert control over this body, which apparently had both legislative powers (defining Jewish law) and executive powers (enforcing Jewish law).

Sarah. Or Sarai, the wife of Abraham and the woman destined to bear the long-awaited child who would fulfill the divine promise that Abraham would one day be the father of a multitude of nations and peoples (Gen. 17:15–21).

Saul. A Benjaminite selected to serve as Israel's first warrior-king (ruled 1020–1000 B.C.?). The Bible portrays him as psychologically unstable and shows him routinely neglecting Israelite principles of holy war. David was forced to flee from Saul and eventually succeeded him as king of Israel.

scribes. People sufficiently trained in the art of reading and writing to be employed as government clerks, secretaries, and archivists. Jerusalem scribes transferred ancient Israelite traditions to writing, producing the books that today comprise the OT. By the first century, Jewish scribes served as "teachers of the law," providing religious interpretations of the customary laws in the OT. The NT suggests that, at the grassroots level, many Jews did not consider their interpretations to be authoritative.

Sea Peoples. A term by which the Egyptians lumped together the many peoples—civilian peasants as well as maritime warriors—who migrated into Egyptian-controlled lands as Bronze Age civilization collapsed around 1200 B.C. Many of the maritime warriors seeking to gain political control of these lands (such as the Philistines) originated in the Anatolian-Aegean area.

Second Isaiah. The name given to chapters 40–55 of the biblical book of Isaiah and to the anonymous prophet who composed those chapters around 538 B.C. They celebrate the end of the Babylonian exile, portray Cyrus as Yahweh's messiah, and describe Yahweh's chosen servant as a "light to the Gentiles."

Seder. Jewish ceremonial feast celebrating the Passover, during which the story of the exodus is read from a book called the Haggadah. Part of the reading involves the celebrants identifying themselves and their personal histories with that of the slaves Moses led out of Egypt.

Semitic languages. A family of languages in the Near East, subdivided into East Semitic (Akkadian), South Semitic (Arabic and Ethiopic), and West Semitic (such as Hebrew, Aramaic, Phoenician, and Ugaritic).

Sennacherib. The king of Assyria (ruled 705–681 B.C.) who invaded Judah in 701 B.C. and destroyed many Judaean villages (including the city of Lachish; see Fig. 6.1). The city of Jerusalem miraculously survived the siege, leading to the popular belief that Yahweh would never permit Jerusalem to be destroyed.

Sermon on the Mount. The conventional name given to the ethical teachings of Jesus presented in chapters 5–7 of the Gospel of Matthew.

Shalem. A god attested in second-millennium-B.C. texts from Ugarit, who probably served as patron deity of the city of Jerusalem (or Urusalim, "city of [the god] Shalem") during the Bronze Age. The name occurs in first-millennium-B.C. personal names. It has been suggested that the name of Solomon, king of Jerusalem, invokes this god.

Shalmaneser III. The king of Assyria (ruled 858–824 B.C.) who initiated Assyrian expansion westward. In 853 B.C. he confronted a coalition of kings (including Ahab of Israel) at the battle of Qarqar. Assyrian advances west were stalled as a result of the battle but a century later would revive.

Shalmaneser V. The king of Assyria (ruled 726–722 B.C.) who succeeded Tiglath-pileser III and resumed the Assyrian expansion westward (2 Kings 17:3–6). He laid siege to Samaria, which fell to his successor, Sargon II, a year later (721 B.C.).

Shammaites. A school within the sect of Pharisees that followed the more conservative legal interpretations of Rabbi Shammai (late first century B.C.).

Shechem. A Canaanite city in the central Palestinian hill country attested in the Amarna texts of the LB

Age. It was closely linked to Israelite history: Joshua 24 suggests that a covenant ceremony there drew the various Palestinian tribes into the Yahwist federation, and the first king of the secessionist northern kingdom of Israel made Shechem his capital city (1 Kings 12:25).

Shekelesh. An Anatolian population group constituting a segment of the Sea Peoples who were dispersed throughout the Mediterranean at the end of the Bronze Age. The name is to be identified with Luwian (i.e., southern Hittite) *Sagalessos.*

Shibboleth. A West Semitic word (meaning "ear of grain") that the Transjordanian Yahwists selected as a password, knowing that the Palestinian Yahwists pronounced the initial "sh"-sound differently (Judges 12). This episode attests to the dialectic diversity within early Israel, demonstrating that the early Israelites were not bound together by kinship or even linguistic ties.

Shiloh. An ancient Israelite village in central Palestine where a sanctuary to Yahweh had been located during premonarchic times (see Map 3.1). In an attempt to refute the popular belief that Yahweh would never permit Jerusalem to be destroyed because the temple was located there, Jeremiah recalled that centuries earlier Yahweh had permitted Shiloh to be destroyed even though a Yahwist sanctuary had been located there (Jer. 7:12–14).

Shuppululiumash. The Hittite king (ruled 1375–1335 B.C.) who conquered most of Anatolia and north Syria, including the Mitanni Empire around 1350 B.C. His expansion into southern Syria and Palestine helped escalate the political turmoil of the Amarna Age.

Sicarii. A band of violent Jewish revolutionaries around the time of Christ who often murdered fellow Jews who did not support their religious and political agenda.

Sihon. A warlord, formerly from the LB kingdom of Amurru, who controlled the villages of central Transjordan during the chaotic years after the collapse of the LB Age. His forces were defeated when he deployed them against Yahwist shepherds passing through the adjacent steppeland (Num. 21:21–25).

Stephen. A Hellenistic Jew stoned to death for professing Christian views considered blasphemous by the religious authorities (Acts 6–7). Stephen thus became one of the earliest Christian "martyrs."

Sumerian. The name given to the culture and (non-Semitic) language of southern Mesopotamia during the third millennium B.C. The Early Dynastic III period witnessed the flourishing of numerous Sumerian city-states. After 2400 B.C. Old Akkadian—a Semitic language—became the official language of the political regimes of Mesopotamia, although Sumerian continued as a scholarly language and was revived briefly during the time of the Ur III dynasty (see Table 1.1).

Synoptic Gospels. Designation given to the Gospels of Matthew, Mark, and Luke, in recognition of the strikingly similar way they recount the life of Jesus. These three accounts can be read *synoptically,* i.e., "with one eye."

Taanach. A non-Israelite town in Palestine that King Solomon designated as a provincial capital. Its bureaucrats managed Israelite affairs in place of the old tribal system that had existed a generation earlier (Judg. 1:27; 1 Kings 4:12). See Map 3.1.

tabernacle. Also called the tent of meeting, a portable tent shrine that housed the ark of the covenant in premonarchic times. The tabernacle and ark were located at Shiloh (1 Sam. 2:22), although later biblical traditions depict it being envisioned and ornately built by Moses and the escaped slaves at Mount Sinai (Exodus 27).

Talmud. A comprehensive collection of later rabbinic interpretations of biblical laws amplifying and expanding on the Mishnah. Two variants of the Talmud were published in Palestine and in Babylon around the sixth century A.D.

Tell eth-Thadyen. See "Tuttul."

theodicy. Human efforts to explain why God permits righteous and innocence people to suffer: If God is all-powerful and all-righteous, why does injustice prevail?

theophany. A manifestation of deity to human beings.

Tjeker. One of five contingents of the Sea Peoples coalition who settled on the northern coast of Palestine and Phoenicia. They are probably identical to Sikel people whose name is reflected in the name Sicily.

Topheth. A burial ground south of Jerusalem associated with child sacrifice prior to the reforms of King Josiah (2 Kings 23:10).

Torah. A Hebrew word that, in the general sense, refers to religious instruction. In a more restricted sense it can mean "law" (i.e., legal instruction), whether written or oral. Technically, the word "Torah" designates the first five books (or Pentateuch) of the Hebrew Bible.

Transjordan. A conventional name (going back to Roman times) for the area east of the Jordan River, between the Sea of Galilee and the Gulf of Aqaba (see Map 1.1).

tribe. A self-sufficient residential group that is typically an early form of political organization. Usually marked by commonly shared strategic and economic interests, tribes are comparatively fragile structures comprised of diverse families and other subgroups.

Tribal organization is therefore proof neither of nomadic origins nor of actual kinship bonds among its members.

Troy. A city on the western coast of Asia Minor that was destroyed around 1200 B.C. at the end of the LB Age. Homer's *Iliad* preserves legends associated with the city's final years.

Tuttul. In the Mari period, the Sumerian name of a town in the Euphrates valley, probably to be identified with modern Tell eth-Thadyen (Map 1.1). Like Arabic *thadyen*, Tuttul means "two breasts," and its Amorite equivalent would have been *shadday*. Genesis 17:1 preserves the tradition that Abraham originally worshiped the god of Shaddai, or El Shaddai (NRSV "God Almighty"). This links the Abraham narrative to Amorite traditions of northeast Syria.

Ugarit. LB Age city-state on the coast of Syria; a major archive of Canaanite texts has been excavated there since 1929, providing insight into Canaanite religion and culture.

Ur. Traditional home of Abraham prior to his move to Haran (Gen. 11:31). This ancient city of southern Mesopotamia was important around 2100 B.C. and again during the Neo-Babylonian/Chaldean Empire of the sixth century B.C.

Uriah the Hittite. A non-Israelite soldier from Jerusalem who served in King David's army. He was the husband of Bathsheba and was murdered so that David could marry the widow pregnant with David's child (2 Sam. 11:3).

Wrath of God. A label for the historical processes that are set in motion whenever the religious ethic of the Yahwist covenant is violated.

Yahweh. The name of the biblical God, rendered in most English translations as "the LORD." This name was first revealed to Moses (Exod. 3:13–15). Within official Yahwisticism, Yahweh was the name of the patron deity of the kingdoms of Israel and Judah. After their destruction, those who continued worshiping this god began considering it sacrilegious to pronounce this sacred name.

Yahwism, Yahwist. Terms referring to the worship of the Israelite god Yahweh, and the association of that god with the Mosaic-Sinai tradition. A central theme in Yahwism therefore was the identification of Yahweh with the voluntary ethic embedded in the Decalogue. Because it was antithetical to Baal worship, "Yahwism" must be distinguished from "Yahwisticism." Some Yahwist literature has been preserved in the Hebrew Bible. Yahwism was the "normative" expression of Yahweh worship in the sense that it predated and outlasted state-supported Yahwisticism.

Yahwisticism, Yahwistic. Terms referring to the official state religion of Israel and Judah during the period of the monarchy (1000–586 B.C.). A central theme in Yahwisticism was the identification of Yahweh with the compulsory power of state government, where Yahweh was the patron deity of the state. Because it thus viewed religion and politics as *complementary* processes, "Yahwisticism" should be distinguished from "Yahwism." Some Yahwistic literature, which shows little comprehension of the older Yahwism, has been preserved in the Hebrew Bible. It is doubtful that Israelite villagers identified with this religion. The eighth-century-B.C. prophets, for example, criticized the Yahwistic "prostituting" of the original Yahwist faith.

Zadok. The priest in Jerusalem who served David and Solomon, and whose descendants had a monopolistic hold on the high priesthood until the time of the exile. Because Zadok only appears after David captures Jerusalem (2 Sam. 8:17), and because Zadok's family tree linking him to Aaron is five generations too long (1 Chron. 6:3–8), many scholars believe that he was actually a holdover from the Jebusite regime of pre-Davidic Jerusalem.

Zealots. A Jewish sect in Palestine around the time of Christ. They were violent revolutionaries practicing a politically militant brand of Judaism, whose activities helped to bring about the Jewish War of A.D. 66–70. Their name may suggest that they regarded themselves as righteous agents of God's wrath against those considered God's enemies.

Zechariah. The name both of a postexilic prophet whose career and concerns overlapped those of Haggai, and of the biblical book containing his oracles (chapters 1–6) as well as several other oracles from later periods (chapters 9–14).

Zerubbabel. A postexilic descendant of David's dynasty who attempted to reestablish the Judaean monarchy in Jerusalem, with the encouragement of prophets such as Haggai and Zechariah. His royal ambitions failed to materialize, and Zerubbabel disappeared without a trace from the historical record.

Zipporah. See "Kashites."

Zoroastrianism. A religious system associated with the Persian prophet Zarathustra that viewed the universe dualistically, with the forces of good and evil linked in combat in the parallel worlds of matter and spirit. In the sixth century a form of Zoroastrianism became the official religion of the Persian Empire. Some biblical concepts—like angels, the devil, and the end-times clash of good and evil—seem to derive from Zoroastrian influence on Judaism.

Bibliography

Selected Works by George E. Mendenhall

A complete bibliography of Mendenhall's publications as of 1983 was prepared by Michael O'Connor and published in *Quest for the Kingdom of God: Studies in Honor of George E. Mendenhall*, edited by H. Huffmon et al. (Winona Lake, Ind.: Eisenbrauns, 1983), 293–298. The following works in particular provide a more in-depth analysis and discussion of material presented in this book.

Law and Covenant in Israel and the Ancient Near East. Pittsburgh: The Biblical Colloquium, 1955. Reprinted in *BAR* 3. General readers can follow this classic and pioneering discussion, which introduces key themes discussed in this book.

"The Census Lists of Numbers 1 and 26." *Journal of Biblical Literature* 77 (1958): 52–66. General readers may feel this discussion (briefly mentioned in chapter 2 of this book) a bit more challenging and specialized.

"The Relation of the Individual to Political Society in Ancient Israel." In *Biblical Studies in Memory of H. C. Alleman,* edited by J. M. Myers et al., 89–108. Locust Valley, N.Y.: J. J. Augustin, 1960. Provides evidence showing that early Israelites did not identify themselves politically; in a volume available mainly in university research libraries.

"Biblical History in Transition." In *The Bible and the Ancient Near East: Essays in Honor of W. F. Albright,* edited by G. E. Wright, 32–53. Garden City, N.Y.: Doubleday, 1961. Scholarly assessment of the state of biblical history, introducing elements of the "field theory of religion"; in a volume available mainly in university research libraries.

"The Hebrew Conquest of Palestine." *BA* 25/3 (1962): 66–87. Reprinted on pp. 100–120 of *BAR* 3 (1970). General readers can follow this groundbreaking discussion, related to chapter 3 of this book.

The Tenth Generation: The Origins of the Biblical Tradition. Baltimore: Johns Hopkins University Press, 1973. General readers will find chapters 1, 7, 8, and 9 more accessible and relevant than other chapters.

"The Conflict Between Value Systems and Social Control." In *Unity and Diversity: Essays in the History, Literature, and Religion of the Ancient Near East,* edited by H. Goedicke and J. J. M. Roberts, 169–180. Baltimore: Johns Hopkins University Press, 1975. A good general discussion of a key biblical theme; in a volume available mainly in university research libraries.

"The Monarchy." *Interpretation* 29/2 (1975): 155–170. A readable treatment of subjects covered in chapters 4 and 5 of this book. This journal may not be carried in general libraries.

"Samuel's 'Broken Rib': Deuteronomy 32." In *No Famine in the Land: Studies in Honor of John L. McKenzie,* edited by J. W. Flanagan and A. W. Robinson, 63–74. Missoula, Mont.: Scholars Press, 1975. A scholarly discussion of a subject covered in chapter 4 of this book; in a volume available mainly in university research libraries.

"Social Organization in Early Israel." In *Magnalia Dei, the Mighty Acts of God: Essays on the Bible and Archaeology in Memory of G. Ernest Wright,* edited by F. M. Cross et al., 132–151. Garden City, N.Y.: Doubleday, 1976. General readers may feel this discussion a bit more challenging and specialized; in a volume available mainly in university research libraries.

"The Worship of Baal and Asherah." In *Biblical and Related Studies Presented to Samuel Iwry,* edited by A. Kort and S. Morschauser, 147–158. Winona Lake, Ind.: Eisenbrauns, 1985. A general discussion related to chapter 1 of this book; in a volume available mainly in university research libraries.

The Syllabic Inscriptions from Byblos. Beirut: American University of Beirut, 1985. A highly technical presentation of the results of the author's decipherment of Bronze Age texts discovered in Lebanon.

"The Nature and Purpose of the Abraham Narratives." In *Ancient Israelite Religion: Essays in Honor of Frank Moore Cross,* edited by P. D. Miller et al., 337–356. Philadelphia: Fortress Press, 1987. A readable discussion of the subject also covered in chapter 4 of this book; in a volume available mainly in university research libraries.

"The Suzerainty Treaty Structure: Thirty Years Later." In *Religion and Law: Biblical-Judaic and Islamic Perspectives,* edited by E. Firmage et al., 85–100. Winona Lake, Ind.: Eisenbrauns, 1990. A very readable retrospective related to chapter 2 of this book; in a volume available mainly in university research libraries.

"Prophecy and Poetry in Modern Yemen." In *Archaeology of Jordan and Beyond: Essays in Honor of James A. Sauer,* edited by L. Stager et al., 340–343. Winona Lake, Ind.: Eisenbrauns, 2000. A brief note about the continuity of ancient cultural features in the contemporary Near East; in a volume available mainly in university research libraries.

Other Works

Anchor Bible Dictionary. Edited by D. N. Freedman. 6 vols. New York: Doubleday, 1992.

Anderson, B. *Understanding the Old Testament.* Abr. 4th ed. Upper Saddle River, N.J.: Prentice-Hall, 1998.

Bright, J. *Jeremiah.* Anchor Bible. Garden City, N.Y.: Doubleday, 1965.

Cardozo, B. N. *Selected Writings.* Edited by M. Hall. New York: Fallon, 1947.

De Vaux, R. *Ancient Israel: Its Life and Institutions.* New York: McGraw-Hill, 1961.

Glock, A. "Warfare in Mari and Early Israel." Ph.D. dissertation, University of Michigan, 1968.

Hillers, D. *Covenant: The History of a Biblical Idea.* Baltimore: Johns Hopkins University Press, 1969.

———. *Treaty Curses and the Old Testament Prophets.* Biblica et Orientalia, no. 16. Rome: Pontifical Biblical Institute, 1964.

Meisel, J. *Counter-revolution: How Revolutions Die.* New York: Atherton Press, 1966.

Plumb, J. H. *The Death of the Past.* Boston: Houghton Mifflin, 1970.

Pritchard, J. B., ed. *Ancient Near Eastern Texts Relating to the Old Testament.* 3d ed. with supplement. Princeton, N.J.: Princeton University Press, 1969.

———. *Ancient Near East in Pictures Relating to the Old Testament.* Princeton, N.J.: Princeton University Press, 1954.

Index of Foreign Terms

Index of Scripture and Ancient Sources

Index of Subjects

(**boldfaced** items also appear in the glossary)